Some Assembly Required

A Complete Guide to Technical Communications

First Canadian Edition

Some Assembly Required

A Complete Guide to Technical Communications
First Canadian Edition

Sally L. Lordeon
President, Communique
Fletcher, North Carolina

Celia H. Miles
Asheville-Buncombe Technical Community College
Asheville, North Carolina

Mary Keane
Nova Scotia Institute of Technology

McGraw-Hill Ryerson Limited

Toronto Montreal New York Auckland Bogotá Caracas
Lisbon London Madrid Mexico Milan New Delhi
San Juan Singapore Sydney Tokyo

McGraw-Hill
Ryerson Limited

A Subsidiary of The **McGraw·Hill** Companies

SOME ASSEMBLY REQUIRED
A Complete Guide to Technical Communications
First Canadian Edition

ISBN: 0-07-552670-0

1 2 3 4 5 6 7 8 9 10   BG   6 5 4 3 2 1 0 9 8 7

Printed and bound in Canada.

Editor-in-Chief: Dave Ward
Production Editor: Kate Forster
Developmental Editor: Laurie Graham
Production Co-ordinator: Nicla Dattolico
Cover and Text Design: Dianna Little
Cover Photo: R. Schneider/The Image Bank
Technical Illustrators: Lisa Hastings, Dave McKay
Typesetter: Bookman Typesetting Co.
Printer: Best Book Manufacturers

Canadian Cataloguing in Publication Data
Lordeon, Sally L.
  Some assembly required : a complete guide to technical communications
1st Canadian ed.
Includes index.
ISBN 0-07-552670-0

1. Technical writing.   I. Miles, Celia H.   II. Keane, Mary.
III. Title.

T11.L67 1997   808'.0666   C96-931757-3

Readers wishing further information on data provided through the cooperation of Statistics Canada may obtain copies of related publications by mail from: Publications Sales, Statistics Canada, Ottawa, Ontario, K1A 0T6, by calling 1-613-951-7277 or toll-free 1-800-267-6677. Readers may also facsimile their order by dialling 1-613-951-1584.

Brief Contents

Table of Contents   vii
Preface   xvii

Part One: Identifying Technical Writing   1

Chapter 1: Defining Technical Writing   3
Chapter 2: Your Job and Technical Writing   29
Chapter 3: Types of Reports   47

Part Two: Developing a Plan   73

Chapter 4: Focusing on Writer and Audience Needs   75
Chapter 5: Organizing Your Ideas: Order and Outline   103
Chapter 6: Collecting and Documenting Information   135

Part Three: Constructing the Report   177

Chapter 7: Defining and Describing   179
Chapter 8: Using Graphics   209
Chapter 9: Preparing the Parts of Your Report   241
Chapter 10: Formatting Guidelines   265
Chapter 11: Technical Style: Writing and Editing   285

Part Four: Writing Informational Reports   323

Chapter 12: Progress and Project Reports   325
Chapter 13: Situation and Site Visit Reports   355
Chapter 14: Process Descriptions and Instructions   381

Part Five: Writing Analytical and Persuasive Reports   415

Chapter 15: Analytical Reports   417
Chapter 16: Persuasive Reports   461

Part Six: Business Correspondence   501

Chapter 17: Letters: Form and Tone   503
Chapter 18: Letters, Memos, and Résumés   529

Part Seven: Speaking of Technical Matters: Effective Oral Presentations 575

Chapter 19: Interviews, Meetings, and Seminars   577

Appendix: Employability Skills Profile   599

Index   603

Table of Contents

Preface   xvii

Part One: Identifying Technical Writing   1

Chapter 1: Defining Technical Writing   3
The Communication Process   5
Communication: Situation and Language   6
Technical Communication Defined   7
Recognizing Technical Writing   7
   Technical Writing and "Creative" Writing   9
   Purpose   9
   Content   10
   Audience   12
   Style   16
   What the Professional Technical Writer Values   21
Technical Reports Step-by-Step: How to Use This Book   21
Computer Tips   24
   How Can Writing with a Personal Computer Help You?   24
   Are Any Negatives Involved in Using a Word-Processing Program?   24
Questions for Discussion   25
Exercise   26
Writing Assignments   28

Chapter 2: Your Job and Technical Writing   29
General Career Areas   30
   Health-Care Careers   30
   Engineering and Science Careers   31
   Business Careers   31
Specific Job Roles   32
   Project Specialist   32
   Project Participant   34
   Project Manager   35
   Reviewer or Evaluator   37
   Investigator or Researcher   38
   Department Head or Manager   40
   Combined Roles   42

Workplace Needs: Keeping Track of Business and Keeping
Business on Track   42
   Time Means Money   42
   A Specific Audience Requires Concise Facts   43
   Employer Expectations Must Be Met   43
Questions for Discussion   44
Exercise   44
Writing Assignments   45

Chapter 3: Types of Reports   47
Informational Reports   49
   Specific Kinds of Informational Reports   51
Analytical Reports   61
   Specific Kinds of Analytical Reports   62
Persuasive Reports   65
   Specific Kinds of Persuasive Reports   66
Questions for Discussion   69
Exercise 1   69
Exercise 2   70
Writing Assignments   71

Part Two: Developing a Plan   73
   Chapter 4: Focusing on Writer and Audience Needs   75
Selecting a Topic   76
   Writing Situations: Workplace and Classroom   76
   A "Workplace" Topic   77
Focusing on Specifics   81
   Methods for Limiting a Topic   82
   Visual Devices: The Inverted Pyramid and Wedge   83
Identifying Your Objectives   85
Targeting Your Audience   88
   A Workplace Audience   89
Determining the Type of Report   94
   The Decision-Making Process   94
Questions for Discussion   100
Exercise   100
Writing Assignments   101

   Chapter 5: Organizing Your Ideas: Order and Outline   103
Choosing an Order   104
   Chronological Order   104
   Spatial Order   105
   Enumeration   105

Cause and Effect   107
Comparison and Contrast   108
Problem–Solution   110
Methodology–Results   111
Order of Emphasis   113
Making an Outline   114
Why Outline?   114
The Controlling Sentence   117
Outline Formats   122
Conventions of Outlining   124
Computer Tips   130
Outlining in Word Processing   130
Using Specialized Software   130
Questions for Discussion   131
Exercise 1   131
Exercise 2   132
Exercise 3   133
Exercise 4   133
Writing Assignment   134

Chapter 6: Collecting and Documenting Information   135
Step 1: Finding Information   136
Use Individual and Community Resources   136
Use Library Resources   146
Step 2: Converting Information for Your Use   155
Take Notes   155
Create a Rough Draft   161
Distinguish Fact, Inference, and Opinion   162
Step 3: Documenting Your Sources   164
Use Methods of Documentation   164
Avoid Plagiarism   171
Computer Tips   172
Computerized Online Catalogue   172
Information Retrieval Services   172
Questions for Discussion   173
Exercise 1   173
Exercise 2   175
Writing Assignments   176

Part Three: Constructing the Report   177

Chapter 7: Defining and Describing   179
Definitions   180
Parenthetical Definitions   180

Sentence Definitions   182
Operational Definitions   183
Expanded Definitions   184
Definitions for Your Specific Audience   188
Placement of Definitions in Reports   190
Product Descriptions   193
Uses and Content   193
Placement of Product Descriptions   198
Mechanism Descriptions   199
Uses and Content   199
Placement of Mechanism Descriptions   204
Questions for Discussion   206
Exercise 1   206
Exercise 2   207
Writing Assignments   208

Chapter 8: Using Graphics   209
Types of Graphical Support   210
Tables   211
Figures   216
Citation, Placement, and Discussion of Graphics   233
Computer Tips   236
Questions for Discussion   237
Exercise   237
Writing Assignments   239

Chapter 9: Preparing the Parts of Your Report   241
Transmittal Letter   242
Title or Title Page   242
Wording of Titles   244
Use of Subtitles   244
Placement of Titles   245
Table of Contents   247
Listing of a Report's Topics   247
Listing of Figures   247
Abstract   249
Content and Structure of Abstracts   249
Executive Summary   250
The Information to Include   251
Glossary   251
Introduction   253
Subsections   253

Body of the Report   255
   Appearance   255
   Headings   255
Conclusions/Recommendations   257
   Effective Conclusions   257
   Sound Recommendations   257
   Placement of Conclusions/Recommendations   257
List of References (Works Cited or Bibliography)   259
Appendix   259
Summary: Order of the Parts   260
Computer Tips   261
Questions for Discussion   262
Exercise 1   262
Exercise 2   263
Writing Assignments   263

Chapter 10: Formatting Guidelines   265
Distinctions between Informal and Formal Reports   266
Aspects of Formatting   268
   Alignment   269
   Binding   271
   Bullets   271
   Citations   271
   Colour   272
   Corrections   273
   Graphics (Figures)   273
   Headings   273
   Margins   276
   Neatness   277
   Numbering   277
   Paper   277
   Paragraphing   278
   Photocopying   278
   Print   279
   Quotations   279
   Spacing   280
   Underlining   280
Computer Tips   281
   Text Formatting   281
   Page Formatting   281
   Advantages and Precautions   281
Questions for Discussion   282
Exercise 1   282

Exercise 2   282
Writing Assignments   282

Chapter 11: Technical Style: Writing and Editing   285
Writing: Step-by-Step   286
   Step 1: Assemble Your Notes   286
   Step 2: Review and Sort Your Note Cards   286
   Step 3: Decide Where to Start   286
   Step 4: Rough Out a Paragraph Based on Your Notes   286
   Step 5: Start Writing   288
Editing: An Essential Ingredient   288
   Step 1: Edit for Clarity   290
   Step 2: Edit for Conciseness   297
   Step 3: Edit for Coherence   302
   Step 4: Edit for Conventions of Standard English   305
   Step 5: Edit for Consistency and Accuracy   314
Questions for Discussion   321
Exercise   321
Writing Assignments   322

Part Four: Writing Informational Reports   323

Chapter 12: Progress and Project Reports   325
Progress Reports   326
   Reasons for Writing Progress Reports   326
   Content in Progress Reports   328
   Form in Progress Reports   331
   Order in Progress Reports   332
Project Reports   340
   Reasons for Writing Project Reports   340
   Content in Project Reports   343
   Form in Project Reports   345
   Order in Project Reports   346
Questions for Discussion   350
Exercise   351
Writing Assignments   353

Chapter 13: Situation and Site Visit Reports   355
Situation Reports   356
   Reasons for Writing Situation Reports   356
   Content in Situation Reports   357
   Form in Situation Reports   361
   Order in Situation Reports   361
Site Visit Reports   368

Reasons for Writing Site Visit Reports   368
Content in Site Visit Reports   369
Form in Site Visit Reports   372
Order in Site Visit Reports   372
Questions for Discussion   376
Exercise   376
Writing Assignments   377

Chapter 14: Process Descriptions and Instructions   381

Process Descriptions   382
Reasons for Writing Process Descriptions   382
Content in Process Descriptions   382
Form in Process Descriptions   387
Order in Process Descriptions   389
Instructions   395
Reasons for Writing Instructions   395
Content in Instructions   395
Form in Instructions   404
Order in Instructions   405
Questions for Discussion   410
Exercises   410
Writing Assignments   411

Part Five: Writing Analytical and Persuasive Reports   415

Chapter 15: Analytical Reports   417

Preparing to Write an Analytical Report   419
Step 1: Identify the Objectives   419
Step 2: Find Useful Information   419
Step 3: Place Raw Data in Outline Order   420
Interpreting and Analyzing the Information   420
Examine All Data Objectively   420
Assess the Data's Relevance   421
Planning Graphics   421
Writing Style   422
Writing an Evaluation Report   422
Reasons for Writing Evaluation Reports   422
Evaluative Areas and Criteria   424
Appropriate Evaluative Strategies   425
Valid and Logical Conclusions   426
Content in Evaluation Reports   427
Feasibility Reports   441

Reasons for Writing Feasibility Reports   441
Key Assumptions and Constraints   442
Content in Feasibility Reports   443
Form in Feasibility Reports   446
Questions for Discussion   458
Exercises   458
Writing Assignments   459

Chapter 16: Persuasive Reports   461
Proposals and Responses to RFPs   462
Proposals   464
Proposals in the Workplace   464
Persuasive Writing   465
Accent the Benefits   467
Difficult Issues   468
Graphics   468
Proposal Organization   469
Proposal Formatting   473
Responses to Requests for Proposals   483
Reasons for Responding to a Request for Proposal   484
Kinds of Responses Requested   485
Content in Responses   491
Form in Responses   492
Questions for Discussion   498
Writing Assignments   498

Part Six: Business Correspondence   501

Chapter 17: Letters: Form and Tone   503
Business Letter Forms   504
Parts of a Business Letter   505
Return Address and Date   509
Inside Address   511
The Attention Line   512
Salutation   513
The Subject Line   514
Body   515
Complimentary Close   515
Signature and Identification   516
Reference Initials   518
Enclosure or Enclosures   518
Copy Notation   518
P.S.   519
Appearance: General Guidelines   519

Tone   520
Questions for Discussion   525
Exercise 1   525
Exercise 2   526
Writing Assignments   528

Chapter 18: Letters, Memos, and Résumés   529
Inquiry Letters   530
Responses to Inquiries   536
Order Letters   538
Complaint Letters   540
Adjustment Letters   543
Transmittal Letters   543
Job Application Letters   546
  The Beginning   550
  The Middle   551
  The Ending   552
Résumés   555
  Content in Résumés   556
Follow-Up Letters   560
Memos   566
  Memo Headings   566
Questions for Discussion   571
Exercise 1   571
Exercise 2   572
Writing Assignments   572

Part Seven: Speaking of Technical Matters: Effective Oral Presentations   575

Chapter 19: Interviews, Meetings, and Seminars   577
Speaking Situations in the Workplace   578
Connecting Oral and Written Reports   580
The Responsibilities of Speaker and Listener   580
Speaking for Yourself: Attending a Job Interview   582
  Preparation   582
  Presentation   584
Speaking with the Team: Participating in Meetings   586
Speaking for the Team: Presenting a Technical Seminar   587
  Defining the Task   589
  Identifying Your Objectives   589
  Targeting Audience Needs   590
  Gathering, Analyzing, and Organizing Information   590
  Preparing Visuals   590

Practising the Presentation   593
Delivering the Presentation   594
Conclusion   596
Questions for Discussion   596
Exercise   596
Speaking Assignments   597

Appendix: Employability Skills Profile   599

Index   603

Preface

As a student preparing for a technical career or as an employee using this book to learn or review the basics of technical communication, you have already realized that your work environment requires you to communicate constantly. You experience daily the need to speak convincingly, listen actively, read intelligently, and write clearly. Moreover, you are having to develop these communication skills fast so that you can complete tasks and deliver assigned projects on time.

The Corporate Council on Education of the Conference Board of Canada lists communication as the first of those academic skills "which provide the basic foundation to get, keep and progress on a job and to achieve the best results." Canadian employers, the Council says, need a person who can

> *Understand and speak the languages in which business is conducted*
>
> *Listen to understand and learn*
>
> *Read, comprehend, and use written materials, including graphs, charts, and displays*
>
> *Write effectively in the languages in which business is conducted.* [1]

This textbook focuses on technical writing. It guides you through the basics of the writing that initiates, informs, and documents the business of the workplace. At the same time, it illustrates how, as a technical writer, you will depend upon effective reading, listening, and speaking skills to achieve the best results. Whatever technical field you are studying, I hope that you will find the information in this book

- readable and easy to use in this course.
- readily transferable to other courses.
- useful and relevant in the workplace.

---

[1] The Corporate Council on Education, *Employability Skills Profile: What Are Employers Looking For?* Ottawa, Ontario: The Conference Board of Canada, 1996.

In this first Canadian edition of *Some Assembly Required: A Complete Guide to Technical Communications,* I have respected the goals set by the United States authors, Sally Lordeon and Celia Miles, and I have followed their instructional plan quite closely. However, I have widened the focus (1) by expanding the sections on job application letters and résumés to include job search strategies, and (2) by adding a chapter on the oral presentation of technical information. These changes respond to the suggestions of some helpful Canadian reviewers and reflect my own experience of Canadian college and workplace needs.

The text contains seven parts:

Part 1 introduces you to technical communication, the technical writing situation, and the types of reports most generated in the workplace.

Part 2 leads you through the essential planning tasks in technical report writing: selecting an appropriate topic, identifying your objectives and targeting your audience, and determining the type of report to write. This part also reviews information gathering and the work journal.

Part 3 guides you through the building stage of preparing reports: defining and describing, using visual aids, preparing the various parts of reports, formatting, and editing conventions.

Part 4 deals with reports that supply information, often the short reports of everyday work situations: progress, project, site visit, and incident reports; process descriptions and instructions.

Part 5 moves into reports that, as well as supplying information, require analysis and persuasive strategies — usually such longer reports as evaluation and feasibility reports and proposals.

Part 6 discusses business correspondence: its appropriate form, tone, and conventions, and the types of letters that you are most likely to write on the job. It also covers the job search process, enabling you to combine what you have learned about gathering, analyzing, and organizing information, so that you can present it confidently and persuasively in the application letter and résumé.

Part 7 shows you how to plan, organize, and deliver oral presentations of technical information in a variety of situations: the job interview, business meeting, and public seminar.

Throughout all the chapters, you will find activities that ask you to reinforce the principles discussed by answering questions. Like Lordeon and Miles, I have tried to make the assignments at the end of each chapter relevant to both the academic and work environments.

For instructors, I have developed a Canadian edition of the manual, which includes suggestions for exercises, tips for team teaching, and additional worksheets, suitable for reproducing, that will aid students as they move through the production of effective and valuable technical documents.

ACKNOWLEDGMENTS

The Canadian content and approach to this text have been supported by the following people who have contributed their expertise and experience:

Colleagues at the Nova Scotia Community College, Institute of Technology. Thanks especially to Susie Kuhner, Lynn Allison, Paul Batson, James Blinn, Cynthia Rogers, Gerry Rideout, Jim Kerr, and Shelley Zwicker.

Thanks also to NSCC Institute of Technology graduates: Greg Backman, Joe Boutilier, Cyril Dempsey, Bill Johnson, Robin Hylands, Russell Kehoe, Paul Landry, Will Lawrence, Joey Liska, Scott MacLeod, Robert McKay, Mark MacLeod, Glen Morton, Simon Petitpas, Chris Rogers, Gary Shore, Liling Tang, Jeff Vienneau, and Gail Wright, Howard Harawitz, President, Brooklyn North Software Works, Halifax, NS; Dan Dawson, Canadian Coast Guard; Louise Dawson, Institute of Technology; Michael Gaccioli, Institute of Technology.

Thank you to the Canadian reviewers for their helpful comments: Denis Beaulieu, Southern Alberta Institute of Technology; Joanne Beger, Northern Alberta Institute of Technology; Denise Blay, Fanshawe College; Michael Godfrey, Dawson College; Brian Hatton, Mount Royal College; Ricki Heller, Seneca College; Freda Hemeon, Technical University of Nova Scotia; Rudy Spence, British Columbia Institute of Technology; John Stonehouse, Camosun College; Leo Wisted, New Brunswick Community College; Larry Yanchynski, Red River Community College.

The publishing team at McGraw-Hill Ryerson also deserve mention: David Ward, Laurie Graham, and Margaret Henderson.

Finally, special thanks go out to my family across Canada, for their wisdom and encouragement: Patrick (Nova Scotia), Vannaver (Saskatchewan), and Leland and Patricia (British Columbia).

Mary A. Keane
Halifax, Nova Scotia

Some Assembly Required

A Complete Guide to Technical Communications

First Canadian Edition

IDENTIFYING TECHNICAL WRITING

Objectives

When you have finished Part One — Chapters One, Two, and Three — you should be able to do the following:

◆ Understand the communication process.

◆ Define technical communication as a part of that process.

◆ Recognize situations that require technical writing.

◆ Distinguish technical writing from other writing in terms of purpose, content, audience, and style.

◆ Relate technical writing skills to the expectations of the workplace.

◆ Describe the three general types of reports based on their purpose:

    informational

    analytical

    persuasive

◆ Recognize the three specific kinds of reports within each general type.

Chapter ONE

Defining Technical Writing

I t's 7:30 on Monday morning, and recently graduated tech-nologist Jenny MacDougall is beginning her third week of work at Crescent Electronics. Checking her E-mail, she finds a message from Tom Abriel, her supervisor and project manager:

| MAIL | | Sun 26 May 15:34:03 ☐ Private |

From: Abriel <ABRIEL_TOM@crescent.com> **CC:**

To: Jennifer <MACDOUGALL_J@crescent.com> **BC:**

Subject: Logos Parts and Testing

Message:
Please do the following:
1. Confirm price and delivery for remaining parts for the Logos project.
2. Set up beta testing as we discussed Friday.
Let me know when you've finished.

Regards
Tom

Attach: Message

Send Cancel Address Print Attach

Jenny immediately begins searching the catalogues and parts lists. She locates three suppliers Crescent usually deals with, and prepares to fax an inquiry, starting with Brandon Instruments.

CRESCENT ELECTRONICS   TEL: (507)555-xxxx   May 27/96   9:13 P.01

CRESCENT ELECTRONICS LIMITED
Tel: (507) 555-xxxx
Fax: (507) 555-xxxx

Fax Message

TO: Brandon Instruments Inc.
DATE: Mon 27 May 09:13:22
FROM: Jennifer MacDougall, Engineering

No. of pages (including this one): 1

MESSAGE

Please fax me a price and a rush delivery date for the following parts in quantities of 1,000:

Part number	Description
BLC3704A	chopper-stabilized op. amp.
BLE1256T	analog timer
BLF2682S	frequency synthesizer

If you have any questions, please call me at (507) 555-xxxx, ext. 621.

If you have not received all pages, please contact (507)555-xxxx.

Jenny sends the same fax to the two other suppliers: Simmonds Distributors and Loranco. However, she is uncertain about the second assignment. She assumes that the beta testing (preliminary tests of the product at the customer's site) is also for the Logos project, but being new both to the job and to the company, she needs to make sure.

"I'd better be clear about what I need to know," Jenny says to herself.

She jots down a couple of questions on her notepad and picks up the phone....

As this scene illustrates, Jenny's business day — a typical business day — starts with communication and puts into action all those skills she had developed during her technical training:

- ◆ Reading — interpreting the information
- ◆ Writing — gathering, organizing, and sending the information
- ◆ Speaking — formulating questions, then asking them
- ◆ Listening — preparing to listen actively, then noting significant points of the response

Of course, Jenny had acquired communication skills long before she entered technical training. Reading, writing, listening, and speaking had been developed formally in school, and informally outside school. Learning to communicate effectively enabled her to gain technical knowledge, complete her training, and get a job with Crescent Electronics, where, in turn, she could apply and communicate that knowledge to conduct business. To better understand the function of communication, let's examine the communication process.

THE COMMUNICATION PROCESS

Three key factors govern any communication process: sender, message, receiver. As Figure 1.1 shows, the sender (writer or speaker) transmits a message (information) to a receiver (reader or listener) to achieve a response. When the receiver responds or reacts, the communication process is under way. The roles are reversed, and the original receiver becomes the sender. If the responses are the ones desired, then the communication has succeeded.

Communication fails, however, when the message meets with interference. The reader or listener may be distracted by the noise

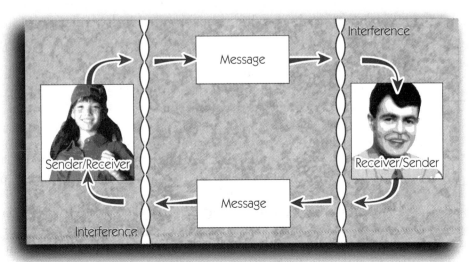

Figure 1.1 *A model of the communication process.*

of a busy construction site, high-traffic area, or overcrowded office. The receiver may then have to apply reading or listening skills more carefully to overcome the interference. The message may also be lost through the sender's lack of knowledge or judgment — the writer or speaker may inadvertently trigger the receiver's hostility, defensiveness, or even withdrawal from the communication situation. The sender may then have to reconsider the situation, learn more about the receiver, and take a different approach.

COMMUNICATION: SITUATION AND LANGUAGE

We all participate in such general communication processes as inviting a friend to lunch, sending greeting cards, reading books as we travel to work, listening to the car radio, or watching a movie. In these situations, we may be the sender or the receiver; in many situations we are both. For example, Jenny MacDougall invites her friend Danielle to lunch because she wants to tell Danielle what it's like working for Crescent. The invitation is personal, the lunch is informal, and Jenny's purpose is achieved through the easy, loosely structured flow of friendly conversation. Danielle's purpose is also achieved; she wants to hear Jenny's news, and to share some of her own.

Whatever our communication role, we all use language — verbal (the words we speak or write) and nonverbal (the signals our body language sends). We use language to convey messages that describe, narrate, explain, question, negotiate, or persuade, and it is extremely important that we know how to match the language with the situation. In informal or familiar situations, we may do this quite unconsciously. For example, when Jenny telephones Danielle, there is no need to formulate questions or take notes. The situation is personal and requires no detailed preparation. The verbal exchange at lunch is conversational, with a liberal use of colloquialisms and slang; the body language is animated, with plenty of hand gestures. The communication is spontaneous and appropriate.

In contrast, Jenny MacDougall's communication with Tom Abriel and with Brandon Instruments is more formal. She plans her approach to completing her assigned tasks, and she uses the tools of communication in her office. Her description of the parts to be ordered is in the precise terminology of her field, and her fax message is direct, concise, and courteous. At Crescent Electronics, Jenny is a technical communicator and has the responsibility of keeping the project on track.

TECHNICAL COMMUNICATION DEFINED

Technical communication is a form of communication used in the workplace and by almost any professional. Industry, science, engineering, business, health-care, and law enforcement professionals all rely on the precise transmission of information for the successful delivery of products and service. The General Competencies Section of the *National Standard — Electrical Technologies* aptly sums up the responsibilities of the technical communicator when it describes the occupation of Engineering Technologist as

> *inherently that of a communicator — one who ensures that information flows accurately and smoothly between engineering offices, the skilled trades, and other stakeholders in the workforce. While the tools of communication have become highly sophisticated, the original purpose remains, requiring a Technologist to be skilled in presenting and explaining technical issues to colleagues and to others.*[1]

In the technical communication process, the sender (or senders) transmits a technical, scientific, or industrial message to a receiver (or receivers) to achieve a technical, scientific, or industrial response. The presentation may be written or oral, and many business situations call for both kinds. Let's look more closely now at written technical communication to see what it is and how it differs from other kinds of written communication.

RECOGNIZING TECHNICAL WRITING

You are already a technical reader. In your normal day at college or work, you read a variety of technical material. At home, you have technical documents stored safely for when you need to use them. Indicate with a check mark which of the following you have read or consulted in the past two weeks:

_____ A popular magazine
_____ A recent best-seller

_____ A letter from a friend
_____ A poem

_____ Your car owner's manual
_____ Instructions for programming a remote control

_____ A credit application
_____ A chapter in a science, mathematics, or engineering textbook

---

[1] Canadian Technology Human Resources Board, *National Standard — Electrical Technologies* (Ottawa: CTHRB, 1994).

The items you checked in the left column probably represent your leisure or spare-time reading — reading you *chose* to do. You read those items "to relax," "for pleasure," or "to learn something new."

The items you checked in the right column probably represent your functional reading — reading you had to do to perform a task. You needed to know *how* to do something, to prepare for class, to apply for a loan. The information would enable you to complete business.

Most of the technical material you read is task- or work-related. For example, have you read any of the following material on the job in the past few weeks?

◆ A procedures manual
◆ An accident or loss report
◆ A policy statement
◆ A case history
◆ Instructions for operating machinery
◆ Specification sheets

You would have read such documents because a workplace situation demanded your attention and response.

This is not to say, however, that reading technical literature is not satisfying and enjoyable. An electrical technology student, returning from contact training with a local aircraft parts manufacturer, described enthusiastically how, in his spare time, he was able to "devour" the innumerable drawings, specification sheets, and parts lists he found on the office shelves. In his passion for all things aeronautical, Will had fortunately landed "in his element," and he was able to enjoy this part of the learning experience. Of course, these documents had not been produced for entertainment, but for the technologists and technicians who had to modify designs, troubleshoot problems, or maintain and repair the equipment.

Will's story, moreover, illustrates the importance of reading technical literature. At first you may find technical journals and books difficult to understand because they are dense with information, examples, and calculations. Nevertheless, reading in your technical discipline is essential for you to keep up with the rapidly changing and increasingly sophisticated nature of the technologies. It is highly likely, though, that you already enjoy reading the material of your field. You have chosen the technical career area that suits your aptitudes and fulfils your aspirations, and so you are willingly committed to the ongoing intensive and extensive reading so necessary for success.

Technical Writing and "Creative Writing"

As a reader of technical documents, you will have observed that the kind of writing they contain differs from what is known as "creative writing." First of all, though, you should remember that all writing is creative: Words are one vehicle or medium for communicating ideas, concepts, and information. In the "creative writing" process, the writer (sender) conveys the message he or she wishes to the reader (receiver) to produce a response. Second, you should recognize that in composing the message, the "creative writer" employs the rules, patterns, conventions, and techniques of the craft to achieve the best results. However, the term "creative writing" refers to the kinds of messages contained in novels, short stories, essays, plays, and poems. And in high school or college, you have had the opportunity to examine, paraphrase, evaluate, and write this kind of literature.

In contrast, technical writing is communication (in such fields as science, engineering, and industry) that originates primarily to convey specific information for a specific purpose to specific readers. It differs from "creative" or highly personal writing in four basic ways:

1. Purpose, or *why* you write
2. Content, or *what* you write
3. Audience, or *who* reads what you write
4. Style, or *how* you write

Purpose

The primary purpose of technical writing is utilitarian: to inform so that tasks can be performed and decisions made. It presents data, analyzes that data, and, with that data, influences direction and decisions. In the professional world, technical writing is like the concrete base of a building rather than its ornamental grille work or intriguing design. The scientist or software developer who is carving out new territory must document the discovery or modification for the employer or for those who will use the product. The purpose of technical writing is "to get the job done" efficiently and accurately. It often achieves that purpose in one or more of the following ways:

It informs. Technical writing *tells* how to maintain workplace safety, what went wrong with an assembly line, how to operate equipment, what happened at a construction site.

It analyzes. Technical writing *diagnoses* why a system does not work, how a process can be streamlined, why an environment is changing, what the advantages are of maintaining, expanding, or selling a business.

It influences. Technical writing *sells* or *persuades* by showing how a company can save money, what changes are necessary to improve a situation, what can be done to counteract or take advantage of emerging trends or practices.

Nontechnical and technical materials are produced for different purposes and usually from different motivating circumstances. Experience, memory, and feelings may inspire a writer to create, re-create, or interpret a situation for anyone who *chooses* to read about it. However, a technical writing situation often involves a "middle person" who recognizes a need for documentation and *assigns* a writer to that task: designing a manual, explaining a procedure, tabulating investigative results.

The technical writer is not usually emotionally prompted to write; the prompting is external — based on the needs of a job. The goal is a clear and accurate recording of factual data, not feeling. The reader seldom reacts on an emotional or personal level, but uses the document to learn, to decide, or to act.

Technical writing serves a functional reading need and is usually the product of scientific investigation and methodical documentation.

Content

Technical writing documents the operations of the workplace. It tracks the progress of projects; it describes, instructs, explains, persuades, or questions. Readers of technical documents should never have to ask, "What does this mean?" There should be no ambiguity, no room for different interpretations.

This lack of ambiguity is a significant difference between technical and "creative" writing. Writers of detective *stories* or of science *fiction* will intentionally evoke several interpretations. Their readers can enjoy solving a "who-dun-it" or guessing the fate of Jean-Luc Picard in his voyages through the galaxy. On the job, however, technical readers cannot afford ambiguities; they want answers. From an inspection report, for instance, they will need to know quickly and exactly what equipment needs repair or replacement, what parts and service will cost, and what delays are involved. Technical documents must clearly define problems and recommend solutions. Conflicting interpretations can cause loss of time, of money, even of life.

The product warranty and service information shown in Figure 1.2 is an example of technical writing familiar to consumers. Notice that it advises the reader exactly what the warranty covers, what it does not cover, and how to obtain service under warranty. It leaves no room for possible misunderstanding.

WARRANTY

Northern Telecom Canada Limited, 2920 Matheson Blvd. East, Mississauga, Ontario, L4W 4M7, warrants this product against mechanical or electrical failure for a period of twelve (12) months from the date of original purchase. Northern Telecom shall, at no charge and at its option, repair or replace a defective machine or component thereof with a new or factory rebuilt machine or component. Proof of original purchase date is to be provided with machines returned for warranty repair.

Exclusions and Limitations

This warranty does not apply to damages or failures resulting from:
-failure to comply with warranty service procedures or owner's guide
-improper installation
-repair by unauthorized persons
-modifications or unauthorized attachments

Warranty Service

Should your unit fail during the twelve (12) month warranty period, please return it to the place of purchase for repair service or replacement. If this is not convenient, call our service HOTLINE number for further information.

Service Hotline

As a further service to help you enjoy your new Northern Telecom Delegate, should you encounter any difficulty with your unit, call our toll-free Service HOTLINE 1-800-361-7800. For your convenience our Service HOTLINE number has been affixed to the bottom of your Delegate.

Figure 1.2 *Technical writing such as this warranty is familiar to most readers.*
Northern Telecom Delegate Telephone Answering Machine Owner's Guide, Publication number PO698010, Issue number 1. Reprinted with permission of Northern Telecom Canada Ltd.

Technical writing records data in business, science, industry, and all professional areas. The data in a technical report can be

◆ measured
◆ observed

◆ quantified
◆ tested
◆ verified

Technical writing can be analyzed logically and evaluated scientifically. It is highly specific and detailed. In brief, technical writing leaves its readers with *increased knowledge* and *satisfaction*.

Activity 1

Read the following brief passages. Place a *T* in front of those you think were taken from technical documents. Place a *C/P* before those you think are examples of creative or personal writing.

_____ a. Eighteen-bit digital-to-analog (D/A) convertors process the digital signal using eight-times-over sampling (352.8-kHz) digital filters. Each channel uses separate convertors to minimize interchannel crosstalk. Direct wire connections shorten the length of the electrical signal path and reduce signal interference.

_____ b. Surrounded by the great tumble of jagged grey stones wrenched through the centuries from the encircling mountains, the grey stone hut was almost invisible. Like a reptile patterned to the foliage of its habitat, this mountain dwelling glimpsed from a road deep in the mountains of Greece seemed itself to have become part of the wild landscape. — Wilma Dykeman, *Explorations*, p. 10.

_____ c. Variables may be (but are not limited to) arrays, strings, data structures, short integers, long integers, signed, unsigned, floating point or fixed point. Some variables, known as *pointers,* contain the memory addresses of other variables. In general, use the smallest and simplest variable that will hold the information required for the task at hand. — Howard Harawitz

You probably had no difficulty recognizing selections *a* and *c* as technical material. Selection *b* creates atmosphere and mood, rather than conveys technical data, and the chances of your reading such an item in the industrial, scientific, or business workplace are slim.

Audience

Audience simply means your readers. Your audience may be specific individuals (often easily identified by name or by position) or a general group with common interests. In both cases, they are reading for specific purposes. As a technical writer, you seldom write "for just anyone who might be interested." Your readers' interest is typically dictated by a need to know the information: to understand a subject, perform a task, or make a decision. Even if you are preparing a sales brochure for the general public, you are essentially targeting those consumers who have a particular interest in your product. In the latter case, you *want* them to know that they have a need for the information and the product.

Your audience may be *external* or *internal*. The *external* audience may be a customer, a member of the general public, or a representative of another organization. The *internal* audience may work in your own organization or department. A service writer in the automotive industry, for example, deals with both kinds of audience: listening to the customer (external) and writing up the problem for the mechanic (internal). Your audience will vary in levels of expertise, education, and experience. They may be experts in your field or in another field. Their roles and occupations will differ: supervisors, engineers, home owners, the company president, a potential customer, the lead chemist, the new lab technician. They may see a report just minutes or hours after you complete it; they may not see the document at all, but may attend an oral presentation or demonstration; or they may read only a section or a summary.

Understanding who your readers are, why they are reading, what they already know, and how much they need to know about the subject influences many writing decisions about content and style. You consider their position, background, and interests, and the use they will make of the information you are communicating. For example, you may write a technical report for your manager. Figure 1.3 shows a brief memorandum report to a specific person within an organization. The writer assumes the reader has some background information.

You may write a technical manual for distribution to all users of a certain product — for many different readers. Figure 1.4 shows one page of a set of instructions that accompanies a household appliance. These instructions are intended for a large audience with varying degrees of knowledge about the piece of equipment.

In some ways, readers of technical materials are an easy audience to write for. For example, they often know what they are looking for in reports, and they recognize the value the information has for them. Technical readers usually exhibit some or all of the following characteristics:

◆   They will need to read the material.

HAMPSTEAD, INC.

MEMORANDUM 302
January 23, 19--

To: A. Gudowski, Operations Manager
From: C. T. Chenard, Quality Control Engineer
Subject: Inspection of Tubular Casing #599-01

A recent review of operations revealed a duplication of quality control efforts relating to tubular casing #599-01. The supplier inspects these casings at its facility and, according to Hampstead's policy as stated in Memo 189 (September 11, 19--), they are again inspected here.

Hampstead's quality policy is now that it no longer requires specialized test fixturing at both facilities. (See Memo 221 for a statement of that policy.)

Thus the test data gathered at our supplier's facility on the spring rate will be the data used to determine acceptability of tubular casing #599-01. The current supplier (Solo/Beckton Industries) has been asked to continue to assist Hampstead by doing the following:

1. Select five (5) component pieces and serialize as 1 through 5.
2. Obtain a total of eight (8) readings on each of the components.
3. Remove the components from the nest after each reading.
4. Collect data on a monthly basis.
5. Transmit data to Hampstead within two days of testing.
6. Yearly (on or near June 30), consolidate testing data and send summary to Hampstead.

We expect that the supplier's testing will be sufficient for maintaining our revised "dock to stock" policy.

Figure 1.3 *This technical memo is addressed to a specific audience (one individual).*

- They will want to read the material.
- They will read for information.
- They will know something — possibly a great deal — about the subject.
- They will read quickly but carefully.

Periodic Maintenance

Temperature-Pressure Relief Valve Operation

The temperature-pressure relief valve must be manually operated at least once a year.

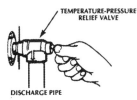

TEMPERATURE-PRESSURE RELIEF VALVE

DISCHARGE PIPE

> — **WARNING** —
>
> **The temperature-pressure relief valve must be manually operated at least once a year. Caution should be taken to ensure that (1) no one is in front of or around the outlet of the temperature-pressure relief valve discharge line, and (2) the water manually discharged will not cause any property damage or bodily injury. The water may be extremely hot.**
> **If after manually operating the valve, it fails to completely reset and continues to release water, immediately close the cold water inlet to the water heater, follow the draining instructions, and replace the temperature-pressure relief valve with a new one.**

Failure to install and maintain a new properly listed temperature-pressure relief valve will release the manufacturer from any claim which might result from excessive temperature or pressure.

> — **WARNING** —
>
> **If the temperature-pressure relief valve on the appliance weeps or discharges periodically, this may be due to thermal expansion. Your water heater may have a check valve installed in the water line or a water meter with a check valve. Consult your local Sears Service Center for further information. Do not plug the temperature-pressure relief valve.**

Draining

The water heater should be drained if being shut down during freezing temperatures. Also periodic draining and cleaning of sediment from the tank may be necessary.

1. Before beginning turn "OFF" the electric power supply to the water heater.

> — **WARNING** —
>
> **HAZARD OF ELECTRICAL SHOCK! Before removing any access panels or servicing the water heater, make sure the electrical supply to the water heater is turned "OFF". Failure to do this could result in DEATH, SERIOUS BODILY INJURY, OR PROPERTY DAMAGE.**

2. CLOSE the cold water inlet valve to the water heater.

3. OPEN a nearby hot water faucet and leave open to allow for draining.

4. Connect a hose to the drain valve and terminate to an adequate drain or outdoors.

5. OPEN the water heater drain valve to allow for tank draining.

   NOTE: If the water heater is going to be shut down and drained for an extended period, the drain valve should be left open with hose connected allowing water to terminate to an adequate drain.

6. Close the drain valve.

7. Follow "Filling the Water Heater" instructions in the "Installing the New Water Heater" section.

8. Turn "ON" power to the water heater.

> **CAUTION**
>
> Never use this water heater unless it is completely full of water. To prevent damage to the tank and heating element, the tank must be filled with water. Water must flow from the hot water faucet before turning "ON" power.

Figure 1.4 *This page of instructions for maintaining an electric water heater is intended for a general audience.*
Periodic Maintenance from Sears Electric Water Heater Owner's Manual, publication number 0291289-00, page 17. Reprinted with permission. Copyright © Sears Canada Inc.

♦ They may read only part of the material.

♦ They will sometimes know you.

    Identifying your readers as specifically as possible helps you target their needs and avoid including unnecessary details or omitting necessary data. When you know exactly who will read a report, you may take into account

- their motive for reading
- their years of experience with the organization
- their need for theory or for practical application
- their attitude toward the subject matter and you, the writer

You will then be able to adapt your message to get the best results.

Chapter Four focuses in more detail on audience analysis and its significance in the preparation of effective technical reports.

Style

Style is *how* you write — a component different from *what* you write. It is a pipeline, a channel, a means of getting information (content) from you to the reader.

You already have a style — a way you communicate (with or without words) what you are and what you think. Consider, for example, the different ways you and several friends might relate the same facts about an incident. The language's extensive vocabulary and the possibilities for various sentence patterns create innumerable ways of expressing the same content. Given identical data with which to work, few writers communicate that data in precisely the same manner.

The goal of effective technical writing style is to make information flow easily and clearly so that readers can make prompt and efficient use of it. Technical style emphasizes objective reporting with no leeway for different interpretations. Accurate information combined with a lucid and concise style produces a readable and useful technical report. Some general characteristics of what technical writing style has and what it avoids are shown in Figure 1.5.

Style, in all writing, is a matter of making choices in two areas: words and sentence structure. In technical writing, a major goal of those choices should be *clarity* and *conciseness*. An ideal technical style does not interfere with the understanding of content and does not call attention to itself.

In the following pairs of sentences, for example, note that both the "poor" and the "better" choices mean the same thing. However, the writer makes very different word and sentence structure choices to express that meaning.

POOR: I forward my apologies for being remiss as regards the tardy submission of the requisite report.

TECHNICAL WRITING STYLE

What It Has

1. A tone appropriate to the specific situation (businesslike, definite, user-friendly)
2. Directness
3. Highly specific and concrete words that cannot be misinterpreted
4. Emphasis on factual data, statistics, and measurable elements
5. Logical explanations that lead to credible conclusions
6. Absolute adherence to the conventions of the language in which business is being conducted
7. Use of graphics to clarify and support prose
8. Objectivity
9. Graphics

What It Avoids

1. Irony and sarcasm
2. Emotionally charged words
3. Liberal use of first- and second-person pronouns
4. Liberal use of contractions and informal punctuation such as dashes and exclamation marks
5. Vagueness and verbosity
6. Excessive technical jargon
7. Colloquial (conversational) expressions and slang
8. Sentence fragments and run-on sentences
9. Unsubstantiated personal opinion and bias

Figure 1.5 *Characteristics of technical style.*

BETTER: I am sorry the report is late.

POOR: Both times and instructors noted on class registration calendars or elsewhere are not guaranteed and should not be considered a contract. Time schedules and curriculum offerings are subject to change without notice.

BETTER: Class schedules change. Please check with your advisor before registering.

As these admittedly exaggerated examples show, vocabulary and sentence structure do not just happen. They are the result of choices you make on the basis of an understanding of your audience.

The two sets of instructions shown in Figure 1.6A and 1.6B further illustrate how the same kind of content can be expressed very differently. Of course, Figure 1.6B is a spoof, showing by ridicule how *not* to write.

Whether your readers are coworkers, technicians, managers, executives, or consumers, they will react to your document first as individuals; and an effective technical style matches their needs and background. They should respond positively to the content, not negatively to an obscure style.

Chapter Eleven discusses several elements of effective technical style. However, the following principle is a general aid in recognizing whether you are producing readable sentences.

The principle of the two *P's* — *pause* and *paraphrase* — helps you write at an appropriate level and avoid negative responses from your readers. Ask yourself these two questions about your sentences:

CHOCOLATE CHIP COOKIES

1	cup margarine or butter, softened
1	cup firmly packed brown sugar
$\frac{1}{3}$	cup sugar
2	eggs
$2\frac{1}{4}$	cups all-purpose flour
1	teaspoon baking soda
$\frac{1}{3}$	teaspoon salt
1	teaspoon vanilla extract
$1\frac{1}{2}$	cups semisweet chocolate morsels
1	cup chopped pecans

Cream margarine. Gradually add sugar and beat until light and fluffy. Add eggs, and beat until well-blended.

Combine flour, baking soda, and salt. Add to creamed mixture, stirring well. Add vanilla, chocolate morsels, and pecans.

Drop dough by tablespoonsful, $\frac{1}{2}$ inch apart, onto an ungreased cookie sheet. Bake at 375° (190 degrees Celsius) for 8 to 10 minutes or until lightly browned. Cool slightly on cookie sheet; then gently remove to wire racks.

Yield: 7 dozen cookies.

Figure 1.6A *These two sets of instructions (recipes) show that content can be expressed in very different styles (see Figure 1.6B).*

CHOCOLATE CHIP COOKIES

Total Lead Time: 35 minutes

Inputs:

1	cup packed brown sugar
$\frac{1}{2}$	cup granulated sugar
$\frac{1}{2}$	cup softened butter
$\frac{1}{2}$	cup shortening
2	eggs
$1\frac{1}{2}$	teaspoons vanilla
$2\frac{1}{2}$	cups all-purpose flour
1	teaspoon baking soda
$\frac{1}{2}$	teaspoon salt
12	ounce package semisweet chocolate pieces
1	cup chopped walnuts or pecans

Guidance:

After procurement actions, decontainerize inputs. Perform measurement tasks on a case-by-case basis. In a mixing-type bowl, impact heavily on brown sugar, granulated sugar, softened butter and shortening. Coordinate the interface of eggs and vanilla, avoiding an overrun scenario to the best of your skills and abilities.

At this point in time, leverage flour, baking soda, and salt into a bowl and aggregate. Equalize with prior mixture and develop intense and continuous liaison among inputs until well coordinated. Associate key chocolate and nut subsystems and execute stirring operations.

Within this time frame, take action to prepare the heating environment for throughput by manually setting the oven baking unit by hand to a temperature of 375 degrees Fahrenheit (190 degrees Celsius). Drop mixture in an ongoing fashion from a teaspoon implement onto an ungreased cookie sheet at intervals sufficient enough apart to permit total and permanent separation of throughputs to the maximum extent practicable under operating conditions.

Position cookie sheet in a bake situation and surveil for 8 to 10 minutes or until cooking action terminates. Initiate coordination of outputs within the cooling rack function. Containerize, wrap in red tape, and disseminate to authorized staff personnel on a timely and expeditious basis.

Outputs:

Six dozen official government chocolate-chip cookie units.

Figure 1.6B *Chocolate chip cookies the bureaucratic way.*
This recipe used with permission of The Washington Post.

PAUSE: Can the reader read through my sentence aloud without pausing for breath?

PARAPHRASE: Can the reader paraphrase (put into other words) my meaning fairly easily and quickly?

You can attain clarity and conciseness by limiting abstract terms, by avoiding too much jargon, and by being conscious of long sentences. Don't make your busy readers look up words in a dictionary or reread excessively verbose (or wordy) sentences in order to understand your report.

Activity 2

Apply the principle of the two *P*'s, *pause and paraphrase*, to the following prose examples.

a. Potato varieties with pigmented skins owe their colour to anthocyanins dissolved in the cell sap of the periderm and cells of the peripheral cortex. It is difficult to say whether this is due to a process of active migration of the anthocyanin from the periderm and cortex or to primary protection within the flesh of the tuber.

Can you read through each sentence aloud without pausing? Can you paraphrase each sentence easily? Write your version of the sentences.

_____

_____

_____

b. The study of the interface between interpersonal behaviour and mass media, this course seeks to further understand the symbiotic relationship between mediated behavioural modes and interpersonal communication through the integration of the theory and practices common to both fields of study and research.

Can you read through the sentence aloud without pausing? Can you paraphrase it easily? Write your version of the sentence.

_____

_____

You probably found these examples difficult or impossible to paraphrase. To avoid similar problems of style in your own writing, quietly read your sentences aloud to yourself and apply the two *P*'s. As a writer, you are responsible for making your sentences clear and readable.

What the Professional Technical Writer Values

Before leaving this chapter, read the Society for Technical Communication's Code for Communicators, which appears in Figure 1.7. You can see that professional technical writers strive to convey subject matter accurately rather than to express an individual style. They recognize the value of their readers' time and strive for clear, concise communication. They also recognize their responsibility to their colleagues, to continuing education, and to the advancement of their profession. The profession or workplace for which you are training will almost certainly have its own written code of values and ethical behaviour. For any writing you do in your workplace, the STC Code for Communicators should provide useful guidance on style and your responsibility to your readers.

TECHNICAL REPORTS STEP-BY-STEP: HOW TO USE THIS BOOK

Becoming a competent technical writer requires that you understand the principles of effective technical communication and that you develop these through lots of practice. This text shows you step-by-step the process of beginning, researching, writing, and editing different types of reports. It also includes computer tips at the end of selected chapters.

Here is a chapter-by-chapter overview of exactly how this book presents the material that will help you become a competent technical writer:

Chapter One, as you now know, identifies technical writing as part of the technical communication process, and distinguishes technical writing from other types of writing in terms of purpose, content, audience, and style.

Chapter Two provides an overview of the needs of the workplace and the different kinds of responsibilities you may have for generating reports.

Chapter Three discusses the different categories of technical reports (informational, analytical, and persuasive) and illustrates them, so that you will know what various technical documents look like and in what circumstances they are produced.

ſociety for technical communication

Code for Communicators

As a technical communicator, I am the bridge between those who create ideas and those who use them. Because I recognize that the quality of my services directly affects how well ideas are understood, I am committed to excellence in performance and the highest standards of ethical behaviour.

I value the worth of the ideas I am transmitting and the cost of developing and communicating those ideas. I also value the time and effort spent by those who read or see or hear my communication.

I therefore recognize my responsibility to communicate technical information truthfully, clearly, and economically.

My commitment to professional excellence and ethical behaviour means that I will

◆ Use language and visuals with precision.

◆ Prefer simple, direct expression of ideas.

◆ Satisfy the audience's need for information, not my own need for self-expression.

◆ Hold myself responsible for how well my audience understands my message.

◆ Respect the work of colleagues, knowing that a communication problem may have more than one solution.

◆ Strive continually to improve my professional competence.

◆ Promote a climate that encourages the exercise of professional judgment and that attracts talented individuals to careers in technical communication.

Figure 1.7 *Code for Communicators.*
Reprinted with permission from the Society for Technical Communication, Arlington, VA.

Chapter Four shows you how to develop a report plan that focuses on writer and audience needs: selecting manageable topics, identifying your objectives, targeting your audience, and determining the appropriate type of report needed.

Chapter Five shows you how to order a large body of material and how to organize it in appropriate outline form.

Chapter Six reviews strategies for finding printed information in and out of libraries, encourages you to go beyond printed sources for valid primary data, and explains how to record your findings, keep track of your research in a journal, and document your sources.

Chapter Seven discusses and illustrates two major elements in technical writing: defining terms and describing products and mechanisms.

Chapter Eight discusses different kinds of visual aids in reports: when to use them, how to produce them, and where to place them.

Chapter Nine shows you how to build the various parts of reports — from the title page to the appendix — and gives examples of each component.

Chapter Ten explains how to put your report together in a format that is appealing, appropriate, and effective.

Chapter Eleven gives you writing and editing guidelines for producing reports that are readable and effective, that use standard English, and that apply appropriate technical writing conventions.

Chapter Twelve discusses two kinds of informational reports — progress and project reports — and shows you how to write each one.

Chapter Thirteen deals with two other kinds of informational reports — situation and site visit reports — and shows you how to write each one.

Chapter Fourteen discusses two final types of informational writing — process descriptions and instructions — and shows you how to write them.

Chapter Fifteen presents two types of analytical reports — evaluation and feasibility reports — and shows you how to write them.

Chapter Sixteen discusses the two main types of persuasive reports — proposals and responses to requests for proposals — and shows you how to write them.

Chapter Seventeen introduces you to business correspondence that accompanies the activities of the workplace, and illustrates various formats and components of business letters with an emphasis on appropriate tone and appearance.

Chapter Eighteen shows you how to write internal and external correspondence, including the following types of letters: inquiry, response to inquiry, orders, complaint, adjustment, and transmittal.

Computer Tips

You are encouraged to become familiar with a personal computer and a word-processing program as you begin your technical writing course. If you already type, you will find keyboarding easy. If you do not type or have used a computer only for games or other nonwriting tasks, you will find using a word-processing program much easier than you may have expected.

How Can Writing with a Personal Computer Help You?

Word processing does not think for you. It does, however, make the process of writing easier, faster, and more fluid than handwriting or typewriting your text. It rewards you too. You are proud of your reports, which look professional and have no strike-overs, no evidence of "white out," and no erasures.

Specifically, using a word-processing program enables you to do the following:

◆ *Rough out your thoughts quickly and make changes easily.* You can delete, add, and move words, sentences, paragraphs, and whole sections without having to rewrite entire pages.

◆ *Get help with spelling.* Most word-processing programs include a spell-check that signals most misspellings, although you cannot rely on it absolutely.

◆ *Get help with vocabulary.* You can quickly find the "perfect" word if a thesaurus is built into your program.

◆ *Get help in generating ideas.* You can brainstorm with a computer by using programs that guide and assist you in the composing process.

◆ *Get help with the final editing.* You can use programs that check your grammar, stylistic choices, and sentence length.

◆ *Feel more in control of your writing.* If you do not like what you read on the screen, you can change it or delete it instantly. You see your product differently once it is removed from your own personal handwriting — and you treat it differently. You modify and reorganize your text more readily — because it is so easy to do — and the result is a higher-quality, more polished report.

Are Any Negatives Involved in Using a Word-Processing Program?

There are very few negatives in using a word-processing program, and two of them have to do with being a beginner, not with the concept of word processing:

1. *Learning time.* You do have to invest enough time to learn the basics of any program you are using. A computer does exactly what it is told to do. Sometimes new users, intimidated by all that a word-processing program can do and perhaps overwhelmed by the user's manual, give the wrong command by mistake or press the wrong key in haste. Expect some initial frustration if you are

unfamiliar with keyboarding. Within days of beginning to use word processing, you will become comfortable with it. And your time investments will start to pay you many dividends as you write more reports.

2. *Unrealistic expectations.* You may expect too much from a word-processing program. Remember, it is only a piece of equipment — created to serve your needs. It cannot know what you mean. It can do only what you tell it. It can help you create the perfect-looking report (headings, margins, and so forth), but *you* make the decisions.

Using a word processor gives you a sense of control over your writing. You begin to look at writing as a *process*, a process that you control. Because you can make changes easily and quickly, you find yourself expecting your reports to be as professional as your readers expect them to be.

The Computer Tips sections in selected chapters of this text will help you with specific areas of technical report writing.

It also introduces job search strategies to support application letters and résumés.

Chapter Nineteen examines the role of oral technical presentations in the workplace. It reviews audience and situation analysis, and shows you how to plan, organize, and deliver presentations of technical information for three specific kinds of situation: job interview, project meeting, and public seminar.

From the beginning of your technical writing experience (choosing or being assigned a topic and considering the audience) to the final formatting and editing stages, this text guides you through the steps of producing effective reports. Depending on your special needs, you can also use the chapters out of sequence. For example, you may need to start with memo or letter writing. You can use Chapters Seventeen and Eighteen right away as there will be cross-references to help you.

Writing valid technical reports is a process you can follow and a skill you can master. Your future employers will value highly your technical writing expertise.

QUESTIONS FOR DISCUSSION

1. At Crescent Electronics (pages 3–4), why did Jenny MacDougall need to telephone her supervisor, Tom Abriel?
2. Why did she write down her questions on a notepad before she telephoned him?
3. What does her approach to the job tell you about the technical communication situation and process?

4. What tools or technology did Jenny use on the job?
5. What would you say are the differences between technical writing and "creative writing"? Do you see any similarities?
6. Why is it important to read technical literature?
7. What are three key factors that govern any communication process?
8. What is the primary goal of effective technical style?
9. What are the responsibilities of a technical writer?

EXERCISE

Read the following selection from Howard Harawitz's *Programming Tips Manual* and answer the questions that follow.

A Few Comments Are in Order

Documenting computer programs takes time. Not documenting *can take even more time.*

Without proper documentation, a program constructed of many modules can be a nightmare to debug or modify.

Despite the best of intentions, almost no one keeps up-to-date information that is separate from actual program source code.

The most useable information about how a program works and how it is constructed can be found in the program code itself. More often than not, eliciting this information is a tedious and difficult task, even if we ourselves were among its authors.

If there is any reasonable way to provide good documentation within the program itself, it certainly deserves our consideration.

Fortunately there are a few simple things that a programmer can do that will greatly improve the intelligibility of his or her program source code.

First, comment your programs as you write them. *It's all too easy to promise yourself to add comments once the "programming" is done, and then forget about it in order to go on to the next "real" programming task.*

When I was in the Sixth grade, I had a sheet metal shop teacher who insisted that "cleaning up was part of the job." As a twelve year old, I resented being pressured to clean up as I worked — but I did develop the habit of doing it. To this day it has consistently served me well — not only when working in the shop, but at home in the kitchen and while writing computer programs.

Comments do not have to be lengthy. Neither do they have to be added to every line of code. Commenting, like other aspects of computer programming, is an art. Skill in this area will develop as you practice.

The general principle is to use comments to clarify those parts of your program which cannot be readily understood by someone with your own programming skills.

Even if you are in a situation where others will be working on your programs, write your comments so that they will be helpful to you whenever you return to your programs to modify or repair them. If you find your own documentation helpful, the odds are that others will too.

Learn to use a proper combination of both macro and micro comments as you work.

A macro comment is a heading that describes the overall task that a section of code is trying to accomplish. Very often it will be only one line — e.g., "Print total balance."

Sometimes additional macro commenting is necessary to outline a principle or special method being used. A macro comment is the appropriate place for a description of any unusual mathematical formula or algorithm.

A micro comment is a very brief description of a single line of code. It is usually tacked on to the end of a line with which it is associated. With a high level language like BASIC, micro comments should be used sparingly. Assembly language programs generally require more micro comments because the language is inherently obscure.[2]

a. List five characteristics of effective technical writing style demonstrated in the passage.

_____

_____

_____

_____

_____

....

[2] *Programming Tips Manual* (1993). Reproduced with permission of Howard Harawitz.

b. For whom do you think this manual was written? Explain briefly.

_____

_____

_____

c. Do you think the story of a lesson learned in the sixth grade is appropriate for this document? Consider the audience and situation, list your points, and then discuss with your group the reasons for your answer.

_____

_____

_____

WRITING ASSIGNMENTS

1. Informally interview two people you know who are employed in a trade or profession. Ask them to describe the technical writing they do on the job. Find out as much as you can about the kinds of writing they work on during the course of a week, and ask them if they have taken any special training in writing. Then write a paragraph summarizing their comments.

2. Each of the following terms has at least one general meaning and one technical meaning:

   Matter
   Tolerance
   Force
   Work
   Pitch
   Pressure
   Worm
   Program

   Choose one of these terms and (a) use it in a sentence to define its general meaning and (b) define it as it is used technically.

   Example: energy.

   General: He was accustomed to speaking with great energy (or vigour).

   Technical: The wind that turns a windmill is an example of kinetic energy, or the energy of motion.

Chapter TWO

Your Job and Technical Writing

Now that you understand what technical writing is and how it differs from other kinds of writing, a reasonable question to ask yourself is this: "Why and when will I have to prepare a technical paper or report for my job?"

After you graduate and obtain the job you have been preparing for, you will have many occasions to use what you have learned about technical writing. Effective technical writing skills help you perform your job responsibilities efficiently, quickly, and intelligently. The value you add to your job abilities with these sharpened writing skills will be evident throughout your career. Typically, a person who can communicate will be hired or promoted before one who cannot.

GENERAL CAREER AREAS

Jobs in all career areas involve responsibility. The jobs that you and your fellow students are preparing for, however, require specialized training and knowledge. Your jobs will demand more than just the usual responsibilities of any good employee: getting to work on time, doing quality work, getting along with coworkers.

The kinds of jobs you and your fellow students will hold are as varied and unique as each of you. All these jobs require specialized knowledge. They also require the ability to communicate that specialized knowledge to other people. Many of you will have careers in the following areas:

◆ Health care and social sciences
◆ Agriculture
◆ Law enforcement
◆ Engineering and science
◆ Business and marketing

All these career areas share a common characteristic: *They require accurate technical writing skills as a part of their responsibilities*. Frequently, entry-level employees may write such simple messages as memos or purchase orders, but as they gain experience and knowledge, the demand and need for more formal technical reports increase proportionately. Let's take a look at a few of these career areas and at their technical writing possibilities.

Health-Care Careers

People with careers in the field of health care have numerous responsibilities. Whether your job is in nursing, X-ray technology, or therapy, you will have important information (learned in the classroom and accumulated on the job) that must be communicated accurately and on time.

As a health professional, you may be asked to do the following:

◆ Report on patient progress and physical or mental reactions.
◆ Report results of and reactions to various tests.
◆ Report on the use of special equipment.
◆ Write a manual on an instrument upgrade.

Health-care professionals often evaluate situations for the institutions in which they work. They may be required to do the following:

◆ Justify a staffing change.

◆ Recommend new equipment.

◆ Evaluate a new procedure.

Depending on your specific position, the responsibilities will vary, but communicating information will be required as a part of your job.

Engineering and Science Careers

People with careers in engineering and science may work as technicians, computer programmers, marine biology technologists, and so forth. The following is an example of a project in the computer field.

> You are working as a computer programmer for a software development firm. As part of a recent assignment, you have developed a software program that numerically sorts age, weight, and food consumption amounts for an aquarium in British Columbia. This program will ease the workload of the researchers tracking the habits and growth patterns of the mammals being studied.
>
> As another part of your job, you are expected to document the logic and steps you used to develop the software program so that your knowledge and expertise can be shared throughout the programming department.
>
> Since there is no technical writer on staff, you are also expected to write the instructions for the researchers who will use this program to enter, manipulate, and store their data.

Engineering and science professionals are continually required to document their methods, results, and procedures as an integral part of their job responsibilities.

Business Careers

The business field covers a vast number of career possibilities. Accounting, quality control, sales, customer service, administrative planning, and personnel are just a few. Although many of these career areas have distinctly different knowledge and training requirements, the business environment frequently requires professionals in one area to interact with individuals in other areas of business. These interactions are usually for the purpose of communicating information. For example:

- The accounting department must obtain this month's billing figures from the sales department.
- The quality control department must learn from other departments the number of usable parts.
- Administrative managers must know how effectively all departments are operating.

Business professionals are continually required to report, evaluate, propose, analyze, and recommend information and solutions. The technical writing possibilities are numerous — and are usually a required part of the job function — regardless of the specific position or the specific business.

SPECIFIC JOB ROLES

Within all general career areas, you will have a specific job function, and you will play a specific role. The role will probably fit one of these categories:

- Being responsible for doing all parts of a project
- Being part of a team
- Leading a team

Following are some specific roles typically found in most career areas. Although the job titles and tasks vary from company to company and sometimes overlap, each role carries a responsibility to communicate specialized knowledge to others. Therefore, each demands good technical writing skills.

Project Specialist

Depending on the job situation in which you are working, some projects may be assigned solely to you — one individual who is expected to take the project or assignment from inception to completion. The assignment may require you to research, develop, design, implement, and evaluate a project. Although you will probably use other resources inside and outside the organization, the primary responsibilities for completing all tasks and for ensuring the desired end result of the project are yours. For example, you could be the specialist or consultant for one of these projects:

- Determine whether your company's new synthetic fibre is suitable for children's clothing.
- Investigate the feasibility of a new store location.
- Evaluate the effectiveness of a new blueprint copy machine.

◆ Develop and install a new lubrication system for your plant's conveyor belts, then show how to maintain it.

◆ Identify the best food service company for your plant's cafeteria.

◆ Develop a simpler method to test the acid levels of soil.

Information is an important by-product of any project. Collected during the project and after its completion, information gathered by a project specialist must be documented and shared with other people in the organization — especially when a person is working alone. Reports prepared while a long project is ongoing assure other interested people (managers, customers, coworkers) that progress is being made and that the end result can and will be accomplished. Reports prepared at the end of a project document important methods, processes, resources, and considerations for future projects, or for further development of the project just completed.

Figure 2.1 shows the type of information that typically evolves from a project for which a project specialist is solely responsible.

If you are a project specialist, your organization expects you to apply your specialized knowledge to a project; it also expects you to

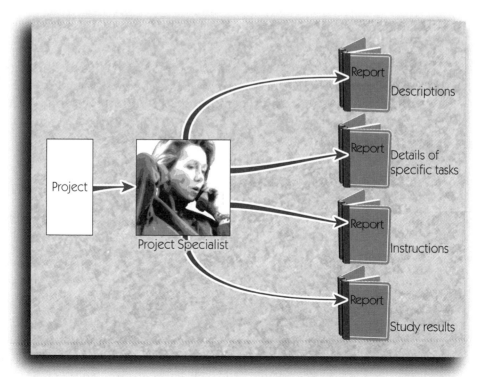

Figure 2.1 *A wide range of information flows from a project specialist's role.*

document your methods, findings, and evaluations so that they can be studied and reviewed by others. To produce the documents that meet the responsibilities of a project specialist, you must be a competent technical writer.

Project Participant

Most jobs require us to work as members of a team. Each person on the team has specific responsibilities that reflect his or her specialized knowledge and training. Teams are frequently developed for projects with a number of different (yet related) components that must be considered or accomplished. For example, project teams are often organized for assignments such as the following:

◆ Improve the purchasing system at Casey Ship Builders Inc.
◆ Determine the need for a new CAD system in A-B Graphics' drafting department and evaluate the effectiveness of a particular system.
◆ Install a new drug distribution system at Foothills Hospital and train technicians to use it.
◆ Investigate the major causes of home fires in Victoria County and implement a community-wide fire prevention program.

Regardless of the specific project, the single most important characteristic of any effective project team is that everyone on it has the same goal: a successful completion. Whether the team is large or small, whether the project is simple or complex, the members of successful teams communicate continually among themselves. Moreover, both your team coworkers and your management will want answers to questions such as these:

◆ Are you on schedule?
◆ Are you within budget?
◆ What tasks have you completed so far?
◆ How much time did these tasks require?
◆ Were there any problems?
◆ What still needs to be done?
◆ Is there anything that needs to be added to the original scope of the project?
◆ At the project's completion, how would you rate the outcome overall?

This list is not exhaustive but represents questions that team members typically address. Whatever your specific job on the project or your specialized knowledge regarding it, you will probably be expected to write and record information that answers such questions to ensure a successful project. Figure 2.2 shows typical types of information generated from a project in which there are several participants.

Some of the information will be needed from all members of the team — tasks completed, for example. Other information will be required of individual members in terms of their specific job function on the team. Regardless of the source of information, the need to document it is an integral part of a successful project's natural flow.

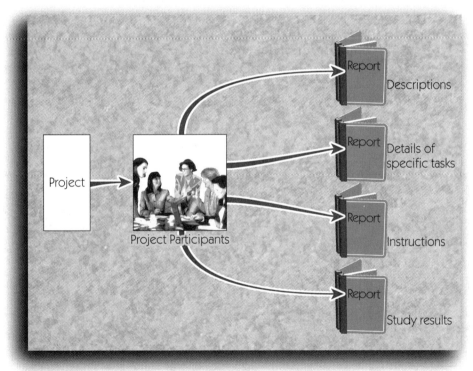

Figure 2.2 *A project participant generates valuable specific information.*

Project Manager

Every team involved with a project has a key individual who tracks its overall progress. As project manager, you not only collect the various reports from your team members, but you also gather, assimilate, and summarize these reports in a concise document for upper management or for your customer(s).

The technical writing responsibilities of a project manager may include determining and speculating on the stages or discrete steps of a project before it is actually undertaken. (Are necessary personnel available? Is there sufficient time? Has enough money been budgeted?) Here the project manager's report or study states whether or not this project can be achieved in the time allotted and with the resources available to the team that will undertake it. The manager is also responsible for compiling and summarizing the results of all phases of the project after it is completed, including the tasks performed, the schedule, the budget (actual and projected), and any changes or revisions in the original schedule or budget.

The typical types of information that flow from a project manager's job responsibilities are shown in Figure 2.3.

A project manager's technical writing skills must span many communication levels. As the leader of a project, you must report to your team members, to your management, and in many cases to your customer(s).

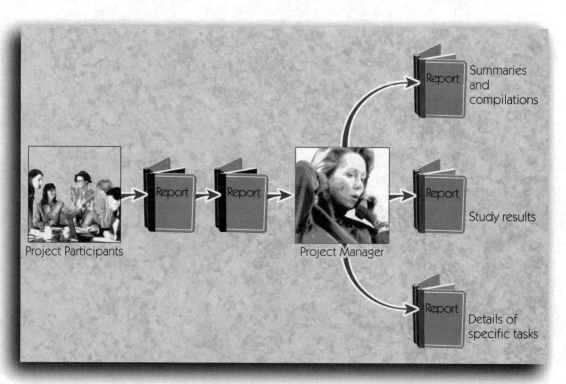

Figure 2.3 *An integral part of the project manager's role is assimilating and summarizing information for upper management and customers.*

Activity 1

Read the following descriptions of people in various on-the-job situations. Relate each situation to the typical job role of a project specialist, project participant, or project manager by writing *PS*, *PP*, or *PM* to the left of each description.

_____ a. An engineer who leads a project to design a water bath system for newly machined parts

_____ b. A city government employee who is solely responsible for implementing new zoning changes

_____ c. A member of the personnel department who helps a team implement a matched savings program for full-time employees

_____ d. An agricultural specialist who develops an easy, reliable way of ensuring balanced pH levels in all types of soil

_____ e. An X-ray technologist who is a member of a task force asked to cut a hospital's film costs

Reviewer or Evaluator

Reviewers or evaluators of projects or proposed projects also need good technical writing skills to produce effective reports for the decision makers in an organization. Reviewers and evaluators are usually required to compile a report that details their findings on a specific assignment. Depending on what their managers or customers want, they may also need to make recommendations based on these findings.

As a project reviewer or evaluator, you may be responsible for producing documents that show the end results of the following efforts:

◆ Reviewing the methods and final results of a new building project that your organization just completed

◆ Evaluating the overall performance of a project team that created and produced a proposal for a power plant

◆ Evaluating the effectiveness of an existing warehouse system

◆ Reviewing the tentative staffing schedules of a new branch store

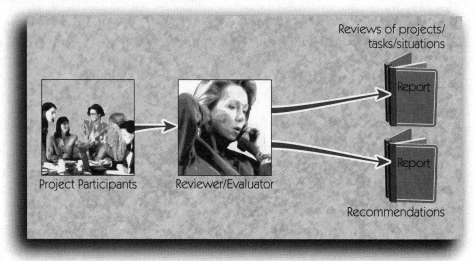

Figure 2.4 *A reviewer or evaluator needs good technical writing skills to document findings and recommendations effectively.*

♦ Describing the damage to machinery and physical plant after a flood at a plant

♦ Making recommendations for any of the preceding projects

The flow of information that emerges from having the responsibilities of reviewer or evaluator is illustrated in Figure 2.4.

Investigator or Researcher

Investigators or researchers have some of the same job functions and generate some of the same types of information as do specialists, project leaders, and reviewers or evaluators. Often, however, these investigators or researchers are expected to report in deeper detail, and they often are looking for specific factors to include in their reports. As an investigator, you might, for example, typically be given one of the following assignments:

♦ Obtain the details of a crane accident at the container port.

♦ Investigate foundation cracks in the outpatient surgery wing.

♦ Check into the effectiveness of a ventilation system in an elementary school.

♦ Investigate traffic congestion problems at a new intersection.

Investigators and researchers also usually respond to their assignments with written verification of their findings. The information they provide is typically heavily slanted toward the scientific or technical — sometimes because of the subject matter and sometimes because their documents are given to other scientific or technical personnel.

More important, researchers are usually assigned to solve a specific problem or to answer a specific question, so their reports state the problem or question, show the methods used for research, then solve the problem or answer the question. Their reports do not merely inform their readers on the subject of their research. Here are some examples of typical problem-solving questions:

♦ How can we prevent further heavy equipment accidents at the container port?

♦ What is the fastest method of repairing the outpatient surgery wing's foundation cracks and related structural problems?

♦ Should the ventilation system at the elementary school be repaired or replaced?

♦ Would a traffic light ease congestion at the new intersection? If so, can we afford it?

The information flow that typically evolves from the job responsibilities of investigators or researchers is shown in Figure 2.5.

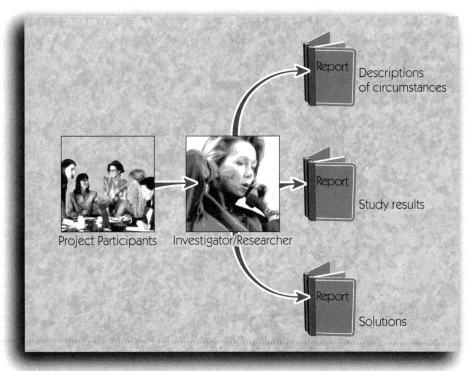

Figure 2.5 *An investigator or researcher often writes reports that examine facts in depth and propose solutions to problems.*

Department Head or Manager

Department heads and managers have many responsibilities to communicate clearly and concisely. As part of their job, they must do the following:

- Write effective technical reports and analyses for upper management and customers.
- Document and communicate information clearly and effectively to their staff.
- Make sure that the members of their staff communicate information effectively to them.

These individuals usually have to produce weekly or monthly reports on the activities of their departments or units. Often, these reports must then be summarized in quarterly and annual reports. In addition to some of the same reports described earlier for other job roles, department heads and managers must have the technical writing skills necessary to produce documents such as the following:

- A report that persuades upper management to implement formal training classes for department computer users
- A convincing discussion on the need to add one more nurse to the daytime shift
- A statement of the department's sales objectives for the new fiscal year
- A response to a potential customer's request justifying costs for the company's water purification system
- A report that documents the department's achievements for the past fiscal year
- A paper that recommends and justifies new market directions for the department's sportswear products

Figure 2.6 shows the typical types of information that flow from the role of department head or manager.

The sources of information emerging from the department head or manager can change, depending on the situation. Such individuals sometimes ask members of their staff to gather the information needed in their technical reports and then pull it all together into a concise, effective document. At other times, they assume the sole responsibility of gathering and writing up the information. At still other times, department heads and managers may assign a member of their staff (quite possibly *you*) to be in charge of generating the entire report. In any case, department heads and managers usually have the responsibility of giving final approval to all documents,

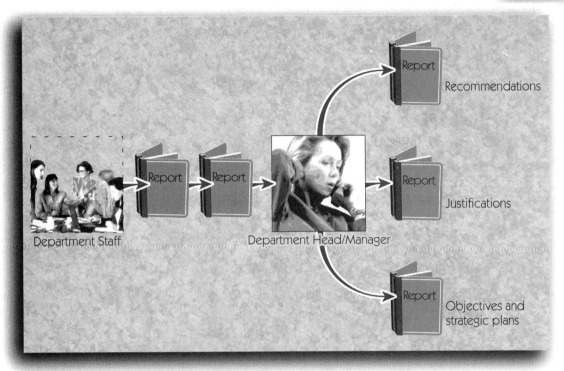

Report — Recommendations

Report — Report — Report — Justifications

Department Staff   Department Head/Manager

Report — Objectives and strategic plans

Figure 2.6 *Clear, concise reports that recommend and justify are routinely required of department heads and managers.*

regardless of who generated them. Therefore, good technical writing skills and the ability to detect such skills in others are essential to these individuals.

Activity 2

Read the following descriptions of people in various on-the-job situations. Relate each description to one of these typical job roles: reviewer or evaluator, investigator or researcher, department head or manager. Write *RE*, *IR*, or *DM* in front of each description.

_____ a. A quality control technician who evaluates existing machine assembly procedures

_____ b. A marine biologist who researches the cause of a disease called red tide

_____ c. An auto mechanic who investigates the fuel emission systems of all cars that use leaded fuel

———— d. A branch store manager who leads her employees in a customer satisfaction campaign

———— e. A member of the city's law enforcement agency who reviews proposals for new patrol cars

Combined Roles

As you may have noticed, most of the job roles we have been discussing overlap frequently: A department head is often also a project manager; a project specialist is often a reviewer or evaluator as well. When Hector Cacho, a nurse at Foothills Hospital, worked with the Computer Services Department in developing a program to track and schedule nursing work shifts, he functioned in three different roles.

As an *investigator/researcher*, Hector helped the computer programmer identify all the scheduling needs that had to be met in the program (various work shifts, specific nursing units, personnel names and availability). As a *project participant*, Hector worked closely with the programmer, answering questions about shift times, getting personnel rosters, locating data items on the screen menus, and assisting with project reports. Finally, as a *reviewer/evaluator*, Hector tested the effectiveness of the program (for ease of use, for accuracy in scheduling) when the project was near completion and helped the programmer write the user instructions.

The technical writing skills you will have acquired by the time you finish this text will serve you in many ways as you enter the workforce as a well-trained and knowledgeable individual.

WORKPLACE NEEDS: KEEPING TRACK OF BUSINESS AND KEEPING BUSINESS ON TRACK

Careful maintenance of records is vital to the success of any organization. No project should be stalled when the personnel fall ill, take vacations, gain promotion to another department, or lose their job. Most organizations, realizing that it is not "good business" to have valuable knowledge locked in just one person's head, require detailed reporting. Work logs or project diaries keep track of operations, assist the compilation of more formal project reports, and can be used as evidence in contract disputes.

Time Means Money

No organization, for-profit or not-for-profit, has enough resources to accommodate poorly spent time or wasted efforts. The longer an employee takes to complete a task, the more the organization spends in time and resources. Whenever any task is accomplished efficiently and effectively, everyone benefits — the employee, the organization, and the customer.

Technical writing is an integral and important part of the workplace. Since time is money for most organizations, the amount of time you, as a professional, spend in reading and preparing information is an important consideration. When you have the skills and ability to produce required documents clearly, concisely, efficiently, and on time, you become a valuable asset to your workplace.

A Specific Audience Requires Concise Facts

Busy, successful organizations want to learn quickly the relevant facts required to make sound managerial decisions. Therefore, they want technical reports that can be read quickly and understood clearly. Your technical reports can meet these workplace demands only when you thoughtfully determine (1) who your readers are and (2) what they need to know. To write competently, you will need to

◆ select only the strictly relevant information.

◆ organize it to address all the important questions.

◆ present it clearly and concisely.

You will be the functional expert on your job and often the best resource for the best information. You will routinely be expected to communicate.

Employer Expectations Must Be Met

Most employers expect the qualities of a good report to go beyond the accurate communication of the information itself. For a moment, visualize yourself not as the writer of a technical report but as the supervisor who requested the material. Beyond "the facts," what would you expect of the report?

As a technical reader, your employer (as well as your coworkers and customers) expects — and respects — a report that meets the following criteria:

1. *On time.* A late report is of little use, especially when the information it contains is needed for decision making. Success in business is based on informed decisions and therefore relies on the timely submission of data. Most agencies that fund projects, for example, automatically reject reports or proposals that arrive even one day past deadline. In the construction industry, late bids are not accepted.

2. *Professional in appearance.* A report that is messy in any way — wrinkled, stained, marked, torn — implies sloppiness in other areas. The reader consciously or unconsciously connects untidy presentation with untidy thinking, and may have difficulty treating the content seriously. A professional appearance encourages a professional response.

3. *Easy to read.* A good report not only contains valid information but inspires the reader to read it. Eye appeal in technical documents may be subtle, but most people who read and write them are quite open and direct about its importance. Long, single-spaced paragraphs with little visual relief (headings, uncluttered illustrations, tables, ample margins, use of white space) are less likely to be read carefully or at all. Attractive document design invites the audience to read on.

QUESTIONS FOR DISCUSSION

1. Why will technical writing skills be important to you on the job?
2. Why is it so important to meet business deadlines for report submission?
3. You have probably been advised not to "judge a book by its cover." Does this advice hold true for evaluating technical documents? If not, why not?
4. Some people might argue that there is no such role as a project specialist, for nobody works alone. Compare the roles of project specialist and project participant and state your view.

EXERCISE

Assume that your classroom, workshop, laboratory, or office needs redesigning and refurbishing. You have been asked to assemble a team to plan and implement the project.

1. Name your role and list some of the tasks that include writing.

_____

_____

_____

_____

_____

2. Name at least two roles for people working on or connected with the project and list their writing tasks.

WRITING ASSIGNMENTS

1. Talk with two people who currently have jobs in your major field of study. Ask what types of information they frequently see in their positions, and ask how often they see each type (daily, weekly, monthly). Summarize each person's responses to your questions.

2. Ask one of the following people to discuss his or her typical technical report writing tasks:

   a. A professional in your college administration
   b. A local government official
   c. A human services professional in your community
   d. A professional technical writer

   Then describe these tasks and relate them to the job roles discussed in this chapter.

3. Talk with an employer in your major field of study. Ask what factors or qualities he or she thinks are most important in any technical report that comes across his or her desk and why. Write a paragraph stating this experienced person's opinions.

Types of Reports

As you have seen in Chapters One and Two, technical writing arises from a specific need and addresses a specific audience. You also know that effective technical writing is interconnected with reading, speaking, and listening, and that the responsible technical writer does not function alone. Successful technical documents are the products of focused communication and consultation.

Technical writing, as you have learned, is a vehicle for conveying specific information, and a report does exactly that: It brings or carries back information. The dictionaries tell you that the word *report* is derived from the Latin *reportare (re* or *back* and *portare* or *to carry)*. Technical reports vary greatly in length, degree of formality, components or elements, and purpose.

The three broad categories used in this text are based on the general *purpose* of a report. Keep in mind, however, that many reports have more than one objective. Three main purposes or objectives of technical reports are to inform, to analyze or evaluate, and to persuade. Reports with these goals as their major purpose are respectively classified as follows:

◆ Informational reports
◆ Analytical reports
◆ Persuasive reports

These labels refer to the overall objective of a report or to the particular emphasis given in the report, which in turn is based on the needs and expectations of the audience. To help identify the type of report you need to write, ask the following questions about *your* purpose:

◆ Am I simply reporting facts and data?
◆ Am I analyzing, interpreting, evaluating something?

♦ Am I attempting to influence a decision?

Then, to doublecheck, rephrase the questions in terms of the main response you want from your *audience:*

♦ Will the audience use the report to *do* something?
♦ Will the audience use the report to *understand* something?
♦ Will the audience use the report to *decide* something?

Informational reports describe situations without giving any analyses, interpretations, or recommendations. They present readers with information so that *they* can do their own analyzing, interpreting, and recommending. Analytical reports go one step beyond informational reports. They describe *and* analyze situations, but they do not make judgments for or present recommendations to readers. Persuasive reports also describe and analyze, but they take the final step in technical report writing and present a clear recommendation for readers to consider and to act upon.

As shown in Figure 3.1, information is the base of all reports. Once writers have the necessary information, they may use it to write analytical and persuasive reports.

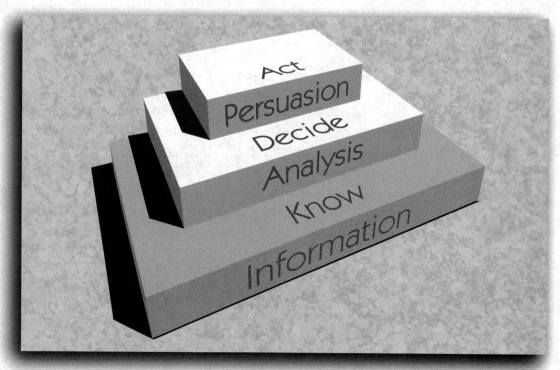

Figure 3.1 *Information is the base of all technical reports.*

The type of report you write usually depends on your reason for writing. In the classroom, you may have the option of developing your own reasons. In the workplace, the reasons for writing will usually be predetermined for you. As shown in Figure 3.2, each type of report answers certain basic questions.

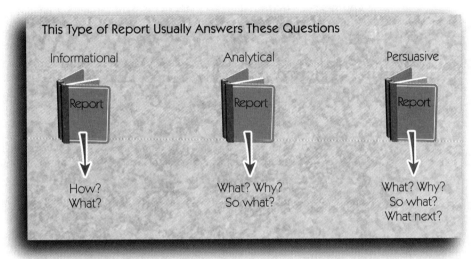

Figure 3.2 *Different types of technical reports answer different questions.*

The same general topic can be used for a strictly informational report, an analytical report, and a persuasive report. (See Table 3.1.) The following general topics are illustrated for each of the three different types of reports:

◆ Making an architectural addition to a heritage property
◆ A security lighting project for a university campus
◆ Tax breaks for industry
◆ Equipment for a clinic
◆ Bed-and-breakfast ratings

INFORMATIONAL REPORTS

Informational reports convey *facts*. Such reports indicate what is or what *was* or, occasionally, what *will be*. They may tell how to do something. They do not give the writer's opinion of what *should be* or *should have been*. They do not assess, judge, justify, propose, or recommend.

Informational reports, then, relay facts without apparent bias or feeling. The key word here is *apparent*. While you may be inclined to agree or disagree with, like or dislike, oppose or advocate what-

TABLE 3.1

TYPES OF REPORTS AND DIFFERENT APPROACHES

Informational	Analytical	Persuasive
How does a heritage home owner obtain approval for adding a sunroom to her city property?	Why does the municipality strictly regulate extensions to residences in the city?	The necessity for regulating the construction of extensions to city residences.
What is the condition of the exterior lighting on St. Brigit's University campus?	Why has the university retained a consulting firm to inspect the exterior lighting system on campus?	The need to upgrade the exterior lighting on St. Brigit's campus.
What tax breaks are available for a new company locating in a specific region in a specific province?	Why have advertised tax breaks failed to attract new industry to a region?	The advantages of tax breaks for new industries to a region.
What specific equipment is required for a local clinic?	Which new cancer-screening equipment —scanner X or scanner Y—is more suitable for a local clinic?	The time benefit of a clinic's purchasing your company's innovative diagnostic machine.
How are bed-and-breakfast ratings determined?	What has been the effect of a newly implemented bed-and-breakfast rating standard on rural operators?	The probability of improving the quality of bed-and-breakfast operations by implementing a provincial standard.

ever you are reporting, your attitude toward the material must be as objective and neutral as possible.

Total impartiality is difficult to achieve, but the attempt to provide facts without bias is a major characteristic of informational reports. Readers expect informational reports to give them facts so they may proceed with some action or make some decision themselves. They do not expect the data or information to be coloured by the writer's choice of judgmental words or slanted language. Good informational reports typically tell a reader *how* and *what*. They do not say *why* except in factual ways that can be verified.

To write an informational report on each of the five general topics noted on p. 49, you might consider answering questions such as the following:

♦ How does a heritage home owner obtain approval for adding a sunroom to her city property?

♦ What is the condition of the exterior lighting on St. Brigit's University campus?

♦ What tax breaks are available for a new company in a specific region of a specific province?

♦ What specific equipment is required for a local clinic?

♦ How are bed-and-breakfast ratings determined?

Activity 1

Read the following pairs of sentences. Check the sentence in each pair that is strictly informational. Underline any words that show the writer's attitude.

_____ a. Store your diskette in a smoke-free environment.

_____ a. You should never store a diskette in a smoke-filled room.

_____ b. Lot 135-VT was rerouted through Saskatoon on August 31, 1995.

_____ b. The manager neglected to plan properly for the most efficient routing and consequently had to reroute through Saskatoon on August 31, 1995.

_____ c. The institution's personnel turnover rate between June 1994 and June 1995 was 39 percent in managerial positions and 27 percent in hourly paid positions.

_____ c. The institution's personnel turnover rate between June 1994 and June 1995 was an unusually high 39 percent in managerial positions and only 27 percent in hourly paid positions.

The second sentence in each pair does more than just state facts. An attitude is also evident. Sometimes only a word or two (*unusually* and *only* in the last pair of sentences, for example) will be enough to change the statement from strictly informational to "information plus interpretation."

Specific Kinds of Informational Reports

There are many kinds of informational reports, and their names vary from company to company. The most frequently written ones are briefly described here.

Progress and Project Reports

Progress and project reports are time- and task-related documents. Sometimes referred to as status reports, they may describe specific elements — especially the completed, continuing, and anticipated work — on a project that spans a time period of more than a few days. They may describe all job efforts of a specific person within a specific time frame or the combined achievements to date on a specific project or of a group of people. As an employee, for example, you may have to report periodically on activities. Figure 3.3 illustrates how one employee documents the monthly progress of all his efforts to develop new business.

If you are in charge of a project that extends over months or years (a construction job, the marketing of a product, the installation of new equipment, the training of personnel, the completion of a project funded by government agencies or the private sector), you will be required to report at specified intervals on the status of that particular project. Figure 3.4 shows a project report on what has been completed to date in the development of a new computer program for a section of a large hospital.

Readers of progress or project reports want answers to questions that relate to time and tasks:

♦ How much work has been accomplished?
♦ What work is currently being done?
♦ How much work is yet to be done?
♦ Is the project on schedule and within budget? If not, why not?
♦ Are there any foreseeable situations that might affect the completion of the project as planned?

Situation Reports

Situation reports (sometimes called incident or accident reports) are related to events or conditions. They may detail what has happened in a particular situation or they may describe a present condition or detail a "static" situation, such as the inspection of a workplace or piece of equipment. If the subject is an event, such as an accident in the workplace, the document may be called an occurrence report. Many occurrence reports are made by filling out appropriate forms supplied by a company or agency. Law enforcement and health-related personnel, insurance agents, and supervisors in industry, among others, often rely on forms. But in just as many cases, a narrative report is expected, a "report in your own words," which is usually more detailed than the information on a form. As illustrated in Figure 3.5, an accident at a plant may require a

MONTHLY PROGRESS REPORT

March 19--

Submitted by: Patrick Ryan, Sales Engineer

Overview

During most of March, I prepared and submitted two major Control Switch proposals to the following utility customers:

- Stewart Valley Light & Power
- Prince David Water Commission

These proposals have a total sales potential of $235,000. Early customer feedback indicates favourable reviews of the documents, particularly of the Stewart Valley proposal (a $155,000 Control Switch package).

Specific Tasks Undertaken

1. Information included in the Stewart Valley proposal, which I began work on in mid-February, was finalized when the Design Engineering and Manufacturing departments sent firm cost figures. I sent the document to the customer on March 8, five days before submission deadline.
2. I prepared and submitted information on an $80,000 Control Switch package to the Prince David Water Commission on March 21. The package is our standard midrange control boxes.
3. Barbara Lewis, at our Lower Mainland sales office, has been keeping close watch on the customer's reactions to our proposal. Stewart Valley comments to date indicate that we are the top contender, pending further scrutiny of our document. Official bid acceptance will be made on April 10.
4. Follow-up phone calls to our Northern sales office indicate that Prince David is questioning the size specification of the control boxes. I have a meeting scheduled for April 5 to provide customer with further clarification.
5. I began development efforts for a technical sales and specification sheet on our new Control-X switches. Targeted print date is May 15.
6. I spent March 8 and 9 with the engineering manager and MIS director of Midland Manufacturing. They are seriously considering ordering CNC control box assemblies for their new high-tech machine lathes. After their tour of our facilities and a meeting with our key engineering and manufacturing people, I believe we have a chance at winning this potential $400,000 order.

Figure 3.3 *Example of a brief progress report.*

PROJECT REPORT

Project: Development of Poison Control Data Program for Emergency Room
                    Computer
Submitted to: Marie Gionet, Director of Programming
Submitted by: Jacob Smicer, Programmer
Date: April 3, 19--

Overview

Program development is on schedule and within the number of work hours allocated. The program should be installed and ready for data input and record generation on May 1.

Work Completed to Date

1. Tuan Lee, Poison Control Centre director, defined all screen menus; all menus are
   now installed in the program.
2. Lee also identified all required data input fields; the top half of the data screen
   now contains these required, colour-coded fields.

Work in Progress

1. The optional data fields are being implemented on the bottom half of the screen.
2. Clear and concise error messages are being developed and installed to enable
   program users to correct data input errors easily.

Work Left to Do

1. Lee must identify specific reports to be generated from the data bank. A meeting
   is scheduled for April 11 so that we can define these requirements.
2. We must create and install record-generating parameters into the program. This
   should take about seven programming hours.
3. User instructions have to be documented. Writing, testing, and producing the
   documentation should take two days.

Anticipated Problems

None

Forecast

We should complete, install, and document the program by May 1, and emergency
room users should be able to begin data input that same day.

Figure 3.4 *Example of a brief project report.*

LOSS REPORT

For: Allison Trust Brokers
By: Matthew S. Pendeen

Account: 15900-Z288
Date of Loss: July 16, 19--
Date of Inspection: July 8, 19--
Loss No: AC-12

Summary
The failure of two of three single-phase 480/240 v transformers interrupted the power supply to the freezing department of Acme Foods.

Description
The equipment discussed is one of two 480/240 v AC 50 KVA single-phase transformers connected in delta/delta to supply 320 v AC 60 Hz three-phase power for lighting, motor controls, and motor operation in the freezing department.

Each transformer is a single-phase 480 v/120–240, 50 KVA, single-phase, Class AA, Type DB, ADD polarity, 3.8% impedance with Class B insulation, manufactured by Nappier Upton in 1979; their serial numbers are Q-4680 and Q-3254. These transformers were protected on the primary side by a fused disconnect manufactured by WTB, Cat. F277,200A, 600 VAC, three-phase 480 v with standard 60 hp–120 hp maximum. The secondary side is protected by a fused disconnect manufactured by Vestron Electric, Type A Cat. 64448 600 A, 3-pole, 600 VAC.

These transformers have been in continuous operation since 1980 without failures, repairs, modifications, or preventive maintenance. They are suspended from the overhead, where the ambient temperature ranges from 27 to 32 degrees C.

Incident
On Monday, July 16, 19--, at 9:15 a.m. lighting in the freezing department went out. The supervisor reported sparks emitting from transformer Q-4680 and immediately opened the primary disconnect.

An electrical contractor was called, and he inspected both transformers. He noted the following: The conductor above the x-3 connection on transformer Q-4680 was burnt in two; the clamp bar below the connection was burnt in two; the secondary winding was open.

The damaged transformer (Q-4680) was disconnected and the other transformer was placed back in 240 v three-phase service at around 10:45 a.m. Lighting was restored at the same time and two of the three conveyor lines in the freezing department were started. After a short period, the other line was started. About 30 minutes later (approximately 11:15), lights in the freezing department flickered, and sparks erupted at one of the light panels.

The electrical contractor (still at the plant) determined that the secondary windings of the transformer were open and the conductor at the x-2 connection and the clamp bar were burnt in two. Senior management decided to install a 150 KVA transformer, available locally and immediately.

At 4:00 p.m. the new 150 KVA transformer was delivered, and installation was completed by 9:00 p.m. on July 16, 19--. The plant resumed normal operations at 7:00 a.m. on July 17, 19--, with the new 150 KVA transformer supplying power to motors, and the remaining 50 KVA transformer supplying power to lighting and motor control.

Damage and Repairs

Damage to transformer Q-4680 was confined to an open secondary winding and a 5cm half round clamp bar. Ten conductors in the conduit below the light panel were damaged. The transformer has salvageable parts and could be kept for spare parts.

The installation of the new transformer included the following: 36 metres of 500 MCM and 14 metres of 00 conductors, 10 small lighting conductors in the conduit, 5 metres of 10cm conduit, and 3 metres of 5cm flex. Repairs were completed on July 17, 19--.

Interruption to Production

This incident prevented 36,788 kilos of vegetables from being processed while the freezing department was down. Thirty-eight employees were sent home at about 12:00 noon.

Cause

A short in No. 1 lighting panel conduit caused the loss of transformer Q-4680. An intermittent short in the light panel caused the second overload after the system was re-energized briefly.

Special Investigation

The x-3 terminal on transformer Q-4680 was thinned and pitted, which could have caused a high resistance at the terminal connections.

Loss Estimate: $15,000

Figure 3.5 *Example of a situation report.*

situation or occurrence report that gives complete details. As you read the report, do not expect to understand all the technical terms. The very specific audience (a plant manager or insurance adjuster) would understand them.

Situation reports answer such typical questions as these about an event, incident, or condition:

- What was the situation?
- What exactly happened?
- Was anyone involved?
- What was the specific time frame?
- What were the causes?
- What was done by responsible personnel?
- What were the consequences or results?
- What should happen next?

Site Visit Reports

Site visit reports describe visits, trips, observations, or actions taken at a location other than the writer's own worksite. For example, an employee might be asked to visit a plant, an institution, a region, or a specific department of a large company. Such visits are often referred to as field trips because they require leaving one's normal place of employment and going into the "field." Site visits are necessary when industries are thinking of relocating; when inspectors need to review local situations or to conduct tests; when companies are checking on policies, procedures, or equipment used by others; when someone is needed to assist temporarily at another site or location. People who make site visits document what happened, what they saw and learned, and the impressions they gathered. Figure 3.6 shows a site visit report responding to a request for a safety procedure check.

Site visit reports always relate to a place and the reason for the visit. They answer questions such as these:

- What site was visited?
- When was the site visited?
- Why was the visit made?
- Who was involved?
- What precisely was gained or accomplished?
- What are the implications for our company?

TO: E. J. Gunn, TMM Portsea
FROM: Janis Milon, Portsea CG Radio
DATE: August 18, 199x
SUBJECT: Tower Safety Procedures, Arbour Transmitter Site

I checked safety procedure conformance at the Arbour site on August 17, 199x, with G. Cottreau, Co-op Student, attending. The following safety procedures were noted:
- The number of each tower is marked on the tower base.
- The Antenna Layout Drawing (MM-104-012-AL) is prominently displayed on the equipment room wall.
- The Tower Shut-Down Procedure is also prominently posted next to the antenna layout drawing. However, the procedure needs clarification.

Actions Taken
I have clarified the steps in the Tower Shut-Down Procedure as follows:

Tower Shut-Down Procedure

When a tower is to be shut down for antenna maintenance, the following procedure is to be used:

1. Using the tower markings and antenna layout drawing as references, the technician shall confirm which tower is to be de-energized.
2. The technician shall put the associated transmitter in LOCAL control, and shall shut off the transmitter high voltage.
3. The technician shall place on the transmitter front panel a red tag or equivalent sign which shall readily indicate that the transmitter has been shut down for maintenance.
4. From electrical panels A, B, or C, the technician shall shut off the A.C. breakers associated with the transmitter and the tower to be de-energized.
5. The technician shall put a red tag on each of these affected A.C. breaker panels. On the red tag, the technician shall write the reason for the shut-down, with the technician's signature.
6. At the de-energized tower, the technician shall ground the antenna feed points.
7. Where it is impractical for the technician to ground the feed-points, the technician may delegate the feed-point grounding procedure to the rigger. The technician shall witness the feed-point grounding.
8. The antenna system is now ready for maintenance.
9. Normally, the technician who shut down the system will remain at the site during the antenna system maintenance, and shall be responsible for re-energizing the system and restoring the service. However, if that technician is unavailable at the site, he/she shall be consulted before the antenna system is re-energized by other technicians.

With your approval, this procedure will supersede that displayed at the Arbour site.

Figure 3.6 *Example of a site visit report.*
Adapted with permission from Canadian Coast Guard.

Process Descriptions and Instructions

Documents that tell readers how something is done or how to perform some action are called process descriptions or instructions. They describe a process so that readers understand the methods and general procedures necessary to achieve a specific result. A process description might present an overview of how equipment works or how a procedure is handled. Instructions show precisely how to do something, how to proceed step-by-step through a series of sequential actions. As illustrated in Figure 3.7, instructions must be clear, concise, and complete.

Sometimes the difference between a process description and a set of instructions is slight. When the reader wants to know how an assembly line operates or how paint is produced, for example, a process description is needed. When the reader needs to know exactly how to set up the assembly line or exactly what tasks are required and in what order to produce a certain shade of paint, instructions are required. Whether the information is needed for *understanding* how the process works or for actually *doing* the process usually determines the form of the material. These informational documents rely heavily on showing as well as telling. Instructions are usually numbered or listed, are succinctly written, and are usually shorter than other types of technical information. Readers expect to understand exactly how something is done or to be able to follow easily the process for efficient performance of a task. Process descriptions and instructions answer questions such as these:

◆ What are these instructions used for?
◆ What materials or supplies are needed?
◆ What equipment is needed?
◆ What safety measures must be taken?
◆ What level of expertise is expected?
◆ What is the first step in the process?
◆ What is the second, the third, the fourth, the final step?
◆ What problems may occur?
◆ How are problems overcome?
◆ What will be the final outcome?
◆ How will I know that I have done everything correctly?

Compare the instructions for setting up the 5-in-1 Remote Control shown in Figure 3.7 with the following description of a process excerpted from a student report shown in Figure 3.8, in which Joseph Boutilier briefly explains how repeater software works.

Clearly, the remote control instructions intend the reader to *act;* the repeater software description intends the reader to *understand*.

SETTING UP THE 5-IN-1

Follow these steps to set up your 5-in-1.

1. Remove the battery compartment cover and install four fresh AAA Alkaline batteries (Radio Shack 23-555) as indicated by the polarity (+ and −) symbols marked in the compartment.

   Note: Do not place objects on the top of the remote control after you install the batteries. This can press down keys and reduce battery life.

2. Refer to "Manufacturer's Codes" and write down the codes for your original remote control on the provided label.

3. Press the device key for the remote you are replacing (TV, VCR, CABLE, AUX 1, or AUX 2).

4. Press down and hold PROG until the red indicator blinks twice, and continue holding it down as you enter the 3-digit manufacturer code.

   For example, to replace a Panasonic TV's remote control (manufacturer code 051), you would press:

   TV—PROG—0—5—1

5. When the indicator blinks twice again, release PROG.

6. Point the 5-in-1 at your device and press POWER. The device should turn on (or off, if it was on).

Repeat Steps 2–6 for additional devices.

Note: The punch-through feature is automatically turned on for the TV's volume and mute controls. This means that when you select CABLE and press one of the volume buttons or the MUTE button, the remote actually sends the codes to the television, and not the cable converter. If you want to use your cable converter's volume and mute controls, disable the punch-through feature for these buttons. See "Punch Through".

If the remote does not operate your device, try other codes listed in "Manufacturer's Codes" for your brand of TV, VCR, or cable box.

If your device still does not respond, follow the steps outside outlined in "If you Have Problems".

Note: When the 5-in-1's range decreases or the 5-in-1 operates erratically, replace the batteries.

Caution: Be sure to have the fresh batteries ready to install before you remove the old batteries. The 5-in-1's memory only lasts about a minute without the batteries. If the memory is lost, simply re-enter the 3-digit codes for your remote control products.

Figure 3.7 *Example of step-by-step instructions.*
Five-in-One Remote Control Owner's Manual, pages 6 and 7. Radio Shack. Reprinted with permission of InterTAN Canada Ltd.

The software for this project was written in CBM BASIC V2. It is the standard operating system of the VIC20/C64 computer line. A complete program is listed in Appendix A.

The program itself is a continuous loop. The program begins by initializing the communication bus to and from the controller circuit board. After entering the loop, the program checks the status of the input lines, checks either timer, updates the video display, and acts on the inputs if necessary. Actions that the controller might take include keying the transmitter, sending a tone, or producing a series of tones that together form Morse code.

Figure 3.8 *Example of a process description.*
From The Design and Construction of a Radio Communications Repeater Controller *(1993). Used with permission of Joseph Boutilier, EMT.*

ANALYTICAL REPORTS

Analytical reports build on information, going beyond the mere giving of data. They interpret the facts. These reports often try to find a cause or causes of a problem, and they may show long- or short-range consequences. For example, the gathering of data about weather patterns would provide the content for an informational report. An analytical report based on those data might provide a tentative forecast of future weather patterns. Analytical reports may compare and contrast sets of data for the purpose of determining what works best under what circumstances. They may review with the intention of determining who or what caused something, such as an industrial accident or a labour grievance, for example. Often longer than informational reports, analytical reports analyze and evaluate relevant data and typically contain conclusions based on that data. Analytical reports usually deal with *why* something is so and answer questions such as the following:

◆ Why does the municipality strictly regulate extensions to residences in the city?

◆ Why has the university retained a consulting firm to inspect the exterior lighting system on campus?

◆ Why have advertised tax breaks failed to attract new industry to a region?

◆ Which new cancer-screening equipment — scanner X or scanner Y — is more suitable for a local clinic?

◆ What has been the effect of newly implemented bed-and-breakfast rating standards on rural operators?

Activity 2

Read the following pairs of report titles and check the title in each pair that seems analytical rather than only informational.

_____ a. Long-Term Disability Insurance: How to Claim

_____ a. Long-Term Disability: An Analysis of Provincial Recipients

_____ b. Uses of a VersaCAD System in a Small Drafting Firm

_____ b. The VersaCAD 5.0 System: Alternatives to Problem Areas

_____ c. Improving the Purchasing Process at Casey Boat Builders: Cost and Time Factors

_____ c. How to Complete a Purchase Order

_____ d. WHMIS Courses for Community College Students

_____ d. The Effectiveness of WHMIS Instruction at Cunnard Campus

Specific Kinds of Analytical Reports

Various reports have the specific goal of analyzing and interpreting material. Two major ones, evaluation and feasibility reports, are discussed below.

Evaluation Reports

Evaluation reports present data and the writer's judgment of that data. The writer measures the accumulated data against criteria or a set of standards, draws inferences and presents conclusions. Here the writer must go beyond the *what* and conclude *why* and *so what*. For example, if A, B, and C are true, then D follows. If Tony Alveriso was injured by a piece of metal flying from a machine, if Jane Allen was injured a few days later at the same machine, and if two other employees reported seeing stray scraps of debris falling from the machine, and these facts are verified, then an inspector can infer or conclude that there is a safety problem with the machine. Inspection reports that detail the review of a facility, program, piece of equipment, procedure, or policy typically do more than report; they evaluate. They point out weaknesses, flaws, and measures needed to correct problems, as well as positive points, policies, and procedures. Because evaluation reports tend to be fairly long, Figure 3.9 shows only a summary of an evaluation report.

EVALUATION OF REMOVAL TECHNIQUES OF ORGANIC SPECIES IN UTILITY POWER PLANT COOLING WATER SYSTEMS

Summary

The presence of algae in the secondary loop of power plant cooling water systems has recently received attention throughout the utility industry. These organic species contribute to operational chemistry control problems and possibly to corrosion concerns. A significant amount of data must be collected before the role of organic contamination in secondary systems can be addressed fully.

The initial phase of this evaluation project, which is covered in this report, focused on two sites: Jones Plant and Brown Plant. At Jones, historical plant data and a special six-month online monitory program identified an unmeasured acidic species as the source of pH/cation conductivity mismatches. The program followed up that finding with an online organic acid survey and a brief study of organic removal techniques. This report describes the results of these tests.

Analysis of Jones's makeup water determined that neutral, nonvolatile organics are present. The neutral organics decompose and result in formic, acetic propionic, and lactic acid in the secondary system. These short-chain organic acids account for the mismatches in measured cation conductivity and measured inorganic ions. Makeup resins were investigated as a possible source of the organic contamination and were determined to be noncontributory to the organic contamination at Jones. This project evaluated laboratory filtration and carbon absorption attempts. These methods were unsuccessful in reducing the organic contamination levels of the makeup water.

Cooling tower cation conductivities at the Brown Plant during initial start-up operations led to a sampling program that helped identify the source of the high cation conductivity. This program involved a variety of analysis techniques (for example, ion chromatography) to detect the species contributing to the elevated cation conductivity. Autoclave testing was used to determine whether several vapour phase inhibitors were responsible for the organic species in the secondary cycle.

These initial analytical and evaluation tests are part of a larger program to identify and to quantify the type, source, and transport of organic species in power plant secondary cooling systems. An industry-wide sampling survey of approximately 17 plants is currently being performed. This survey is collecting data that can subsequently be used to address corrosion concerns and possible removal techniques.

Figure 3.9 *Summary of an evaluation report.*

Evaluation reports answer questions such as these:

◆ Is the project meeting its objectives?

◆ How well or to what extent is it doing so?

◆ What improvements are needed?

◆ What factors are influential in determining the status of the project (time, money, personnel)?

◆ Why is the project not going well (behind schedule, over budget)?

◆ Why is the project going well (on schedule, within budget)?

Note that answering the last question provides important information for the success of future projects. It also recognizes the efforts of personnel involved in planning and implementing the project.

Feasibility Reports

Feasibility reports, or studies, assess the practicality of a proposed project or change. They assist readers in deciding whether a possible course of action is worth pursuing, whether something can be done within reason (is "feasible"), and whether that course of action is economically or technically likely to succeed. These reports consider all (or at least significant) facets of a proposed or continuing action and conclude that an action is justified or that it is not. Before major design changes are made, before companies locate or relocate, before organizations make major policy shifts, before most changes occur, a feasibility study is carried out to help answer the basic question "Does proceeding with this action make sense?" A full-length feasibility report is included in Chapter Fifteen.

Questions such as the following are usually addressed in any feasibility report:

◆ What is the current situation?

◆ Is sufficient need shown to warrant the action?

◆ Is sufficient capital available?

◆ What legal concerns must be considered?

◆ Is the technology available if needed?

◆ Are appropriate personnel available?

◆ What are the long-range benefits?

◆ What are the costs?

◆ What are the long-range problems?

◆ What will be the social and/or environmental impacts?

PERSUASIVE REPORTS

The main purpose of persuasive reports is to influence decisions in determining a course of action. They are concerned with the action-oriented question "What next?" They must contain data, and they must give an interpretation of that data. Both data and interpretation, however, are presented with the clear intent of getting something done in a specified manner or within a specified time or by a specified organization or individual. Most often both the title and the body of a persuasive report will contain specific words that clearly show that the writer's purpose is to influence or persuade.

In terms of the five general topics noted on p. 49, you might write persuasive reports to show the following:

◆ The necessity of regulating the construction of extensions to city residences

◆ The need to upgrade the exterior lighting on St. Brigit's campus

◆ The advantages of tax breaks for new industries in a region

◆ The time benefit of a clinic's purchasing your company's innovative diagnostic machine

◆ The probability of improving the quality of bed-and-breakfast operations by implementing a provincial standard

Activity 3

Check the following report titles that you consider to be persuasive.

_____ a. Proposal for a Tanker Truck Refuelling Process

_____ b. The Need for Improved Water Treatment Facilities in Sackville

_____ c. Effects of Upgrading Computer Facilities at Jubilee Road School

_____ d. Building a Regulated Adjusted DC Power Supply

_____ e. Departmental Procedures Following the Use of Deadly Force

_____ f. Ultrasonic Cholangiography: Its Purpose and Procedure

_____ g. A Dental Survey of Bear River Child-Care Centre

_____ h. Improving the Security System at Echo Lake Recreational Centre

_____ i. A Rationale for Implementing Distance Education Courses
at Maitland High School

_____ j. A "Plot for the Future": A Food Bank U-Plant Initiative

Specific Kinds of Persuasive Reports

Proposals and responses to requests for proposals are the two most
frequently written kinds of persuasive reports. Each is described
below.

Proposals

Proposals do just what their name indicates: They propose — a
change, a solution, an action. A solicited proposal is written in
response to an invitation. If a writer initiates a proposal without an
invitation, it is called unsolicited. Proposals point out a problem or
need and state a suggested solution. The writer (representing one
person, a department, or an organization) wants something to be
done. For example, an administrator may want to reinstate a certain
form of insurance, a department may want to reorganize, a company
may want the federal government to provide funds for certain training programs, a radio station may want to change its format.

A proposal is a strong statement that shows why, how, in what circumstances or conditions, and with what results some action should
be undertaken. As such it gives specific details intended to convince
the reader of the validity of a decision or action. Figure 3.10 on pages
67 and 68 illustrates a proposal for a change within a company.

Readers expect proposals to answer many questions, such as the
following:

- Exactly what are you proposing?
- Why are you proposing it?
- What is the current situation?
- What are the benefits of accepting the proposal?
- How much financing is involved?
- How much time is required?
- How will the work be accomplished?
- How many people are involved?
- What facilities and equipment are required?
- How will you evaluate the outcome?
- Why should *you* be awarded the contract or why should *your*
proposal be accepted?

PROPOSAL FOR INSTALLING AN IN-HOUSE PVC PIPE-THREADING MACHINE

Submitted to:
Carl W. Treadway, Owner Treadway Manufacturing Company

Submitted by:
Manuel Fuente, Supervisor
March 18, 19--

Summary

Designing, constructing, and using a CNC PVC threading machine in-house will eliminate delays by our supplier (Sigma) and will expedite prompt deliveries of exact dimension PVC pipe. Treadway has both cost-effective technology and efficient personnel to improve the current manufacturing situation.

Current Situation

As you are well aware, Treadway Manufacturing is having serious problems in getting prompt and efficient service on the threading of PVC pipe. So far this year, our company has been late in delivering orders for PVC pipe of 20–30-cm diameter a total of 21 times.

One major buyer (Omni, Inc.) cancelled its contract, and others expressed dissatisfaction with our delivery dates. The Order Department reports that it is not unusual now to have a buyer ask, "Are you sure you can get the pipe to us on time?" For each of the 21 late deliveries, Treadway was ready with all orders except those for 20- and 30-cm pipe.

All PVC pipes are threaded by Sigma here in Braeside, and it has difficulty with the larger pipe sizes. According to Sigma, two problems prevented prompt delivery of the pipe:

1. Setting up a manual lathe requires approximately two hours.
2. The first piece of pipe (or sometimes the first few) must be scrapped because the lathe operator considers them practice runs.

Solution

I am proposing in-house threading of PVC pipe. Treadway already does the slotting of its PVC pipe before shipping it to the main plant in Hamilton for cleaning, packing, and shipping to the customer. A natural extension of this procedure is also to do the in-house threading of the pipe. One of our technicians, Louis Tomblin, has designed a computer numerically controlled (CNC) PVC threading machine that would not only solve these late delivery problems, but would also solve some of our quality control problems.

Tomblin's machine design is shown in detail in the appendix to this proposal. The CNC threading machine cuts male acme threads on one end of the pipe and female acme threads on the other and threads pipe sizes from 10 to 30 cm. Basically, the machine consists of the following components:

- A motorized horizontal rotary holding fixture
- A reciprocating carriage

- A table with shaft support rails
- Two stepping motors

Operation of the machine requires the following equipment:

- A computer
- A translator

The machine can produce a double-lead acme thread on the O.D. (outside diameter) and I.D. (inside diameter) of a piece of PVC pipe using a CNC reciprocating carriage not equipped with helical interpretation, with a cycle time of approximately four minutes. Several pages of design features are attached to this proposal.

Benefits

By using an in-house CNC PVC threading machine, Treadway would eliminate the problem of late delivery by our supplier (Sigma) and of occasionally misaligned threads and subsequent loss of time due to practice runs. Applying this latest technology within our own plant site gives us greater control over manufacturing/delivery schedules and quality.

Implementation

Treadway has a technician who can oversee the construction of the threading machine and can complete the necessary calculations to set up the CNC operation. Total implementation should take approximately 120 days.

A recent graduate of Hamilton Tech can train any Treadway worker to use the machine in a matter of hours. Maintenance will be minimal. A service contract on the computer is an option open to consideration.

Costs

The entire project should come in under $4,000 since most of the construction can be completed by Treadway technicians. A certified electrician must be employed to wire the translator, computer, and stepping motors.

A general estimate of costs follows:

Computer	$2,500
Translator	125
Materials and motors	1,000
Electrician's charges	175

A detailed breakdown of costs is also attached to this proposal.

Conclusion

Installing an in-house PVC pipe-threading machine will greatly improve the efficiency and effectiveness of Treadway Manufacturing. I would appreciate a meeting to explain the details and to gain project approval.

Figure 3.10 *Example of a brief proposal.*

Responses to Requests for Proposals (RFPs)

Responses to requests for proposals (RFPs) indicate specifically what an entity can do to meet a stated need and specifically how it can do so. RFPs document expectations on the part of a company or agency, often a governmental one, that wants a job done; they are invitations to submit bids. When an RFP is made, the problem or need has already been recognized, and certain characteristics of the solution have already been identified. You, the writer, are being requested to respond to the recognized need by supplying specific, detailed information about how you or your organization can precisely meet the need. An RFP is illustrated in Figure 16.5.

Readers of responses to RFPs expect answers to questions such as these:

◆ What are the size specifications of any equipment needed for the job?
◆ What is the scope of delivery, installation, and maintenance service provided?
◆ What is the specified function of equipment or range of service?
◆ What detailed and exact costs are involved?

QUESTIONS FOR DISCUSSION

1. What are the three general types of reports based on purpose?
2. What forms the base of all reports?
3. Name some of the reports written in industry. Explain how they use information as a base.
4. What is the main difference between giving instructions and describing a process?
5. How do evaluation reports differ from feasibility reports?
6. What are the distinguishing characteristics of a proposal? Of a response to an RFP?

EXERCISE 1

a. You have been asked to write a report on Foamcore insulation. Below are three statements expressing the intent of the report. Beside each one, indicate whether a report based on that statement would be informational (*I*), analytical (*A*), or persuasive (*P*):

_____ 1. This report shows how Foamcore insulation is installed in a standard mobile home.

       _____ 2. This report shows the advantages of installing Foamcore insulation in the standard mobile home.

       _____ 3. This report shows the components that make up Brand X , Brand Z, and Foamcore insulation used in standard mobile homes.

b. You have been asked to write a report on the parking problem at Hometown Institute of Technology. For each type of report, write a sentence that clearly states your purpose.

1. Informational: _____

_____

2. Analytical: _____

_____

3. Persuasive: _____

_____

c. You have been asked to write a report on poor television reception in the Appletree Valley. Again, write a sentence that clearly states your purpose in each type of report.

1. Informational: _____

_____

2. Analytical: _____

_____

3. Persuasive: _____

_____

EXERCISE 2

Assume that your supervisor, Jason Peters, calls you to the office and says the following:

a. Jason: "We've decided that we want to ask our regional offices to assume responsibility for certain programs, including employee assistance. That will mean a change in some key administrative posts, so they may not want to take it on; however, overall the company expects to save money and to improve morale. Send me a proposal for the changes in a couple of weeks so that I can present them at the next board meeting."

What kind of report does Jason expect? _____

What influenced your answer? _____

b. Jason: "As you may know, I'm meeting with our Alberta rep next month, and he'll want to know how the employee assistance program here works. Can you get me a report on that, including our procedures and our policy regarding spousal and family support?"

What kind of report is Jason requesting? _____

Identify any specific word(s) or phrase(s) that influenced your

answer. _____

c. Jason: "Say, I've heard there's some dissatisfaction with our employee assistance program. Since we're committed to it for at least three years, please investigate the situation and see what the underlying trouble areas are. You might start with the personnel director, who's been keeping tabs on it. We need to know just how serious the problems are at this point."

What kind of report does Jason expect? _____

How do you know? _____

WRITING ASSIGNMENTS

1. Look closely (as a technical writer might) at your footwear. For five minutes, jot down all the facts (just the facts) about your shoes (colour, cost, material, and so on).
   a. Write a paragraph that conveys only *information* about your footwear. Keep the tone neutral and objective.
   b. Write a paragraph in which you *analyze* your footwear. You may, for example, compare your shoes with others, or you may evaluate their value and usefulness. Assume that a friend has asked for your analysis of the shoes before he or she buys a pair.

c. Assume that you work for the company that produced your footwear. In a paragraph, *persuade* your friend to purchase the brand you are wearing.

2. You have just finished contract training with Loranco, and your supervisor, Ted Chapman, recommends that you be offered an entry-level position (full-time). Loranco has just landed a large contract and is hiring 10 new workers. The only problem is that Ted Chapman wants you to start one week before your final term ends. You have told James Flinn, your department head, of this important offer and you request permission to leave the program one week early. At first, Mr. Flinn is reluctant to approve the request: The final week is examination week and special arrangements would have to be made with your instructors. However, he asks you to put the request in writing.

Write a memo requesting that you be allowed to leave the program early. You may support your request with some of the following information:

◆ Name of your program
◆ Your current status in college (number of courses completed)
◆ Average marks for terms completed
◆ Particular achievements
◆ Work (amount and kind) needed to graduate
◆ Expected graduation date
◆ Value of job opportunity

You also know that a similar request was made three years ago and the instructors were willing to make special arrangements for the student to write examinations early.

Use the memo format illustrated in Figure 3.6 as a model, or use a template provided by your word processor.

Part TWO

DEVELOPING A PLAN

Objectives

When you have finished Part Two — Chapters Four, Five, and Six — you should be able to do the following:

◆ Focus on specific writing and audience needs in effective reports by taking these steps:

Selecting an appropriate topic
Identifying clear objectives
Identifying audience characteristics
Determining the specific kind of report needed

◆ Organize ideas clearly according to the following types of order:

Chronological
Spatial
Enumeration
Cause and effect
Comparison and contrast
Problem–solution
Methodology–results

◆ Create effective topic or sentence outlines that have the following characteristics:

Traditional or decimal format
Clear and complete controlling sentence
Logical and full development
Parallel structure

◆ Collect valid information from both nonprint and print resources in the community, college, and workplace.

◆ Take notes and integrate summarized, paraphrased, and directly quoted material into a rough draft.

◆ Cite sources and document references correctly.

Chapter FOUR

Focusing on Writer and Audience Needs

ompetent reporting requires efficient planning. To produce a successful report, you will need to

◆ Select a topic.

◆ Focus on a specific aspect of the topic.

◆ Identify your objectives.

◆ Target your readers and their needs.

◆ Determine the kind of report that will best meet your objectives and your readers' needs.

SELECTING A TOPIC

For most beginning classroom writers, selecting a topic is one of the most difficult tasks in preparing a technical report. In the workplace, however, technical reports are typically assigned by a supervisor, or they are an expected, routine part of the job.

Writing Situations: Workplace and Classroom

On the job, you write a report because someone needs the information for a specific purpose and at a specific time. As an employee, you will be assigned a task and be expected to document it. For example, a supervisor may say, "Check this situation out and get a report to me in two weeks." You will then plan, conduct, and document your investigation or inspection in an appropriate report and deliver it to your supervisor by the deadline set.

As a student, you have the challenge of finding a topic suitable for the course requirements, working within formal guidelines, and having deadlines established by the instructor or technical advisor. The report may be a requirement for graduation and accepted as part of the certification process by your professional body. In such a case, you may be working for your writing instructor, an instructor in your discipline, and possibly an outside firm that can offer a suitable project and is willing to participate in your training.

If you are employed, either full-time or part-time, you should choose a report ideally from your actual work situation or related to some aspect of your field that you would like to develop further. This is your opportunity to apply directly the writing principles that you are learning here. The following are hypothetical examples of writing opportunities in different fields.

Manufacturing: You work at a local carpet manufacturing plant that is considering an expansion of its storage facilities. Your supervisor asks for a review of the current storage space and for some suggestions for increasing storage space at minimal cost.

Entrepreneurship: You intend to open a small engine repair business in your area and have explored two or three locations. Before proceeding further, you must provide your lending institution with a report that will influence its decision on whether and to what extent to finance your project. The report must contain a complete business plan. You must detail each location, its advantages and drawbacks, potential clientele, monthly costs, projected revenues, and payoff dates.

Quality Assurance: Your firm is now committed to the implementation and documentation of an ISO 9000 Quality Management System. You are now a member of a group whose task it is to write procedures and work instructions for your department. Your document will include appropriate graphics.

Productivity Improvement: You have been asked to examine the procurement (or purchasing) process at your plant and to recommend means of reducing time and cost involved. You will need to examine each step of the process carefully, from raising the requisition slip to issuing the purchase order. Then you will decide on the most feasible productivity improvement measures and make recommendations from your data.

A "Workplace" Topic

Many of you will have written book reviews or researched topics for term papers or projects. Such research reports have helped you learn to retrieve printed information from libraries. You have then synthesized the data, organized it, and written the report. Literature searches resulting in written literature surveys fulfil an important purpose: They furnish much-needed up-to-date information. However, finding information that is not readily accessible in printed sources is also essential to keeping current with developments in your field. Remember, too, that effective technical reports in the workplace are not usually generalizations about a topic but rather responses to specific job-related problems and needs.

For example, a local condominium corporation made the following project available to two mechanical engineering technology students. This energy study and design project for an 84-unit condominium enabled the students to apply their technical knowledge and gain valuable experience in problem solving, project management, and technical writing.

The proposal for this project originates from the need to examine long-term cost containment measures for the condo building. Concerns are particularly acute because all the building's space heating and hot water is electric. Space heating for the units is controlled by individual room thermostats in each unit (baseboard heaters), and hot water is provided from a central hot water tank.

In essence, all of the building's electrical consumption is supplied through one metered supply. The cost of providing heat and hot water services to individual units is levied through the condominium fee.

The current annual expenditure for electricity is in the range of $90,000 to $100,000. Identification of energy-saving mechanisms and practices are considered an essential long-term cost containment strategy. The focus of the study is expected to be principally in the area of mechanisms and systems, the largest of which are heating components.

One of the obvious potential areas to mitigate costs is hot water heating. Design options for alternate energy use, such as passive solar panels, need to be investigated and ultimately specified with projections on energy recovered (added) through such systems.

A financial analysis is necessary to justify investments in capital proposed. Disaggregating the costs for each of the major energy uses in the building would be needed to isolate hot water heating and other costs.

The outcomes of this project are expected to include

◆ A complete energy use/cost profile for the building
◆ Design options for systems to mitigate energy use
◆ Estimates of the capital expenditures required as well as financial justification for the investment
◆ A practical plan for implementation

As you can see, this energy study and design project addresses a particular problem and illustrates how technology responds to human needs. You can therefore find possible workplace topics all around you — in the fast-food industry, your campus, local governmental agencies, local department stores, and your neighbourhood, and at your job. Here are just a few possibilities:

Food management: How a franchise is set up for a fast-food restaurant.

Office technology: How to plan and implement "one-stop shopping" for students registering at your campus.

Transportation and communications: How to persuade your local traffic authority to reduce the increasingly heavy traffic on residential streets in your part of the city.

Construction technology: What planning and implementation procedures are involved in extensive renovations at your local airport.

Engineering technology: Designing a smoke alarm for the hearing impaired, modifying the braking system on a mountain bike, investigating Programmable Logic Control (PLC) for a local application.

Public administration: Determining the effectiveness of some local ordinance.

Business and marketing: Setting up a small business in a section of your town or county.

Health-care services: Choosing a new piece of equipment for the laboratory where you work.

Examine briefly just one of these possibilities: choosing a new piece of equipment for your laboratory. It would be simple and easy — but not very effective — merely to write a general review of the value of the piece of equipment. As an example, consider a recently upgraded X-ray machine that many hospitals would like to have but have managed without because it is very expensive. A valid technical report on this topic might do the following:

♦ Demonstrate the specific uses of the machine in your lab.

♦ Describe its benefits for users (technicians).

♦ Explain its benefits for patients at the lab.

♦ Discuss its costs in relation to its perceived need.

If you are employed, it is quite reasonable to assume that you are currently working on a project that requires documentation. If this is not the case, ask your supervisor for the opportunity to investigate and report on something that would have real value for the company: the progress of some new construction, determining the cost of equipping offices or labs, surveying employees' reaction to specific company policies, or documenting a new or revised process.

If you are not currently working and cannot relate your report to an actual workplace situation, confer with instructors in your major field of study. Ask whether any of the following ideas might be good possibilities: comparing two pieces of equipment or two processes, investigating a new procedure in your field, or reviewing policies and suggesting improvements in some area. Your instructors can help by pointing out "problem" areas that may lead to a topic, by indicating the availability or lack of resources on topics you have in mind, and by indicating whether a topic is too simple or too complex.

Activity 1

If you are employed, confer with your supervisor and make a list of possible topics for a report. In the blanks below, list them in order of preference, with the one you like best first.

If you are not employed, confer with instructors in your major field and make a list of possible topics for a report. In the blanks below, list them with the most appropriate first.

_____

_____

_____

_____

Review the topics you listed in Activity 1 and start to narrow the list by asking yourself this question: "Is the topic researchable in terms of the time and resources available to me?"

Time: As you consider your answer for each topic, remember that you are limited by time — in the classroom, in the workplace, and in your personal life. The few weeks assigned for the completion of your report may not allow you enough time to receive information from some individuals, agencies, or companies. People and organizations will not necessarily work within your time frame. Material that you need in January may not arrive until June. Also, if your topic requires that you travel to another city or province to investigate some situation, consider carefully and realistically just how much time you have and what alternative means of information gathering you have. Do not underestimate the time you will need for investigation and research.

Resources: As a student, you may very well have a major industry as a resource. For example, you may have been on contact training, or you may be reporting on a work term. You will then have specific reports to write: an application of business computer programming, the building of a firestation in a rural county, an aspect of airport improvement, negotiating a contract, preparing a bid, upgrading a piece of equipment, public relations, and writing service orders. Whatever topic you choose, you must consider the resources available (space, equipment, components) and the time allotted for the activity. It is important that you consult with your supervisor or instructor and that you modify or abandon a topic for which you have insufficient time, money, and other resources. Unquestionably, a topic awaits your investigation and documentation!

As a student, you also must consider your present understanding of the topic. Read two or three articles dealing with the potential topic. If you really do not comprehend them fairly well, then — at this stage of your education and knowledge — the topic is too technical or specialized. You are not expected to be a Certified Engineering Technologist, a hydrologist, or an accountant at this point. Select a topic about which you already know a good deal, not one that leaps far ahead of where you are now educationally.

Reading ahead: However, if you are allotted sufficient time for your report, you may well read ahead of your topic and even teach yourself new concepts before they are covered in your course. One aspect of adult education and of continuing learning is seizing any opportunity to teach yourself. Students undertaking report projects that require two semesters or one year often are able to learn on their own and ahead of their courses those concepts essential to the projects they have chosen. For example, by reading manuals and consulting with instructors, students have taught themselves a new programming language or advanced mathematical concepts necessary to the completion of their project. This kind of self-directed learning is extremely important not only to the topic at hand but also to a successful career. In any technical reporting situation, learning how to learn is an essential characteristic of the successful student. Therefore, consult with your instructors or work supervisors about your topics.

You will also find that no technology or discipline is isolated; it depends upon other technologies or other fields for its successful application. For example, if you are upgrading a tensile testing machine, you will need to consult outside the discipline of mechanical engineering technology. You will need to have an electronics or computer technologist work with you. Perhaps this is the most satisfactory aspect of working in any field or technology: You will quickly discover the interdependence of technical disciplines, and you will develop flexibility in your workplace simply because you have learned some appropriate skills from another discipline or technology.

FOCUSING ON SPECIFICS

Selecting a viable topic that has value in the workplace is a good first step for your technical report. You now must limit this topic so that it is manageable.

Methods for Limiting a Topic

Begin early to narrow your topic. Start by using these easy methods for limiting its scope: space, time, specific terminology, and journalistic questions. Depending on the topic, one of these methods should help you narrow a broad topic into one that is manageable for a technical report.

1. *Space (locale).* Most technical reports deal with a highly specialized locale. In a limited number of pages, you cannot adequately treat a topic on a world-wide basis. When appropriate, restrict it to a definite location.

2. *Time.* Most technical reports deal with the current situation, but some may compare an earlier situation with the current one, and some may project into the future. When applicable, limit your topic to a specific time frame.

3. *Specific terminology.* By moving from the general term to the specific one, from the unmodified to the modified, you begin to focus on a certain aspect of a topic. State exactly the people, places, and things with which the report will deal.

   Look at how the first three methods help narrow the following topics:

   > *Space (locale).* Limit "national parks" to "Waterton Lakes National Park."
   >
   > *Time.* Limit "X-ray technology" to "X-ray technology in 1996."
   >
   > *Specific terminology.* Limit "employee absenteeism" to "maintenance personnel absenteeism."

4. *Journalistic questions.* Another effective method of limiting your topic is to ask the questions common in journalism: what, why, when, where, how, and who. If, for example, you have selected "Desktop Publishing" as a possible topic, ask the following questions:

   ◆ *What* is it?
   ◆ *Why* was it developed? *Why* is it used? *Why* am I writing about it?
   ◆ *When* is it used? *When* is it better than other alternatives? *When* is it not useful?
   ◆ *Where* is it used? *Where* is its use not advised?

◆ *How* is it used? *How* is it different from its predecessors or counterparts?

◆ *Who* uses it? *Who* finds it most beneficial?

Apply all these journalistic queries, when appropriate, to focus the scope of your topic.

Activity 2

From Activity 1, select one topic that you determined was best suited for a technical report and ask journalistic questions to focus it.

Topic: _____

What? _____

Why? _____

When? _____

Where? _____

How? _____

Who? _____

The topic should now be sufficiently focused for a valid technical report.

Visual Devices: The Inverted Pyramid and Wedge

When applying any of the four methods for limiting a broad topic, you may also find it helpful to use one of these visual devices: the inverted pyramid or the wedge. Such devices allow you to *see* the narrowing process.

The *inverted pyramid* helps "funnel" a topic, level by level, until you arrive at a specific aspect of it. Figure 4.1 shows how to use the method of space in an inverted pyramid. Note how this visual device helps the writer narrow the topic to an increasingly specific locale. Figure 4.2 shows how an inverted pyramid and the method of *time* help move the topic from general to specific.

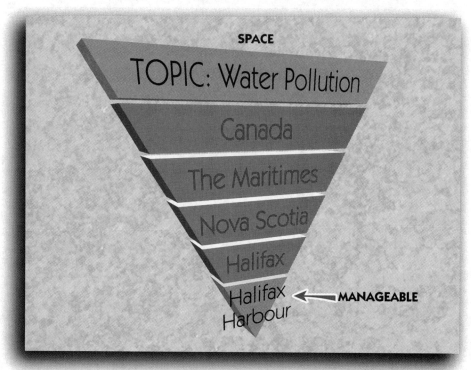

Figure 4.1 *This inverted pyramid helps the writer limit a topic according to space or locale.*

To limit a topic, you may prefer to use the *wedge*. Think of the topic as a pie, and then reduce the size of the pie or topic by slicing it into increasingly smaller wedges. Look at the example shown in Figure 4.3, where the writer uses the method of *specific terminology* and slices the broad topic into a manageable one.

If you are interested in the general topic "Plastics," as another example, you could start by imagining it as a giant pie. You then could apply the method of *journalistic questions*, or any of the methods, to limit the scope. By asking "*What* aspect of plastics?" you might first slice down your topic to the *uses* of plastics. Since this is still far too general to be manageable, you might then ask "*Where* are they used?" and cut the wedge into an even smaller section on the uses of plastics in *automobiles*. For a well-focused topic with a reasonable scope, you could then ask "*How* are they used in automobiles?" and arrive at a topic specific and small enough to deal with: "Uses of Plastics on Automotive Exteriors."

As a student writer, you will find these methods and devices helpful as you select and limit your technical report topics.

Figure 4.2 *With the help of this inverted pyramid, the writer narrows a topic according to time.*

IDENTIFYING YOUR OBJECTIVES

The next task in planning for your report is to identify your reasons for writing. You must have a clear understanding of your objectives. Identifying them helps ensure that all the information you present has the following qualities:

◆ *Importance.* The subject matter has a real and specific value to the individual(s) or organization for which it is written. The readers must know "what's in it for them." The information helps the audience make a decision, take a specific action, or solve a problem.

◆ *Relevance.* All the information included has a direct connection with the report's main topic and with the writer's main objectives. The information addresses all the questions that the audience expects to be answered.

You have selected and narrowed a good topic for your report. Now identify specifically what you intend to do with the topic —

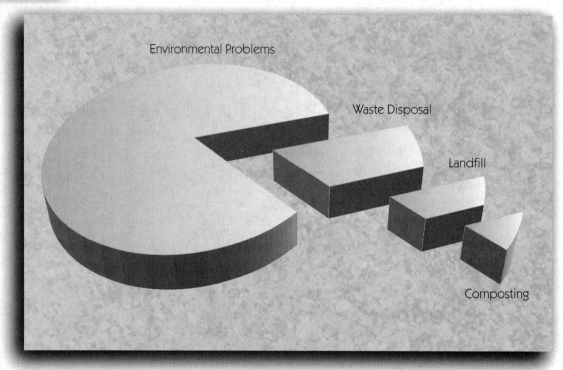

Figure 4.3 *Viewing a topic as a pie, the writer slices a topic into wedges by means of specific terminology.*

what your main objective is. An objective is the *reason* you prepare a report. It keeps you moving forward in a steady direction. A writer who has a clear main objective achieves far more than one who does not, and a writer with a *written* objective achieves the most of all.

Begin to identify your main objective by asking, "Why am I writing this report?" Try to state your answer as an infinitive phrase, that is, *to do something*. Use a *specific* verb (rather than a broad or general one) that clearly states the objective, or what you intend to accomplish, in the report. Understand that an objective for a technical report is not "to tell about my trip" or "to report on my test results." Clarity and specificity are needed to keep a writer focused and moving forward in a definite direction. In the sampling of verbs that follow, the verbs in the left-hand column are too broad and vague to give much direction when stating a main objective. The verbs in the right-hand column create a far more specific mission for a writer.

Too Broad and Vague	More Specific and Directed
Inform/familiarize	Instruct, verify, substantiate, document
Discuss/examine	Evaluate, determine, investigate, compare, recommend
Obtain/get	Persuade, convince, gain approval for, motivate

The vagueness of the verbs in the left-hand column could actually deter a writer from accomplishing his or her intended objective in writing the report. The verbs in the left-hand column could mean any of the more specific words in the right-hand column; yet many of the more specific verbs have different meanings from one another.

Here are some of the sufficiently focused topics mentioned earlier in this chapter and the ways in which a writer might identify a specific objective in writing about each topic:

♦ *To convince* my local government to proceed quickly with their initiative to clean up Halifax Harbour.

♦ *To verify* the work completed, in progress, and still to be done on pollutant cleanup in Halifax Harbour.

♦ *To evaluate* the impact of incinerating waste at Bagtown landfill.

♦ *To compare* the durability of plastics to metal in automobiles.

♦ *To instruct* my readers on how to replace a plastic fan drive assembly in an automobile.

A report may have more than one objective:

♦ To compare the capabilities of Software A and Software B *and* to recommend which my company should buy.

♦ To determine the feasibility of opening a small engine repair business in Digby Neck *and* to recommend a specific location for it.

♦ To convince my manager to buy a specific computer for my department *and* to get me the training to use it.

When planning a report, be sure to identify and state all your main objectives for writing it. Then continually remind yourself of these objectives to keep all information relevant to your topic and to keep all your efforts directed to the job at hand.

Activity 3

Read the sample topic and *specific* objectives given below. Next, in the spaces that follow, list a topic on which you might like to write a report. Finally, using specific verbs, state your objective(s). A sample topic and objective have been supplied.

Topic: <u>Machine operator training programs in a man-</u>
<u>ufacturing plant</u>

Objective(s): <u>To evaluate the effectiveness of</u>
<u>machine operator training efforts in manufactur-</u>
<u>ing companies and to convince my supervisor to</u>
<u>implement training programs at our plant</u>

Topic: _____

Objective(s): <u>To</u> _____

_____

_____

Take a closer look at your stated objectives in Activity 3. Can the verbs you used in them mean something other than you first intended? If so, you need to find more specific verbs. If not, you have set your writing efforts in a specific direction.

As a bonus, if you eventually decide to use the topic and accompanying objectives that you wrote in Activity 3, you can turn your objective statement into a controlling sentence by simply prefacing it with "The purpose of this report is …." For example, if your objective was "To document the advantages of using paper rather than plastic bags at the Farmers' Market," your controlling sentence could be: "The purpose of this report is to document the advantages of using paper rather than plastic bags at the Farmers' Market."

TARGETING YOUR AUDIENCE

The next task in planning your report is an essential one: analyzing your audience. An audience analysis is a valuable tool in helping you make some important choices in writing any kind of report. Identifying your audience helps ensure the *appropriateness* of all information included. That is, you should aim all information specifically at the audience's technical, authority, and interest levels.

Equally important, you should consistently consider the audience's main purpose in reading the report.

A Workplace Audience

When the report is a classroom assignment, it is often tempting to write for the instructor, as you probably do when writing themes and term papers in other classes. A technical report, however, should be written for those in a workplace environment or for your fellow students. When you have difficulty targeting a workplace or technical audience, write for a real one. If you have a job (part- or full-time), consider writing a report for one or more managers or colleagues in the company for which you work.

If you are not employed, set up a hypothetical situation for a company or organization in your area. Then write the report as if you are an employee who is asked, "Can you give us a report (or a proposal) on your findings (or ideas)?"

When you are actually on the job, you will not have to "imagine" who the audience is. Nevertheless, you will have to do some detective work to pinpoint specific characteristics of your readers. You should determine their technical and authority levels, their general attitudes, and especially their purpose for reading the report.

Audience Technical Level

The first point to consider in targeting the needs of your readers is their *technical level*, which reflects the depth of their knowledge of the topic. Your audience's technical level should guide the amount of background material you include in the report, the terms you define (as well as the method you choose to define them), and the type and number of visual aids you use. By identifying the audience's technical level and adjusting the report's content accordingly, you can always answer the question "Is my audience capable of understanding this point?"

Essentially, audience technical levels may be divided into three major ranks: low, medium, and high. To help you in your reports, Table 4.1 correlates these levels to some specific audience needs.

As you face important choices in the preparation of your report, consider these audience technical levels and needs. They directly affect the appropriateness — and effectiveness — of the information in your report.

Audience Authority Level

Another characteristic that can help you target your readers is their *authority level:* (1) as it relates to you and (2) as it relates to the rest

TABLE 4.1

AUDIENCE TECHNICAL LEVELS, CHARACTERISTICS, AND NEEDS

Technical Level	Typical Audience	Background Material	Definitions Needed	Visual Aids Needed
Low	The general public, consumers, laypersons	Detailed descriptions of how things look/work/develop	Careful explanations of all specialized terms and all abbreviations when first described, clarification of basic principles	Simple drawings, pie graphs, actual photos
Medium	Top managers, customers, operative personnel, production workers	Overviews of mechanisms/products/process	Limited use of jargon, clear and concise explanations of essential terms and concepts	Graphs that show trends and movement, organization charts and flowcharts, tables that clearly summarize data
High	Peers, experts	No background material	Only unusual abbreviations and terms defined	Line graphs that show minute changes or increments, illustrations that show internal structures or pertinent details, bar graphs that show multiple clusters of data

of the organization. This consideration helps you determine whether your audience has the authority to act on the information in your report and whether you are preparing an appropriate report for the appropriate audience.

For example, a report that asks the chief executive officer of Queen Elizabeth Hospital to buy a different film for the Radiology Lab is inappropriate and, at best, will only be rerouted to the radiology director. Likewise, a report that asks your immediate supervisor to make a company-wide change is also inappropriate and may not get rerouted anywhere.

This audience characteristic may also be divided into three basic levels: low (cannot act on any request without higher-level approval), medium (can grant permission or confirm actions for limited requests), high (has authority to confirm or deny actions on major corporate issues). Determine whether your audience's authority level is appropriate to any requests or recommendations included in your report.

Audience Purpose

In addition to identifying your reasons for writing the report, you must identify the audience's *purpose* for reading it.

- *To learn* (Is the project on schedule? What happened at the Moncton plant? How do I operate this machine?)
- *To evaluate* (Is Model X or Model Y better? What do the test results show? Is Penticton a good location for a new warehouse?)
- *To act* (Should I buy ABC Electric control boxes? Should we change the registration process at XYZ Community College? Should I improve our filing system?)

By pinpointing exactly why readers are interested in the report, you save valuable time (theirs and yours) by preparing a report that meets their specific needs. You should anticipate your readers' question: "What's in it for us?"

Audience Attitude

Yet another audience characteristic to target is your readers' *attitude* — toward you or toward the subject. Here are three general attitudes of readers:

- *Agreeable.* Are they reading the report because they are interested in (or have even initiated) the subject matter?
- *Antagonistic.* Are they reading the report with a preconceived negative view of the subject matter? (Do they think it costs too much, is not necessary, has already been done?)
- *Apathetic.* Are they reading the report only because their manager told them to?

Audience attitude may have a significant impact on the type of information you include in a technical report, the formality or informality of the report, and the number and kinds of visual aids you include in the report. "Agreeable" readers, for example, need not be so thoroughly convinced of the benefits of buying a new computer as "antagonistic" ones. "Apathetic" readers, on the other hand, may need a report that contains vivid visuals to spark their interest. Always consider the general attitude of the readers and the way they may receive your report when it is placed in their hands.

The Major Audience Characteristic

The final aspect of analyzing your audience may be the most important: What one *major characteristic* of your readers may help or hinder you in achieving your objectives? This characteristic may be one that you have already identified: for example, the readers want to learn how to assemble a fan drive, the readers are unaware that a problem exists, or the readers have a high technical background.

The audience's major characteristic may also be some other factor that you know from personal experience could influence your report's success: For example, the readers frequently resist change, the readers are ready to embrace change, the readers are dedicated to improving working conditions, or the readers often encourage innovative ideas. Carefully consider any possible conditions or tendencies that may affect your report's success.

Your Approach to the Audience

Once you have completed your audience analysis, you can tailor the report's overall approach, or emphasis, to the readers' main interests or concerns. The overall approach will be different for each type of reading audience: An organization's top managers have different business interests from those of its production workers; customers have different reasons from coworkers for reading about your company's product.

If the objective of the report, for example, is to convince the audience of the value of a new production technique that your department has just perfected, the approach — for the same topic but for different readers — would probably change as follows:

Audience	Approach/Emphasis
Top managers	Saves money and time
Production workers	Streamlines assembly process
Potential customers	Improves product quality and reliability
Others in your field	Solves a production problem

You would include much of the same information in each of these approaches, but you would emphasize the specific aspect that is of greatest interest to each audience.

Approach for a Mixed Audience

Many workplace reports are produced for more than one reader or group of readers. For example, the energy study and design project (pages 77–78) will be documented for several readers. As you will see in Chapter Fifteen, students Liling Tang and Mark MacLeod are writing their document for a condominium corporation board. Their transmittal letter is addressed to Mr. Dromlewicz, a board member and mechanical engineer, who has authorized the study. The chair and other members of the board will read the abstract and conclusion sections. They may also read the introductory sections and the cost comparisons. However, they will rely on Mr. Dromlewicz and other technical consultants to scrutinize the technical details.

In this case, the writers have a clear objective and emphasis — cost containment. Therefore, they make sure that the abstract, conclusion, and introductory sections are targeted to a more general audience and that the technical details are fully documented for Mr. Dromlewicz.

You should be aware that substantial technical documents may never be read in their entirety by one person. Portions of them may pass through many departments and may be acted on or consulted days, months, or even years later. However, pinpointing the objectives and identifying the audience(s) of your report will guide you to write a productive document.

Activity 4

In the space provided, write your choice for a topic. Next identify your *specific* objectives. Then identify your audience. *Note:* if you are writing for a hypothetical audience, select those characteristics you have observed (through study or workplace experience) that a middle manager or customer — or whoever you have decided will be reading the report — will have.

Identifying My Report Objectives and Audience

Topic: _____

Objectives:

My main objective(s) is (are) to _____

_____

_____

Audience: _____

My audience's technical level is _____

My audience's authority level is _____

My audience's purpose in reading my report is to

_____ Learn   _____ Evaluate   _____ Act

_____ Other (Explain)

My audience's attitude toward me or my topic is

_____ Agreeable   _____ Antagonistic   _____ Apathetic

My audience's major characteristic is _____

Use this worksheet for every technical paper and report that you write.

The worksheet can also be used for planning an oral technical presentation, as shown in Figure 19.2, p. 591.

DETERMINING THE TYPE OF REPORT

The last task in planning a report involves answering one more question: "Which specific kind of report fits my topic, my objectives, and my audience?"

You already know the following:

◆ The typical types of information generated in the workplace
◆ The three types of reports — informational, analytical, and persuasive — and the various kinds of reports encompassed by each major type
◆ The planning tasks required for appropriate topics, objectives, and audience

You can now decide what type of report to write.

The Decision-Making Process

In college and at work, you make decisions all the time: which courses to take next year, which graphics software to use for a technical presentation you are to give, which person to hire. Most often, the decision-making process begins by your looking at all the choices: the available courses and meeting times listed in the course catalogue, the graphics presentation packages available at your office, the pile of résumés on your desk.

The process of deciding continues as you establish the facts you have about each choice: Only one elective course fits your schedule; Microsoft Office, which contains PowerPoint, is installed on your local area network (LAN); only one person has the knowledge, skills, and years of experience requested in the advertisement. These facts help with your decisions by allowing you to narrow your list of possible choices:

◆ Because it is the only course offered at a time that fits your schedule, you will take Developing Effective Proofreading Skills.

◆ Because PowerPoint is an effective graphics package available at your office, you will use it for a slide show in your seminar.

◆ Because her résumé describes the characteristics you require in an employee, you will interview Louise Dubinsky.

By looking at the choices and then applying the facts you have on each choice, you subtract one possibility at a time until you make a decision. On the basis of choices and known facts, you draw a valid conclusion. This is a decision-making process.

Steps in the Process

The same decision-making process applies when you determine the specific kind of report to write. There are three steps in the process:

1. Identify the choices (types of reports).
2. Establish known facts (the report topic, objectives, audience).
3. Apply the facts and narrow (subtract from) your choices until you arrive at a clear decision.

To see this decision-making process in action, let's look at how it helps one student determine what kind of report to write for a work situation and a class assignment.

> Steve Yoshida, a marketing major at ABC Community College, also works part-time at Midway Manufacturing. A keen observer as well as a hard worker, Steve notices that employee productivity is suffering at Midway because the office copy machine has only limited capabilities. Employees have to sheet-feed originals one page at a time, separate multiple copies into various piles, and then collate and staple them by hand. Steve sees an opportunity to save employees time, to improve productivity for the company, and to write an effective report for his technical report writing class.

Steve begins the process of selecting the kind of report he should write by completing Step 1 (identifying his choices): the general types of reports (informational, analytical, and persuasive) and the specific report choices within each category (see Figure 4.4).

In Step 2, Steve establishes the known facts about his report by completing an objectives/audience worksheet as shown in Figure 4.5.

Step 3 of the process now becomes a matter of applying the known facts to the preliminary choices and then eliminating choices and drawing a conclusion. Figure 4.6 shows Steve's thinking as he first considers each type of informational report: progress report, project report, situation report, site visit report, process description, and instructions.

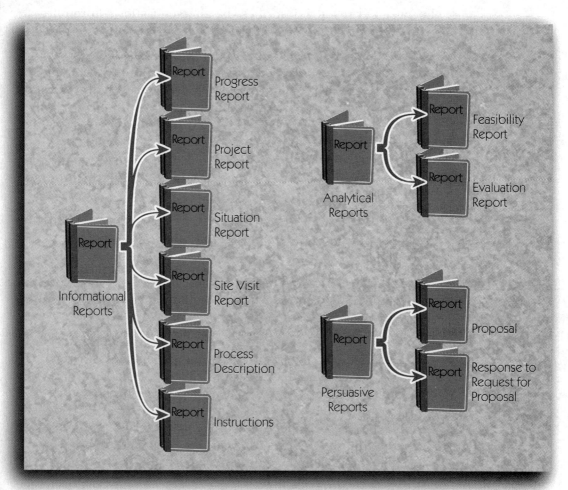

Figure 4.4 *The first step in determining the specific kind of report to write is identifying the available choices.*

IDENTIFYING MY REPORT OBJECTIVES AND AUDIENCE

Topic: Model XYZ Copier with Automated Sheet Feed,
                    Collator, and Stapler

Main objective(s): To convince my supervisor of the need for a new
                    copier and to recommend the purchase of the
                    Model XYZ Copier

Audience: Jessie Cole, Supervisor

My audience's technical level is medium.

My audience's authority level is high.

My audience's purpose in reading my report is to learn and then to decide
on action.

My audience's attitude toward me or my topic is agreeable.

My audience's major characteristic is a desire to improve business operations.

Figure 4.5 *Well-defined objectives and audience establish the facts in a report-writing situation.*

Notice that the decision-making process has triggered the need in Steve's mind for including a piece of important information in the report: how the process of making multiple copies will be streamlined with a copy machine that has more automated features. Steve knows his supervisor well enough (as he points out on the "major characteristic" line of Figure 4.5) to determine that streamlining may be a strong factor in convincing Jessie Cole to agree that there is a need. Yet Steve's clearly established objectives remind him that he wants to accomplish more than just to convince his supervisor of a need; he also wants to recommend a solution (the purchase of the Model XYZ copy machine).

Since there are still more choices to consider, Steve next looks at each report possibility in the analytical category: feasibility report and evaluation report. Figure 4.7 shows Steve's thinking process as he considers each kind of analytical report.

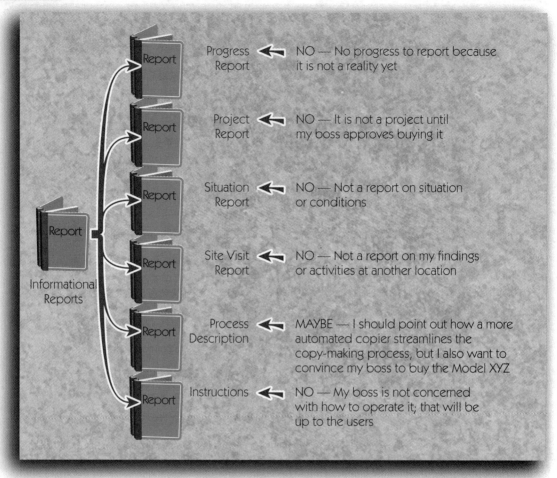

Figure 4.6 *In considering known choices and facts, a writer begins to decide on a report type by first reviewing the various kinds of informational reports.*

He decides that the type of information presented in analytical reports is not relevant to his main objectives. These reports would be relevant if Steve's supervisor had said: "Look into some new copy machines and find out what we need to make copies faster and better" or "Look into the copy machine requirements of our department and find out whether we have the space and the need to buy a larger or better one."

Neither statement was made to Steve, however. He analyzed the needs of the department and evaluated various copy machines *in preparation* for his report. No doubt he will use some of the information gathered in this preparation stage within his report, perhaps to help justify the purchase to his supervisor.

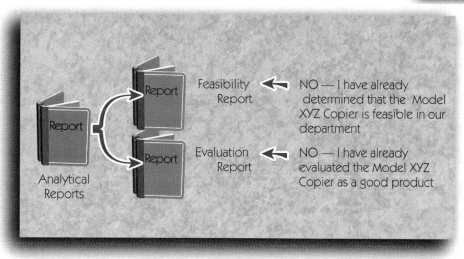

Figure 4.7 *A writer's thought process in considering analytical reports.*

As shown in Figure 4.8, Steve then considers the report choices in the last major category: persuasive reports. After examining the possibilities, he decides that the kind of report needed to accomplish his defined objectives and to reach his target audience is a *proposal*.

Advantages of Using the Process

The short time that it takes to go through the entire process of deciding on the best specific kind of report helps the writer avoid taking

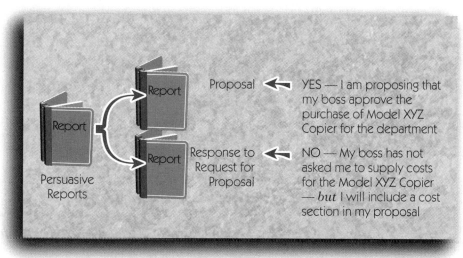

Figure 4.8 *A writer applying known facts to choices available in persuasive reports.*

the wrong direction. Had Steve stopped at the first possibility (process description), he would not have even considered the best report choice (proposal). He would have wasted valuable time preparing an inappropriate or ineffective report. Completing the process also helped Steve identify two important sections to include in his proposal: a description of how an automated machine streamlines the copy-making process, and a cost section that shows the capital investment required.

As you go through the process of deciding which kind of report will best achieve your specific objectives, make sure you continue until you have answered *yes, no,* or *maybe* to each possibility. The process will help assure that you have made the right choice and will help you pinpoint any other sections or information that you should include.

QUESTIONS FOR DISCUSSION

1. What is meant by *focus* in a technical report?
2. What visual devices do you prefer to use in narrowing your report topic?
3. What are four easy ways to restrict a general topic?
4. Can you name any other courses to which you can apply your ability to focus?
5. Why should a writer identify the objectives of a technical report?
6. Why and how should technical report writers analyze their audience?
7. How can the decision-making process help you produce the right type of report?
8. Can you suggest ways in which you can apply the decision-making process to other areas of your life (study, work, home)?

EXERCISE

Read the following report topics. Check the ones that are sufficiently focused and appropriate for an effective technical report.

_____ a. How to fold and pack a parachute.

_____ b. The progress made to date on a warehouse expansion project.

_____ c. What everyone should know about the human brain.

_____ d. What every hiker should know about bears in Waterton Lakes National Park.

_____ e. Methods of composting in your city garden.

_____ f. Which treatment of mastitis is more effective with machine-milked dairy herds.

_____ g. Which marketing approach should be used to attract more people to enrol as full-time students.

_____ h. Whether the production of a new synthetic dress fabric is economically feasible.

_____ i. Installation and care of a computer communications modem.

_____ j. Whether we will run out of natural gas.

WRITING ASSIGNMENTS

1. A friend of yours in the personnel department (or in a Human Resource Management course) has been given one week to produce a short report on how to help several employees transferred to his organization become comfortable and productive. They have come from branches that have been closed through sweeping cuts to the organization. He has been asked to suggest ways to help them cope with the transition. He is in a state of panic about the short lead time for this assignment. Write a paragraph convincing him that he should invest some time in developing a good plan for the assignment. Then provide him with a useful example.

2. Select one of your fellow students as a potential reader of one of your future technical reports. Spend at least five minutes or fill a sheet of notebook paper (whichever comes first) listing every characteristic you can think of about this person that might influence what you will include (or exclude) in the report.

3. Choose two of the following broad topics and use the inverted pyramid or wedge to narrow them to a manageable size for a technical report:

    radar

    corrosion

labour relations in the construction industry
forestry management
surround sound
sensors
safety in the workplace
dealing with change
ergonomics
ethics
the environment

Chapter FIVE

Organizing Your Ideas: Order and Outline

So far in the report-writing process, you have (1) selected and limited your topic, (2) determined your objectives and audience, and (3) decided on the specific kind of report to write. You are now ready to think about how to arrange, or *order*, your information and ideas.

Whenever you write anything — a letter to a friend, a poem or a song, a memo to a supervisor, a short or long report — you impose an order on the information you communicate. Sometimes you organize "naturally," such as when you chronologically narrate the events of your last few weeks in a letter to a friend. In a memo to a supervisor, however, you consider carefully which point to make first and which to put last.

Effective arrangement is a vitally important aspect of presentation. A report is not a haphazard assembly of discrete data. It is a collection of significant points, each supported by evidence, to achieve a purpose. A boat-builder, for example, designs and constructs a craft for a specific purpose and user. The result is an assembly of components selected and organized for racing, sailing, fishing, transport, or rescue. As a technical report writer, your responsibility is to organize your information so that it is meaningful and useful to your reader. Similarly, all the chess pieces in a box are of no use to the player until they are arranged on the board. It is only then that the game can have any meaning or purpose. All effective communication is governed by an arrangement, reflecting meaning and purpose, that guides the reader through it.

When starting a technical report, you may find it helpful to think first of *ordering* your material and then of *outlining* it, which is simply giving a format to the order.

CHOOSING AN ORDER

Ordering, or methodically developing, your information requires you to make a series of decisions. You decide which "block" of information your audience will see in each section of the report. Then you put the material into outline form. The information itself, the needs of the audience, and the kind of report needed determine what order you use.

Here are some types of order for arranging a large body of information:

◆ Chronological
◆ Spatial
◆ Enumeration
◆ Cause and effect
◆ Comparison and contrast
◆ Problem–solution
◆ Methodology–results

Some report situations require you to use a combination of types of order, although typically one arrangement dominates. For example, a proposal to reduce energy costs in an apartment building may be governed by the problem–solution arrangement, but it must also include a section on cost comparisons.

Chronological Order

Chronological order relates material in a time sequence. It is sometimes called a natural order because the events on paper are related in the same order as they occur in reality; the writer does not arbitrarily impose an organization. For example, when you instruct someone in how to administer CPR, install a new printer, or set out new seedlings, you start with the first step and move naturally through each succeeding sequence of actions. The order is characterized by transitional words such as *first*, *second*, *next*, and *finally*. Chronological, or time, order is used in two main situations: (1) when describing a process, a "how-to" report, and (2) when narrating an event, a "what happened" report.

Progress reports, project reports, process descriptions, instructions, and situation reports are usually written in chronological order. This order is illustrated in Figure 5.1. Joey Liska reports in January on his design project to be completed in May. He chooses chronological order to lead his supervisor through the work completed, problems encountered, and work remaining.

Purpose Statement: This report documents the work completed, problems encountered, and work remaining in the design, testing, and construction of a radio-controlled aerial photography system.

Work Completed Since 15 January 199x
- All encoder parts ordered and received, with exception of one transformer.
- Encoder and transmitter breadboarded.
- Preliminary encoder test results.

Problems Encountered
- No concrete data or guidelines yet received from investigation of federal government guidelines on wireless transmissions.
- Transmitter design work delayed

Work to Be Done
- Encoder and decoder go to printed circuit board layout.
- Boards to be designed (OrCAD), etched, and stuffed.
- Testing in mid-March.

Figure 5.1 *Example of chronological order.*
Adapted with permission of Joey Liska.

Spatial Order

Spatial (or space) order shows the physical appearance of something. The writer starts the description at an obvious point — such as the first component or the most noticeable part. With phrases such as "to the left," "behind," and "in front of," this order guides readers visually and directionally so that they have a vivid and accurate image of a tangible object, product, or place. For example, to describe the floor plan or layout for installing a computer workstation in an office, use spatial order. To describe the parts of an assembly robot, use spatial order. Typically, two types of situations call for this type of order: (1) describing a location, and (2) describing a piece of equipment or a product.

Enumeration

Enumeration, or the listing of points, is often used in technical reports. Many times you do not need to show specific kinds of relationships among the sections of a report. For example, you enumerate when you identify the factors influencing employee choice of food services or when you indicate the four significant elements in deciding on a location for a shopping mall.

If you have several points to make, you usually begin with the most important and end with the least important. You put "first things first." As shown in Figure 5.2, for a report analyzing the effects of the purchase of certain equipment on a plant, three results are listed, or enumerated. This example starts with the most important result (increased production) and ends with the least important (reduced downtime).

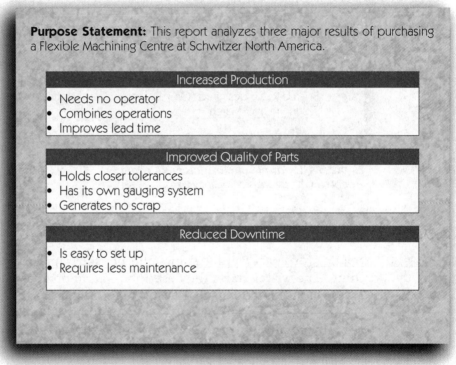

Purpose Statement: This report analyzes three major results of purchasing a Flexible Machining Centre at Schwitzer North America.

Increased Production

- Needs no operator
- Combines operations
- Improves lead time

Improved Quality of Parts

- Holds closer tolerances
- Has its own gauging system
- Generates no scrap

Reduced Downtime

- Is easy to set up
- Requires less maintenance

Figure 5.2 *Example of order by enumeration, from most to least important.*

Activity 1

Indicate how each report topic listed below would be developed by placing a *C* (chronological), an *S* (spatial), or an *E* (enumeration) to the left of it.

_____ a. Constructing a wind-powered generator

_____ b. Factors influencing employee absenteeism

_____ c. Setting up an automated enrolment and registration system

_____ d. Description of the new laser printer in Room 229

_____ e. Types of shopping malls

Cause and Effect

Cause and effect is the type of order often used in analytical reports. When a report shows *why* something happened, *why* something is true, or the consequences of an event or decision, it shows cause and effect. The writer starts with a fact or verifiable situation and then either looks back and shows *why* that is the case or looks forward and shows *what* the effect(s) will be if the situation remains.

For example, you know for a fact that on a certain three-kilometre stretch of highway, 14 serious accidents have occurred in the past two years. If you are asked to find the reasons for this situation, you start with the known *effect* (the number of accidents). You then must find and analyze the *cause(s)* (perhaps inadequate turning lanes or banking of the road). You might go on to discuss the expected consequences or effects of leaving the current situation unchanged (increased congestion and accidents, for example) or the anticipated effects of making changes in the current situation (improved traffic flow, decrease in accidents, for example).

Frequently, a situation has more than a single cause and more than a single effect. Always, however, to start a report of cause–effect order, you must have a beginning status point, a fact or belief. You then look to see *why* (causes) or *what next* (effects).

Activity 2

Begin to analyze one of the following situations that applies to (or closely approximates) your experience. State the situation or problem more specifically. Then list three possible causes (the *whys* of the situation) and three possible effects, or consequences (the *what nexts* of the situation).

If you would find it more useful, choose a situation or problem not listed below.

a. While you are currently achieving excellent results in most work projects (or courses), you are not doing well in one particular assignment (or course).

Problem Statement (specify the problem assignment or course)

_____

_____

Causes: (1) _____

(2) _____

(3) _____

Effects: (1) _____

(2) _____

(3) _____

b. Several stores at your local mall are closing.

Problem Statement (specify which stores at which mall)

_____

_____

Causes: (1) _____

(2) _____

(3) _____

Effects: (1) _____

(2) _____

(3) _____

Comparison and Contrast

Comparison and contrast are used for analyzing in detail the similarities or the differences between any two objects, processes, procedures, or policies. When you emphasize the ways in which things are alike, you are comparing; when you emphasize the ways in which they are different, you are contrasting. Normally, with any two items (tourism on Prince Edward Island and Vancouver Island, the management styles of two corporations, the benefits of two employee retirement or health plans), you will find both likenesses and differences. What you want to stress determines which type of order you choose.

Use comparison or contrast when a supervisor asks for an investigation and report on two possible computer software packages for the drafting department, for a document on the status of the company in 1992 and in 1996, for an analysis of the organization of two departments.

When you know the two items to be discussed, you will determine two or more bases of interest on which to compare or contrast them. For example, as you investigate two different heating systems for your company's warehouse, you might decide to consider these three bases: cost, comfort, and convenience.

Once you know the two *items* to be compared or contrasted and the *bases* to be considered, group or arrange your information so that your audience can follow your thinking. You have two options:

◆ *Item.* Discuss one item according to all your bases and then the other item. With this option, you devote the first half of your report to one item and the second half of the report to the other item.

◆ *Basis.* Discuss each basis of comparison or contrast first by one item and then by the other. If you choose this option, you will have as many main sections as you have bases of consideration.

Both options are acceptable arrangements. Figure 5.3 shows how the same information in a report may be arranged by *item* or by individual *basis* of comparison or contrast.

However, if you have an assignment that requires you to select some expensive new equipment for your workplace, for example, you will have to compare and contrast many similar items. Reporting your selection must include a thorough comparison–contrast of more than two items and a ranking of those items. In this case, you may find it more appropriate to organize by basis, and support your findings with a chart.

Activity 3

You have been tasked to cost and recommend some new computer equipment (antivirus software, style checkers, monitors, printers, scanners, multimedia systems, etc). Consult a well-known personal computing magazine and observe how the publication organizes by

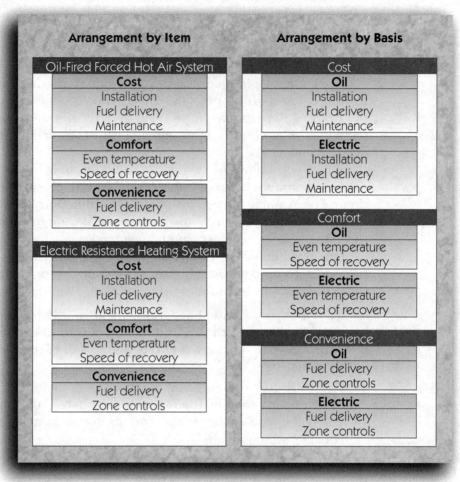

Figure 5.3 *Example of ways to order by comparison and contrast.*

comparison–contrast. Decide whether you will organize your information by item or by basis. Discuss your decision with the class.

Problem–Solution

Problem–solution order is used in reports that propose a change. You show that there is a problem or difficulty, and you show how it can be resolved. Fairly short memos and longer proposals advocating change typically use this order. For example, writing to convince managers to implement a change in downtime or in personnel benefits requires that you lead them through a logical sequence:

1. Review of the current situation (problem)
2. Proposed change (solution)

3. Advantages of making the proposed change
4. Disadvantages of not making the proposed change.

The inclusion of the fourth step depends upon the urgency of the situation or need.

The problem–solution order is illustrated in Figure 5.4 for a report proposing a change in equipment to increase efficiency and produce a higher-quality product.

Thesis Statement: Tallison Manufacturing Company should convert from a mechanical press brake to a computerized numerical control (CNC) brake.

Review of Current Situation

Advantages of mechanical press brake
  • Efficient in running small parts
  • No capital outlay
Disadvantages of mechanical press brake
  • Unsafe for running large parts
  • Inefficient setup operation
  • Maintenance requirements
  • Potential lack of accuracy

Converting to a CNC Brake

Initial capital outlay required
Operator retraining required

Anticipated Results of Converting

Increased quality of parts
  • Less retooling
  • Greater accuracy
Cost-effectiveness
  • Less maintenance
  • Less downtime
Increased safety

Figure 5.4 *Example of order by problem–solution.*

Methodology–Results

Methodology–results order is used when the report writer does primary research and readers need to know specifically how the data were gathered as well as what findings were obtained. For example, if your assignment is to assess the training needs of industry in your college region, you would first discuss your *methods* of collecting data (questionnaires, interviews, or data from existing programs) and then discuss your findings, or the *results*. For readers to accept your stated results, they must know the processes by which you arrived at those results.

Figure 5.5 illustrates the methodology–results type of order for a report that assesses the oral health status of preschoolers at a day-care centre.

Purpose Statement: The purpose of this report is to assess the general health status of preschoolers at the Snowcamp Day-Care Centre and to make recommendations as needed to improve their oral health status.

Methods of Assessment	Results of Assessment

Dental indices
  • DMF/DEF index
  • PHP index
Interviews
  • Staff
  • Students
Questionnaires
  • Students
  • Parents
  • Teachers
Direct observation
  • Inside facilities
  • Outside
     Playground
     School buses
	Dental health
	  • Plaque
	  • Caries
	Knowledge and attitudes
	  • Students
	  • Teachers
	Safety
	  • Inside facilities
	  • Playground
	  • School buses
	Nutritional status

Recommendations for Implementing Dental Health Program

Student-oriented
  • Swish program
  • Field trips to dental offices
  • Programs presented by dental hygiene students
Teacher-oriented
  • In-service program each fall
  • Incorporation of dental health into curriculum
Closer relationship with public health department

Figure 5.5 *Example of order by methodology–results.*

Order of Emphasis

With most of the types of order that we have been discussing, you must decide whether to state your most important point first and the least important last, or vice versa; that is, start with the least important point and lead up to the most important. In technical writing, starting with the most important point is in almost every case the more effective strategy. Remember that the person or organization requesting the report is interested in the major findings and will expect to read those first. Some reports will have more than one reader and will be passed, for example, through many departments from the Chief Executive Officer to Engineering, to the Chief Technologist, and on to Sales. Your readers will be looking for answers or recommendations, and most technical reports begin with a section summarizing the main conclusions and recommendations. Your technical readers need answers quickly. For them, time is money.

Let's say you are enumerating the following main points (arranged alphabetically here) in a report about reducing loss due to shoplifting at a local department store:

◆ Electronic devices
◆ Employee awareness
◆ Proper labels
◆ Security guards

After analyzing the data, you decide that "employee awareness" is the most important item and "proper labels" is the least important. Accordingly, you arrange the main sections of your report as follows:

1. Employee awareness
2. Electronic devices
3. Security guards
4. Proper labels

Remember that ordering by emphasis can fit in well with using chronological order. In your report on reducing loss through shoplifting, you would recommend that the reader

1. implement an employee training program.
2. install a more effective electronic monitoring system.
3. hire a different security service.
4. use sensitized labels.

These steps are chronological *and* in order of emphasis.

Effective ordering means that the sections of a report are in a sequence that best suits the information, the objectives, and the readers of the report.

MAKING AN OUTLINE

In long reports, the table of contents gives the audience a first indication of the information presented and its sequence. In shorter reports of two or three pages, the headings and sections of the report guide the readers.

As an employee, you may rarely be asked to show anyone your plan of organization beforehand. When you write as a student, however, your instructors often require outlines to ensure organized and complete reports. Seeing a proposed outline for a report or research project allows instructors to assist you before you go on to write your final draft. All readers expect the same thing of a finished report: clear organization that they can follow easily.

Why Outline?

Outlining is more than just an academic exercise or a formal structure. It is a well-known and helpful strategy. Just as builders and architects must move ideas from their heads to blueprints before those ideas are put into practical use, outlines help writers visualize the finished product.

As a technique for both *selecting* and *maintaining* an order for a report, the outline gets you started and keeps you on track. It prevents digression (just as a blueprint discourages a builder from tucking in an extra room at the last minute) and the haphazard presentation of material.

An outline is an arrangement of material within a specified format to provide the writer with a clear guide or roadmap for conveying information. An outline can help you do the following:

◆ Generate and develop ideas.

◆ Evaluate ideas and logic.

◆ Avoid digression.

An outline assists in the thinking or "generating" stages of report writing. After you have brainstormed or listed potential points that you want to make, outlining shows whether and how they hang together, or form a cohesive whole.

Outlining helps you focus on specifics so that readers follow your reasoning and accept your overall contention or conclusion. An outline requires "two-legged" support for every point made. One specific item is not sufficient to support a broader, more general point. For each statement that is more than just a fact, ask and answer at least twice *what*, *why*, or *how*. Trying to divide every point into at least two subpoints shows you just how much information you need, how much you have, which points require more research, and perhaps which ideas can be combined.

Outlining helps you evaluate a listing of the points you intend to cover. You see (as if viewing a skeleton or an X-ray) the basic structure of the report. This skeleton structure usually reveals whether you have omitted vital points, have attached irrelevant information, or have failed to show a logical relationship between each subpoint and the point above it.

Very few writers start with a clear sense of what to include in what order. They start with "everything" they want to say in much the same way that the names of all your friends and relatives rush to mind when you organize a wedding. Only later when you make the invitation list or organize accommodations according to groupings do you begin to categorize. You may start a report with a list of all you want to include, but very early you begin to group or categorize information so that you can manage it and the audience can follow it.

Assume, for instance, that you are writing about setting up a crime prevention program in Northcliffe, a retirement village located on the fringe of an area that has a high crime rate. Your purpose is to show residents resources available to them so that they will be encouraged to start the program. Preliminary investigation and consultation with a residents' committee have given you the list of ideas shown below.

Ideas for Report
Police will help.

Monthly meetings of residents.

Assistance from larger community.

Hot line possible.

Volunteers to hand out material.

High school volunteers possible.

Fear of purse snatching and burglars.

Patrol cars on routine basis.

Do-it-yourself battery-powered security systems best.

Speakers available on legal aspects.

Local newspaper will print pamphlets.

Area churches involved.

Lighting inadequate on some streets.

Videos and posters free from community police office
(Bravo Zone).

Residents will gain satisfaction, feeling of value.

Some municipal grants for seniors possible for extra expenses.

You realize that these ideas are not all equal. Just as you might
organize a grocery list into the general categories of "meats, vegetables, and fruits" or "frozen, fresh, and canned," you identify major
areas of assistance under which other items logically fall. As you
look at the following ordering, can you see that some points (true
and interesting though they may be) are unrelated to the others and
that one point stands alone?

Ordering of Ideas

Assistance from police department

    Speakers available on legal aspects.

    Videos and posters supplied free.

    Patrol cars on routine basis.

    Hot line possible.

Assistance from area churches

Assistance from residents

    Volunteers to distribute information.

    Fear of purse snatching and burglars.

    Do-it-yourself battery-powered security system best.

    Monthly meeting to report.

    Gives residents satisfaction and feelings of self-worth.

Assistance from larger community

    Pamphlets printed at cost by local newspaper.

    Municipal government funding possible for extra costs.

    Lighting inadequate on streets.

    High school volunteers available to assist in distributing
    window stickers.

Activity 4

Study the material shown in the ordered list above.

a. Which two points should be omitted because they do not belong
    with the other items in the group?

b. What item needs to be incorporated into another section or to be developed further with more supporting details?

You probably noticed that the two comments about residents' fear of purse snatching and resident satisfaction do not logically support "assistance from residents," and that "assistance from area churches" should either be placed under "assistance from larger community" or be developed with subpoints.

An outline has two elements: (1) a sentence that limits and controls the material and (2) the body of main and supporting points.

The Controlling Sentence

The first step in making an effective outline is writing an effective controlling sentence. This sentence that states exactly the objective or conclusion of the report is called a thesis statement, a purpose statement, a content statement, or simply a controlling sentence. Like a signpost, this sentence directs the reader to the contents of the report.

When your objective is to draw a conclusion in the report, write a *thesis sentence*. This shows your conclusion, which is based, of course, on substantiated data, not simply opinion. When your objective is to present data only, write a *purpose* or *content statement*. A purpose statement emphasizes why the report was written, and a content statement emphasizes what the report contains. These statements leave the drawing of conclusions to the audience.

When you are assigned a report, determine what is expected of you: just the facts, or the facts *and* the conclusions. In a classroom situation, you may wonder how you can start with a thesis or conclusion before you have completed the research. Investigators usually start with an expected conclusion or an anticipated result. In pure research situations, this anticipated result is called a hypothesis. For example, agricultural scientists place varieties of grain in certain growing environments (such as soil conditions) because they anticipate a certain result. Their experiments then either prove what they thought would be the case (the hypothesis) or disprove it. If you start a research project with a purpose statement, you can always change it to a thesis statement when you are far enough along to be sure or fairly sure of a conclusion supported by the data.

When you have difficulty stating in one sentence all that you intend to do in the report, visualize a situation such as this:

The historic building your company occupies and owns requires extensive renovations to meet its expanding business needs and to satisfy local government health and safety regulations. Your supervisor wants you to investigate the possibility of leasing space in a new office tower or renovating the existing building. The report will be presented to the board of directors at its next meeting.

In consultation with the appropriate departments, you investigate renovation and moving costs, real estate opportunities, and image factors — all the factors you think must be taken into account before reaching a critical decision involving the company's future. And you submit your report.

A colleague from the marketing department sees your supervisor and says, "I understand you've got a report on leasing space in that new tower on the wharf rather than patching up this old house! What does the report cover?"

If you have presented *only* the facts, your supervisor should reply with almost exactly the same sentence of purpose that controlled your report: "The report compares the costs, the safety aspects, and the expansion factors to be considered in deciding between renovating our existing premises and moving into new rental property."

If you have both investigated *and* made a recommendation, the supervisor would likely respond with your conclusion (in less formal language than that in the report): "We should move up to the tower because it's got the space we need, the vacancy rate is high and the rent is accordingly low, and it will provide us with the upscale image we must cultivate to remain competitive." Alternatively he might say "we'll stay here, hire a reputable architect, and maintain the tradition of stability and service our customers expect from this historic address. We'll also save money!"

A reader should be able to sum up exactly *what* a report covers or *what* it concludes. When you start with a clearly stated objective in one well-written sentence, the chances are excellent that your audience will finish with a clear understanding of your material.

Activity 5

Read the following controlling sentences, and identify each as either a thesis statement (*T*) or a purpose/content statement (*P/C*). You will recognize some of the material from preceding chapters.

_____ a. This report documents the design of a new security lighting system for St. Brigit's University.

_____ b. The limitations imposed on small business owners in the Rockingstone area are legally indefensible.

_____ c. The purpose of this report is to explain the guidelines inspectors used in determining rural bed-and-breakfast accommodation ratings.

_____ d. This report describes the main objectives of the Regional Solid Waste Management Project Group and its strategies for a successful resolution to the present controversial waste management problems.

_____ e. Construction on Highway 101 is running behind schedule and over cost at its midpoint.

_____ f. Well-conceived and efficiently implemented automation will improve Leland's Heating and Air Conditioning Company's inventory control.

_____ g. Scanner X and Scanner Y are compared on three bases: cost, ease of operation, and range of procedures.

A controlling sentence has these characteristics:

◆   It is a complete declarative sentence.
◆   It is clear, specific, and concise.

Writing a complete sentence requires a complete thought expressed with a subject–verb relationship. A complete declarative sentence starts with a capital letter, ends with a period, and makes sense. An incomplete sentence (a sentence fragment) is often a phrase that simply announces the topic. A complete controlling sentence goes beyond just restating the topic and indicates what you intend to do with it or what you expect to conclude about it. The controlling sentence should not be a question. Although the writing process often starts with a question, the purpose of most reports is to answer questions.

Activity 6

Which of the following are complete sentences and which are fragments? Place an X in front of each sentence fragment and a check mark in front of each complete sentence.

_____ a. The time and cost of repaving Highway 101 compared to repaving the Lighthouse Route.

_____ b. Tax breaks have failed to attract a significant amount of new industry to the Niagara region for three reasons.

_____ c. How quality circles can solve work productivity at Simmonds Brake Company without a great investment of time or money.

_____ d. Simmonds Brake Company can implement the quality circle concept with relatively little investment of time or money.

_____ e. Setting up a yearly golf tournament with provincial and city officials, celebrities, and local business partners to provide funding for literacy programs in the province.

_____ f. The province's literacy program coordinator should organize an annual golf tournament with provincial and city officials, celebrities, and local business partners to fund literacy programs throughout the province.

_____ g. The costs and considerations involved in upgrading the kitchens of CCCC (Crusty Comestibles Catering Corporation).

Activity 7

Read the following questions; choose one; and, in the space provided, rewrite it as a declarative sentence with appropriate punctuation. You will have to supply details for completeness as shown in the first example. A sample has been completed for you.

What main factors will influence whether Simmonds Brake Company decides to implement the quality circles concept?

Both employee acceptance and management cooperation will influence Simmonds Brake Company's decision to implement quality circles.

a. What is the perceived impact of contracting out for maintenance services upon the maintenance personnel in this institution?

_____

_____

b. What can be done about the stress level of the remaining employees after a series of layoffs at Thornville Industries?

_____

_____

c. Can Mercury Communications Inc. justify the purchase of a new, expensive multimedia system?

_____

_____

A good controlling sentence states exactly what you intend to do, cover, or conclude in the report so that readers do not wonder about your point, intent, or conclusions. The use of specific terms results in conciseness and clarity. Specific terms have specific meanings and leave little or no room for interpretation.

Look at the following list. Notice that for each vague or general term in the left-hand column, the reader needs specific information.

Vague/General Terms	**Interpretations/Questions**
Several	How many?
Contact	Telephone? Fax? E-mail? Write? Meet?
Some	Three, four, five …?
Program	College? Software?
Large	How large?
Tomorrow	What date?
Early	How early is early?

Activity 8

In the following sentences, circle any vague and general words that lead to a lack of conciseness or clarity. Choose one of the sentences and rewrite it, adding specific words or details you may have to invent, so that the sentence is clearer. The first sentence has been rewritten for you.

This report considers all the factors that might influence a small business in deciding whether to go with quality circles to help the company.

<u>This report analyzes three main factors that will influence Simmonds Brake Company's decision to implement quality circles: employee acceptance, management cooperation, and management training</u>.

a. Several points should be taken into account when a small business decides on its accounting procedure.

_____

_____

b. This report discusses pollution in the local area.

_____

_____

c. Radar has had an impact on our lives.

_____

_____

d. This report shows that the engine is now running smoothly.

_____

_____

Outline Formats

After you have chosen an order for your material and written an effective controlling sentence, you must decide (1) whether to write a traditional or decimal outline, and (2) whether to write a topic or sentence outline.

Traditional Form

The traditional outline form is undoubtedly familiar to you. You have seen it throughout your school years. In this form, Roman numerals mark main sections of a report, and capital and lowercase letters, Arabic numbers, periods, parentheses, and indentions indicate more and more specific points, or details. The following outline shows only three levels of headings, usually all that are needed for a technical report.

Title of Report

Controlling Sentence: All main section headings must relate directly to this sentence.

I. First Main Heading
    A. Second-Level Subheading (supports I)
        1. Third-Level Subheading (supports I.A)
        2. Third-Level Subheading (supports I.A)
    B. Second-Level Subheading (supports 1)
        1. Third-Level Subheading (supports I.B)
        2. Third-Level Subheading (supports I.B)
II. Second Main Heading
    A. Second-Level Subheading (supports II)
    B. Second-Level Subheading (supports II)
        1. (supports II.B)
        2. (supports II.B)

Note that this abbreviated traditional outline shows only two entries at each level. You may need more than two.

Decimal Form

In technical writing, a decimal outline form is more popular than the traditional (or alpha-numeric) form. The decimal form, which eliminates the use of Roman numerals and letters, is shown below.

Title of Report

Controlling Sentence: This thesis, content, or purpose statement must be a complete sentence.

1. First Main Heading
    1.1 Support for First Main Heading
    1.2 Support for First Main Heading
        1.2.1 Support for 1.2 Heading
        1.2.2 Support for 1.2 Heading

2. Second Main Heading
    2.1 Support for Second Main Heading
        2.1.1 Support for 2.1
        2.1.2 Support for 2.1
    2.2 Support for Second Main Heading
    2.3 Support for Second Main Heading
3. Third Main Heading
    3.1 Support for Third Main Heading
    3.2 Support for Third Main Heading
        3.2.1 Support for 3.2
        3.2.2 Support for 3.2

The intent of a decimal outline is the same as that of a traditional outline. Each entry stands in logical relationship to the entry level above it; the progression of main to lesser points is the same. Only the notation system is different.

Topic Outline

Topic outlines are usually brief and written in much the same way as a list. By means of single words or phrases, each entry announces the topic to be discussed. Topic outlines may be the first attempt (a rough draft) at getting some control over the material, or they may be sufficient for many short reports. A topic outline is shown in Figure 5.6.

Sentence Outline

Sentence outlines require that each entry be a complete sentence. Rather than announcing the coverage of a section, each sentence asserts a point or completes a thought. Thus, sentence outlines are more complete than topic outlines. You may start with a topic outline but be required to turn in a sentence outline for a longer report. A sentence outline is shown in Figure 5.7. Notice that this outline covers the same material as that presented in the topic outline in Figure 5.6. Although the topic outline could serve as a guide for the writer, the sentence outline is more complete.

Conventions of Outlining

Certain conventions (expected behaviour or treatment) have developed as part of the formal outline. Two conventions that govern outlining are partners and parallelism:

◆ Each entry must have a *partner* of equal value.
◆ Equal-value entries should be *parallel* in structure.

Purpose Statement: This report describes the New Reader Program located in the Regional Library, Didsbury, Manitoba.

1. Established in 1990 to address literacy needs of community
    1.1 to provide reading classes for adults
        1.1.1 upgrading
        1.1.2 family literacy
    1.2 funded by various agencies
        1.2.1 federal, provincial, and municipal governments
        1.2.2 nongovernmental, service organizations, and churches
        1.2.3 partnerships with computer industry
2. Staffed by Qualified Personnel
    2.1 Coordinator/Counsellor
        2.1.1 Conducts outreach
        2.1.2 Administers programs
    2.2 Teachers/Volunteer Trainers
        2.2.1 Literacy Tutors
        2.2.2 ESL Literacy Teachers
3. Accessed by a variety of clients
    3.1 Adults who want to learn to read
        3.1.1 Reading for job change
        3.1.2 Reading for personal or family reasons
        3.1.3 Reading for the first time
    3.2 English as a Second Language (ESL) Adults
        3.2.1 English for upgrading
        3.2.2 ESL Literacy for Adults (not literate in their first language)

Figure 5.6 *Example of a topic outline in decimal form.*

The *partner* convention means that nothing stands alone. To argue any proposition effectively, any general statement requires at least *two* points that validate or add detail to it. While more than two subentries may support an entry, no entry should be supported by only one subentry. Logically, each subpoint supports the level above it. When you have only one supporting point, incorporate it into the level above it. Can you see the flaws in the following outlines?

Flawed Outline 1
1. Oil-fired forced hot-air system
    1.1 Cost
    1.2 Comfort
    1.3 Convenience

Purpose Statement: This report describes the New Reader Program located in the Regional Library, Didsbury, Manitoba.

1.   The program, established in 1990, is designed to respond to the specific needs of the Didsbury community.
      1.1.1   The program provides reading classes and tutoring for adults.
      1.1.2   There are also classes for families to learn to read together.
    1.2   The program is funded by a number of agencies.
      1.2.1.   It receives federal, provincial, and municipal funding.
      1.2.2.   Nongovernmental organizations, service organizations, and churches also contribute funds.
      1.2.3.   The program has formed a partnership with an international computer firm.
2.   The program is staffed by qualified personnel.
    2.1   The program is administered by a Coordinator/Counsellor.
      2.1.1   This person conducts outreach activities.
      2.1.2   This person is responsible for administering the entire program, including budget, staff, teaching personnel, and volunteer training.
    2.2   The program has two qualified adult literacy practitioners and five volunteers.
      2.2.1   The two practitioners teach small classes, tutor one-on-one, and train volunteers, who give extra help to the clients.
      2.2.2   Of the two practitioners above, one has experience in teaching ESL literacy.
3.   The program is accessed by a variety of clients.
    3.1   There are 25 adults who want to learn to read.
      3.1.1   Eighteen adults need to read for changing job responsibilities, and four of these want to be able to read to their children.
      3.1.2   Seven adults, who are landed immigrants not literate in their first language, need to read for survival.

Figure 5.7 *Example of a sentence outline in decimal form.*

2.   Electric resistance heating system
    2.1   Cost

Flawed Outline 2
1.   Fuel delivery
    1.1   Cost

      1.2 Installation

      1.3 Maintenance

  2. Comfort

      2.1 Even temperatures

      2.2 Speed of recovery

  3. Fuel delivery

      3.1 Convenience

      3.2 Zone controls

In the first outline, 2. must have more than the one entry "Cost" to support it. In the second outline, 3.1 ("Convenience") is the broader point, and 3. ("Fuel delivery") should be a supporting point.

The *parallelism* convention means that entries of equal value should be written in a similar grammatical structure. For example, all the entries on the same level (main headings, second-level headings, and so on) might be expressed as nouns, all as gerunds (verb forms ending in *ing*), or all as infinitive phrases (*to* plus verb forms). This sameness of grammatical construction often occurs without your even thinking about it.

Notice the examples below. The items on the left are in parallel form. The items on the right lack parallelism:

Steps in Fishing	Steps in Fishing
Fly tying	Tying flies
Catching	Catching fish
Cleaning	To clean them
Cooking	Have someone cook them

Here is another set of parallel (left-hand column) and nonparallel (right-hand column) entries:

Cost	How Much It Costs
Installation	Installing
Fuel delivery	Fuel
Maintenance	Maintenance cost
Comfort	Comfort
Even temperatures	Temperatures are even
Speed of recovery	Recovery speed
Convenience	Its convenience
Fuel delivery	Delivering fuel
Zone controls	Controls are zoned

Activity 9

In the following listings, check any item that is not parallel with the others and rewrite it in parallel form.

a. Steps to be followed in case of fire

_____ Maintain calm.

_____ Walk quickly to the nearest fire exit.

_____ You should use the stairs; it is not safe to use the elevator.

_____ Leave the building.

_____ Wait outside until the klaxon sounds.

b. Decisions in setting up a CPA firm

_____ Acquiring physical facilities

_____ What personnel are needed

_____ Developing client contracts

_____ Promoting a professional image

c. Increased strengths of epoxy mixed with concrete

_____ Greater tensile strength

_____ Has more flexibility potential

_____ Higher resilience

_____ Greater compressive strength

A good topic outline provides the main headings and subheadings of a report. A good sentence outline supplies key words for headings *and* the topic sentences of paragraphs. Although you may write more than one paragraph per entry, prepare at least one paragraph for each entry of the outline. Use the outline checklist shown in Figure 5.8 to ensure that your outlines are valid and correct.

Deciding on an order and then outlining your points are essential steps in producing well-organized technical reports. Although these steps take time, they ultimately save time. They require logical thinking and lead to logical, coherent reports.

OUTLINE CHECKLIST

When you have completed your outline for a report, use this checklist to be sure that the outline is complete, clear, and in correct form.

1. Is the outline headed by a controlling sentence?
2. Is the controlling sentence clearly either a thesis statement or a purpose or content statement?
3. Is the sentence a complete declarative sentence with a subject and verb?
4. Do you have at least two main headings for the body of the report?
5. Are the parts of the outline logically arranged?
6. Are you consistent in using the traditional form or the decimal form?
7. Have you checked for proper punctuation (periods and decimal points)?
8. Is the outline uncrowded, spaced appropriately on the page, and easy to read?
9. Have you indented properly and consistently?
10. Can you write at least one paragraph (short or long) about each entry?
11. Does each entry have a "partner" of equal value? (No 1 without a 2, etc.)
12. Are complementary entries parallel in structure?
13. Does a quick look at the outline reveal the scope of your report and your method of developing it?

You should have checked (✔) all questions.

If you are uncertain about the answers to any of these questions, ask your instructor to review your outline.

Figure 5.8 *Review and check the questions listed here each time you develop an outline.*

Computer Tips

In the "generating" stage of writing, when you are both creating and imposing some order on your ideas, think of word processing as the "softcopy" stage. Word processing enables you to put your ideas on the screen rather than on "hardcopy" paper as they occur to you, to create more freely because you know you can invent and eliminate easily. A computer allows you to change, manipulate, and restructure your points with a few keystrokes.

When you are ready to create an outline or organize your points, you can use features incorporated into word-processing programs or use software programs specifically designed to help in organizing.

Outlining in Word Processing

Several word-processing programs such as *DisplayWrite 5* and *Microsoft Word* incorporate advanced features that can assist you in organizing ideas. While programs vary in the way in which and the degree to which they assist with outlining, the outline feature usually offers these advantages:

◆ You can view the outline (in some high-end programs) in the corner of the screen as you create.

◆ You can choose the traditional outline or the decimal outline.

◆ You can rearrange the points in the outline as you reorganize your thoughts, and the program renumbers all levels and indents them appropriately.

◆ You can expand your points with supporting details while leaving the original outline entries on the screen.

Using Specialized Software

Other programs, such as *Writer's Helper* and *ThinkTank*, are designed specifically to help in the organizing stage of writing. Ranging from the fairly simple to the sophisticated, these programs lead writers in brainstorming strategies, making lists, and answering questions about a subject. They may also ask the writer to consider (and respond to) questions about audience and purpose.

Your college library or writing lab may have these or other software programs that help in organizing and outlining reports.

QUESTIONS FOR DISCUSSION

1. What does the term *ordering* mean?
2. Name and briefly describe at least one type of order you have already used in writing for another course, for work, or for a personal situation.
3. You have been asked to write instructions for ensuring safety in your lab, office, or home. What type(s) of order would you choose?
4. Your supervisor has money in the budget for upgrading equipment (computer, furnishing, or similar). He asks you to investigate specifications, quality features, cost, delivery, and special deals, and to report your findings to him in writing. Which type(s) of order will you use?
5. How can an outline help you in questions 3 and 4?
6. What is the difference between a purpose or content statement and a thesis statement?
7. Which do you find more helpful — a sentence outline or a topic outline?
8. How can the "partner" convention in outlining make your report more logical?
9. Explain parallelism.

EXERCISE 1

Assume you work for Ace Manufacturing Company at a middle management level. Your supervisor asks for a report that addresses each of the following questions or situations — stated informally here. What kind of order would you expect to use for each? Indicate chronological (*C*), spatial (*S*), enumeration (*E*), cause and effect (*CE*), comparison/contrast (*CC*), problem–solution (*PS*), or methodology–results (*MR*).

_____ a. "Which medical insurance plan — Atlantic Medical or Gold Sceptre Medical — offers Ace employees the most for their money?"

_____ b. "There's been a problem lately with Department 22, especially with returns from Machine 205. See what can be done about it."

_____ c. "Our shareholders need an in-depth survey of the quality of our products, our image in the marketplace, and our potential for increasing our market share."

_____ d. "Employees are complaining about the crowded lounge areas. We believe we can allot more space to each area. Give us a report on how to best use the space."

_____ e. "Assembly line 4 needs to be reorganized. Give the maintenance crew a set of instructions for rebuilding it as efficiently as possible."

_____ f. "What facts should we take into account as we decide where to locate our new packaging plant?"

_____ g. "What would happen in terms of our workforce and our tax situation if we located our new packaging plant in the adjoining county?"

_____ h. "What steps are involved in setting up a child-care centre for employees' children?"

_____ i. "What seems to be causing the excessively high rate of absenteeism among the clerical staff?"

_____ j. "Write a user's manual for the new computer in the maintenance area."

EXERCISE 2

Review the outline shown here, and then follow the instructions below it.

Thesis Statement: Using a computerized accounting system at Hanson Photographics will save time, increase accuracy of accounts, and help control operations.

I. Saves time
   A. Updating accounts
      1. Eliminating repetition
      2. Correlating transactions
   B. Inventory can be updated
   C. Payroll
II. Increases accuracy
   A. Using memory units
III. Operations controlled
   A. Printing documents
      1. Retrieving documents
   B. Filing documents

a. Circle any flaws in the conventions of partners and parallelism in the outline. Write a corrected version of the outline.
b. Rewrite the outline in the decimal form.

EXERCISE 3

Look through a newspaper or magazine for advertisements that contain parallelism (headings, descriptions, slogans). Discuss how parallel structures invite the reader to buy.

EXERCISE 4

Suppose that you are organizing a small conference for the local chapter of your professional association. You have made arrangements with the hospitality department of the local college to cater for the 150 delegates coming in from across the province. It is just two days to the conference opening and everything is coming together. You check items on your planning list and then turn to your mail. The first letter you open is from Herbert Lang, hospitality coordinator. The body of the letter is shown below:

Dear Ms. Yanowski:

Unfortunately for you and for my department, our College Board of Governors has established a new policy that restricts the hospitality department of this campus from catering for outside organizations.

The reason for this is that, as you may know, my department has been deluged with requests for catering from all over the region. I have been short staffed, and the students are increasingly resistant to the long hours spent after their daytime course work. In addition, costs have risen, and we cannot continue to provide the quality service to which our clients have become accustomed.

I deeply regret that we will be unable to serve you in the future and sincerely hope that you will understand our position. However, as your conference starts in two days, I have received special permission from the Board to proceed with the arrangements and look forward to serving you this coming Wednesday. By the way, the menus you chose have been confirmed and preparations are well under way. We have taken note of the special menus ordered for two guests and we can assure you that shellfish will not be included in any meals. As usual, we guarantee your satisfaction.

a. Explain your reactions as you read the letter!

b. Apart from the content, what was the main problem with this letter?

c. Reorganize and rewrite the letter to eliminate the kind of reaction you experienced at a particularly busy time.

WRITING ASSIGNMENT

The ordering of information or material applies to paragraphs as well as to reports. The length and depth are different but the principles are the same.

The following topics do not require much outside research. Writing on any one of them will give you experience in ordering information before you write a longer report. Choose and complete *one* of these paragraph writing assignments:

a. In a paragraph for either your work supervisor or an instructor in your major study area, document your workday. Use *chronological* order.

b. Look at the layout of your classroom, laboratory, or shop. Describe it as technically as possible. Use *spatial* order.

c. Jot down the typical costs of attending college this term. After you have made a list of all items, group them into three or four main kinds of costs and write a paragraph using the order of *enumeration*.

d. Refer to your responses to Activity 2, pp. 107–108. Choose one of the sentences for which you gave possible causes and effects. Expand your responses into a paragraph ordered according to *cause and effect*.

e. Write one or two *comparison* or *contrast* paragraphs showing the similarities or differences between two products.

Collecting and Documenting Information

Although written for different purposes and for different audiences, all technical reports share a common characteristic. They are information-based and rely heavily on factual, verifiable content. Collecting valid information and documenting it appropriately are vital to producing effective reports.

The information-gathering process is divided into three basic steps:

Step 1: Finding information
Step 2: Converting it for your use
Step 3: Documenting it appropriately

STEP 1: FINDING INFORMATION

When starting a report, you are usually familiar with the general subject you are writing about, and you may know a great deal about the topic. Some reports, in fact, are based almost entirely on a writer's experience, observation, or performance (progress, project, and site visit reports, for example).

However, many writing situations, especially those resulting in long analytical and persuasive reports, require more information and validation than your experience and knowledge alone can provide. You will gather information from a variety of print and nonprint sources, from agencies, and from people in the community and in the workplace. You may use your college and local libraries and their online services for background material and data; however, to encourage you to think of technical reports as different from term papers, this chapter begins with community and individual resources. In the workplace, you would probably explore these resources first. The flowchart in Figure 6.1 gives an overview of a typical research process from the beginning of your information gathering through some potential data resources to the completion of the process.

Use Individual and Community Resources

A few minutes spent looking through the Yellow Pages Infoguide and Index of your telephone directory may produce several ideas for potential sources of information. Also check the Blue Pages for government listings (federal, provincial, and municipal). Check these places in your community for useful printed material:

Chamber of Commerce

Better Business Bureau

Industrial and business parks

Hospitals

Social work agencies

Fire and police departments

Charitable and nonprofit organizations

Manufacturing plants

Newspaper offices

Service clubs

Other colleges and universities

Professional organizations such as the Institute of Electrical and Electronics Engineers, the Canadian Council of Professional

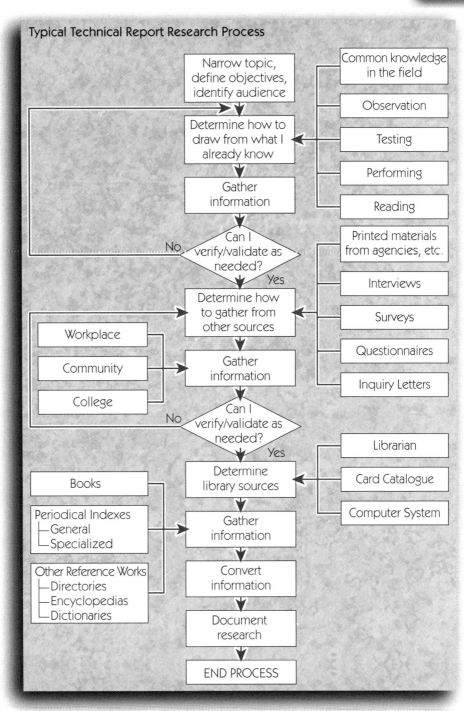

Figure 6.1 *This flowchart displays the typical research process for a technical report.*

Engineers, Canadian Federation of Independent Business, Canadian Institute of Fisheries, Canadian Bar Association, and the Canadian Manufacturing Association

These and other sources can supply brochures, in-house or trade journals (those distributed primarily for a specific readership and not always on library shelves), advertising material, manuals, policies, laws and statutes — almost anything you can name.

For technical reports, you can expect to use a great deal of material not found in print. This primary source material may be based on your own experience or on the experience of others, as the following listing shows:

Writer's Experience	Experience of Others
Testing	Personal interviews
Experimenting	Telephone interviews
Observing	Inquiry letters
Performing	Surveys and questionnaires

The Writer's Experience

Actual testing and experimenting in a laboratory or in the field usually supplies much useful data for a report — especially in engineering, environmental, and scientific fields. For example, here are some possibilities for testing and experimenting:

Conduct an air, noise, or water pollution study.
Test certain metals for various characteristics.
Test the drinking water of homes for lead, or test homes for the presence of radon gas.
Count and classify trees in a downtown area.
Conduct an energy audit of a building.

Using your work-related knowledge and hands-on experience may form the basis of or add data to a report if readers will accept it as valid. For example, consider the following situations:

As a computer programmer, use your knowledge to write programs or to evaluate programs at work.
As a shipyard employee, write a proposal for improving efficiency in handling purchasing procedures.
On the basis of your experience as an equipment operator at a manufacturing plant, compare the efficiency and usefulness of new machinery.

Your objective observations are also a valid source of data. For example, you might do the following:

Observe procedures at work for safety infractions.
Visit a plant to study its new assembly line operations.
Take a traffic count to determine potential market sites.
Ride with a police officer to observe behaviour.
Study procedures at a blood donor clinic.

Just how much information of this sort that you incorporate into a report depends entirely upon the subject and the purpose. You must treat all material objectively and fairly; the data gathered from your experience must be valid and verifiable; that is, another impartial observer should be able to arrive at similar data. Your feelings should not influence your presentation of data.

The Experience of Others

Your college, community, and workplace can be considered as being like a card catalogue of resource people for a report. The difference is that knowledgeable people are not always neatly categorized and easy to find. Nevertheless, they offer an often untapped and very valuable pool of information.

When you have a report assignment, immediately brainstorm to think of people who can supply pertinent information. Your immediate reaction may be, "Oh, I don't know anybody in that field," or "Well, I know two or three people, but they're probably busy." Brainstorming and talking with others, however, will usually reveal several names. For the most part, people will find time to talk with you about a worthwhile report project when you seem to know what you want from them.

Assume that you are writing a report on radon gas in homes. Who could help you? Several possibilities come to mind: chemistry instructors, environmental science instructors, local directors of civil preparedness or emergency services, sellers of and testing labs for radon gas detector kits, fire department personnel, poison control centre personnel, or hospital personnel. You can probably think of others. Do not overlook the assets in your "community catalogue." You can gather information in several ways, both oral and written.

Interviewing   Interviewing is an effective means of getting valid and useful information, but it is not necessarily easy. It requires preparation and persistence beforehand; it requires politeness and more persistence during the interview; and later it requires proper use of the information gathered.

When you have found a resource person, prepare carefully for the interview. Communicate exactly what you would like from the interview and exactly what you intend to do with the information. Do not go to an interview with the attitude that "we're just going to talk about radon gas." If you "just talk," you may emerge from the interview with lots of information not suited to your purpose and many questions left unanswered. You need to go to the interview with a list of focused questions.

Here are some pointers to help make personal interviews successful:

1. Know your subject matter. You want information and opinions from the interviewee; nevertheless, you should have read sufficiently in the area to know what questions to ask.

2. Write out the questions you have before you arrive at the interview. It is a good idea to put one question at the top of a clean (lined) sheet of paper. That way you have plenty of space to write without crowding the page. And go equipped with a firm legal pad or notebook; a flimsy set of loose papers is hard to write on.

3. Explain your purpose for the interview and indicate how you will use the information. Be honest about your degree of knowledge, but do not say "Just tell me everything you know about my topic."

4. Ask in advance whether you may use a tape recorder. If the person objects or appears reluctant, do not insist. You might point out, however, that for questions eliciting technical data, a tape recorder will help ensure accuracy.

    If you do use a tape recorder (and it should be small and inconspicuous with a long-playing tape, just in case you are given more time than originally scheduled), also take notes. Often interviewees will be more relaxed if you are doing something while they are talking.

5. Be on time for the interview. Not being able to find a parking space or having to stay late for a class will seem a very poor reason for delaying a busy person who is taking time to talk to you.

6. Be courteous. Express appreciation for the interview at the beginning and again as you are leaving.

7. When you do not understand what the interviewee means or do not know the meaning of a term or concept, ask for

clarification. Most people are glad to expand on what they have said to make it clearer.

8. Offer to allow the interviewee to see the results of the interview in the form of your report. Sometimes the person may ask to review your material before you hand it in.

9. If you have been allotted a certain amount of time, end the interview promptly when the time is up. Of course, if the interview is going well, the interviewee may disregard the original time allotted.

10. Within a few days, write a brief note thanking the person again for the interview and information.

As soon as possible after the interview, listen to the tape and/or review your notes. Take time to fill in the gaps and clarify any vague points while the interview is fresh in your mind.

In writing the report, integrate relevant comments and pieces of information from the interview wherever they fit naturally or logically into the report. Do not simply transcribe or summarize the interview as a separate section. It helps to put information from the interview on note cards so that when you begin to organize your material, you can see where it all fits into the report.

Telephone interviews are helpful when people are not available locally or simply do not have time to talk with you in person. The same courtesies apply to in-person and telephone interviews. Here, too, plan your questions and know exactly what information you want.

Interviews give a human element to a report. The testimony, opinions, and attitudes of individuals in positions of authority often add an important dimension to a report. You will probably be surprised at the knowledge and insights you will gain from interviewing.

Inquiry Letters   If interviews are impractical, inquiry letters can sometimes elicit helpful information. Before you write an inquiry letter, decide exactly what kind of assistance you want, and do not expect too much. Answering letters takes time and thought, so make your request clear and the response easy. Effective inquiry letters are discussed in detail in Chapter Eighteen.

Surveys and Questionnaires   Surveys and questionnaires are a means of gathering written information from more than one or two people, usually from a representative cross-section of a group.

One individual's views of, say, the efforts to revitalize a certain downtown section are interesting, especially if that person has special insight about the project, but the views of dozens of people give a report a stronger impact.

The size of a sample is important. For valid results, survey as many people within a group as possible. For example, collecting information from the first 50 teenage shoppers who enter a mall store may give a valid indication of the opinions of that age-group toward that store. Surveying only three shoppers will not allow you to draw a valid conclusion.

Here are some possibilities for conducting an on-the-spot survey or sending out questionnaires:

Poll fellow students regarding some problem or policy at school.

Survey fellow employees about proposed changes in benefits, working conditions, or salary options.

Question business owners about the impact of a new mall in their vicinity.

Survey consumers concerning the effects of price increases or changes in a company's product packaging.

Conducting effective surveys and mailing out questionnaires take both time and financial resources. You should, for example, include stamped, return-addressed envelopes for the easy return of written questionnaires.

These five suggestions for creating surveys and questionnaires will help you gain information that can be efficiently tabulated:

1. Always explain clearly but briefly the purpose of the questionnaire or survey. Indicate who you are, your position, your reasons for requesting the information, and what use (a report, for example) you will make of the results. Develop the "you attitude" and tell respondents what's in it for them. Offer to send copies of the tabulated results to the respondents.

2. Make questions easy to answer. Closed-ended questions give respondents a limited selection of items or answers from which to choose. Open-ended questions ask respondents to write out answers; questions that require even only one or two sentences typically go unanswered.

   Multiple-choice questions that require circling a response or checklist questions that require only a check mark response usually get a high rate of return. Even if you ask only for a yes, no, or maybe, list those choices and ask only for a circle or check mark — not a written word.

You may want to include an option labelled "Other" followed by space for answering. When a response requires phrases or sentences, give lined space for answers and limit it to two lines.

3. State your questions clearly but in such a way that the answer you want is not obvious. A slanted questionnaire is useless. Use objective, neutral terminology, not emotionally charged words that reveal your point of view.

4. Express sincere appreciation for the participants' cooperation and help.

5. If possible, limit your questions to one page or at most one page double-sided. Busy people are more likely to fill out a short questionnaire than to wade through a long one.

An example of an effective survey is shown in Figure 6.2. As the survey is a double-sided tear-out sheet in a mail-order seed catalogue, the name and return address are shown in the catalogue itself. This concise survey demonstrates

◆ an inviting attitude ("We need to know how to serve you better")

◆ a "what's in it for the customer" statement ("a survey with a reward!" and better service)

◆ the use of closed-ended questions (Check the boxes in response to "what kind of gardening do you do the most?")

◆ the use of open-ended questions ("What other products would you like us to offer?")

The survey is designed to find essential information for the business, so that product decisions can be made wisely. Notice, too, that the survey contains no slanted questions. For example, the company wants to find out how the customers feel about using the Internet. While the survey describes the Internet as a powerful method of communication, it does not *persuade* the customers that they should use the Internet for ordering. The questions "Are you interested in a computerized form of the catalogue?" and "Do you have an e-mail address?" are for information — they do not suggest that customers should use the Internet.

Surveys and questionnaires are excellent sources of information when they are well planned and well worded. When they exhibit evidence of haste and little consideration for the respondent and material (as illustrated in the sample in the following activity), they yield poor results.

We want to know more about our mail-order customers!

We need to know how to serve you better and the best way to do this to have you fill out the survey below. Now wait, this is not your ordinary survey, this is a survey with a reward!

Fill out the survey, enclose it with your mail order form and receive free, your new variety seed sample with your order. That's right, a new variety that is not yet made available in our catalogue. These new varieties are suitable for our Maritime climate.

Please check the box at the end of the survey to indicate which seed you would prefer.

What type of gardening do you do the most?

❏ Vegetable
❏ Herb
❏ Flower
❏ Container
❏ Bulb

What is the approximate size of your garden?

_____ sq.ft. or
❏ 250 sq.ft.
❏ 1000 sq.ft.
❏ 5000 sq.ft.
❏ 20,000 sq.ft.

Do you have a green house or solarium that you use for gardening purposes?

❏ Yes ❏ No

What other products would you like us to offer?

_____

See over

Do you have children (or grand children) that are interested in gardening or you would like to see interested in gardening?

❏ Yes ❏ No

What is your favourite vegetable and flower that you grow?

Vegetable   _____

Flower   _____

Do you own or have access to a personal computer with a modem

❏ Yes ❏ No

Are you interested in a computerized form of the catalogue?

❏ Yes ❏ No

In this new electronic age there are many alternative ways of communication. The "Internet" is one of the most powerful. We would like to know how you feel about it.

Do you have an e-mail address?

❏ Yes ❏ No

Would you use the computer and Internet to:

(Check all that apply)
❏ Look for information
❏ Internet discussion groups
❏ Ask specific questions
❏ Source and order garden products

Other_____

Other comments are appreciated

_____

_____

What sample of new variety seed would you like sent to you?

❏ Vegetable ❏ Flower

Figure 6.2 *This concise survey illustrates one effective method of collecting information.*
Reprinted with permission from the Halifax Seed Company, Inc. 130th Anniversary Catalogue, 1996.

Activity 1

Assume you have received the following questionnaire from a fellow student. Fill it out as requested, and then answer the questions that follow it.

Dear Student:

I am required to do a survey for one of my classes. Fill out the questions that follow and return this sheet to Box 879. It has to be in my box by next Friday.

1. Have you ever filled out a questionnaire?

   _____ Yes   _____ No   _____ Can't remember

2. What is your reaction when you get a questionnaire in the mail?

   _____

3. If you have filled out other questionnaires, what is your attitude toward the task?

   _____ a. I like to help by giving my views.

   _____ b. I resent being asked for my views.

   _____ c. I have no feelings about the task.

   _____ d. I feel uncomfortable about the task.

4. Describe what an effective questionnaire or survey should do:

   _____

5. Which of the following describes an appropriate tone of a survey or questionnaire?

   _____ a. Very personal

   _____ b. Objective and neutral

   _____ c. Demanding

   _____ d. None of the above

* * * * *

a. Now that you have completed the brief questionnaire, circle the number(s) of the question(s) you consider well constructed.

1　2　3　4　5

b. Rewrite the opening three questions to create a more courteous tone and to be more specific.

_____

_____

_____

c. Did you answer questions 2 and 4?　_____ Yes　_____ No

How could they be improved?　_____

_____

When you gather data through surveys and questionnaires, you must inform readers of the methodology used (how you chose your participants, for example, and how many there were). When possible, place your data within a larger context by comparing it to similar studies. When readers accept the validity of a survey or questionnaire, they are more likely to accept conclusions drawn from the results.

In addition to information from community and individual sources, you will usually want to find what authorities in the field have said about your report topic, you will need to read background material, you will wish to clarify points and concepts, and you may gather statistics from reputable studies — in short, you will need to use library resources.

Use Library Resources

Libraries are reservoirs of information, great storehouses of print and nonprint sources on practically every subject. If you do not know your college and community libraries very well, this is a good time to become familiar with all they offer.

Here are several types of printed material available in most libraries:

Abstracts	Handbooks
Bibliographies	Indexes
Books	Journals
Dictionaries	Magazines
Directories	Magazines
Encyclopedias	Yearbooks

How to Find a Book

There are three efficient ways to find a specific book: (1) check the card catalogue, (2) conduct a computer (online catalogue) search, and (3) ask a librarian. A fourth and time-consuming way is simply to drift through the stacks (shelves of books) and hope you come upon just what you need.

The Card Catalogue   The card catalogue, undoubtedly already familiar to you, is a listing or cataloguing (on index cards) of all the books that the library has on its shelves.

Libraries use either the Dewey decimal classification or the Library of Congress (LC) classification. The Dewey decimal classification has 10 major categories designated by numbers. The 600s, for example, deal with technology and applied science, including (among others) the fields of medicine, business, and the mechanical trades. The Library of Congress classification has 20 major categories indicated by letters of the alphabet; for example, the sciences (computer science, microbiology, and others) are found under *Q*. In both classification systems, the main categories are further divided into more specific areas. You should know those categories of most interest to you.

Activity 2

a. Which classification system does your college library use?

_____

b. Which classification does your local library use?

_____

c. From either classification, find at least one area in which you might locate information for a report in your field. Write the name of the area and its number or letter here:

_____

From these cataloguing systems, a "call number" (consisting of the classification category, author number, and copyright date) is given to each book in the library. Books are shelved according to their call numbers so that you can find any book in a specific place on a specific shelf. A Library of Congress call number with each item identified is illustrated below.

RA	Indicates Public Health category
1231	Subdivision within the category
.M5	Further subdivision
T38	Author number
1988	Copyright date

In either classification system, all books are listed in the card catalogue under three headings: author, title, and subject.

Each card contains several items of information in addition to the author's full name, the book's main title, and its subtitle (if any). It tells whether a book is illustrated and indexed, the number of pages, copyright dates and reprints, and publishing information.

Until you recognize the names of authorities and writers in your field, you should start your library search for sources with the subject card catalogue. For example, if your interest is mercury and its potential dangers, you can find out whether your library has books on that subject by looking under the main subject word, *mercury*, in the card catalogue. A subject card for mercury is shown in Figure 6.3.

When you know the title of a book, the card catalogue shows whether your library has it and, if so, lists other items about the book. Figure 6.4 shows a sample title card.

If you know the author is Joyal Taylor, for example, an author card (illustrated in Figure 6.5) tells you that your library has *The Complete Guide to Mercury Toxicity from Dental Fillings*.

Note: An excellent report topic may be too specific to appear in the *title* of a book. Do not be discouraged. New products and concepts take a few years to get into books. In fact, topics in the titles of books are very likely too broad to be treated adequately in a report of 10 to 30 pages. You will, however, be able to find the titles of several books in your field of interest. Check them out and review their tables of contents for appropriate chapter titles and their indexes for references to your topic.

Computer Systems   Computer systems of cataloguing books are replacing card catalogues in many libraries. Your college has probably put its book listings in a computer database or is in the process of doing so. Online systems give clear instructions at the computer

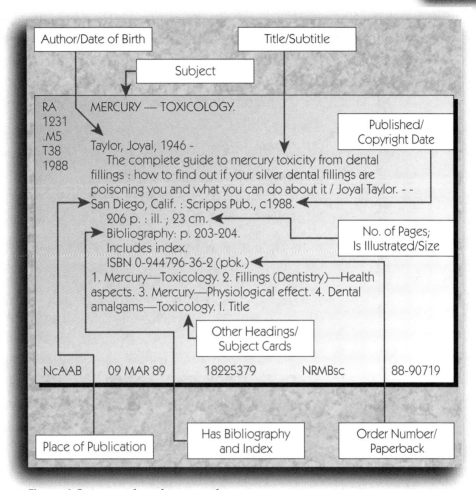

Figure 6.3 *A sample subject card.*

terminals for bringing up the system and locating books. For example, the system may give computer screen instructions as shown in Figure 6.6.

Most systems have a "browse" option on their menus. Like the subject cards in the card catalogue, this option lists all the books under various key headings. (Refer to the Computer Tips section at the end of this chapter for more information on how libraries are using computers.)

Librarians   Ask library personnel for help when you cannot find books you need in the card catalogue or online system. Librarians may have suggestions about finding material outside the college library. They know whether new books have arrived but have not yet been catalogued; they may direct you to other related sources. When you have questions about any of the library's resources, ask for assistance. Librarians are well known for *liking* to help!

| RA 1231 .M5 T38 1988 | The complete guide to mercury toxicity from dental fillings

Taylor, Joyal, 1946 -
    The complete guide to mercury toxicity from dental fillings : how to find out if your silver dental fillings are poisoning you and what you can do about it/Joyal Taylor. - - San Diego, Calif. : Scripps Pub., c1988.
        206 p.: ill.; 23 cm.
        Bibliography: p. 203-204.
        Includes index.
        ISBN 0-944796-36-2 (pbk.)
1. Mercury — Toxicology. 2. Fillings (Dentistry) — Health aspects. 3. Mercury — Physiological effect. 4. Dental amalgams — Toxicology. 1. Title |

Figure 6.4 *A sample title card.*

| RA 1231 .M5 T38 1988 | Taylor, Joyal, 1946 -

    The complete guide to mercury toxicity from dental fillings : how to find out if your silver dental fillings are poisoning you and what you can do about it/Joyal Taylor. - - San Diego, Calif.: Scripps Pub., c1988.
        206 p.: ill.; 23 cm.
        Bibliography: p. 203-204.
        Includes index.
        ISBN 0-944796-36-2 (pbk.)
1. Mercury — Toxicology. 2. Fillings (Dentistry) — Health aspects. 3. Mercury — Physiological effect. 4. Dental amalgams — Toxicology. 1. Title |

| NcAAB | 09 MAR 89 | 18225379 | NRMBat | 88-90719 |

Figure 6.5 *A sample author card.*

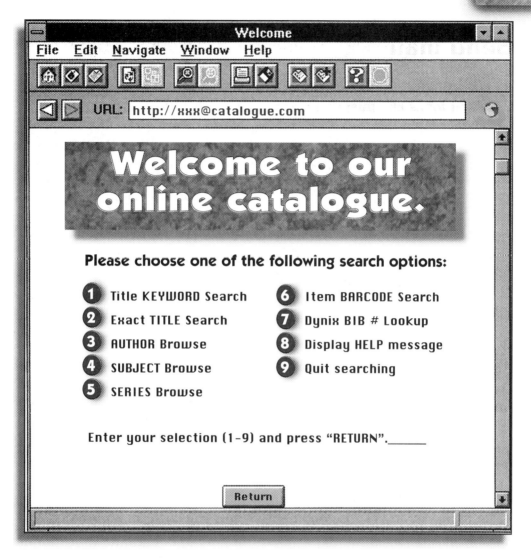

Figure 6.6 *Instructions for using a computerized system.*

Use whatever methods work for you in locating appropriate books. For technical reports, books are especially helpful for background information; for general overviews of subjects; and for concepts, definitions, and theories.

Very recent statistical data, however, may not yet be in books. The very process of getting data gathered, written, edited, published, advertised, bought, and then processed (ready to be put on the shelf) by a library system takes several years. A research study conducted in 1984, for example, is usually first published in a journal and then in a book; it might be ready for college readers by 1992.

For recent studies and up-to-date information on products and processes, look for magazine and journal articles and use indexes to help you find them.

How to Find Indexed Periodicals

Indexes tell you what has been written on almost any subject within a certain time frame. Usually they are published monthly or quarterly and bound yearly. They are also available through computer searches. Like the card catalogue, indexes do not contain the material itself. They list what is available, where to find it, and usually its format (number of pages and illustrations, for example).

Indexes are a necessary research tool both on the job and in college. Some of the most useful ones are discussed next.

Readers' Guide to Periodical Literature   The *Readers' Guide* is a monthly listing of magazine articles in hundreds of mostly general-interest magazines. It lists articles by author and by subject. An explanation on the inside cover of each booklet and bound volume tells how to use the guide.

Always begin with the most recent listing and work backward so that you can locate the most up-to-date information available. If you have a subject in mind, start with that and narrow it as needed. When you know authors in the topic area, look up their names.

Every college library has the *Readers' Guide*. It is a good starting point, especially for topics of popular or general interest. A sample listing for an article in the *Readers' Guide* is shown here:

> *Mercury in the body*
>   *See also*
> *Mercury poisoning*
> *How safe are your dental fillings? [mercury amalgam fillings] il Glamour 85:330+ My '87*

This entry tells you that an illustrated (il) article entitled "How Safe Are Your Dental Fillings?" can be found in volume 85, the May 1987 issue, of *Glamour* magazine. The article starts on page 330. It relates to mercury amalgam fillings and was probably written by someone on the magazine's staff since no author is given.

The *Readers' Guide* may not list articles of a highly technical nature, and it does not index all periodicals. Other indexes you may consult include *Ulrich's International Periodical Directory* and *Popular Periodical Index*. If the index you use does not list several articles dealing with your topic, look under another subject word. You may need to refine or narrow the topic further.

Specialized Indexes   Indexes are available for almost every profession or field of interest, some dating back to the 1800s. Depending on your report topic, the following indexes may be helpful:

Accountants' Index
Applied Science and Technology Index
Biological and Agricultural Index
Business Periodicals Index
Canadian Business and Current Affairs Index
Consumer's Index
Cumulative Index to Nursing and Allied Health Literature
Current Law Index
Education Index
Engineering Index
Environment Index
Index to Dental Literature
Index to Legal Periodicals
The Matthews List
New York Times Index
Quarterly Cumulative Index Medicus

Check with your college and public libraries to determine the availability of other indexes. If you find an article indexed for a magazine not carried by the college or community library, don't give up. Your instructors or other people in the field might subscribe to the magazine or have a connection to the Internet, or the material might be available through interlibrary loan. For a reasonable fee, you may also be able to acquire an off-campus borrower's card at a local university library. With this card, you might be able to access a number of postsecondary institution or professional association libraries, depending on agreements existing between these institutions.

Other Reference Works

In addition to books and indexes, libraries have a wealth of other reference works in print, on microfilm, and on microfiche. The *Statistics Canada Catalogue* gives census data; an almanac such as *Economic Almanac* gives facts and figures about business and industry. This section discusses only the three most important reference works: directories, encyclopedias, and dictionaries.

Directories   Directories are listings of companies, corporations, and businesses. Especially helpful for business-related reports, they contain information about the size of a business, its status, investment opportunities, and products. Here are three of the better-known directories:

The Canadian Almanac & Directory
Canadian Trade Index
Dun and Bradstreet
Fraser's Directory
Scott's Manufacturer's Directories (All Provinces)
Standard and Poor's Register
Sweet's Canadian Construction Catalogue
Thomas' Register of American Manufacturers

Encyclopedias   Encyclopedias provide broad reviews and previews of topics and definitions of concepts and terms.

If a subject is unclear in your mind and you cannot put your thoughts into words, the solid background information in an encyclopedia article is beneficial. However, in a technical report, do not quote or paraphrase much (if any) material from these general sources. You are probably familiar with general encyclopedias such as the *New Encyclopaedia Britannica* and the *Canadian Encyclopedia*. Other specialized encyclopedias include

Encyclopedia of Biological Sciences
International Encyclopedia of the Social Sciences
McGraw-Hill Encyclopedia of Electronics and Computers
McGraw-Hill Encyclopedia of Science and Technology

Dictionaries   Use dictionaries primarily to check spellings, word origins, and acceptable usage of terms — not for technical content. These standard dictionaries are available in most libraries:

Funk and Wagnalls New Standard Dictionary
Gage English Dictionary
Oxford English Dictionary
Random House Dictionary of the English Language
Webster's Third New International Dictionary

For technical coverage, one of these specialized dictionaries may be more helpful than a general one:

Dictionary of Business and Science
Dictionary of Computing
Dictionary of Criminal Justice
Dictionary of Economics and Business
Dictionary of Robotics

Dictionary of Scientific and Technical Terms
Funk and Wagnalls Dictionary of Electronics
Stedman's Medical Dictionary
Thorpe's Dictionary of Applied Chemistry

Check your library to see which are available to you. You may find that some material (back copies of newspapers, journals, dictionaries, and indexes) is stored on microfilm, microfiche, or CD-ROM. Your librarian will help you use the information technology.

Never assume, however, that if you cannot find material in the college or public library nothing is available on the topic. Libraries are the most convenient information storage areas. For technical reports, they often supplement, validate, and help to verify data gathered elsewhere.

STEP 2: CONVERTING INFORMATION FOR YOUR USE

After you determine which sources will provide you with appropriate data, the next task is to gather the information and convert it into a document that is uniquely yours in terms of wording and organization.

Creating a report from the many pieces of data gathered from printed and nonprint sources requires (1) taking useful notes and (2) transferring those notes to a rough draft. A third step is then the proper and clear documentation of your sources.

The rest of this chapter discusses and illustrates each task.

Take Notes

As you read articles, sections of books, manuals — any printed material — you should take notes. It is unrealistic to think that you will remember all that you read over a period of days and weeks.

Remembering other papers you have researched, does the following scenario seem familiar?

At lunch hour, you rush to the library and find an article on your topic. You begin to read and jot down useful information in the order in which you read it. Thirty minutes later you have three or four handwritten pages of notes on the material. You do this several times before the report is due. Preparing the first rough draft, you have before you almost 20 pages of notes from eight different sources. Now you must find the information a second time — and in your hurriedly scrawled handwritten notes.

You may jot down information on legal pads, notebook paper, or possibly on a computer. You may photocopy material to take home and review later, marking or highlighting the relevant parts. However, there are two effective ways of organizing your research material: using a research journal or using note cards. The method you choose will depend on the length of the research period and the nature of the project or report.

Start a Research Journal

One way to keep track of research or of a prolonged work project is to keep a research journal, sometimes referred to as a work journal, learning journal, or laboratory notebook. For example, if you are reporting on a project you are undertaking for a technical instructor or for a work term supervisor, you should note your activities and observations in a bound notebook.

This journal has at least three advantages:

1. It is a complete record of all your research activities.
2. It can provide a useful form of communication between your research or work supervisor and you.
3. It can be used as a record in registering for a patent on your invention or product.

You should take care to organize the journal carefully. Here are some suggestions:

◆ Date each entry.
◆ Record library search activities.
◆ Record significant points from interviews with contacts.
◆ Begin a working bibliography.
◆ Keep copies of inquiry letters and responses.
◆ Devote a section to summaries of articles under specific headings.
◆ Make notes of questions for your supervisor.

If your research is likely to result in a marketable product, you may wish to patent your design or product. In this case, you should record your activities in a bound notebook. Dates, test results, sketches, and notes are important data which should be written in ink. Number each page. Do not use correcting fluid (white-out); rather, draw lines through errors and across unused portions of the page. Do not remove any pages. Initial and date your corrections. Keep the notebook confidential and in a safe place. Such precautions will facilitate patent registration. Your librarian will be able to help you with information on patenting and may be willing to demonstrate a patent search. (Many libraries now charge a fee for such services.)

On the job, your journal or work diary can become a useful record for your company and may, if needed, provide legal evidence of worksite activities if contract disputes or accidents occur. Many companies have preprinted forms for recording daily or weekly activities. A construction company superintendent, for example, may use a form to record the following information: project number, date, location, trades on site, trades finishing, weather, specific problems, visits from government inspectors, supplies ordered, and change orders. A work log also keeps track of time and costs.

Using Note Cards

Using note cards to transfer information from the original source to a rough draft is an efficient way to go about accumulating information and fitting it into your report.

Put relatively small bits of information on individual note cards, and label them for easy retrieval when you begin the rough draft. Here are some pointers for using note cards efficiently:

◆ Use 3- by 5-inch note cards, preferably lined.
◆ Put three items on each card:

1. What you plan to use in the report (the note itself).
2. Where you got it (the source).
3. Where you anticipate it will fit into the report (the section heading of the report or entry in the outline).

◆ Use LARGE, legible letters.
◆ Limit the length of the note. Put only what you can see at a glance and read rapidly. Do not write complete sentences here — just basic information. Create your own sentences later.
◆ List the source briefly: Use only the author's last name (or a brief title notation) and the exact page(s) on which you found the information. Later you will give all the bibliographical information in the List of References.
◆ Use the key word(s) from your outline for the note heading. This heading indicates — as you take the notes — where you expect to use them in the report.

There are three ways to take notes from a printed source:

◆ Copy directly and exactly.
◆ Paraphrase.
◆ Summarize.

Copying the original material directly is the easiest way to take notes, but it is *not* recommended. In fact, you should use very little directly quoted material in a report. You may quote controversial statements or clearly opinionated material directly to preserve the original flavour, but do not directly quote routine information.

Quite often you may feel "I can't say it better" or "There is no other way to say it." However, you *must* say it differently; otherwise, the report will be mostly the words of other people rather than your own. Make it a habit from the very beginning not to copy very much directly, because later you will not be inclined to put the material into your own words. However, for the rare occasion when you need a direct quotation, notice that the note card illustrated in Figure 6.7 clearly shows quotation marks around the quoted material.

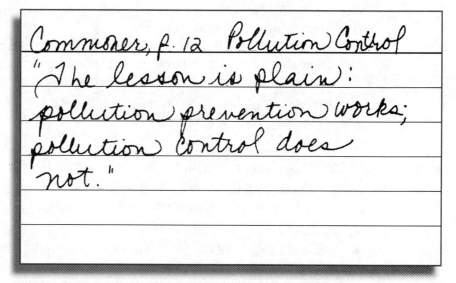

Figure 6.7 *Sample note card with directly quoted material.*

Paraphrasing is one step removed from direct quotation. To paraphrase means to keep essentially the same order of sentence structure and perhaps a few of the same words as the original, but not exactly the same words in exactly the same order. A sample note card showing a paraphrased note is illustrated in Figure 6.8.

Summarizing the information is the preferred way to reshape the original material for *your* report. Of course, summarizing is more difficult than quoting directly and paraphrasing. You must take the time to *understand* the material and then put it into your own words. You must still give credit to the original source for the ideas and information, but the writing is now totally yours. A sample note card of summarized material is shown in Figure 6.9.

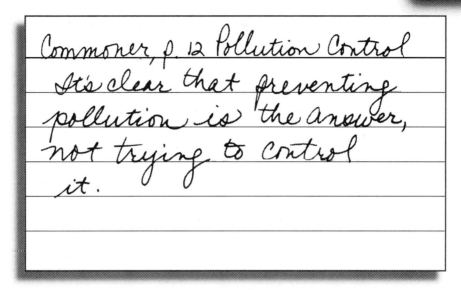

Figure 6.8 *Sample note card with paraphrased material.*

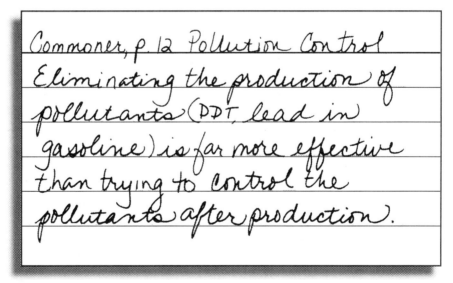

Figure 6.9 *Sample note card with summarized material.*

Activity 3

Assume you are taking notes on this chapter for a section of a report with the heading "Library." On each note card, include a heading, the source, and the brief note itself.

a. Reread the section "How to Find a Book" (pp. 147–152) and make a note card of directly quoted material.

b. Reread the section "Librarians" (pp. 149–150). Paraphrase it on the note card below. Again include all parts of a note card.

c. Reread and then summarize the section "The Experience of Others" (pp. 139–146).

```

_____

_____

_____

_____

_____

_____

_____
```

Create a Rough Draft

Using an appropriately organized research journal helps you create a first rough draft of a report. You may find that the early stages of your research form the background section of your introduction, in which you briefly review the literature and/or describe similar studies or examples of your topic (or technical project).

Your final draft will also benefit from your keeping a detailed and orderly journal. For instance, the chronological listing of your activities may provide a firm basis for a report section requiring a step-by-step explanation of a procedure, and you can copy exact test results and analysis straight into the final draft. Finally, keeping a working bibliography in your journal will cut down your time and effort in compiling the final bibliography, list of references, or works cited. From your journal bibliography, you may select and transfer the appropriate entries into your final draft.

Using note cards also helps you create a first and rough draft. With your outline as your guide, review all note cards and separate them according to their headings.

Since you took notes over a period of time, you will probably have cards with repetitive and irrelevant information. Put aside any notes that repeat information and veer off topic. The number of card stacks should equal the number of main headings in the outline. Then sort the cards further to match the subheadings in the outline.

Use the key words or phrases from the outline entries to create headings for the report. Use the sentence outline entries as topic sentences under the headings. Find all the note cards relating to one heading, and from the notes, construct rough paragraphs. Do not try for perfection here. Expect to modify, refine, and reword most sentences as you write your rough drafts. However, a good outline means that you have the beginning of paragraphs under headings in the report.

Remember, you do not have to write the rough draft in the order in which the reader will read the report. If you feel comfortable with the stack of note cards relating to section 3.2 of the report, for example, write that section first.

When you feel overwhelmed — as both experienced and inexperienced writers sometimes do — by the extensive amount of material you have gathered, the outline should give you a sense of control and direction. As you constantly decide what to use and what not to use, do so on the basis of the outline. Yes, you may change the outline, but it is still the road map or guide sheet. Just as starting a long journey is less intimidating when you have directions, planned stopover sites, and a final destination, constructing a report is easier when you have the same kind of assistance from an outline.

Distinguish Fact, Inference, and Opinion

Technical writing is essentially factual writing with logical inferences used as needed and little or no opinion expressed. In converting information for your report, you need to recognize the differing characteristics of fact, inference, and opinion.

A *fact* is a statement that can be verified by others or by the experience of the writer. It has been "proved" (to the extent that anything can be) either by scientific studies or by human experience and is generally accepted as true. That the sun has risen every day of our lives is a fact.

An *inference* is a belief based on fact. It is a logical assumption derived from fact or experience. That the sun will rise tomorrow is an inference based on past data and experience. Although you assume that the sun will rise, only after it has done so can you announce it as fact. Any statement made about the future is an inference based on what has occurred in the past.

An *opinion* is a view or feeling that may or may not be based on fact or inference. That the sun rises too early on workdays is an opinion. Opinions alone are not valid in technical reports; they must be supported and substantiated by proof, at which point they become fact or inference.

The following examples may clarify the differences among facts, inferences, and opinions.

FACT: Walking along, you are suddenly knocked to the ground by a speeding bicycle rider. A purse falls from the cyclist's shoulder.

INFERENCE: The bike rider was female. (This may or may not be true; it is based on the assumption that generally females carry purses and generally males do not.)

OPINION: All women cyclists are dangerous and careless. (From one experience, you may form an opinion, but you cannot expect readers to regard it as anything other than opinion.)

FACT: Cordless drill Brand Q has a speed range of 0-44/ 0-1,100, has 5 clutch positions, weighs 4 pounds, is equipped with a screwdriver bit, and costs less than $250.

INFERENCE: Cordless drill Brand Q will meet the needs of the typical homeowner for most tasks.

OPINION: Cordless drill Brand Q is fantastic. I like it!

Facts should form the basis of any report; from facts, inferences are made and conclusions are drawn. The difference between an inference and a conclusion is a matter of degree. A conclusion is typically a more absolute and decisive statement.

Opinion statements are rarely needed in technical reports. Regardless of personal opinions, you must state facts, substantiate any assumptions, and draw conclusions based on those facts.

Activity 4

Indicate whether each of the following statements is a fact (*F*), an inference (*I*), or an opinion (*O*) by placing the appropriate letter in front of it.

_____ a. In 25 years the common wooden sleepers (railway ties) will be collectors' items for antique dealers.

_____ b. A study by the Swiss National Railways found that wooden sleepers last approximately 18 to 25 years and steel sleepers last 25 to 100 years.

_____ c. Steel sleepers will replace wooden railway ties because they are more economical.

_____ d. A composite asphalt with 5 percent (by weight) scrap polyethylene added resists cracking at lower temperatures than does "normal" asphalt.

_____ e. Composite asphalt is a ridiculous attempt to change a perfectly good asphalt mix.

_____ f. Composite asphalt is more likely to be used in colder regions of the country where winter temperatures drop below zero.

_____ g. The SuperBrand motorized band saw has a 16" blade-to-frame capacity.

_____ h. SuperBrand's saw is a real value!

_____ i. Anyone can accurately cut wood, plastic, sheet metal, and aluminum with SuperBrand's saw.

STEP 3: DOCUMENTING YOUR SOURCES

You have found information for a report, you have taken notes on the information, and now you must give credit to the originators of the information.

Here are three good reasons for documenting and citing your sources:

◆ To give credit to whoever is responsible for the material
◆ To demonstrate that you recognize authorities in the field, authorities who lend credibility to your statements
◆ To tell readers where they might look for further information on the same subject

Appropriately giving credit to the original source prevents plagiarism, a serious offence that is discussed later.

Use Methods of Documentation

Direct your readers to your sources of information by using a standard style of documentation. Style guides vary, so choose one that is best suited to your field, discipline, or situation. Your instructor or employer can advise you of the preferred format: the Modern Language Association (MLA), the American Psychological Association

(APA), the *Chicago Manual of Style,* the Council of Biology Editors (CBE) *Style Manual,* or other.

Adequately and accurately informing readers of the origin of information requires two tasks:

◆ Compiling and including, at the end of the body of the report, a list of references or works cited

◆ Placing citations to specific sources as needed within the body of the report

Make a reference or bibliography card for each source (book, article, manual, whatever) you use. Depending on the type of source, items for a reference card include the following:

BOOK: Author(s) or editor(s) — name(s) exactly as given on title page
Title (and subtitle) — underlined
Edition number if other than first edition
Facts of publication: place of publication, publisher's name, and latest copyright date

ARTICLE: Author(s), if given
Title of article — in quotation marks
Name of magazine or journal — underlined — and volume number and date
Page numbers of entire article

INTERVIEW: Name and position (if relevant) of person interviewed
Date of interview

Include all information about where to find the source. A sample reference card is shown in Figure 6.10.

Produce a List of References

The *List of References* (also titled "Bibliography," "Works Cited," or simply "References") follows the body of the report and conforms to specific stylistic expectations. You use *Works Cited* when you list the works you specifically cite; you use *Bibliography* or *References* when you list the works to which you have referred throughout your research and which may be additional, useful information sources for your reader. Follow the style guide carefully and consistently.

One way to indicate different kinds of sources in a list of works cited is shown in Figure 6.11. The form of the entries follows the MLA guidelines. When a source does not fit any of the examples shown, use a *who, what, where, when* order for giving all available information so that the reader can find the same material:

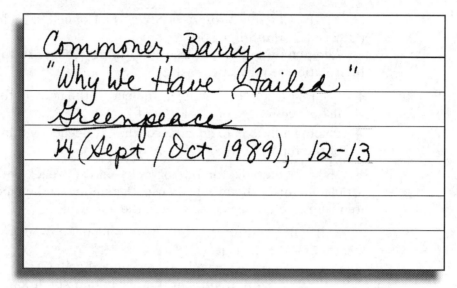

Commoner, Barry
"Why We Have Failed"
Greenpeace
14 (Sept/Oct 1989), 12-13

Figure 6.10 *Sample reference bibliography card.*

- *Who* (individual, company, or organization) is responsible for it
- *What* it is (its title, caption, etc.)
- *Where* it originated or where it can be found
- *When* it was released (published, handed out, etc.)

When you do not have *all* the above information, write what you do have in the order listed above.

Generally, follow these conventions in listing references: (1) underline titles of books and long documents, names of magazines, journals, and newspapers; (2) use quotation marks around titles of articles in magazines, journals, newspapers, and titles of short pieces of information (pamphlets, brochures, etc.).

For all printed material, remember that the whole is underlined and a part of the whole is placed in quotation marks. Thus, you would underline the title of a book (the whole) and place quotation marks around the title of a chapter (part within it).

In the sample list of works cited illustrated in Figure 6.11, notice the following:

- Entries are alphabetized by author (individual or responsible company). Alphabetize by the first main word of the title if there is no author.
- Entries are double-spaced, with double-spacing between entries. (Alternatively, the entries may be single-spaced, with double spacing between entries.)

WORKS CITED

Doucet, Marie-Josée. (Hydrologist.) Personal Interview. Wetlands Management Program, Calgary, AB, May 10, 1994. [Personal interview]

Hamblin, Kenneth W. Earth's Dynamic Systems. 6th ed. New York: Macmillan, 1992. [Book with one author]

Hammer, Donald. Creating Freshwater Wetlands. Chelsea, MI: Lewis Publishing, 1992.

Journal of Hydrology 141 (1993). Special Issue on Hydrogeology of Wetlands.

Mairson, Alan. "The Everglades: Dying for Help." National Geographic, April 1994: 2–35. [Magazine article with one author]

Stone, J. A., and D. E. Legg. "Agriculture and the Everglades." Journal of Soil & Water Conservation 47,3 (1992): 206–15. [Journal article with two authors]

Wright, Gail M. "Wetlands in Our Environment." Technical Paper. Halifax: NSCC, Institute of Technology, 1994. [Unpublished technical paper]

Figure 6.11 *Sample list of references with types of works shown in brackets.*
Adapted with permission of Gail M. Wright, Earth Resources Technology Graduate.

Activity 5

Arrange the following five references in the correct form for a list of references. Remember to alphabetize.

a. A book called Quality Is Free written by Philip B. Crosby and published by McGraw-Hill Book Company in New York, with a copyright date of 1984

b. A pamphlet entitled SPC Mitutoyo System with a date of 1986 and available through the Mitutoyo company

c. An interview with the quality control supervisor at Micro Switch, Joseph Ramirez, conducted on June 17, 1990

d. An article by Margaret Strus, titled Self-Assessment — Determining which assessment is right for your needs, published in the Fall 1995 issue of the Canada Quality Journal and appearing on pages 11 to 15 of volume 1, no. 3.

e. The third edition of a book by Elwood S. Buffa and Jeffrey G. Miller titled Production-Inventory Systems Planning and Control, published by Richard D. Irwin at Homewood, Illinois, in 1968

1. _____

_____

_____

2. _____

_____

_____

3. _____

_____

_____

4. _____

_____

_____

5. _____

_____

_____

Use Citations

Technical writing generally has simplified the methods of citing sources and uses fewer citations than do other kinds of writing. This is because many reports rely heavily on the author's own experience, observation, and testing.

Citations are used for two reasons:

◆ To explain material in the text
◆ To give credit in the text to the original source

Explanatory Notes   Occasionally, you may want to comment on text material without interrupting the narrative. In this case, use a citation "signal" such as an asterisk (*) — or use a number if you anticipate more than one such note in the text. Position the asterisk or superscript number after the word or idea you wish to explain or comment upon. At the bottom of the page, place the same signal and your commentary. For example, you may have found two contradictory pieces of data and feel you must indicate this. The explanatory note would be handled as illustrated below.

TEXT: The Metropolitan Water Commission stated in May that more than $2 million would be appropriated by Watborough for improvements to the system.*

FOOTNOTE: *Commissioner Watkinson reportedly has indicated that the system could be *replaced* at a cost of $2.5 million.

Use explanatory notes sparingly in technical reports. They tend to distract the reader.

Source Citations   The in-text citation system is one efficient method recommended by the MLA. This system dispenses with the use of footnotes and endnotes, and makes it easier for the reader to recognize the source of a citation. There are two methods to cite your sources within the text, illustrated here with examples from the text of a research paper on wetlands and the environment:

1. Put the author and page number in parentheses at the end of the sentence.

EXAMPLE: It is estimated that one third of all North American birds rely on wetlands at some stage of their lives (Hammer 70).

2. Put the author(s) in an introductory (or signal) phrase, and the page number in parentheses.

EXAMPLE: According to Stone and Legg, an excellent example of integrated decision-support systems is the Nitrate Leaching and Economic Prediction Program (206).

You may decide to include the copyright date in the parentheses (Hamblin 1992, 14) if your references include more than one work by the same author.

Reading a report with the above citations, you could turn to the Works Cited shown in Figure 6.11 to find full publication information about these books and article. Including such information is essential as it enables an interested reader to discover more about the topic.

Whether quoting directly, paraphrasing, or summarizing, whether stating someone's opinion, statistics, or concepts, you must document the source. For some of the information collected, these questions may occur to you:

QUESTION: Everybody knows this information. It's in all the books. Do I have to give credit?

ANSWER: You do not have to cite material that is considered "common knowledge in the field." This may be a questionable area for you now, but it will become less so as you work and read widely in your field. If you find the same information in several places and if it is not documented there, you can assume it is common knowledge for technical readers, though perhaps not for Communications instructors. When in doubt, ask your instructor or go ahead and document the information.

QUESTION: I found the same thing in three articles. Which one do I give credit to?

ANSWER: When you find the same information in several places, you can use the most recent source or the best-known source. Obviously a 1990 date seems more valid than a 1972 date for statistical data, and a well-known scientist's views carry more weight than those of an unknown. However, you can cite more than one source for the same information if there is a good reason to do so. For instance, if an interviewee confirms data found in a book, cite both sources.

QUESTION: How many citations do I have to have? How many references must I have?

ANSWER: There is no prescribed number. Use as many references and citations as you need to give credit for all information taken from someone else. Print-oriented research typically requires more source references than a report based on firsthand information.

Keep in mind that a report is a valid, verifiable, and accurate collection of information. Readers tend to accept its points and conclusions when they are well documented.

Avoid Plagiarism

Plagiarism is a term often heard in writing courses. Bluntly, plagiarism is academic shoplifting. It is taking someone else's words or ideas and using them as if they belonged to you and had originated with you, the equivalent of slipping a piece of merchandise into your pocket and considering it yours because it is now in your possession. Plagiarism is typically heavily penalized. The policy for a course and/or college is usually put into writing to avoid any misunderstanding.

Plagiarism is the result of any of the following:

◆ Directly quoting the words of an author and omitting the required quotation marks. (Even if a report writer cites the source properly, without quotation marks around a direct quotation, the reader assumes that the idea belongs to another but that the wording is the writer's own.)

◆ Summarizing ideas or information from another source and omitting proper credit to that source (including page numbers).

◆ Paraphrasing too closely the words of another, thus leaving the impression that the ideas are one's own.

Give credit for whatever you use from another source. Never leave the impression — even accidentally — that exact words (quoted), similar words (paraphrased), or ideas (summarized) that you did not originate are yours. When you are uncertain about citing a source, give credit. Leave no doubt about your academic and professional honesty.

As a beginning writer in a field, you may be thinking that you will have to give credit for *everything* in a report. This will not be the case. As you organize the material, you will be surprised at how much does not require a citation. For example, as noted earlier, you need not give credit for information that is common knowledge (well-known dates, data, concepts, elementary material, and situations that are noncontroversial and accepted by all authorities) or for processes that you have observed firsthand or completed yourself. You would not, for instance, have to cite sources for Ohm's Law, the date of the D-day invasion, or the need to clean surfaces before soldering.

Good technical reporting is a combination of finding necessary data and information to complete the writer's objectives, converting and thus reshaping that material into a useful report, and giving credit for any assistance and any material taken from others.

Computer Tips

Finding usable and up-to-date technical information can take so long that you are left with too little time to analyze the data and write the report. Computer searches expedite the process.

Most libraries now use computers to (1) list their own holdings and (2) access national and international databases to show what has been published in a variety of fields. You may access the following services.

Computerized (Online) Catalogue

All the library's book holdings or possibly all its holdings have been placed into its computer system. Users may key in title, author, and subject words; they may also ask for materials by format (videocassette, for example) or other means to determine what is available. Information very similar to that supplied in the card catalogue appears on the screen. A computerized search for books is much quicker than thumbing through a card catalogue and can provide a useful beginning bibliography.

Information Retrieval Services

Hundreds of computerized databases list periodical articles and abstracts in many fields. A library may subscribe to more than one bibliographic database. Educational Research and Information Service (ERIC), Scisearch, and Chemical Industry Notes are three well-known information retrieval systems.

A library may use disks that contain regularly upgraded bibliographies, or it may be connected by telephone line and computer to databases. Users may have to pay a fee to cover the cost of the telephone and the time spent in the search, or the search may be free.

Databases give a quick, complete, current (and sometimes overwhelming) listing of up-to-date articles. Librarians can help in selecting appropriate key words (descriptors) that narrow the number of possibilities.

Generally, for a list of articles on a topic, you decide on key words and type them in. The database tells you the number of articles found with those key words in their titles; that number indicates whether you need to make your key words more specific (a listing of a hundred or more articles containing the word *abuse*, for example, is not very helpful). You can then ask for titles, possibly abstracts of the articles, and a printout.

Your library may also access the On-line Computer Library Centre (OCLC), which supplies information about library locations and materials available through interlibrary loan from almost 3,000 libraries. Your library may be connected with the Internet.

Firmly entrenched as valuable research tools, computers can make the search for up-to-date materials an exciting adventure.

QUESTIONS FOR DISCUSSION

1. What resources are available to you as a technical writer?
2. Why is keeping a research journal useful and productive?
3. What are the characteristics of a successful survey?
4. How can encyclopedias help beginning technical writers?
5. Why is it important to cite your sources?

EXERCISE 1

This exercise is designed to acquaint or reacquaint you with your college library.

a. What classification system does your college library use?

_____

b. Does your library have a computerized cataloguing system? If so, what is it called?

_____

c. List three general categories of either the Dewey decimal or the Library of Congress classification (whichever your college library uses) that you expect to use in your college studies:

_____

_____

d. Does your library have open stacks? (Are individual students allowed to find their own books?)

_____

e. Find a book directly related to your major area and preferably to a report topic. Write its call number here:

_____

Write the information about it that you would include on a reference (bibliography) card:

Author: _____

Title: _____

Place of publication: _____

Publisher: _____

Date of publication: _____

f. In the *Readers' Guide*, find an article related to your major field
    and complete the following information about the article.

Author: _____

Title: _____

Name of magazine: _____

Number of pages in article: _____

Date and volume number of magazine: _____

Is the article illustrated? _____

g. Find another *index* that you might use in your field and write its
    name here:

    _____

h. List at least three magazines which might be helpful in your
    field as you write technical reports:

    _____

    _____

    _____

i. Name one general encyclopedia that your library carries:

    _____

j. Name one unabridged dictionary in your library:

    _____

k. Indicate with a check mark which of the following resources are
    available in your library.

    _____ *Dictionary of Economics and Business*

_____ *Fraser's Directory*

_____ *McGraw-Hill Encyclopedia of Science and Technology*

_____ *New York Times Index*

_____ *Public Affairs Information Service Bulletin*

_____ *Scott's Manufacturers Directories*

l. During what hours is your college library open on Tuesday? On Saturday? On Sunday?

_____

m. If you need a book not available at your library, is it possible to get the book without leaving campus? If so, how?

_____

_____

EXERCISE 2

Below are questions you might want answered, and sources in which you might look for answers to those questions. Put the number of the correct source in the blank to the left of each question.

1. Card catalogue
2. *Readers' Guide*
3. Questionnaire
4. Librarian
5. Interview
6. Observation or experience
7. Dictionary
8. *The Matthews List*
9. Inquiry letter
10. Encyclopedia

_____ a. How do students feel about the college attendance policy?

_____ b. Does your library have an Internet connection?

_____ c. Are there any books on using the Internet?

_____ d. What exactly did *The Globe and Mail* editorialize about the World Economic Forum in early 1996?

_____ e. What is DNA?

_____ f. What are recent trends in the management of hazardous waste?

_____ g. How do local authorities respond to environmental emergencies such as tanker truck oil spills?

_____ h. What is the concept of total quality management, and when and where did the concept originate?

_____ i. What does the Better Business Bureau advise about dealing with bogus telephone offers of prizes? (The local director has no time for an interview.)

_____ j. What are the flaws in the registration process at your college?

WRITING ASSIGNMENTS

1. When you are assigned a report, keep a logbook of all the activities and tasks in which you engage that relate to the production of the report. Assume that a supervisor at work then asks for a three-page summary of all that was involved in finishing the report. Review your logbook and summarize your work on the report.

2. Use the directories or indexes in your library to conduct (1) a product search, and (2) a job search. Describe the product and write a brief profile of a company to whom you might wish to apply for a job when you have graduated. Briefly explain how you found the information.

3. If you now have a topic for an assigned report, write 7 questions (in complete-sentence form) that you might ask a prospective interviewee. If you do not have a topic for a report at this time, think of a topic on which you would like to do a report and write 10 clear and specific questions (in complete-sentence form) to ask a prospective interviewee.

4. Class Project: In groups, develop a questionnaire to be sent to local organizations that employ your college's graduates. Ask 10 to 20 easy-to-answer questions about what should be taught in a technical writing course so that graduates will be well prepared to write on the job. If time permits, ask your instructor if it is feasible to send out the best questionnaire, so that you can tabulate, analyze, and report the results.

CONSTRUCTING THE REPORT

Objectives

When you finish Part Three — Chapters Seven through Eleven — you should be able to do the following:

- Write different kinds of definitions as appropriate for your audience.
- Describe mechanisms clearly.
- Describe products clearly.
- Recognize the value and function of graphics in reports.
- Create different kinds of graphics and place them appropriately in reports.
- Write the following sections of reports as needed:

   Transmittal letter
   Title and title page
   Table of contents and list of figures
   Abstract and executive summary
   Formal introduction
   Conclusions and recommendations
   List of references
   Appendices

- Distinguish between formal and informal report formats.
- Recognize the importance of appropriate formatting for technical reports.
- Produce visually appealing reports that meet the formatting criteria of the classroom and the workplace.
- Approach writing as a step-by-step process.
- Edit reports for

   Clarity
   Conciseness
   Coherence
   Conventions of standard English
   Consistency and accuracy

Chapter SEVEN

Defining and Describing

"After all, engineering writing is not like riding a bicycle; it is not a skill that's once learned and forever the same. Rather, engineering writing is like bicycle racing; it's an ongoing activity requiring constant attention, variation, and practice."

William E. McCarron, "The Power of Analogy in Engineering Writing," IEEE Professional Communication Society, April 1987

Defining and describing are important parts of technical writing. Often, technical reports deal with complex terms, concepts, equipment, mechanisms, procedures, or projects. One of your goals as a technical report writer is to help your specific audience understand — in small, digestible bites — everything in the report. One of your jobs, therefore, is to break down the complex and present it so that it is simple and clear. Accurately worded definitions and descriptions are effective means of achieving your goal.

Definitions and descriptions appear in many workplace documents:

Business and marketing: Product literature and proposals contain physical descriptions, operating overviews, descriptions of special features and benefits, and definitions of all specialized terms.

Engineering and science: Manuals and feasibility studies contain vividly described procedures and clearly defined concepts.

Health care and social sciences: Instructions and evaluations contain precise descriptions of administering treatment and detailed definitions of important principles.

The major difference between a definition and a description is as follows:

◆ A *definition* is a clear, concise statement of the meaning of a term or phrase.
◆ A *description* is a detailed picture in words of how something appears, works, or behaves.

Sometimes definitions and descriptions are supplemented with visual illustrations that serve as additional *support* for verbal definitions and descriptions.

The following sections of this chapter explain how to develop effective definitions and descriptions. Consider this information as a general guide and modify it to serve your specific purpose, audience, and situation.

DEFINITIONS

Good technical writing is clear, concise, and unambiguous. A reader should always know precisely what you mean when you use such terms as *upload* or *O-ring* or *efficiency* or *market share*.

Methods of defining should be based on the following:

◆ The technical level of the audience
◆ The complexity of the subject
◆ The scope of the objectives

Generally, make a definition long enough so that your audience understands it clearly. Some terms for some readers need only a brief one- or two-word definition. The same terms for other readers may require a fuller, more in-depth definition. An audience analysis (as described in Chapter Four) helps with these choices.

Parenthetical Definitions

To use a parenthetical definition, you place a word or phrase (enclosed in parentheses) directly after the term. Parenthetical definitions allow the audience to get a quick understanding of a report's specialized terms with little interruption to the reading flow. All levels of audience benefit from clear parenthetical definitions, but high-level technical readers especially appreciate them.

A parenthetical definition is ideal when you can clarify a term in the report with a synonym (something the term is equal to) or with a simple phrase.

EXAMPLE: For a greener lawn, use a fertilizer that balances your soil's acidity (sourness) and alkalinity (sweetness).

EXAMPLE: The U-bend was first exposed to temperature stress
with an annealing (heat-treating) process at 182
degrees Celsius.

Parenthetical definitions also are effective when you use an
acronym (abbreviation) of a term. For example, rather than repeating the cumbersome term *linear variable displacement transformer*
throughout the report, use an acronym in its place.

EXAMPLE: The transducer chosen for deflection measurement was
a linear variable displacement transformer (LVDT). An
LVDT …

When using parenthetical definitions, always define the term the
first time you use it. Thereafter, it is not necessary to define it again
unless the report is lengthy (several long sections). If you have not
used the term since Section 1, readers may appreciate the courtesy
of having the term defined again in Section 4.

Activity 1

In the space provided to the right, write a one-word parenthetical
definition that may be more familiar to your report audience than
each of the following terms:

a. distilled   _____

b. conduit   _____

c. centrifugal   _____

d. velocity   _____

e. phobia   _____

f. acuity   _____

In the space provided, write a one-phrase parenthetical definition
that may be more familiar to your audience than each of the following terms:

g. binary   _____

h. indigenous   _____

i. diameter   _____

j. prestressed concrete   _____

Sentence Definitions

Some terms may require more than just a word or a phrase in parentheses to establish a clear definition, especially for an audience with a low or medium technical level. In such cases, develop a formal sentence definition. A formal sentence definition always contains these three elements:

1. The term being defined
2. The class or specific group to which the term belongs
3. The distinguishing features that make the term different from other items in its class

EXAMPLE: An electroencephalograph is an instrument that measures the changes in electric potential produced by the brain.

This sentence definition contains the *term* (electroencephalograph), the *class* to which it belongs (instrument), and the *distinguishing features* that make the term different from other instruments. (It measures the changes in electric potential produced by the brain.)

When using a formal sentence definition, state the term first. Then give the "class" to which the term belongs. The class will always be a noun. Never use *is when* or *is where* directly after the term you are defining. Such phrases result in a grammatically incorrect sentence and a vague, rambling, and often inaccurate definition.

INCORRECT: A theorem *is when* you demonstrate a geometric truth.

CORRECT: A theorem is a statement of a geometric truth to be demonstrated.

Finally, add the distinguishing features that make the term different from all other terms. Be precise. Avoid circular definitions (defining a term with itself) such as this: "Creativity is being creative."

Sentence definitions also are effective in clarifying terms that may have different meanings for different readers. For example, the term *full-time employee* may mean someone who works no less than 40 hours per week, or it may mean someone who works more than part-time (25 hours or more per week). So that the reader has a clear understanding of the term, stipulate the meaning as shown next. Underline or italicize the term, or put it in quotation marks.

EXAMPLE: In this report, the term *full-time employee* means all Crescent Electronics personnel who work no fewer than 40 hours per week.

By using all three elements — term, class, and distinguishing features — you can develop clear and precise formal sentence definitions for your audience.

Activity 2
....

a. List five terms from your major field of study that would need sentence definitions to help a reader with a medium level of technical background in your field understand them.

_____   _____

_____   _____

_____

b. Choose one term and write a sentence definition of it.

_____

_____

Operational Definitions

An operational definition outlines the functions or workings of an object or process, usually in two or three sentences, and is often effective for audiences with a medium level of technical knowledge. Such a definition gives readers a general understanding of how something operates.

Perhaps, for example, you have an idea about how your company's product, a viscous fan drive assembly, can be improved. The plant manager likes the idea and wants you to propose the change to division headquarters. You have determined that the division's management knows what a viscous fan assembly is but not how it operates in an automobile. Understanding this operation is important if management is to realize the value of the idea. Here is an operational definition you might provide for these readers:

EXAMPLE: A viscous fan drive assembly is a thermostatically controlled fan clutch that provides air flow to an automotive engine when it needs cooling. Typically mounted on the engine water pump, the unit's thermostatic coil is positioned as close to the radiator as possible to accurately sense changing temperatures. When the coil senses the radiator is heating up, it opens the valve and engages the unit; conversely, when the coil senses that the radiator and engine are cooled, it closes the valve, disengages the fan drive, and returns the unit to idle speed.

Note that in this example, the first sentence contains the essential elements of an effective sentence definition: term, class, and distinguishing features. The next two sentences briefly explain how the fan drive assembly operates.

If, on the basis of your audience analysis, you find that a term needs more than a two- or three-sentence definition to explain its operations adequately, a mechanism description may be necessary. This description gives specific details about the item, often describes relationships between its parts, sometimes gives readers with a low technical level some background information, and is placed in a separate section of the report. The "how to's" of writing a mechanism description are detailed later in this chapter.

Expanded Definitions

Brief definitions — a word, a phrase, a sentence or two — do not always serve your purpose or meet your audience's needs. Knowing exactly what you want (or need) to achieve in the report and recognizing how much your audience knows will determine to what extent specialized terms will be defined. Clearly stated objectives and a thoughtful audience analysis help you decide when, how, and to what extent to expand definitions.

You may expand definitions in several ways; each method serves a different writing purpose for a different type of audience:

◆ Exemplification (examples)
◆ Comparison (noting similarities)/contrast (noting differences)
◆ Illustration
◆ Etymology (word origins and roots)

Choose the method for expanding the meaning of a term based on your purpose for defining it and on what your audience needs to understand about it. The following sections explain the value and purpose of each method and give you some guidelines for using them effectively.

Exemplification

Use exemplification to expand a definition when a concrete example (or several examples) will help further clarify the specific meaning of the term. (This textbook uses exemplification often to help you understand important points.) The following example defines and then exemplifies the term *social stressors:*

EXAMPLE: Social stressors are sudden traumatic events in an individual's life that allow little or no time for preparation or controlled reaction. The social stressors often occur very quickly. For example, social stressors may be the death of a loved one, marriage failure, loss of one's job, or a sudden financial crisis.

Just as exemplification helps readers with a low or medium technical background (the general public and customers, for example) understand a term or concept more clearly, it can also help employees understand the importance of new ways of doing business. For example, the Queen Elizabeth II Health Sciences Centre's quality handbook lists examples of how Continuous Quality Improvement (CQI) works:

♦ *The Pulmonary Function lab and the Respirology Clinic worked together to eliminate the often inconvenient wait faced by many patients. Using redesigned and coordinated appointment schedules, patients are now booked for tests immediately before their appointments with their doctors.*

♦ *A team of food service staff formed a workgroup called Cash in a Flash and tackled the problem of long coffee shop line-ups. New signs, redesigned food displays, and flexible cash floats are just a few of their innovative ideas for getting and keeping those lines moving.*

♦ *Laundry staff called in the expertise of nursing representatives as they examined a long-standing linen supply problem on the units. Their redesigned delivery process and schedule have reduced calls from the nursing floors to the laundry by 88%.*[1]

Comparison/Contrast

Use comparison and/or contrast when the term is completely unfamiliar to your audience. By comparing or contrasting details of the term to a term that is familiar to readers, you help them equate physical or operational characteristics to something that is more recognizable.

---

[1] Reprinted with permission from *A New Way of Doing Business: Victoria General Hospital Quality Handbook.* Copyright 1994, Queen Elizabeth II Health Sciences Centre.

If you know, for example, that some of your readers have never seen a rugby ball, you could begin to describe it by using a comparison such as "It has an oval shape similar to a that of a football." You could then use a contrast such as "Even though a rugby ball can be dribbled with the feet down the playing field, it does not roll as quickly or smoothly as a soccer ball."

You will often find an *analogy* useful when comparing the term to a term that is more familiar to your audience. In his article titled "The Power of Analogy in Engineering Writing," William E. McCarron notes that the "analogy — the ability to put difficult technical concepts in more familiar terms — is a powerful additive to straightforward technical writing," and his engineering writing–bicycle riding/racing analogy provides a powerful beginning to this chapter.

Analogies are frequently used in introductory science or engineering texts and lectures. Technology instructor Susie Kuhner supplies the following classic example of the electricity–water analogy:

Electrical current is analogous to the flow of water in a pipe, where

◆ *The pipe diameter is analogous to electrical resistance. Changing the pipe diameter changes the resistance to the flow of water.*

◆ *The force behind the water that is causing it to flow (for example, the pump or waterfall) is analogous to electrical voltage. The greater the force, the faster the water flow.*

◆ *The rate of flow (that is, how many drops of water pass by a given point in a given time) is analogous to electrical current, which is expressed in amps.*

Here are two examples:

1. *If the pipe diameter is changed to increase the resistance to the water flow, with no change in the force behind the water, then the rate of water flow would decrease as well. Electrically this relationship is expressed using Ohm's law, where current = voltage/resistance (I=V/R). That is, if resistance is increased with no change in voltage, then current decreases.*

2. *Similarly, if the force behind the water, such as the pump, is increased, then the rate of water flow increases as well. Electrically, if the voltage increases with no change in resistance, then current increases proportionally.*

As you can see, an analogy can present a slightly longer, more detailed comparison than the rugby and bicycle examples.

Comparing and contrasting the unfamiliar to the familiar is an effective way of defining new terms or concepts for readers who have a low technical or knowledge level of your subject.

Illustration

Use a drawing or photograph of the object or a depiction of the process to further define a term when a verbal definition seems to need more concrete information. Visual images enhance technical documents for all levels of technical readers, but are particularly user-friendly for readers with a low or medium technical level. While in some instances it may replace a long verbal definition, an illustration more often *supports* the verbal definition and offers readers additional concrete information.

Try to use a drawing or photograph to help define the term more clearly. Experts in the field use illustrations, particularly when these support and sell new concepts or mechanisms. Whether you are defining an object or a process, often a simple illustration will improve your readers' understanding of a term. The illustration in Figure 7.1 shows how basic graphic elements (block diagram with arrows) can help an audience get a clear picture of a complex system.

Developing graphics in technical reports is discussed in detail in Chapter Eight.

Etymology

Use etymology to explain the origins or roots of a term. Etymology can be an effective way of emphasizing a specific aspect of the term that you intend to develop into an important point in the report. This method is often effective for readers with a medium level of technical knowledge, and for those who may have some familiarity with the term but who may not know about an unusual aspect of it. The following example shows how the current meaning of the term *psychosomatic* has deviated greatly from its roots, a point that the writer develops.

EXAMPLE: Psychosomatic disease is a condition that is induced by a tragic event of some sort that brings on an emotional crisis. The primary stressors that induce psychosomatic diseases are social stressors. The term *psychosomatic* is derived from two roots: *psyche*, meaning mind, and *soma*, meaning body. This etymology is relevant because psychosomatic disease is not "all in the mind," as is commonly thought today. Psychosomatic disease is very real, can be diagnosed, and can be manifested physically.

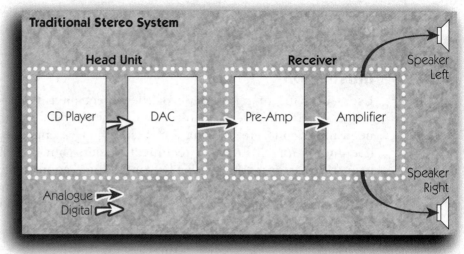

Figure 7.1 *A simple visual illustration supports and clarifies a technical description.*
With permission of Jeff Vienneau.

Dictionaries are excellent sources of etymological information. Such information (often brief) is usually presented in brackets just after the pronunciation of a term. Many research books that go into more detail on the etymological origins of terms also are available.

A note of caution: While most etymologies are interesting to the general reader, be sure you are presenting information that is relevant to your purpose and to your specific *technical* audience.

Definitions for Your Specific Audience

To communicate your meaning successfully, you must suit your definitions to your audience. You will quickly lose your readers if you (1) confuse them by neglecting to define sufficiently something obscure to them, and (2) insult their intelligence by overdefining something they find simple. A thoughtful analysis of your audience and writing situation will prevent you from inadvertently confusing your audience and condescending to them. In oral presentations you can more easily gauge your audience's reaction and respond appropriately; in written reports, you need to consider very carefully specific methods for specific types of audiences. Table 7.1 presents some of these methods and suggests the type of audience for which each is appropriate; use it as a quick reference when you begin defining terms for your reports. Be aware, however, that these are only guidelines and that you should not limit your definition methods to the audiences recommended. Modify these suggestions as situations dictate.

TABLE 7.1

DEFINITION METHODS FOR SPECIFIC AUDIENCES

Method	Characteristic	Typical Audience	Audience Technical Level
Parenthetical	Gives a quick understanding of a term with a word or phrase	Peers, experts	High
Sentence	Restricts a word's meaning according to its class and distinguishing features	Top managers, customers, operative and production personnel, the general public, consumers, laypersons	Medium or low
Operational	Explains briefly the working of an object	Top managers, customers, operative and production personnel	Medium
Expanded exemplification	Clarifies meaning with an example	Top managers, customers, operative and production personnel, the general public, consumers, laypersons	Medium or low
Comparison/ contrast	Equates the unfamiliar with the familiar, often by means of analogy	The general public, consumers, laypersons	Low
Illustration	Supports a verbal definition with a visual image or depiction	Peers, experts, top managers, customers, operators and other production personnel, the general public, consumers, laypersons	High, medium, or low
Etymology	Explains the origins or roots of a word	Top managers, customers, operators, and other production personnel	Medium

Placement of Definitions in Reports

Always define a term before using it in your discussion. The best choices for placing definitions in a report are the following:

◆ Incorporating definitions within the text
◆ Grouping them into a formal subsection in the introduction
◆ Placing them in a separate major section

Another option is to place the definition in a footnote at the bottom of the page on which the term first appears. Although many academic papers use this placement, most technical reports in the workplace do not use footnotes. Footnotes tend to distract readers from the context of the report by directing their attention temporarily to the bottom of the page.

Incorporated Definitions

Many terms can be defined as you introduce or discuss them. As you saw in the section on parenthetical definitions, you can frequently incorporate a brief definition (a word or phrase) into the same sentence in which a term first appears. You should incorporate a sentence definition within the context of the report.

EXAMPLE: Compensation is the addition of specific materials or components to counteract a known error. Without proper compensation, pressure sensors cannot accurately measure pressure.

If you plan to use only a few definitions in your report, include them within the body of the report. A few incorporated definitions will not significantly interrupt the report's reading flow, as long as the definitions fit smoothly into the text.

Definitions in a Formal Subsection of the Introduction

When the terms to be defined number more than five or six, incorporating them gracefully into the context of the report may be difficult — especially if several terms must be defined together. In this case, make a list of the terms and their definitions and place it in the introduction of the report as a formal subsection entitled "Definitions," "Terminology," or "Nomenclature." In his report on the design of a security lighting system for a local university, an electrical engineering technology student places a list of terms at the end of the introductory section, as shown in Figure 7.2.

As a result of increasing assaults at St. Brigit's University campus, the students attending the university have expressed concerns over the lack of light in certain walkways on campus. The University administration has decided to upgrade the lighting to security levels in some heavily used walkways. Flick Engineering is handling this account and is designing a new security lighting system.

This report documents a lighting system for those areas designated as security lighted areas. The design will be presented to Flick Engineering, who may or may not choose the design for the replacement of the older, ineffective lighting system currently in place.

The new security lighting was designed with the aid of the new computer software technology, Genesys....

Terms

Illuminance is the density of luminous flux incident on a surface. It is the quotient of the luminous flux by the area surface when the latter is uniformly illuminated.

Light loss factor (LLF) is a factor used in calculating illuminance after a given period of time and under given conditions. It takes into account temperature and voltage variations, dirt accumulation on the luminaire and room surfaces, lamp depreciation, maintenance procedures, and atmosphere conditions.

A *luminaire* is a complete lighting unit consisting of a lamp or lamps together with the parts designed to distribute light, to position and protect the lamps, and to connect the lamp to the power supply.

Washover lighting is the amount of light illuminating an area outside that area desired to be lit....

Figure 7.2 *This electrical engineering technology report includes a list of terms at the end of the introduction.*
From "A Security Lighting Design" (1993). Adapted with permission of Scott MacLeod.

Figure 7.3 also illustrates how nomenclature is placed in a product data sheet to make the ordering process concise and easy:

HRV600i Product Data
Heat Recovery Ventilator
600 cfm Ventilation Air Capacity

HRV 600i

The **Venmar HRV600i** provides a compact solution to your ventilation needs. Suitable for installation in a ceiling space, mechanical room or suspended from a ceiling, this ESV™ (Energy Saving Ventilator) delivers year-round comfort and sensible heat recovery with virtually no cross leakage. With its rugged polypropylene or aluminum heat recovery cores, it is designed to meet specifications established for a variety of commercial applications.

Applications

- Smoking rooms
- Restaurants
- Office areas
- Strip malls
- Medical clinics
- and others...

Features

- Apparent sensible effectiveness: 70%
- Indoor installation
- Easy to clean, rugged polypropylene heat recovery core
- Optional aluminum core
- Typical payback: under 5 years
- Removal of major serviceable parts in less than 7 minutes
- Complete line of remote controls
- Toll free technical service number

Indoor Air Quality is the single largest issue facing the industry in the 90's. This product is designed to help resolve that issue and to satisfy the ventilation requirements of ASHRAE 62 and other applicable building codes in an energy efficient manner.

The **Venmar HRV600i** Heat Recovery Ventilator saves on operating costs, decreases demand load and considerably reduces capital costs for air conditioning. There is a 2 year parts warranty, and an unequaled 15 year warranty on the heat recovery cores.

CONTENTS

- Unit Nomenclature
- Specification Chart
- Airflow Graph
- Efficiency Graph
- Unit Dimensions
- Guide Specifications Example

HRV600i
Nomenclature   Ordering Example

HRV600i

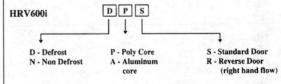

| D | P | S |

D - Defrost
N - Non Defrost

P - Poly Core
A - Aluminum core

S - Standard Door
R - Reverse Door (right hand flow)

Figure 7.3. *This first page of a product data brochure includes the nomenclature section.*
Copyright Venmar Ventilation Inc., 1995. Reprinted with permission.

Definitions in a Separate Major Section

When you have an extensive list of terms and definitions (more than 10, for example), place them in a separate major section at the beginning of the report and use the heading "Definitions" or "Glossary." This concise section serves as a minidictionary for readers who want to check any unfamiliar terms quickly. Figure 7.4 shows the "Glossary" section of a Construction Technology student's work term report on the construction of a sunroom. Understanding the specialized terms enables readers to follow the construction process more easily.

PRODUCT DESCRIPTIONS

Readers must be able to visualize a product and understand its uses before you can convince them to buy it, instruct them how to use it, or help them evaluate its effectiveness. A product description helps accomplish these objectives — to convince, to instruct, to evaluate — by providing an overview of the product's physical appearance and general capabilities.

A visual description of the product is often essential for audiences with little or no technical experience or knowledge. Their basic understanding of the product may be important to the success of your report. However, when writing for the general public or potential customers (refer to Table 7.1 for some other typical audiences with low and medium technical levels), you should include an appropriate product description. Most audiences with high technical levels (peers and experts in the field) may already be familiar with the basic appearance and capabilities of the product or of one similar to it; these readers do not usually need product descriptions.

A product may be a "hard" object such as a CNC lathe or an X-ray machine, or it may be a "soft" product such as an engineering and design service or a haircut. In either case, a clear, vivid description helps your specific audience comprehend the information in technical reports.

Uses and Content

A product description may be used in marketing literature or included as a section within a lengthy report. Most proposals and responses to requests for proposals, often written to managers and marketing personnel rather than to engineers, contain product descriptions. Most equipment manuals and instructions, frequently written to consumers and operators, contain a general description of the physical characteristics of the product. When feasibility studies and evaluation reports focus on a product, the product is always described carefully. A product description, then, helps the audience achieve the following goals:

◆ Grasp the product's overall characteristics and capabilities.
◆ Understand the whole product before dissecting it into parts.
◆ Decide whether the product meets their needs.

GLOSSARY

Bottom chord	The horizontal bottom member of a truss.
Bullfloating	Using a large trowel with an extension handle to eliminate high and low spots and to embed large aggregate particles on a freshly poured concrete surface too large to reach with an ordinary hand trowel.
Cant strips	Triangular-shaped strips of wood used under a membrane to eliminate a 90 degree bend.
Chase	A shaft used to route wires or pipes.
Parge-coating	A stiff sandy cement mix hand-trowelled over unit masonry or a concrete surface. A bonding agent is usually added to the mix.
Screeding	The process of striking off excess concrete to bring the top surface to proper grade.
Soldier course	A course with bricks laid on their ends so that their longest dimension is parallel to the vertical axis of the face of the wall.
Truss webs	The smaller members of a truss that join the top and bottom chords.
Tuck pointing	Pushing mortar into a joint after a brick is laid.

Figure 7.4 *In this report a list of specialized terms appears in a separate section.*
Adapted with permission, Gary Shore, "An Architectural Addition: A Contractor's Perspective," 1995.

Before beginning to write any product description, you should become thoroughly familiar with the product. The key to writing successful descriptions is to know completely what you are writing about.

Although product descriptions usually do not go into great technical detail, they must contain enough specific information about the item so that your audience can form realistic images and can make some initial decisions. Generally, your product descriptions should tell the audience the following:

◆ What the product is
◆ What the product does
◆ How it looks in general
◆ What it is made of
◆ Why they should/are going to use it

Follow these four steps to ensure that you have addressed all of the preceding points:

Step 1: Identify the product.
Step 2: Describe the product's general capabilities.
Step 3: Expand with specific language.
Step 4: Use visual aids.

Step 1: Identify the Product

Begin the product description with a sentence definition that identifies the product (name of product and/or its manufacturer or name of service or its provider), classifies it, and describes how it is used. Here is the first part of a description taken from a product's marketing literature and installation/user instructions:

EXAMPLE: The MicroLight by Techtronics is a peripheral pointing
          device for your computer that allows you to move
          through your menu-driven software programs by
          touching the screen.

Whether writing about a hard item (such as the MicroLight) or a soft item (such as the service contract for the MicroLight), clearly identify the product by using a sentence definition.

Step 2: Describe the General Capabilities

Continue by describing the advantages of the product and its general capabilities. Even though you may choose not to go into great technical detail, be sure your audience can understand your description easily.

EXAMPLE: Some software programs require numerous keystrokes
          to select an item from an onscreen menu. The

MicroLight saves time in executing commands —
and in learning those complex keystrokes. When you
lightly press the *touch pen* to the screen menu, your
software program responds to your command. The tip
of the pen contains a light-emitting ray to which your
personal computer responds instantly when contact is
made to your monitor. This time-saving device is compatible with most menu-driven programs and installs
easily with a tangle-resistant cable into any available
serial port on your personal computer.

Step 3: Expand with Specific Language

Next, describe the physical characteristics of the product. When
writing about a hard item, tell readers the product's size, colour,
materials, design, texture or finish, and any major components.

EXAMPLE: The MicroLight is designed to fit comfortably in the
palm of your hand. Shaped like any writing instrument,
the 7-inch, white *touch pen* is made of smooth space-
age plastic. When not in use, the MicroLight can be
stored in its special holder that protects and darkens
the tip light for energy-saving efficiency. The MicroLight
assembly contains a printed circuit board, coaxial cable,
touch pen, and holder.

When writing about a service — office cleaning, for example —
describe its features, benefits, frequency, and so forth. Explain the
scope and range of expertise available, proven track records, and any
other pertinent information.

A product description — hard or soft — will be meaningful to
readers only if you use specific language. Instead of using vague,
imprecise words, look at these better alternatives:

Rather Than Saying	Use
Large/small	Dimensions (centimetres, metres, height, depth)
Heavy/light	Weights (tonnes, kilograms, grams)
Many/few	Quantities (20, 100, dozens, thousands)
Quickly/slowly	Specific measurements of time (within moments, instantly, four seconds, two hours, 90 days, three years)
Expensive/affordable	Prices and costs (dollars/cents)
Next to/in front of	Direction and position (to the right, to the left, top, bottom)

Specific language, related to specific information, enables a reader to make a sound decision about the product being described.

Activity 3

Read the vague and general phrases listed below. In the blanks provided, rewrite the phrase by using expanded, specific information so the reader can visualize a more precise and vivid image. As needed, invent weights, quantities, and so forth.

Vague and General	Specific and Improved
a. An inexpensive drill	_____ _____
b. A large number of computers	_____ _____
c. A small, compact cabinet	_____ _____
d. A high rate of speed	_____ _____
e. A great deal of experience	_____ _____

Do the phrases you wrote evoke a clearer image of the product or concept?

Step 4: Use Visual Aids

Whenever possible, use an illustration of the product to help your audience understand its physical characteristics. (Remember, however, that an illustration should *support* your verbal description, not replace it.)

Figure 7.5 illustrates a product overview from an introduction to an operator's manual. The audience sees a simple line drawing of the product before reading the instructions for its use.

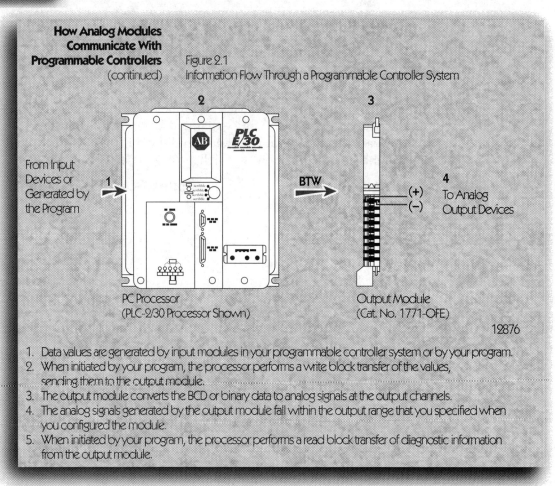

How Analog Modules Communicate With Programmable Controllers (continued)

Figure 2.1
Information Flow Through a Programmable Controller System

2

PLC E/30

From Input Devices or Generated by the Program

1

BTW

3

(+) (−)   **4** To Analog Output Devices

PC Processor
(PLC-2/30 Processor Shown)

Output Module
(Cat. No. 1771-OFE)

12876

1. Data values are generated by input modules in your programmable controller system or by your program.
2. When initiated by your program, the processor performs a write block transfer of the values, sending them to the output module.
3. The output module converts the BCD or binary data to analog signals at the output channels.
4. The analog signals generated by the output module fall within the output range that you specified when you configured the module.
5. When initiated by your program, the processor performs a read block transfer of diagnostic information from the output module.

Figure 7.5 *This operator's manual visually describes a machine's basic operations before presenting specific operating instructions.*
Publication no. 1771-6.5.30, October 1987. Reprinted with permission, Allen-Bradley Company.

Placement of Product Descriptions

In marketing literature, vivid descriptions are usually the readers' first introduction to the product. These descriptions often lead into other information, such as the availability of the product, its special features, and persons to contact for more information.

Similarly, in technical reports — feasibility reports, manuals, proposals — product descriptions are most effective when presented as a subsection in the introduction. Readers need to develop visual pictures of the product as early as possible so that they can relate the information in the rest of the report to something that is now recognizable to them. These descriptions are typically given headings such as "Product Overview" or "Product Description" or "Physical Characteristics."

MECHANISM DESCRIPTIONS

When new items enter the market, mechanism descriptions influence sales. When technicians learn to operate equipment, they need detailed descriptions of equipment and how it works. Both technicians and managers read mechanism descriptions to stay informed of new equipment and upgrades. Effective mechanism descriptions provide vivid word pictures (along with supporting illustrations) to help audiences "see" how an item operates.

Since mechanism descriptions are sometimes aimed at knowledgeable readers with a medium technical level, the terminology may sound foreign to someone in another field. Remember to analyze your readers and determine the extent of their knowledge about a mechanism, as well as what they need to know for your purposes. Then adjust the vocabulary to meet their needs.

Uses and Content

Mechanism descriptions may inform, analyze, or persuade. These descriptions are often part of longer technical reports — manuals and instructions, feasibility reports and evaluations, or proposals. Descriptions may be several brief paragraphs to sell the mechanism in marketing literature, or they may be long narratives in reports and journals to keep employees up-to-date in their fields. Your audience and your purpose will determine the extent of the description and the depth of explanation needed. (Refer to your objectives and audience analysis worksheet in Chapter Four.)

Technical descriptions should be highly specific and as objective as possible. Descriptions written to sell a mechanism may obviously be somewhat subjective; those written to inform a worker must be completely objective. However, all technical readers want information — and specific details.

Generally, mechanism descriptions should provide the following specific information:

◆ What the mechanism is and how it works in general
◆ What the principal function or purpose of the mechanism is
◆ What the mechanism looks like
◆ What the mechanism's principal parts are and how they work

Follow these four steps to ensure that you have addressed all the preceding points:

Step 1: Identify the mechanism
Step 2: Describe the operating functions and parts
Step 3: Expand with specific language
Step 4: Use visual aids

Step 1: Identify the Mechanism

Effective mechanism descriptions begin with a concise sentence definition. Give the mechanism a name — for example, *internal gear pump* or *hydraulic excavator* or *pneumatic load assist system* — then identify the manufacturer when possible. Follow the sentence definition with an explanation of the mechanism's distinguishing feature — that is, features that make it different from other machines.

Step 2: Describe the Operating Functions and Parts

Mechanism descriptions are sometimes a natural extension or expansion of operational definitions and should give readers a deeper understanding of how the mechanism works.

These descriptions go further than operational definitions by giving the reader background information about why the mechanism was developed, what specific problem it will solve for the user, and so forth. Mechanism descriptions specifically mention or list major components and often describe the relationships between these parts:

EXAMPLE: The notched escape wheel, which is the major component in the mechanism, is rotated about its central axis and is set into motion by the energy stored in the wind-up spring.

To write an effective mechanism description, specify the main components to help readers get an overall idea of what the mechanism contains. Next, present specific details in the operational narrative to describe how the mechanism operates. (The extent of these details will vary depending on the audience and your purpose.) Point out clearly the specific uses of the mechanism and any special features. If the overall description is lengthy, include a brief summary paragraph at the end to help your audience understand and review the important points of the description.

A fairly long mechanism description is illustrated in Figure 7.6. As noted in the margins of this illustration, the different descriptive elements provide readers with a vivid picture of the item and the way it operates.

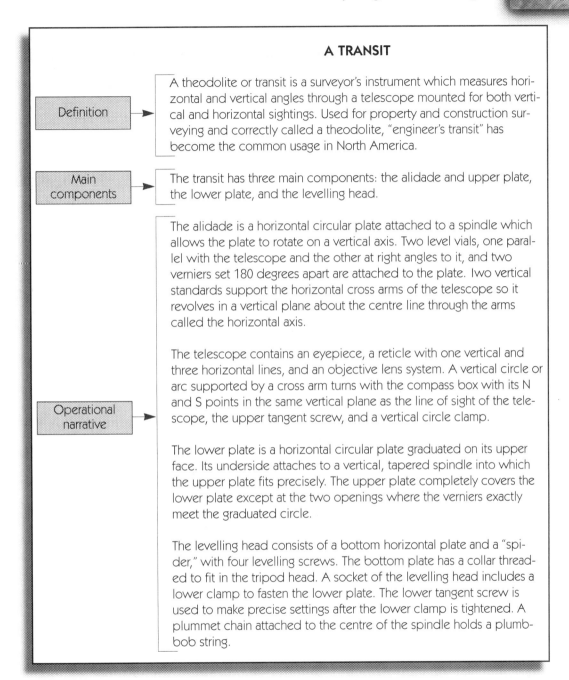

A TRANSIT

Definition ➤ A theodolite or transit is a surveyor's instrument which measures horizontal and vertical angles through a telescope mounted for both vertical and horizontal sightings. Used for property and construction surveying and correctly called a theodolite, "engineer's transit" has become the common usage in North America.

Main components ➤ The transit has three main components: the alidade and upper plate, the lower plate, and the levelling head.

Operational narrative ➤ The alidade is a horizontal circular plate attached to a spindle which allows the plate to rotate on a vertical axis. Two level vials, one parallel with the telescope and the other at right angles to it, and two verniers set 180 degrees apart are attached to the plate. Two vertical standards support the horizontal cross arms of the telescope so it revolves in a vertical plane about the centre line through the arms called the horizontal axis.

The telescope contains an eyepiece, a reticle with one vertical and three horizontal lines, and an objective lens system. A vertical circle or arc supported by a cross arm turns with the compass box with its N and S points in the same vertical plane as the line of sight of the telescope, the upper tangent screw, and a vertical circle clamp.

The lower plate is a horizontal circular plate graduated on its upper face. Its underside attaches to a vertical, tapered spindle into which the upper plate fits precisely. The upper plate completely covers the lower plate except at the two openings where the verniers exactly meet the graduated circle.

The levelling head consists of a bottom horizontal plate and a "spider," with four levelling screws. The bottom plate has a collar threaded to fit in the tripod head. A socket of the levelling head includes a lower clamp to fasten the lower plate. The lower tangent screw is used to make precise settings after the lower clamp is tightened. A plummet chain attached to the centre of the spindle holds a plumb-bob string.

Figure 7.6 *The elements of effective mechanism descriptions help create a vivid, detailed picture for readers. (continued on page 202)*
Adapted from Elementary Surveying, *Eighth Edition, by Russell C. Brinker and Paul R. Wolf, pp. 183–185. Copyright © 1989 Harper & Row, Publishers, Inc. Reprinted by permission of HarperCollins Publishers, Inc.*

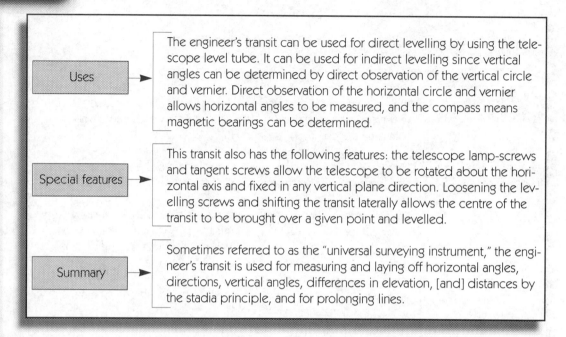

Uses

The engineer's transit can be used for direct levelling by using the telescope level tube. It can be used for indirect levelling since vertical angles can be determined by direct observation of the vertical circle and vernier. Direct observation of the horizontal circle and vernier allows horizontal angles to be measured, and the compass means magnetic bearings can be determined.

Special features

This transit also has the following features: the telescope lamp-screws and tangent screws allow the telescope to be rotated about the horizontal axis and fixed in any vertical plane direction. Loosening the levelling screws and shifting the transit laterally allows the centre of the transit to be brought over a given point and levelled.

Summary

Sometimes referred to as the "universal surveying instrument," the engineer's transit is used for measuring and laying off horizontal angles, directions, vertical angles, differences in elevation, [and] distances by the stadia principle, and for prolonging lines.

Figure 7.6 *continued*

Step 3: Expand with Specific Language

Mechanism descriptions help readers visualize the object and how it works. Whether you are describing the physical characteristics of the mechanism (size, capacity, and so forth) or capabilities (speed, efficiency, and so forth), use words specific enough for your anticipated audience to "see" what you mean.

Activity 4

Read the following description of a hydraulic excavator. Assume you are the purchasing agent for a construction company interested in buying such a piece of equipment. You see this brief description in a magazine dealing with heavy construction.

> *The new hydraulic excavator has a fantastic capability for operating weight and its bucket holds a lot. The backhoe is pretty heavy with a bucket of over two yards; the loader is also fairly heavy with a big bucket. The engine is great with plenty of horsepower. Width and height are sufficient. The digging force of the backhoe, the leader crowding force, and the loader breakout force are high. Its maximum travel speed in both gears is okay and its maximum traction force is rated very high.*

a. Will the equipment meet the needs of your company?

_____ Yes   _____ No   _____ Don't know

b. List at least 10 words that should be more specific and then show how you would improve them.

Vague   **Specific**

_____   _____

_____   _____

_____   _____

_____   _____

_____   _____

_____   _____

_____   _____

_____   _____

_____   _____

_____   _____

Figure 7.7 shows the original description of a hydraulic excavator, taken from the section on new equipment in *Highway and Heavy Construction* magazine. Notice that, for the most part, the nouns and verbs are the same in both descriptions. The description in Figure 7.7, however, includes specific terms, especially units of measurement that are particularly relevant to this kind of equipment.

The description of a semisubmersible drilling rig shown in Figure 7.8 is taken from an introductory guide to the off-shore industry and demonstrates how the vocabulary is adapted to the audience's knowledge.

HYDRAULIC EXCAVATOR MADE FOR HIGH PRODUCTIVITY

The EX700 from Hitachi is a new hydraulic excavator which has an operating weight capability of 154,000 lb. and a bucket capacity of 3.4 to 5.2 cu. yd. The backhoe has a machine weight of 143,000 lb. with 3.4-yd. bucket and the loader has a machine weight of 152,119 lb. with 5.2-yd. bucket. The engine is a 420PS Cummins with SAE HP of 114. Overall width is 11 ft. 5 in. The overall height of cab is 11 ft. 6.5 in. Digging force of backhoe by bucket cylinder is 79,368 lbf; loader crowding force is 99,208 lbf; and loader breakout force is 97,000 lbf. Maximum travel speed is 2.05 mph (1st) and 2.85 mph (2nd). Maximum traction force is rated at 106,000 lbf.

For information circle 253 ❏

Figure 7.7 *Specific terms help readers determine whether this equipment meets their needs.*
Highway & Heavy Construction.

Step 4: Use Visual Aids

A supporting illustration helps the audience understand the mechanism being described. (Note the word *supporting*. An illustration should not replace any part of the verbal description.) In the sample mechanism descriptions illustrated in this chapter, do you get a better understanding of the workings of the mechanisms when an illustration is included? Whenever possible, supplement descriptions with a visual aid.

Placement of Mechanism Descriptions

When you develop a mechanism description for readers, you do so for a good reason — to tell them how an item works and what it does. This information will help them buy, use, or evaluate the item. Therefore, present the description to readers at the beginning of a technical document.

In marketing literature, the mechanism description usually appears after the initial introductory paragraphs. In longer reports — instructions, evaluations, proposals — the description is included as a subsection of the introduction. These descriptions are typically given such headings as "Mechanism Description," "Operating Characteristics," or "Operations Overview."

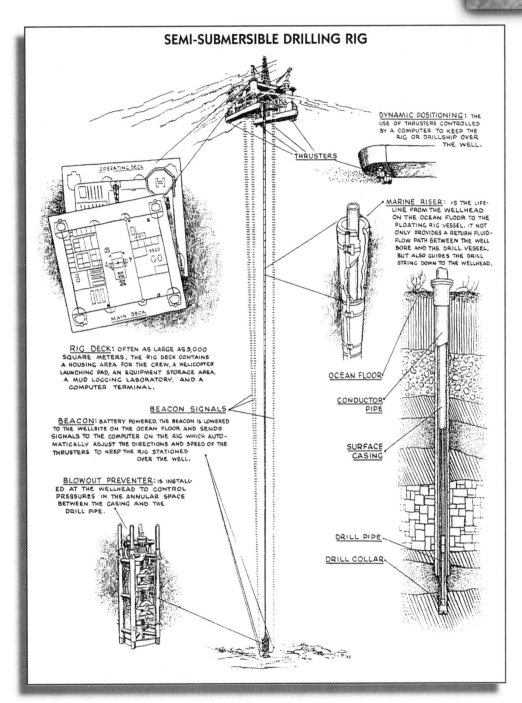

SEMI-SUBMERSIBLE DRILLING RIG

DYNAMIC POSITIONING: THE USE OF THRUSTERS CONTROLLED BY A COMPUTER TO KEEP THE RIG OR DRILLSHIP OVER THE WELL.

THRUSTERS

OPERATING DECK

MAIN DECK

MARINE RISER: IS THE LIFE-LINE FROM THE WELLHEAD ON THE OCEAN FLOOR TO THE FLOATING RIG VESSEL. IT NOT ONLY PROVIDES A RETURN FLUID-FLOW PATH BETWEEN THE WELL BORE AND THE DRILL VESSEL, BUT ALSO GUIDES THE DRILL STRING DOWN TO THE WELLHEAD.

RIG DECK: OFTEN AS LARGE AS 3,000 SQUARE METERS, THE RIG DECK CONTAINS A HOUSING AREA FOR THE CREW, A HELICOPTER LAUNCHING PAD, AN EQUIPMENT STORAGE AREA, A MUD LOGGING LABORATORY, AND A COMPUTER TERMINAL.

OCEAN FLOOR

CONDUCTOR PIPE

BEACON SIGNALS

BEACON: BATTERY POWERED, THE BEACON IS LOWERED TO THE WELLSITE ON THE OCEAN FLOOR AND SENDS SIGNALS TO THE COMPUTER ON THE RIG WHICH AUTO-MATICALLY ADJUST THE DIRECTIONS AND SPEED OF THE THRUSTERS TO KEEP THE RIG STATIONED OVER THE WELL.

SURFACE CASING

BLOWOUT PREVENTER: IS INSTALL-ED AT THE WELLHEAD TO CONTROL PRESSURES IN THE ANNULAR SPACE BETWEEN THE CASING AND THE DRILL PIPE.

DRILL PIPE

DRILL COLLAR

Figure 7.8 *The vocabulary in a mechanism description is adjusted to the audience's knowledge level.*
From Offshore Drilling: Deeper and Deeper. Copyright © Shell Canada Resources Limited, 1982. Reprinted by permission.

QUESTIONS FOR DISCUSSION

1. When and to what extent should you provide an audience with definitions?
2. When is a parenthetical definition used?
3. What three elements are essential in a formal sentence definition?
4. What factors should a technical writer consider in choosing the type of definitions used in a report?
5. When are definitions included in a separate section — entitled "Glossary" or "Definitions" — in a report?
6. Who reads product descriptions and why?
7. Who reads mechanism descriptions and why?
8. What do you look for in an effective mechanism or product description?

EXERCISE 1

Rewrite the following definitions to correct flaws in form or content.

a. Booting is when you start a computer.

_____

_____

b. An assembly line is where products are assembled.

_____

_____

c. An engineering technologist is a person who works on an engineering team.

_____

_____

d. High Pressure Sodium (which is abbreviated HPS) and Metal Halide are both considered HID (which is short for High Intensity Discharge) lights.

_____

_____

EXERCISE 2

The following excerpt from a PharmAction brochure (1995) at a local pharmacy defines and explains angina. Read the passage carefully and answer the questions that follow it.

Angina is a condition often characterized by pain or discomfort in the chest resulting from decreased blood supply to the heart muscle. The pain is usually concentrated in the chest, just beneath the sternum, but it could spread to the arms and neck. The pain normally disappears after a few minutes rest. Angina attacks frequently occur during periods of increased physical activity or emotional stress when the heart is required to beat faster than normal. Angina is not a disease itself but a symptom of an underlying disease of the arteries, often referred to as heart disease. In severe cases, angina can lead to a heart attack.

PREVENTION WITH MEDICATION

Medications known as betablockers, calcium channel blockers and nitroglycerin are used to manage the pain or discomfort associated with angina. Nitroglycerin is available in several formats for prevention:

> *Tablets that are taken once, twice, or three times daily*
> *An ointment applied to the skin*
> *A disk which, when applied to the skin, releases the drug into the blood stream*

The preventive action of nitroglycerin wears off in only hours; so it is extremely important to take the medication as prescribed.

TREATMENT OF ANGINA ATTACKS

Nitroglycerin is also used to treat angina attacks by dilating (opening) blood vessels and restoring blood flow. This helps reduce stress on the heart and the pain it causes.

> *Two forms of fast-acting nitroglycerin are available: sublingual tablets (which melt under the tongue) and sublingual spray.*[1]

a. For what type of audience is this information written?

b. What methods of definition are used?

....

[1] PharmAction patient information pamphlet number 1, April 1995. Reprinted with permission of CommuniMed Incorporated.

c. Why does the writer define *dilating* and *sublingual?*

d. Why does the writer *not* define *betablockers* or *calcium channel blockers?*

e. If you were using the term *sublingual* in a report on angina for an interested colleague, you might use its etymology. Give the etymology of *sublingual.*

f. Why does this brochure *not* use etymology?

WRITING ASSIGNMENTS

1. Choose one term from each list of words given below, or select from your own list of terms from Activity 2. Write a two- or three-sentence operational definition of one of the terms in the left-hand column. Then write an expanded definition of one of the terms in the right-hand column, using one of these methods: exemplification, comparison/contrast, illustration, or etymology.

Pendulum	Leaf insect
Circuit board	Outpatient
Roof truss	Sheet metal
Seawall	Static electricity
Transformer	Market share
General anesthesia	Torque

2. There's a substantial purchase you would like to make to upgrade your computer system for an upcoming multimedia course. Choose a major product that you might sell to realize the money — e.g., your old car, motorcycle, VCR, TV set, monitor, or printer. Write a one- or two-paragraph, specific product description that you could hand to potential customers responding to your advertisement on the bulletin board.

3. Write an analogy to explain one of the following terms or concepts or choose a term from your discipline:

Inertia

Radar

Covalent bonding

Diode

DOS

EIGHT

Using Graphics

enry Luce, a founder of *Time* magazine, once said that "*Time* is interested not in how much it includes between its covers, but in how much it gets off its pages into the minds of its readers." Presenting technical information that stays in readers' minds can be a problem. Supplying graphics is the solution. They summarize and clarify complex technical data; they give perspective and meaning to numbers; they add emphasis and importance to facts; and, above all else, they translate information into images that readers *remember*.

To create memorable visuals, you do not have to be a professional graphic artist. Many word processors provide excellent graphics capabilities, and you will most likely have access to presentation graphics software packages and a computer-assisted drafting (CAD) lab in the workplace or on campus. Depending on the situation — preparing a substantial proposal or bid, for example — you may work with a technical illustrator hired by your organization. However, you should be prepared to take advantage of the readily available user-friendly graphics packages to create your own visuals. If you do not have access to such technology, a straight-edged ruler, some graph paper, a nonsmear pen, and a few coloured felt-tip markers will enable you to make neat, presentable visuals. Be aware that no matter what resources are available, they only help you *produce* the finished visuals. You must still decide *what* information should be summarized, clarified, or emphasized, and *how*.

This chapter examines how technical reports that use visuals help your readers remember important information and explains the best methods for making this information understandable.

TYPES OF GRAPHICAL SUPPORT

In technical reports, two types of graphics are commonly used: (1) tables (tabular data) and (2) figures (graphs, charts, line drawings, and photos). One of your toughest decisions will be to determine the best way to present data so readers understand (and remember) its importance. Do you just string it out in the text?

> *In September 19--, the Engineering Department had 32 people budgeted and two vacancies. In March 19--, the department still had 32 people budgeted but accrued three vacancies, leaving it with 29 employees. (Resignations from employees moving out of province created all three vacancies.) In June 19--, the department filled two vacancies, for a total of 31 employees and one vacancy (32 budgeted).*

Do you list it in a table?

TABLE 1

ENGINEERING DEPARTMENT EMPLOYEE CHANGES

Date	Employees Budgeted	Employees Actual	Position Vacancies
Sept. 19--	32	30	2[a]
Mar. 19--	32	29	3[a]
June 19--	32	31	1[a]

[a] Due to employees moving out of province.

Do you plot it in a graph like the one in Figure 8.1?

Choose the best kind of graphic for your specific purpose and audience. Each visual has its advantages and uses. In these examples, all three versions present the same information and each is appropriate for specific purposes. The textual version, quickly and easily produced, is sufficient for a brief memo report that needs only to relay some facts. (However, reading more than just one or two paragraphs similar to the textual version would probably make the audience dizzy.) The tabular version, clearer yet more time-consuming to produce, is a better choice when you must present several sets of data or when the audience needs to reference and compare exact numbers quickly.

You may think the graph is better still because it is even more visually explicit. But note the difference in emphasis that a bar graph produces: Budgeted and actual employees are proportionately close in number; vacancies are proportionately quite low. If the writer wants to emphasize these factors, the graph is indeed the best visual. If, however, these facts are not significant, then the bar graph is emphasizing data that may not be appropriate for the writer's purposes and for the audience's needs.

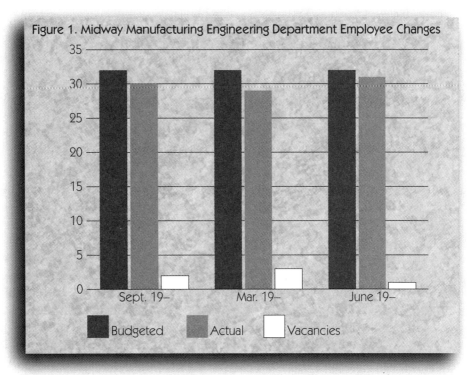

Figure 8.1 *This bar graph shows one way of illustrating data for readers.*

The following sections explain the different kinds of graphics (tables, figures, and their variations) and their uses, along with some rules and guidelines to help you choose and develop the best visual support for your specific purposes and audience.

Tables

Tables are essentially lists: number lists, word lists, or combinations of both. Use tables to present information that audiences need to be able to study and compare easily.

Tables are also a good way to present complete sets of data that can be compared easily, such as mileage distances between cities, acceptable cholesterol levels in adults and children, or replacement parts and numbers for a television. For nearly all technical levels of audiences — low, medium, and high — tables effectively organize and display large amounts of related information.

Basic Table Construction

Understanding some basic construction principles and following certain important rules can help you simplify the organization of data in tables. In tables, information is organized to be read both horizontally (in rows) and vertically (in columns). All the information in one column or row is related in some way. Although tables can vary in layout to accommodate the information being presented, they all share certain basic characteristics. Figure 8.2 shows the major parts of a basic table. The following paragraphs explain the functions of these basic parts, and suggest the best ways to present them.

Table Number and Title   Assign a sequential number to each table so that the reader can easily locate it and you, the writer, can easily cross-reference the number in your text. Number your tables *Table 1*, *Table 2*, and so forth, or number them *Table 1.1*, *Table 1.2*, etc. when there are several numbered sections in your text. (This tells the reader that the table is in Section 1 and is the first or second table presented.) As shown in Figure 8.3, make the table title as explicit as possible so that the reader knows just what is being presented without referring to the text.

Type table numbers and titles in all uppercase letters and centre them over the width of the table, above the data being presented. Solid rules, typed or drawn from margin to margin above and below the table number and title, help distinguish this information from the data presented in the rest of the table.

Column Heads and Side Stubs   Column heads are the labels given to the vertical lists of data in a table; information is always read *down* from the heads, all the way to the end of the table. Type column heads in upper and lowercase, centre each over the column it labels, and either underline each head or draw a solid line from margin to margin underneath all column heads. Side stubs are used to label the information listed horizontally in the body of the table; information labelled by the side stubs is read *across*. Type side stubs in upper and lowercase, and keep all stubs lined up with the left margin. Write heads and stubs as concisely as possible. Long, involved descriptions are difficult to read in tables and are difficult to fit into the limited space available.

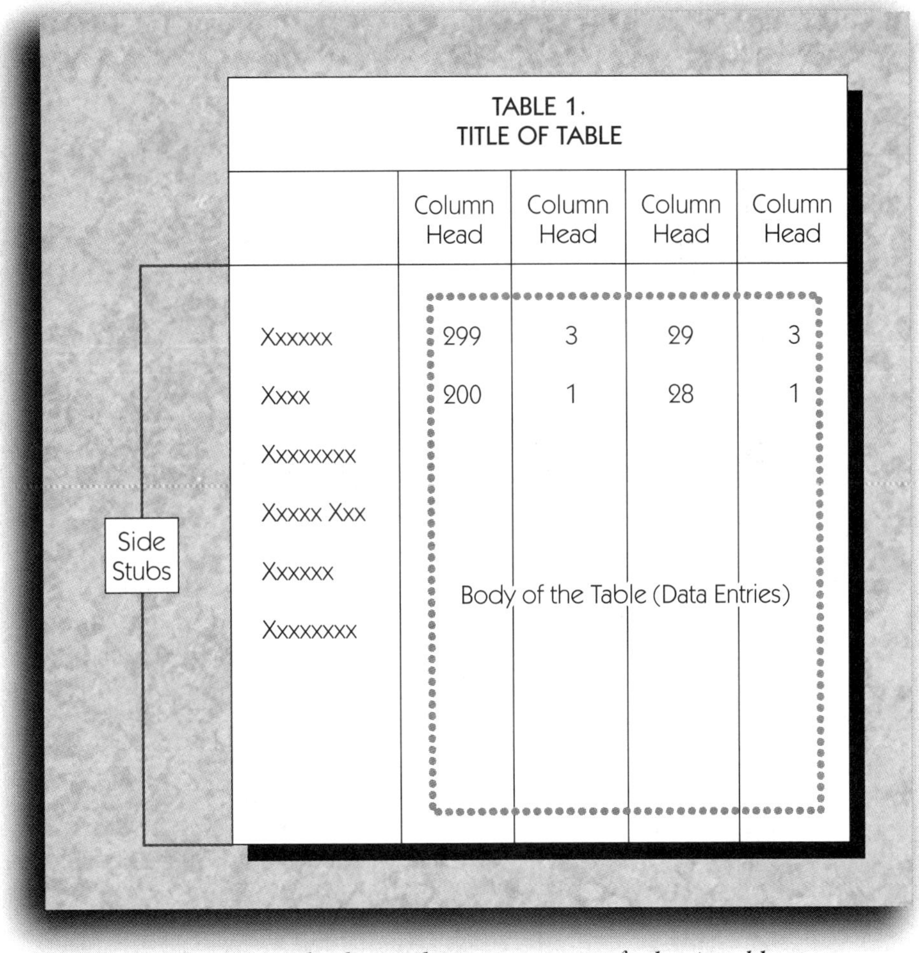

	TABLE 1. TITLE OF TABLE			
	Column Head	Column Head	Column Head	Column Head
Xxxxxx	299	3	29	3
Xxxx	200	1	28	1
Xxxxxxxx				
Xxxxx Xxx				
Xxxxxx	Body of the Table (Data Entries)			
Xxxxxxxx				

Side Stubs

Figure 8.2 *This example shows the major parts of a basic table.*

Footnotes Put details about the table in a footnote (as shown in Figure 8.4). Although footnotes in the body of a report are indicated with numbers, footnotes in tables are designated with lowercase letters. If your word processor can do superscripts (place characters a half-space above the regular typing line), type the footnote symbol in superscript and place a short line above it to separate it from the table data. This method is also shown in Figure 8.4.

The Body of the Table The body of the table contains the data, which may include numbers, words, or both. Numbers may be aligned on the left (easiest to type), aligned on the right (best visually), or aligned on the decimal point (most logical for comparison). Whichever you choose, be consistent. Place all data within the widths allotted for each column.

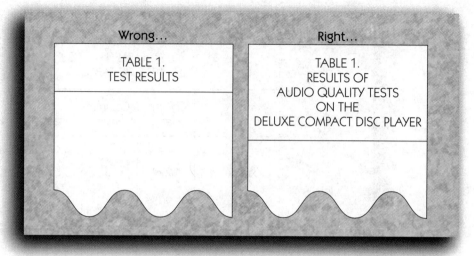

Figure 8.3 *Explicit titles allow tables to stand independent of the text.*

Imagine a grid in the body of the table with each square serving as a data unit that relates to its column head and side stub. Make an entry for each data unit in the body. Do not leave a blank space for a unit when information is missing or inadequate or of little conse-

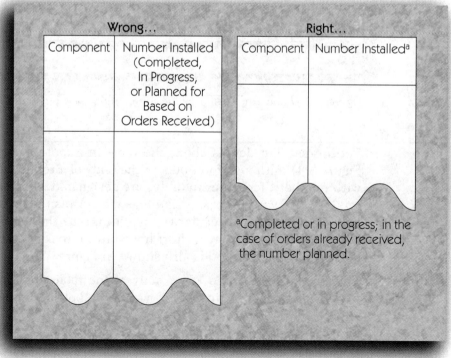

Figure 8.4 *Using footnotes helps make column heads explicit.*

quence. Instead, insert *N/D* (no data) or a double hyphen (- -) or a zero (0) for missing numerical entries, and use the word *None* in word lists. This practice, as shown in Figure 8.5, serves two purposes: (1) It helps you keep data in the correct space, and (2) it assures the reader that you did not merely forget to put data in the space.

Wrong...		Right...	
Estimated	Actual	Estimated	Actual
110	117	110	117
	228	—	228
390		390	—
545	546	545	546
	344	—	344

Figure 8.5 *An entry must be placed in each data unit in the body of the table.*

Useful Suggestions for Tables   A table is a valuable visual aid in technical reports; it helps readers of all technical levels to retain the facts. Here are some guidelines for ensuring clarity in all tabular material:

◆ *Abbreviations.* Use standard abbreviations throughout the table if space limitations prevent using the full word. If your audience would not readily understand your abbreviations, explain them in a footnote in the table.

◆ *Multiple pages.* When tables occupy more than one page, repeat the table number/title and all the heads on the spillover pages. Repeat footnotes only if they apply to the information on the spillover pages.

◆ *Meaningful heads.* Avoid clutter in the body of the table. Never repeat a unit symbol if you can avoid it. (See Figure 8.6.)

◆ *Readability.* Here are several suggestions for making a table more legible for the audience:

Generally, Arabic numerals (1, 2, 3) are easier to read than Roman numerals (I, II, III).

When a table presents long columns of data (particularly numbers), leave a blank space every five lines down the column to help make the data easier to follow.

Ruling between columns and around the table is optional. (Sometimes, too many lines in a table can be confusing.) At the very least, however, add a solid line above the table number/figure and after the last data entry or footnote to signal to readers the beginning and end of the table.

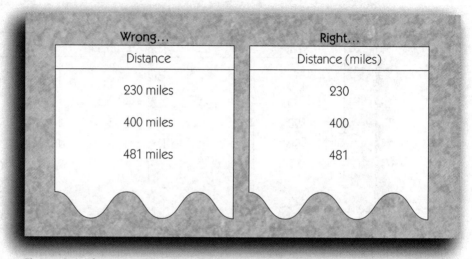

Figure 8.6 *This example shows how to avoid clutter in the body of the table.*

Figures

The main purpose of a figure (any graphic that is not a table) is to help translate information into images that readers can easily absorb and remember. Which of the following statements is easier for you to remember?

FACT 1: A direct-home satellite dish has a diameter of 40 centi-metres.

FACT 2: A direct-home satellite dish is the size of a medium pizza.

Most people would probably remember the tasty image in Fact 2 longer than the statistic in Fact 1. A figure works the same way: It translates potentially dry and difficult data into meaningful images that your audience can retain.

In technical reports, the most commonly used figures are graphs, charts, line drawings, and photographs. There are a number of variations on each of these visual devices; this chapter deals only with the most frequently used and the most easily composed. Regardless of which figure you use, number and label all of them as follows:

Figure 1, Figure 2, etc., or Figure 1.1, Figure 1.2, etc. Follow the figure number with a title, which should be explicit enough to allow the reader to understand the figure without reading the text. Figure numbers and titles may be placed above or below the visual; whichever you choose (check your employer's standards on this), be consistent with all figures. As you write technical reports containing extensive (but perhaps difficult to absorb and remember) data, you will find figures an excellent means of clarifying and emphasizing important information.

Graphs

Graphs — line, bar, and pie — are the simplest forms of figures; use them to depict relationships and trends. These graphs use numbers as their primary means of relating one item to another. Each kind of graph gives the audience a different perspective on the data presented.

Line Graphs Line graphs are the most commonly used figures for presenting trends or movement of data over time. One of the main features of a line graph is its ability to show small increments effectively. This type of detail often interests audiences with high technical levels. Time may be given in months or years, or in smaller increments such as seconds, minutes, hours, or weeks. Use line graphs, for example, to show hourly temperature changes at your local airport, to track the daily fluctuations of the stock market over the last month, to show monthly population growth in Toronto over the last two years, or to demonstrate progress in reducing pollution in the Saint John River over the last three years.

The facts and figures used in line graphs are called data points. As the illustrations in Figure 8.7 show, data points are plotted on a grid structure with a clearly labelled x-axis or horizontal scale (Jan., Feb., March, and so forth) and y-axis or vertical scale (19,000, 20,000, and so forth). When these points are connected with a line (curve), the trends of the data become apparent. Designate the data points with small circles or thick dots (called *tick points*) and, if they enhance the readability of the graph, add the actual grid lines. One rule to remember when labelling x- and y-axes is always to place time increments across the bottom of the graph (on the x-axis).

If you wish to compare the trends of several different kinds of data, you may plot more than one set of data on the same line graph. To avoid possible confusion, use different colours (as in Figure 8.8.) or draw each line differently: Use a solid line for one, a dashed line for a second, and a dotted line for a third. Clearly label each line in the graph or include a legend that defines these lines for the readers.

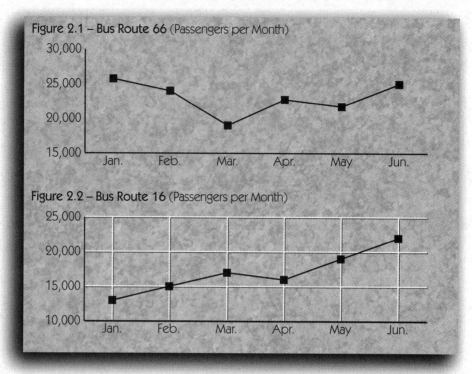

Figure 8.7 *This example shows two ways of depicting data on a line graph: Figure 2.1 uses tick points only; Figure 2.2 adds grid lines.*
Adapted with permission of Susie Kuhner.

A note of caution: Line graphs with more than three curves become difficult to read, even for experts in the field.

In addition to knowing when to use line graphs, you should also know when *not* to use them:

◆   Do not use line graphs to compare size.
◆   Do not use line graphs to emphasize differences among elements.
◆   Do not use line graphs to show how component parts relate to a whole.

These kinds of information are best depicted in other types of figures, which are discussed below.

Bar Graphs   Bar graphs are useful for comparing similarities or for emphasizing differences in several items, and are usually effective for all levels of audiences. Their main advantage over line graphs is their ability to include a large number of items that can be compared simultaneously. Like line graphs, bar graphs are constructed with

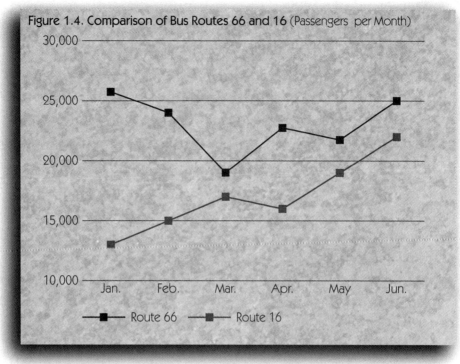

Figure 8.8 *This example shows how to draw and label two curves on a line graph.*
Adapted with permission of Susie Kuhner.

clearly labelled x- and y-axes. Data points, however, are illustrated with bars of various lengths to indicate quantities or values.

In technical reports, three bar graph variations are frequently used: (1) horizontal, (2) clustered vertical, and (3) stacked column. Each variation can be used to illustrate different information for different audiences. As in all graphs, the proportions must reflect the numbers or percentages honestly.

Use a *horizontal bar graph* to compare a number of different elements or to emphasize differences in several items: for example, to illustrate the levels of five different minerals in a community's water supply or to compare the number of emergency room admissions among six area hospitals. As shown in Figure 8.9, a horizontal bar graph clearly compares the proportion of the population covered by a dental plan in the 10 provinces.

Use a *clustered vertical bar graph* to compare size, to compare several related elements over time, or to contrast several elements over time. The time increments used in this kind of bar graph usu-

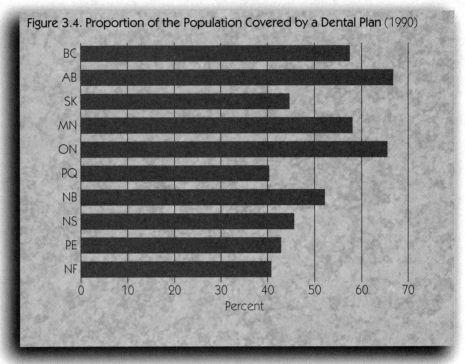

Figure 3.4. Proportion of the Population Covered by a Dental Plan (1990)

Figure 8.9 *A horizontal bar graph emphasizes the differences among several items.*
Adapted from Statistics Canada Catalogue 11-008E, Canadian Social Trends, Summer 1994. Reproduced by authority of the Ministry of Industry, 1996, Statistics Canada.

ally span long periods: months or years, rather than days, hours, or minutes. A clustered vertical bar graph, for example, would aptly illustrate these facts: the number of first-class versus economy airline tickets purchased in the last three years, the number of male students versus female students in your college's engineering program in the last five years, or the import versus export rates in Canada over the last seven years.

As shown in Figure 8.10, bars with varying shades (or different colours) help audiences of all levels distinguish the comparisons or differences within each cluster. Explain the significance of the bar shades or colours used by including your shade or colour code in a legend that defines the various bars. Place the legend anywhere in or around the graph where it can be seen easily without interfering with the data presented.

Use a *stacked column bar graph* (for readers with medium and high technical levels) to show how component parts relate to a

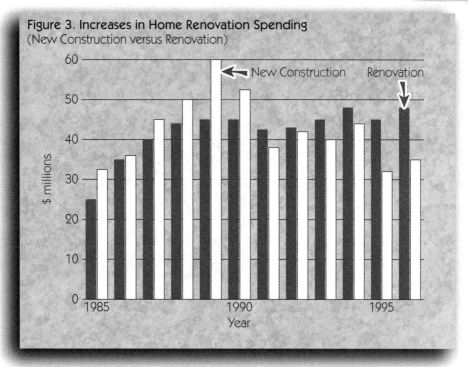

Figure 3. Increases in Home Renovation Spending
(New Construction versus Renovation)

Figure 8.10 *A clustered vertical bar graph groups related elements for easy comparison.*
Adapted with permission of Susie Kuhner.

whole. For example, this type of bar graph could show concisely how much time during the average working day is spent in meetings and on telephone calls, planning, and paperwork, or how much of your total budget is spent on taxes, shelter, food, clothing, and tuition.

Column graphs cannot compare component parts of several wholes. As shown in Figure 8.11, the "whole" must be 100 percent and component parts must relate their portion to the whole. Use varying shades or colours in the bar segments to add definition among the parts, and label each segment clearly with the component name and percent scale.

Pie Graphs   Pie graphs function the same way as stacked column bar graphs: They show the relationship of component parts of a whole at one time. As illustrated in Figure 8.12, however, the pie graph is generally less complex than other graphs, and is often better suited to readers with low technical knowledge levels.

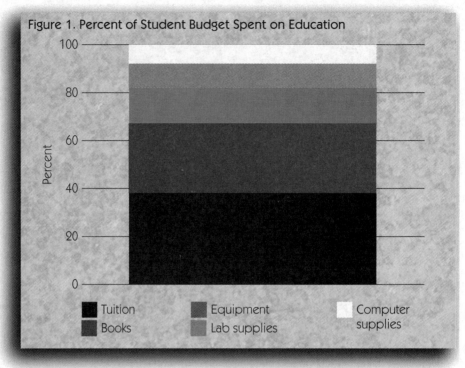

Figure 8.11 *A stacked column bar graph illustrates how component parts relate to a whole.*
Adapted with permission of Susie Kuhner.

The same rules apply for pie graphs as for stacked column bar graphs: The *whole* must be 100 percent, and all parts must add up to the whole. Also, pie graphs can compare the component parts of only one whole. To create a pie graph, draw a perfect circle with a compass and locate its centre. Check the statistics to be illustrated, then use a protractor to determine the precise segments (wedges) within the circle. (Accuracy in scaling the wedges is essential when drawing pie graphs. Follow this scale: 3.6 degrees equals 1 percent.) Colour or shade each pie wedge differently so readers can see the individual parts easily. Label each segment (either outside the circle or within it, if space permits) with the component it represents and the actual number or percentage.

When the whole has more than five or six components, use a horizontal bar graph instead of a pie graph. Additionally, bar or pie graphs should *not* be used to show fine increments or to illustrate movements or trends.

Table 8.1 provides a quick reference for choosing the best graph to illustrate information effectively.

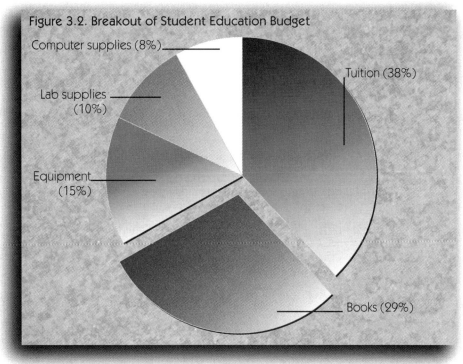

Figure 3.2. Breakout of Student Education Budget

Computer supplies (8%)

Tuition (38%)

Lab supplies (10%)

Equipment (15%)

Books (29%)

Figure 8.12 *A pie graph (using same data as Figure 8.11) illustrates how parts compare to a whole.*
Adapted with permission of Susie Kuhner.

Activity

For the tasks listed below, indicate in the blanks whether you would use a line (*L*) graph or a horizontal (*H*), clustered vertical (*CV*), or stacked column (*SC*) bar graph to illustrate the data. Be prepared to discuss your choices in class.

_____ a. Track the fractional changes in the water table levels in your community over a six-month period.

_____ b. Show the various percentages of age groups (18–25, 26–35, 36–50, over 50 years) of your school's total student population.

_____ c. Compare the number of new construction projects in Edmonton and Calgary for the past three years.

_____ d. Compare the number of existing nuclear power plants in Spain, Canada, the U.S.A., Japan, Britain, and Sweden.

TABLE 8.1

GUIDELINES FOR CHOOSING A GRAPH

Type of Graph	Use to ...	Do Not Use to ...
Line	Show trends or movement of data over time (long or short periods) Show the rate at which things change Show small increments of data	Compare size Emphasize differences Show how components relate to a whole
Horizontal bar	Compare more than five elements Emphasize differences in several items	Show fine increments Show movement or trend
Clustered vertical bar	Compare size of related items Compare items over long time periods	Show fine increments Show movement or trend over short time periods
Stacked column bar	Relate how parts fit into a whole	Show fine increments Show movement or trend
Pie	Show how parts relate to a whole Show parts/whole relationships to a general audience	Compare parts of more than one whole Compare more than five parts in a whole Show fine increments

_____ e. Show the increasing demand over the last three years for fuel-efficient automobiles.

Charts

Frequently, the terms *graphs*, *charts*, and *diagrams* are used interchangeably. In this text, *charts* refer to figures that show relationships but do not use numbers to compare or contrast components. These charts effectively show the relationships of functions, events, or people. Primarily, they use rectangular blocks (or other geometric shapes) interconnected by one or more lines. These lines sometimes include arrowheads to show flow functions. Each block is clearly identified.

Flowcharts   Flowcharts are excellent visual devices for summarizing the major steps in a process from start to finish. Look at the example shown in Figure 8.13 and note how easy it is to read and understand a flowchart. The simple graphic elements (rectangles, lines, and arrows) help audiences of any technical level easily trace

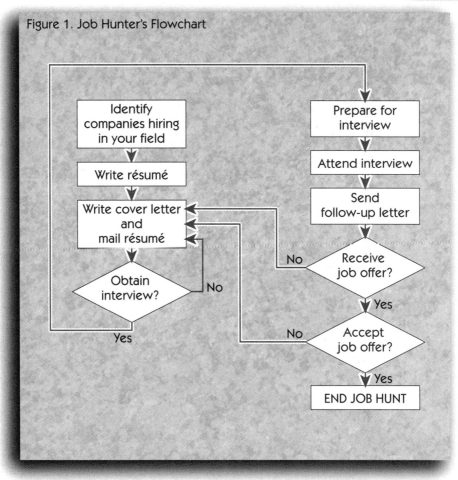

Figure 1. Job Hunter's Flowchart

Figure 8.13 *A flowchart uses basic graphic elements to show major steps in a process.*

the sequence of steps involved in finding a job (and retrace them when the hunt must continue!).

Pictures also may be used in flowcharts to summarize and reinforce key steps in a process, as illustrated in Figure 8.14. Flowcharts with pictures are also effective when you are introducing a process that is new to your audience. Figure 19.4 (page 593) simplifies a process for an audience of low to medium technical levels.

Flowcharts may take more time and artistic talent to produce than other kinds of figures. Most important, you must take special care to determine their appropriateness for your audience. Determine the technical and knowledge levels of your readers (low, medium, or high), and then develop flowcharts that meet their needs best.

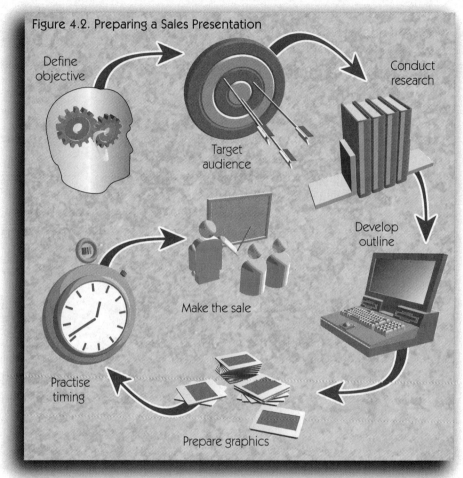

Figure 4.2. Preparing a Sales Presentation

Define objective

Target audience

Conduct research

Develop outline

Make the sale

Practise timing

Prepare graphics

Figure 8.14 *A flowchart with pictures summarizes and reinforces key concepts in a process.*
Adapted with permission of Susie Kuhner.

Organization Charts   These charts are similar to flowcharts, but their main purpose is to display relationships such as these:

◆   The interactions of various departments in an organization

◆   The interactions of various operations in an organization

◆   The authority/responsibility levels of people in an organization

As shown in Figure 8.15, organization charts are arranged from a top-down perspective. These figures are often of greatest interest to upper managers and potential customers. Use only basic graphic elements (rectangles, lines, arrows) to illustrate.

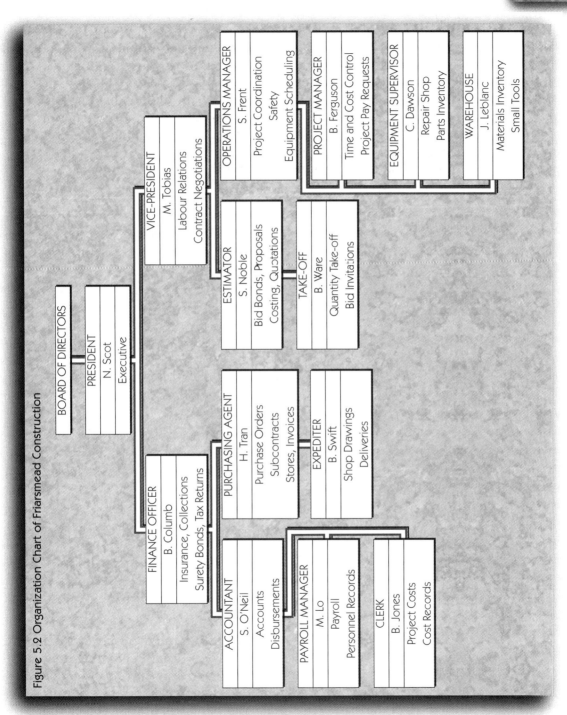

Figure 5.2 Organization Chart of Friarsmead Construction

BOARD OF DIRECTORS

PRESIDENT
N. Scot
Executive

VICE-PRESIDENT
M. Tobias
Labour Relations
Contract Negotiations

FINANCE OFFICER
B. Columb
Insurance, Collections
Surety Bonds, Tax Returns

OPERATIONS MANAGER
S. Frent
Project Coordination
Safety
Equipment Scheduling

PROJECT MANAGER
B. Ferguson
Time and Cost Control
Project Pay Requests

EQUIPMENT SUPERVISOR
C. Dawson
Repair Shop
Parts Inventory

WAREHOUSE
J. Leblanc
Materials Inventory
Small Tools

ESTIMATOR
S. Noble
Bid Bonds, Proposals
Costing, Quotations

TAKE-OFF
B. Ware
Quantity Take-off
Bid Invitations

PURCHASING AGENT
H. Tran
Purchase Orders
Subcontracts
Stores, Invoices

EXPEDITER
B. Swift
Shop Drawings
Deliveries

ACCOUNTANT
S. O'Neil
Accounts
Disbursements

PAYROLL MANAGER
M. Lo
Payroll
Personnel Records

CLERK
B. Jones
Project Costs
Cost Records

Figure 8.15 *This example presents an organization chart for a medium-sized corporation.*

Line Drawings

Lines and solids are the key graphic elements in line drawings. In technical reports, they are frequently used to clarify and simplify complex or detailed objects for readers of all levels or to emphasize important information. For example, a clean, simple line drawing is an excellent way of augmenting a specific written instruction. Readers frequently judge the effectiveness of an operator's or user's manual based on the number and clarity of its supporting illustrations. The sample shown in Figure 8.16 illustrates one way of showing a procedure.

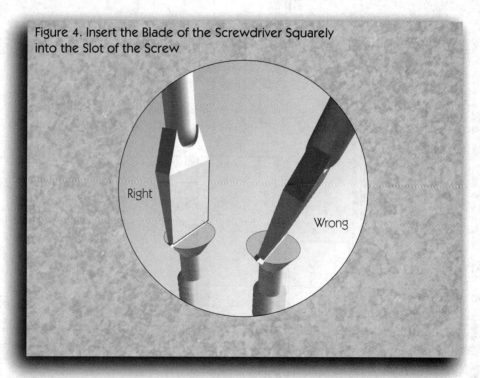

Figure 4. Insert the Blade of the Screwdriver Squarely into the Slot of the Screw

Right

Wrong

Figure 8.16 *A simple line drawing makes these instructions clear.*

Producing effective line drawings requires relatively little artistic talent; however, a keen sense of scale is essential in creating drawings that relay correct perspective. Use good drawing tools — a non-smear pen, a sharp pencil — to produce line drawings. The clean and crisp lines of these drawings make reproducing multiple copies simple and easy. The variations of line drawings described next meet most of the illustrative requirements for technical reports.

Figure 1. Sears/Craftsman® Electric Trimmer

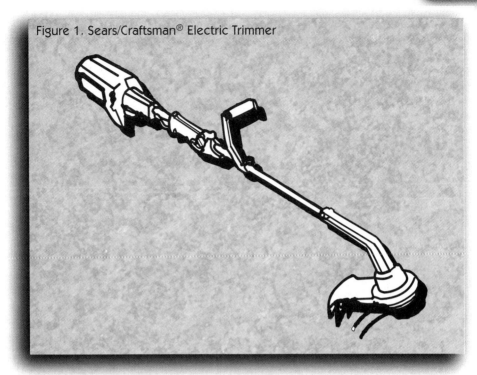

Figure 8.17 *A full-view line drawing clearly illustrates an object for readers.*
Sears Craftsman® Electric Trimmer, from publication number 530-400657-1-01,
October 10, 1992. Copyright © 1992, Sears Canada Inc. Reprinted with permission.

Full Views   These line drawings illustrate a complete object for the
reader and, depending on the purpose of the drawing, offer either a
front, side, back, or three-dimensional perspective. Full views are
frequently used in an introductory or overview section of a report.
(See Figure 8.17.)

Cutaway Views   A cutaway is a view of an object cut to reveal its
internal structure. Frequently, a cutaway view is prefaced with
either a description of the exterior of the object or with an actual
illustration of it (Figure 8.18). The purpose of a cutaway view is to
focus on the inside design of an object.

Exploded Views   There are two versions of this type of line drawing:

◆   An exploded line drawing that shows parts and subassemblies
    separated, with each part projected along the centreline of its
    assembled position. This kind of exploded drawing, as shown in

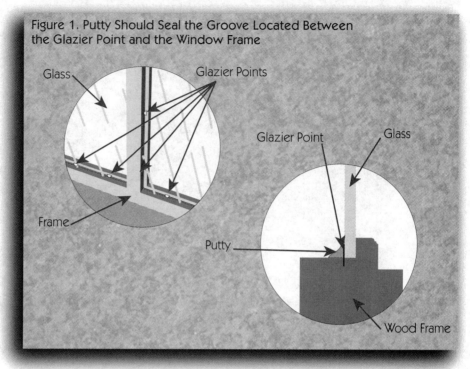

Figure 1. Putty Should Seal the Groove Located Between the Glazier Point and the Window Frame

Glass

Glazier Points

Glazier Point

Glass

Frame

Putty

Wood Frame

Figure 8.18 *This cutaway line drawing shows an interior view of the object.*

Figure 8.19, helps the reader visualize how the object is put together or taken apart.

◆ An exploded line drawing that shows an enlarged view of a small part or component of a larger, more complex object.

The example shown in Figure 8.20 illustrates how an exploded line drawing effectively helps readers focus on a specific part of a larger item. The example in Figure 8.21 shows how an exploded line drawing helps relay important perspective to readers.

Pictograms   Pictograms are symbols, sometimes used internationally, that emphasize an important safety message: *Stop, Danger, Warning, Caution, Hazardous Voltage,* and so forth. Pictograms usually accompany words that clearly state the danger or risk and that describe how to avoid the hazard. (See Figure 8.22.) For many safety and instructional messages, you can use standard illustrations available in art catalogues. When none of the standard pictograms appropriately shows the situation or message (for example, *Keep Hands Away from Moving Gears,* or *Wear Safety Glasses at All*

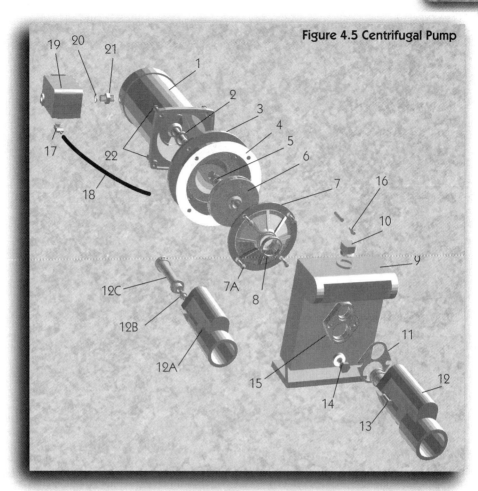

Figure 4.5 Centrifugal Pump

Figure 8.19 *This exploded view shows how parts are assembled.*
From Sta-Rite Owner's Manual. Brochure No. S369 (11/21/95). Reprinted with permission. Copyright 1995, Sta-Rite Industries, Inc.

Times), develop your own to emphasize the nature and consequences of the message.

Photographs

Use photographs when an accurate depiction of a real subject (equipment, products, people, buildings, specimens) must be shown. In many cases, photographs are far superior to line drawings. For example, in an evaluation report, lab test results become more meaningful when actual photographs of the effects of heat on metal pipes are presented for the reader to inspect. In a proposal to a prospective

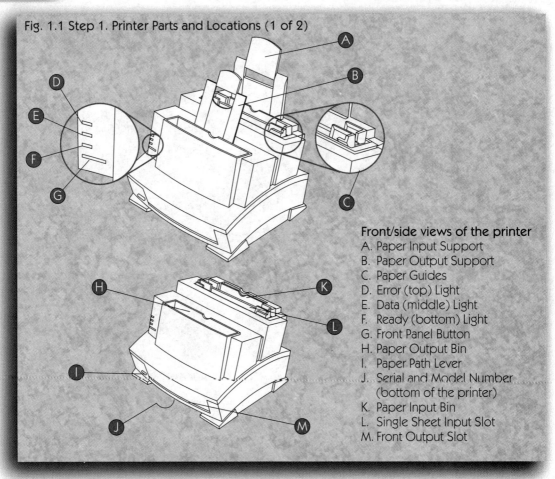

Fig. 1.1 Step 1. Printer Parts and Locations (1 of 2)

Front/side views of the printer
A. Paper Input Support
B. Paper Output Support
C. Paper Guides
D. Error (top) Light
E. Data (middle) Light
F. Ready (bottom) Light
G. Front Panel Button
H. Paper Output Bin
I. Paper Path Lever
J. Serial and Model Number
   (bottom of the printer)
K. Paper Input Bin
L. Single Sheet Input Slot
M. Front Output Slot

Figure 8.20 *An exploded view helps readers locate specific parts of a larger object.*
HP LaserJet 5L Printer, copyright 1995 Hewlett-Packard Company. Reproduced with permission.

customer, the benefit of using graphite mould castings (for their precise detailing abilities) becomes quite clear when the photograph shown in Figure 8.23 is included; a line drawing could not portray this benefit as effectively. Readers of all levels appreciate photographs.

Photographs, however, present some problems for technical report writers; they are often difficult to produce and to reproduce. Only distinct and well-focused photos are of value to a reader. To produce effective photos, you will need either substantial photographic experience or the assistance of a professional. Since techni-

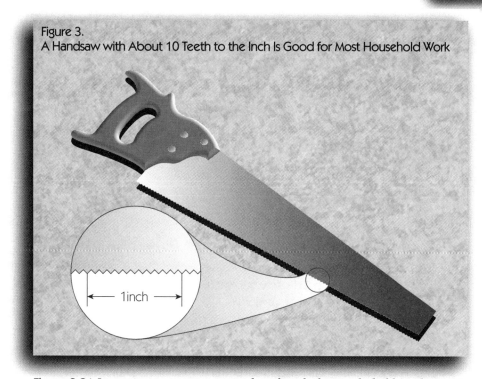

Figure 3.
A Handsaw with About 10 Teeth to the Inch Is Good for Most Household Work

1inch

Figure 8.21 *Important perspective is relayed with this exploded line drawing.*

cal reports frequently are distributed to more than one reader (and there is always a file copy), an original photograph must be included in each report, or the photo must be specially processed (*screened*, as it is called in the printing business) so it can be reproduced clearly. Both options require extra time and money.

CITATION, PLACEMENT, AND DISCUSSION OF GRAPHICS

Each graphic in a technical report must be cited in the text and numbered in order of appearance. Always include a citation in the text to explain briefly what the visual aid shows and why it is in the report, as in the following examples:

EXAMPLES: As the flowchart in Figure 1 shows, ...

Table 1.1 lists the test data obtained ...

The photograph shown in Figure 4 reveals ...

The cutaway drawing of the subassembly, shown in Figure 3.1, illustrates how ...

Important Safety Instructions

⚠ **WARNING**	**To reduce the risk of fire, electrical shock, or injury when using your refrigerator, follow these basic precautions:**

- Read all instructions before using the refrigerator.
- Child entrapment and suffocation are not problems of the past. Junked or abandoned refrigerators are still dangerous . . . even if they will "just sit in the garage a few days."

    If you are getting rid of your old refrigerator, do it safely. Please read the enclosed safety booklet from the Association of Home Appliance Manufacturers. Help prevent accidents.

- Never allow children to operate, play with, or crawl inside the refrigerator.
- Never clean refrigerator parts with flammable fluids. The fumes can create a fire hazard or explosion.

• FOR YOUR SAFETY •

DO NOT STORE OR USE GASOLINE OR OTHER FLAMMABLE VAPORS AND LIQUIDS IN THE VICINITY OF THIS OR ANY OTHER APPLIANCE. THE FUMES CAN CREATE A FIRE HAZARD OR EXPLOSION.

—SAVE THESE INSTRUCTIONS—

Figure 8.22 *A pictogram placed with a safety warning emphasizes the importance of the message.*
Sears Kenmore Owner's Manual for No-Frost Refrigerator, publication number 2176227, July 1994, p. 2. Copyright © 1995 Sears Canada Inc. Reprinted with permission.

Place the graphic as close to the citation as possible. When the table or figure is not a full-page illustration, insert it below the paragraph where it was referenced (ideally, on the same page). For full-page graphics, insert the sheet containing the illustration immediately following the page where the citation appears. Then follow the illustration with a discussion that points out any pertinent data or feature(s) that particularly support your report's objectives. Numbering, citing, placing, and discussing a table or figure in this sequence will help your audience best understand the visual's purpose and function in your report.

If you do not have access to a computer, the list below provides some general guidelines for using visuals in reports handed in for classwork. Your instructor may add to this list.

- ◆ Use black ink — not ballpoint pen and not pencil — as the basic colour.

Figure 8.23 *This photograph shows actual detail much better than a line drawing.*
Reprinted with permission. © 1989 Skyland Tool and Mold, Inc.

◆ For colour, use nonsmear pencils or inks — not crayons.
◆ Type legends and figure numbers.
◆ Give credit to the visual's source (if the visual is not your own).
◆ Use rubber cement or a white paste glue to insert a visual on a page — do not use tape or staples.
◆ Place visuals as close to their citations as possible.
◆ When you place visuals on the same page as your text, allow plenty of white space around them — triple-space above and below.
◆ Place visuals within the standard margins (left/right, top/bottom) of the page.

Whenever you write a technical report, always consider using graphics to help your readers understand — and *remember* — the important information included.

Computer Tips

In the workplace and almost certainly at your college, computer-generated graphics are widely used because of their sharp lines and geometric shapes, their automatic and precise measurements, and the ever-increasing user-friendliness of the available graphics programs. Once you learn how to use the software, you can create and print illustrations that take less time to produce and are frequently of higher quality than hand-drawn visuals.

Listed below are a few currently available software packages (and their manufacturers) that will help you develop professional-looking visuals. These packages range from easy-to-use to complex; the more capabilities you want in a software package, the more skill you will need to use it.

◆ *WordPerfect for Windows* contains many functions particularly useful for technical documents: You can create tables, use special characters, import graphic elements from other programs, and integrate your CAD drawing into your document.

◆ *Microsoft Office* includes PowerPoint, a presentation graphics package, and Excel, a database package from which you can generate spreadsheets, graphs, etc.

◆ *Microsoft Access* is a database management system for Windows which has a *ReportWizards* feature that enables you to create presentation-quality reports with the graphs, charts, and other visuals you need.

◆ *ChartMaster* (Ashton-Tate) is one of the easiest programs to learn and use for drawing line, bar, and pie graphs. It automatically scales and positions graphs, and easily imports data created in other software. *ChartMaster* includes a wide variety of type styles, type sizes, and patterns. Depending on your printer's capabilities, you may choose among eight different colours for your graphs.

◆ *FormTool* (Block Publishing Corp.) allows you to produce tables (or any tabular material) more easily than many word-processing programs, but with several of the same functions: move, copy, insert, and delete. *FormTool* also creates full-page vertical and horizontal lines (frequently with only one keystroke), as well as varying shades, patterns, borders, and type styles.

◆ *OrgPlus* (Banner Blue) allows you to create organization charts easily. It automatically draws and spaces geometric shapes (rectangles, squares, etc.) and offers a number of options such as double borders and type styles.

◆ *Lotus 1-2-3* (Lotus Development Corp.) is actually a spreadsheet program which can produce tables of data and perform mathematical functions. *Lotus* also has the capability to transform the spreadsheet data into line, bar, and pie graphs. Many organizations use *Lotus* to perform other business functions, so it may be the software program most readily available to you in the workplace.

● *Allways* (Funk Software) is used in conjunction with Lotus. *Allways* is simple and easy-to-use, but requires a working knowledge of Lotus (and a developed spreadsheet). This package produces attractive tables with clean, crisp lines and includes a number of type styles, sizes, shades, and colours.

◆ *Harvard Graphics* (SPC Software Publishing Corp.) has extensive capabilities to produce line graphs, bar graphs, pie graphs, and flowcharts with varying graphic elements. It automatically scales and positions graphs according to the data entered. Three-dimensional graphs, varying grid lines, symbols, and colour and shade selections are among its capabilities. *Harvard Graphics* also allows you to import data created in another software program (*Lotus*, for example) and use the figures for plotting its graphs.

In addition, a number of graphic software packages are available for creating freeform line drawings (*PC Paintbrush*, *Publisher's Paintbrush*, and *Lotus Freelance* are examples). These packages require an investment of time to learn but, for many people, they are easier than drawing with a pen. The computer software market changes fast. Before buying or using any package, read the documentation carefully to ensure that it will do what you want it to do, and that it is compatible with your system. Professionals in computer retail stores can assist you by assessing your needs and recommending the best software.

QUESTIONS FOR DISCUSSION

1. How do graphics support text in technical reports?
2. What is a key consideration in choosing the best way to illustrate data in a report?
3. What should you consider when you use graphs?
4. What is the main purpose for illustrating information in a flowchart or organization chart?
5. Describe the advantages and disadvantages of using line drawings versus photographs.
6. Where should graphics be placed in a technical report?

EXERCISE

Match the following terms with the comments that best suit their illustrative purposes.

1. Table
2. Line graph

3. Horizontal bar graph
4. Vertical clustered bar graph
5. Stacked column bar graph
6. Pie graph
7. Flowchart
8. Organization chart
9. Full view line drawing
10. Cutaway line drawing
11. Exploded line drawing
12. Instructional aid
13. Pictogram
14. Photograph

_____ a. Shows readers with low technical levels the relationship of component parts of a whole at one time

_____ b. Shows parts and subassemblies separated, with each part projected along the centreline of its assembled position

_____ c. Presents and lists information that needs to be studied and compared easily

_____ d. Shows an accurate depiction of a real subject

_____ e. Shows relationships and interactions of various departments in an organization

_____ f. Emphasizes the differences in several related elements over time

_____ g. Shows an object cut to reveal the desired parts of the internal structure

_____ h. Summarizes the progression of major steps in a process

_____ i. Shows trends or movement of data in small increments

_____ j. Compares a number of different elements or component parts

_____ l. Shows a complete object with either a front, side, back, or three-dimensional rendering

WRITING ASSIGNMENTS

1. While preparing a report on women students in undergraduate engineering programs, you decide that the following information shows an important trend:

   Based on the figures provided by the Canadian Engineering Human Resources Board, the fall undergraduate enrolment of women in accredited engineering programs rose steadily from 10.8% (3,660) of total enrolment in 1985, to 11.4% (3,771) in 1986, to 11.6% (3,805) in 1987, to 12.3% (4,023) in 1988, to 13% (4,276) in 1989, to 14% (5,013) in 1990.

   Illustrate these figures in a graph that best emphasizes the increasing number of women choosing a career in engineering.

2. Develop a table that lists the courses you have taken so far at college, the course instructor's name, the grade you earned in each course, and your rating (excellent, good, fair, poor) of how valuable you think what you learned in the course will be after you graduate. Remember to apply all the rules of good table construction and readability.

Chapter NINE

Preparing the Parts of Your Report

ll technical reports have at least three basic parts: (1) a beginning, (2) a middle, and (3) an ending. The specific information included in these parts may vary, but their nature is the same.

1. You preview the information to come (introduction).
2. You present the information (body).
3. You review the main points (conclusions/recommendations).

A common axiom from journalism advises the writer: "Tell them what you're going to tell them. Tell them. Then tell them what you told them."

A logical and coherent report depends on this effective writing structure. An outline gives the body an effective order, but a well-organized body of information alone is not sufficient. Introductions and conclusions are essential as they supply readers with the purpose (the *what for*) and the outcome (the *point*).

Depending on the report's purpose, situation, and audience, you may omit some of the components described below. However, you should carefully choose parts that will guide the reader smoothly through the information. This chapter will show you how to compose these important parts so that you can begin to design and visualize a final product.

A *special note*: Although the parts of a report may not improve the *content*, they will improve the *impact* of the information on your audience.

TRANSMITTAL LETTER

A transmittal letter is a business letter that accompanies a fairly formal and long report. Somewhat like the person who introduces (or paves the way for) the main speaker at a dinner or conference, the transmittal letter hands over or "transmits" your report to the reader.

Essentially, the transmittal letter reminds the busy reader (who probably has many projects to supervise) of what prompted the preparation of the report, and prepares him or her to read it.

The letter explains to the reader the following aspects:

♦ Why the report was written
♦ Who requested or authorized it
♦ When it was requested and/or when it is due
♦ The parameters or scope of the report

The tone of a transmittal letter should be courteous and professional. The letter is usually no longer than two or three paragraphs. You may use it to give credit to specific persons who helped you complete the report, indicate any problems you encountered or emphasize your successes, or express willingness to discuss the report's contents personally with the reader or to conduct further research. Figure 9.1 shows an example of a transmittal letter's format and content. (Chapters Seventeen and Eighteen discuss the tone, form, and content of business correspondence in detail.)

In the workplace, the transmittal letter may be attached to the outside of the report, in front of the title. Alternatively, it may be bound in the report, after the title page. Follow the specific procedure of your workplace or course for the placement of this letter.

TITLE OR TITLE PAGE

All reports must have a title. Since the title or title page is the first element of a report that the audience sees, its impact is considerable. Because a first impression is usually difficult to change, make sure the title or title page has these positive characteristics:

♦ It immediately and specifically tells the audience what the report is about.
♦ It is concise.
♦ It is clear enough to attract the attention of all potential readers.

205 Kilbourne Street
Calgary AB T3M 4Z2
May 25, 19--

Dr. G. Liberatore and Mr. T. Lipkus
Communications and Engineering Technology Departments
Drumheller Technical Institute
Lethbridge AB T4E 1G9

Dear Dr. Liberatore and Mr. Lipkus

The enclosed report titled <u>A Security Lighting Design for St. Brigit's University,</u> <u>Blazeborough</u> is submitted in accordance with your instructions of March 1. Responding to the University administration's request for an upgraded system, this report evaluates the present security lighting system at the Northwood Campus and proposes an energy- and cost-efficient upgrade.

You will be pleased to know that Mr. Paul Jamieson of Flick Engineering, the firm contracted to install the new system, has some positive comments on my proposed design, including my use of Genesys software. You will note that the proposed design will improve the lighting particularly for students using the Stanley Street shortcut, an area that the preliminary inspection noted as a significant safety concern.

I wish to thank Ms. Mai Vu, Administrative Assistant in the Department of Engineering, and Mr. Chris Fougère, Plant Superintendent, for providing assistance and information.

I hope that the report meets with your approval and that we can continue to cooperate with Flick Engineering on this project. I look forward to receiving your questions and comments. I can be reached at 555-1213.

Yours truly,

Scott MacLeod

Scott MacLeod

Figure 9.1 *A transmittal letter personalizes a formal report.*
Adapted with permission of Scott MacLeod.

Wording of Titles

Using vague and overly complex terms in a title may irritate — rather than inform — the audience. General terms which do not instantly identify the specific purpose of the report may leave the reader uncertain about exactly what she or he is about to read. Compare these titles:

EXAMPLE: Installing VersaCAD

EXAMPLE: Engineering Department VersaCAD System: Installation Procedures

The first title is concise but not specific enough to indicate the purpose of the report. The audience may wonder whether the report will tell *how* to install the system, *where* it is being installed, and *why*. The second version is clearer, though longer, and has no unnecessary words.

Use of Subtitles

If the report is complex (perhaps it evaluates several different products or it studies more than one aspect of a subject), add a subtitle. Subtitles may also show the purpose or type of report.

EXAMPLES: Effective Formats in Operations Manuals: An Evaluation of Operator Performance

Automating the Moveable Contact Assembly at Sneeds Manufacturing: A Feasibility Study

A subtitle usually follows a colon. Typically, it clarifies or adds to the main title. Occasionally, depending on your purpose and readership, you may use a catchy title:

EXAMPLES: "Look Ma, New Brakes!" The Design, Analysis, and Construction of a Cantilever Brake System for Bicycles[1]

A Bird's-Eye View: A Radio-Controlled Aerial Photography System[2]

These report titles were designed to attract the interest of colleagues, junior students, and a general audience attending an open house where the documented projects were on display. Note that the subtitle gives the reader precise information.

[1] Used with permission of Glen Morton, Mechanical Design Technologist.
[2] Used with permission of Joey Liska, Electronics Technology Graduate.

Placement of Titles

If your report contains fewer than five pages, you may place the title at the top of the first page along with your name, your department and/or title, and the date you are submitting the report.

For longer (or more formal) reports, place the title on a separate page. Ensure that your title page is well balanced, attractive, and uncluttered. Your title page should contain the following information:

◆ Title and subtitle of report.

◆ Name and position of person receiving the report. (If more than one person will be reading the report, you can either list them or designate only the primary reader.)

◆ Firm's name (if needed).

◆ Your name and position.

◆ Date of submission.

Depending on the situation and on the standards of a specific workplace, the title page may also include other information: contract numbers under which the work was done, list of contributors to the report, name and signature of the person authorizing the report. Most companies have a preferred format for title pages and most include a logo identifying the company. Occasionally an *abstract* (described later in this chapter) is placed on the title page, particularly for technical reports written for and by government agencies.

A sample of a good title page for a student report is shown in Figure 9.2. This title page is placed at the front of the report. (When you include a separate title page, you do not need to place the title again on the first page of the report.)

Activity
....

Read the report titles below. Mark *C* in the blank provided if the title seems to indicate clearly what the accompanying report might cover. Mark *U/C* in the blank provided if the title seems unclear.

_____ a. Project Report

_____ b. Project Report on the Seldes System Installation at
Midland Manufacturing

_____ c. Brake System

_____ d. A Cantilever Brake System for Bicycles: Design and
Construction

_____ e. Proposal for Electronic Publishing

_____ f. Proposal for Implementing Electronic Publishing at
          Gracelands Hospital

**A SECURITY LIGHTING DESIGN FOR ST. BRIGIT'S UNIVERSITY
BLAZEBOROUGH, ALBERTA**

Submitted to:
Dr. G. Liberatore
Instructor, Communications
and
Terence Lipkus
Director, Engineering Technology

Submitted by:

Scott MacLeod
Engineering Technology Student
May 19--

Figure 9.2 *A well-balanced title page makes a good first impression on readers.*

TABLE OF CONTENTS

When a report is lengthy (more than five or six pages), include a table of contents (TOC). This "menu" of the items in the report tells the audience the following:

◆ The placement of sections and subsections
◆ The extent and nature of what is covered in the report
◆ The logic of the report's organization or the relationship of the various parts (or sections)

Listing of a Report's Topics

In the TOC, list all major sections and subsections. Every heading listed should be worded exactly as it appears in the report. (The use of section numbers is optional.) Be consistent in capitalization; generally, type major headings in ALL CAPS. Indent subsections to show the relationship of sections and subsections at a glance.

A brief example is given next of a partial table of contents, including section numbers. (A complete table of contents with section numbers omitted is shown in Figure 9.3.)

TABLE OF CONTENTS

Section	Title	Page
	EXECUTIVE SUMMARY	1
1.	INTRODUCTION	2
1.1	Definitions	2
1.2	Background	3
2.	THE CURRENT SITUATION	5
2.1	Quality Control Problems	5
2.1.1	Misaligned Threading	7
2.1.2	Inaccurate Sizing	7
2.2	Equipment Downtime	8

Listing of Figures

When a report contains illustrations (charts, graphs, pictures, drawings), make a separate listing for them. Place a short list (labelled "Figures") on the same page as the TOC. Place a longer list (labelled "List of Figures" or "List of Illustrations") on a separate page immediately following the table of contents.

TABLE OF CONTENTS

Abstract   ii

Table of Contents   iii

Introduction   iv

METHODOLOGY   1

    Interviews   1

    Questionnaires   2

    Indices   4

    Surveys   5

ANALYSIS   6

    Policies and Attitudes   6

    Dental Knowledge   6

    Home Care and Oral Habits   7

    Nutrition   7

    Dental Safety   8

RECOMMENDATIONS   9

References   10

Appendix   11

<u>Figures</u>

1. The sections of a tooth as scored by a PHP index   4

2. The classification of PHP scores   5

Figure 9.3 *This table of contents includes a short list of illustrations.*

Note that you do not need to insert the word "page" in the table of contents.

    The list of figures uses a similar format to the table of contents shown in the previous example. List the figure titles exactly as they appear on the illustrations. Figure 9.3 shows a table of contents that includes a list of figures used in the report.

Place the table of contents (and list of figures, when needed) after the transmittal letter and title page.

Use lowercase Roman numerals for front matter pagination and Arabic numerals for the body proper.

ABSTRACT

An abstract is a concise, clear description of what the report covers. It states only the major areas and main facts — and omits preliminaries, details, illustrations, and examples.

Abstracts have several functions. Their primary purpose is to help readers decide whether they need or want to read the entire document. A quick reading of fewer than 100 words should tell readers whether or not they need the information in a 5,000-word report.

Content and Structure of Abstracts

Abstracts and executive summaries are somewhat interchangeable; most reports contain only one of these components. An abstract (sometimes called a synopsis or summary) usually prefaces a technical report dealing with topics in science, health, or technology. Many published technical reports contain descriptive abstracts which are included in library catalogues or computer databases. Frequently, technical conference planners use a submitted abstract to determine which reports they wish to accept for presentation. Therefore, the abstract must be understandable enough to stand alone in a catalogue or conference program.

Figure 9.4 shows an example of a good descriptive abstract. Notice that it describes when and where the study was done. (Even when the abstract is *in* the report, do not assume the reader "knows" these facts.) The abstract also states the major areas covered in the report (students' understanding, improvement, and correlation, etc.), but it does not state any details or conclusions.

When writing an abstract for a report (and sometimes you are asked to do this before you actually write the document), focus on the main areas that are (or will be) covered. If you've already prepared your outline, look at the major points listed and include only those.

Ranging in length from a brief paragraph to half a typed page, the abstract is typically single-spaced and placed on a separate sheet after the title page and before the table of contents.

TECHNICAL WRITING AND ACADEMIC SUCCESS

By John Chang, Engineering Technology Student
Deer Point Technical Community College

ABSTRACT

In the summer 1990 semester, technical report writing was integrated into the structure of all technical major fields of study at Deer Point Technical Community College. The required coursework consisted of technical reports rather than the traditional textbook-resource papers. This report documents the follow-up evaluation of the overall performance impact of this course on student grades, examinations, and written reports in later engineering courses. Areas specifically addressed in this report are before-and-after comparisons of (1) student understanding of the subject matter; (2) improvement or change in writing and organizational skills; and (3) the correlation of student writing skills to problem-solving skills.

Figure 9.4 *This concise abstract tells readers whether the information in the report will be useful to them.*

EXECUTIVE SUMMARY

An executive summary, which is usually more informative and often longer than an abstract, prefaces a report with a business-related focus (such as a proposal). An executive summary contains tightly written statements of the objectives of the report, its highlights, and its conclusions or recommendations. Executive summaries differ from abstracts in three ways:

1. An abstract prefaces a report that focuses on science, health, or technology; an executive summary prefaces a report that focuses on business.

2. An abstract describes only the major areas or points covered in a report; an executive summary expands on these major areas with concise details and brief conclusions.

3. An abstract rarely exceeds a paragraph; an executive summary often fills a whole typewritten page.

The executive summary is particularly helpful to busy managers who have many reports to read and limited time to spend reading each one. Many organizations require an executive summary for all reports longer than five or six pages.

The Information to Include

Although the executive summary appears near the beginning of a report, it should be the last page you write. To write an effective executive summary, go over your entire report and write down all the headings that precede each section and subsection. Write a sentence about each heading. Condense what you have just composed. Finally, polish the condensed version until it flows smoothly without unnecessary introductory and transitional material.

Tips for writing and formatting a concise executive summary:

◆ Keep to one page or less.

◆ Use bullets to list important highlights in concise sentences. Bullets eliminate the need for transitional phrases, which take up room on the page.

◆ Use concise statements, not long detailed sentences.

◆ Do not include anything that is not in the report.

Figure 9.5 shows an executive summary. Note that this sample gives only the highlights of the main document; readers who want more details can consult the text. Compare this summary with the sample abstract in Figure 9.4 and note the differences in length and details.

Place the executive summary after the table of contents. If the report also contains an abstract (in rare cases), place the executive summary after the abstract.

GLOSSARY

If a list of definitions is needed in your report, include this section (titled Definitions or Glossary) in one of these places:

◆ At the front of the report, following the executive summary and preceding the introduction

◆ At the back of the report, preceding the appendix

EXECUTIVE SUMMARY

One benefit of completing a technical writing course is gaining a facility in document generation, organization, and clarity. The value of this benefit is widely recognized in the workplace. Working engineers are commonly expected to describe clearly their activities in technical reports submitted to their superiors, colleagues, and customers. In fact, the engineering design, analysis, construction, and testing effort is routinely linked to the report-writing effort.

Since Engineering Technology students usually take a technical writing class at Deer Point Technical Community College before their final semester, the possibility arises that the skills learned in this class may also have some value in their later engineering classes. This report documents the follow-up evaluation of overall performance impact of this course on student grades, examinations, and written reports in a later engineering course, ET 217 — Engineering Mathematics.

The evaluative areas investigated in the body of this report are summarized next.

Area 1: Student Understanding of the Subject Matter

- Average test scores were 18 percent higher for students who took a technical writing course the previous semester.
- Homework accuracy was 13 percent higher for former technical writing students.

Area 2: Improvement or Change in Writing and Organizational Skills

- All former technical writing students ranked in the top 5 percent of grades earned for an assigned report on differential and difference equations.
- All former technical writing students ranked in the top 7 percent of grades earned for an assigned report on discrete-time convolution.

Area 3: The Correlation of Student Writing Skills to Problem-Solving Skills

- Visual inspection of all graphs used in the assigned papers prepared by the former technical writing students showed greater analytical skills.
- Mathematical accuracy showed no marked difference between the two groups of students observed.

Conclusion

This study demonstrates that technical report writing can have a marked influence on improved performance of engineering students in their later courses.

Figure 9.5 *An executive summary allows busy managers to scan only the highlights of a long report.*

In the past, glossaries usually were placed at the end of the report, just before the appendix; many writers now prefer to present the glossary before the main text so readers can become familiar with any specialized terms and recall them as they read the report.

INTRODUCTION

The introduction familiarizes the audience with the report's subject material. Think of the introduction as the "Tell them what you're going to tell them" part, in which you state your main objectives for writing the report.

Subsections

The introduction section of a report may include these subsections:

◆ *Purpose.* Explains as fully as necessary the conditions or events that created the need for the report.

◆ *Scope.* Settles any possible doubt about what the report covers and what it omits. (The "Scope" subsection may not be necessary if the title is exact enough.)

◆ *Sources.* Makes a general statement about the source(s) of information and how you obtained the facts in the report. If some information comes from printed sources, they may be named here — provided you include no more than three or four.

◆ *Authorization.* Acknowledges who, when, and how someone authorized the preparation of the report.

◆ *Descriptions.* Includes any product or mechanism descriptions.

◆ *Definitions/terminology.* Lists specialized terms and their meanings (if a separate section is not included in the report).

Figure 9.6 shows an example of an introduction with many of these features.

The introduction follows the executive summary (or glossary, if you have included one in the front of the report). It can be placed on a separate page (or pages), separating it from the body of the report, or it can be placed on the same page as the first major section of the body of the report.

INTRODUCTION

The objective of this report is to determine the need for and the feasibility of implementing a local area network (LAN) computer training program at Midway Manufacturing (MM).

Purpose

The need for this analytical report arose from the number of documented "help" calls received by Computer Services from troubled MM computer users. Most calls for assistance have been resolved easily by the department's hardware and software personnel, which implies a lack of formal user education in even basic computer skills.

Scope

This report identifies the organizational and cost benefits of a formal computer training program at MM, and investigates the economic and logistical feasibility of beginning such a program onsite. Based on the findings of this study, this report includes specific computer courses, teaching resources, and an implementation schedule. It also recommends a budget based on estimated costs.

Sources of Information

A questionnaire and MM user survey prepared and tabulated with the assistance of the Employee Development Department provided significant data in this report. The computer department at Deer Point Technical Community College provided information on developing computer training classes. Area professional computer trainers were contacted as a possible alternative to MM training resources.

Authorization

This report is prepared in response to a request in November from the Director of Operational Services, B. W. Sloane.

Figure 9.6 *This introduction orients readers to the report.*

BODY OF THE REPORT

The body of the report includes facts, figures, and details that inform the audience, explain methodology, substantiate findings, and convince decision makers. It moves point by point to explain and develop the topic. (*Note:* Specific details regarding the content for each type of report are covered fully in Parts Four and Five of this text.) In addition to the content itself, two other elements play a key role in the body of a report: its general appearance and its specific headings.

Appearance

Generally, the appearance of the body in *all* reports follows these guidelines:

◆ For the classroom, your instructor may prefer double-spaced typewritten pages. For the workplace, use the standards set by the organization.

◆ Do not staple or paper clip formal reports. When preparing the final draft of a report, leave $1\frac{1}{2}$-inch margins on the left side so the report can be placed in a binder or secured in a folder. Set the margins on the right, top, and bottom of each page to measure one inch.

◆ Vary the lengths of paragraphs to make the pages more inviting to read. So that pages appear uncrowded, include at least two paragraphs on each page — more, if possible, to provide plenty of white space.

Chapter Ten presents more information on the preparation of a well-formatted report.

Headings

Be sure to include ample but meaningful headings throughout your report. Use the guides (hierarchies) shown in Figure 9.7 to ensure that the audience sees the relationship of one piece of information to another, or one point to another.

Remember, even if someone else types the report, *you*, the author, are responsible for its appearance and for its correct format, grammar, and mechanics.

MAIN HEADING

The main headings correspond to outline entries I, II, III or 1., 2., 3. These announce the major sections into which the report is divided. They are put in all capital letters and can be flush left (as shown above) or centred. Underlining is optional. Use no punctuation following a main heading unless the heading is a question. On the first page of the body of a report, place the main heading approximately 6 centimetres from the top of the page. There must be some text material between headings. When you finish one main section of the report, leave three or four line spaces before the next main heading.

First Subhead

The first subheads correspond to the A, B, C or 1.1, 1.2, 1.3 outline entries. Place these headings flush with the left margin and underline each word. Capitalize the first letter of each word in the heading. Use no punctuation at the end of the heading.

Second Subhead. These headings correspond to those numbered 1, 2, 3 under the A, B, C entries in traditional outlines and to the 1.1.1, 1.1.2, 1.1.3 entries in decimal outlines. They are indented the same number of spaces as paragraphs. Capitalize the first letter of each word and underline all words. Place a period (and double space) at the end of the heading. Begin the first sentence in this section on the same line as the heading.

Figure 9.7 *A consistent hierarchy of headings demonstrates the relationship of the information being presented.*

CONCLUSIONS/RECOMMENDATIONS

A necessary part of informing readers is to finish by "telling them what you told them." Even when the conclusions/recommendations may seem obvious to you, do not assume that they will be equally obvious to your readers.

Effective Conclusions

Depending on the type of report you have prepared, your readers will expect you to take all the information presented in the body of the report and pull it all together in a conclusion. They will expect you to tell them what the data mean overall. Any effective technical report builds on its information and draws sound conclusions for its readers.

Begin the conclusion section by briefly restating the main points. Note the word "restating." This section should contain no information that has not already been included in the body of the report. Using words like "based on," "because of," and "therefore" will help you make smooth transitions in the conclusion as you move succinctly from one major point to another.

Finally, compose a strong, effective concluding statement; leave readers with the *one main idea* that you want them to remember. Figure 9.8 shows an example of how to write an effective conclusion.

Sound Recommendations

If one of your purposes in writing the report is to make specific recommendations based on your findings, be sure that these recommendations are based on sound, logical reasoning already presented in the main part of the report and stated clearly in the conclusions section. The information in the body should build steadily toward these recommendations. As shown in Figure 9.9, succinctly state all recommendations for your audience.

Placement of Conclusions/Recommendations

The placement of the conclusions/recommendations section is optional, depending on the type of report written. Frequently, conclusions/recommendations are placed at the end of the body of the report. However, when you have written an analytical report — such as an evaluation report or feasibility study — you may prefer to put this section before the body of the report. The body then substantiates and reinforces the valid conclusions or recommendations pre-

7. CONCLUSION

There is a growing and ongoing need for local area network computer training classes at Midway Manufacturing. As shown in the computer user survey, MM computer employees have asked for help in achieving the computer skills they need to do their jobs better.

Formal computer training classes will have a positive impact through the organization:

- Administrative personnel will have enhanced planning skills and tools.
- Improved job performance through time-efficient computer applications will result in an improved end product.
- Shared knowledge will enable existing computer personnel to perform more effectively in their own areas of expertise.

When Midway Manufacturing provides its employees with effective computer skills, it is making an investment in today's resources to ensure a more progressive and prosperous tomorrow.

Figure 9.8 *This conclusion briefly restates a report's main points and explains why they are important.*

8. RECOMMENDATIONS

After surveying the current computer users at Midway Manufacturing and investigating the feasibility of developing formal computer training classes, I recommend that Midway implement the following program:

- Onsite classes be held in Employee Development classroom number 2.
- A classroom forum of six participants per session be used.
- Computer Services personnel be used as trainers.
- A descending matrix of users (from department heads to clerical) be used as the class roster.
- A schedule of classes be completed by August 1994.

The findings detailed in this report indicate clearly that Midway Manufacturing's investment today in effective and productive computer skills for its employees is an investment in a more progressive and prosperous tomorrow.

Figure 9.9 *Your recommendations should be displayed clearly and concisely.*

sented earlier. In some cases, the company president or agency director who commissioned your report would wish to read the conclusions and recommendations first, and then pass the report down the line for comments and action.

LIST OF REFERENCES (WORKS CITED OR BIBLIOGRAPHY)

The List of References presents all the sources you either consulted or cited for the report. Most technical reports are derived from *primary* sources (interviews, experiments, surveys, collected data, and so forth), rather than *secondary* sources (such as books and articles). In general, you must include any sources which provided you with background material or substantiated your assumptions.

Chapter Six, "Collecting and Documenting Information," shows the correct form for entries in a list of references. Place the list of references directly after the conclusions/recommendations section, if you included that section at the end of your report.

APPENDIX

The appendix includes all supplemental material related to the report. It gathers into one place all the information which might help a reader seeking further assistance or clarification but which cannot be worked into the body of the report without interrupting the reading flow: texts of interviews, pertinent correspondence, large drawings, detailed cost comparisons, etc.

The following items may also be included in an appendix:

◆ Test results
◆ Lists
◆ Calculations
◆ Specifications
◆ Computer printouts
◆ Questionnaires

Include only one type of material in an appendix and precede it by a separate title page labelled "Appendix." If different kinds of items are included, develop separate appendices and label each title page:

EXAMPLE: Appendix A: Computer Printouts

Appendix B: Questionnaires

Number the pages in the appendices A-1, A-2, A-3 and so forth; then B-1, B-2, B-3; then C-1, C-2. Some reports number the appendix pages consecutively (continuing from the end of the body). Appendices in some industrial reports have no page numbers. The appendix is the last part included in the report.

SUMMARY: ORDER OF THE PARTS

All the parts discussed in this chapter combine to form a well-constructed document. By carefully compiling information into a strong organizational structure, you build clarity and impact into a report. Well-built reports achieve positive results.

To reference quickly the suggested order of the report parts, review the illustration in Figure 9.10, which shows the organization of a report containing most of these parts.

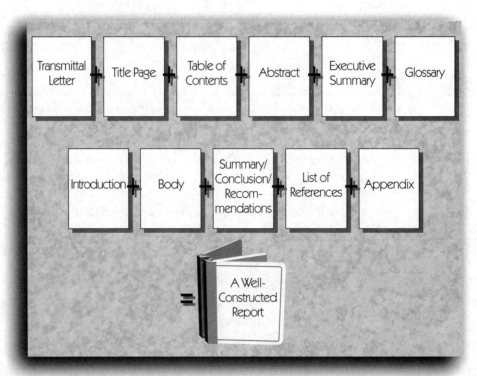

Figure 9.10 *This illustration shows the order of parts in a formal report.*

Computer Tips

A table of contents (TOC) may seem simple enough to construct: Just list the headings of all major sections and subsections and correlate them with accurate report page numbers. But this simple task becomes more complex when you decide just hours before the report is due (and this eventually happens to all report writers) to add or delete some data, to insert or omit a visual aid, or to rearrange some sections of text. These decisions, of course, affect the section order and/or page numbers on your original TOC.

You do not have to forgo these improvements to your report because of a quickly approaching deadline. A number of word-processing programs can do much of the work for you. When the original TOC is generated in a word processor with a special table of contents feature (*Microsoft Word* and *DisplayWrite* 5 are two such programs), any changes can be quickly updated with a simple keyboard command and then reprinted — all with the correct page indentions automatically inserted by the program.

While individual word-processing programs vary somewhat in the exact way they generate a TOC, generally they use the following principle: You create a document in the word-processing program, and then you insert a code (visible only on your computer screen) before the line of text that you want to appear in the table of contents (usually a heading). You specify (via the code) whether the item is a major section or subsection.

When you finish flagging these entries in your word processor, you execute a command and the TOC is generated with the section headings and the number of the page on which each appears. If you ever decide to make any changes to the body of the report, you can simply execute the TOC command again and page numbers will be readjusted accordingly.

Computer-generated TOCs, of course, are only as complete and accurate as you make them. You, the person in charge of this operation, must flag and specify each heading that should be in the TOC; the program does not make these judgments for you. Any additional headings must also be flagged with the code. Check the user's manual for your word-processing program to see if it offers you this handy TOC feature.

QUESTIONS FOR DISCUSSION

1. How can you ensure that your readers' first impressions of a report are positive?
2. How can a report's structure affect the reader?
3. A report is not just a well-organized set of data. Explain.

EXERCISE 1

In the blanks provided, indicate where in a report — title page (*TP*), transmittal letter (*TL*), table of contents (*TOC*), abstract (*AB*), executive summary (*ES*), glossary (*G*), introduction (*I*), body (*B*), conclusions/recommendations (*C/R*), references (*R*), appendix (*AP*) — the following would be found.

_____ a. An expression of appreciation for help in completing the report

_____ b. Authors and titles of books used as sources

_____ c. Names and positions of person(s) who authorized the report

_____ d. The inferences drawn from the body of information

_____ e. Details, facts, figures

_____ f. Writer's name and position

_____ g. Concise statement of what the report covers

_____ h. A listing or "menu" of parts of the report

_____ i. A separate listing of terms and definitions

_____ j. Statement of objectives, main points, and conclusions or recommendations

_____ k. Supplemental material that may be of interest to the reader

_____ l. A section labelled "Scope"

EXERCISE 2

Investigate one or two textbooks from your technical courses and a number of articles from technical journals or magazines. Find examples of

♦ a chapter summary
♦ an article summary or abstract

Then read the entire chapter and the entire article. Note how the headings also help you to summarize the main areas. Discuss your findings with your class colleagues and your instructor.

WRITING ASSIGNMENTS

1. Write an abstract for this chapter that would help readers decide whether they want or need to read the chapter themselves. Try to limit the abstract to no more than 250 words. Remember to mention only the major areas covered in this chapter, not the details.

2. Read a three- or four-page magazine article of your choice. Write an executive summary for your instructor that will give him or her the highlights and pertinent details of the article. (Your summary should be less than one page in length.) Attach the article (or a photocopy of it) to the summary when you hand in this writing assignment.

3. Choose a manageable (suitably narrow) technical topic with which you are thoroughly familiar. Using this chapter as a guide, prepare the parts of your report. If you are already working on a report for a technical course or work assignment, use what you have learned in this chapter to prepare a table of contents and to write some or all of the parts discussed.

Chapter TEN

Formatting Guidelines

Producing an effective report requires attention to the visual elements as well as to the content, attention to the way the material looks on the page as well as to words and sentences. *Formatting* refers to the overall use of *form* to enhance and communicate the message.

Readers always see more than just words; they see the information within a context. That total context is the format. For readers, a "well-formatted" report includes the following:

◆ Material that is easy to read and visually appealing because of its physical layout

◆ Material that is labelled, numbered, and clearly classified for quick accessibility

◆ Material that follows a familiar (or standard) pattern

This chapter briefly distinguishes between informal and formal reports, since their formats are different. It tells and shows you *what to use* and *what to do* to produce readable and professional-looking reports; its emphasis is on formal reports. The different aspects of formatting formal reports are listed in alphabetical order so you can find them easily.

DISTINCTIONS BETWEEN INFORMAL AND FORMAL REPORTS

How to convey information — formally or informally — is always a key decision in report writing. Like instructors, some organizations insist on very specific guidelines; others give writers complete liberty to choose their own formats. Many organizations use standardized preprinted reports for routine purposes. Generally whether a report should be informal or formal is determined by why you are writing (purpose), to whom you are writing (audience), and what you have to say (content). These considerations govern not only the type of research and the tone of the report, but also formatting aspects such as the length, the kind of parts supplementing the body, and the use of graphics.

TABLE 10.1

MAJOR FORMATTING DISTINCTIONS BETWEEN FORMAL AND INFORMAL REPORTS

Feature	Formal	Informal
Length	More than 5 pages	1 to 5 pages
Supplemental parts	Title page	No title page
	Transmittal letter	No letter
	Abstract	No abstract
	Table of contents	No table of contents
	List of figures	No list of figures
	Introduction	Summary statement
	List of references	No list of references
	Appendix or appendices	No appendices
Visual aids	Some/extensive	Limited/none
Headings	Expected	Optional
Binding	Required	Varies

You may present your material in a letter, a memo, or a report of only a few pages (generally considered "informal" reports) or in a long (generally "formal") report. Although exceptions occur often, Table 10.1 shows the major distinctions between formal and informal reports.

Informal reports such as letters and memos are typically single-spaced with double-spacing between the paragraphs. Short informal reports (less than five pages) may be either single-spaced or double-spaced. To increase readability, any short report may contain headings for each section. Note the examples provided of a poor and an improved format (or page design) for a memo report (Figures 10.1 and 10.2) and a letter report (Figures 10.3 and 10.4).

If you examine the formats in Figures 10.1 through 10.4, you will see how important it is for your document to be visually appealing. You can assess the attractiveness of the format more easily without actually reading the text. For example, when you use the print preview command in your word processor, the format of the page is shown, rather than the actual wording. WordPerfect for Windows

TO: _____
FROM: _____
SUBJECT: _____
DATE: _____

Figure 10.1 *A poorly formatted memo is difficult to read.*

TO: _____

FROM: _____

SUBJECT: _____

DATE: _____

Figure 10.2 *A well-formatted memo is easy to read.*

(version 5.1/5.2) reveals the page with lines only so that you can see the impact of the arrangement immediately. In WordPerfect 6.1 for Windows and in other word processors, "view full page" (or two pages) reveals a minute version of the writing, since what you want to see is the overall visual impact, rather than the content. The main point of looking at a page of lines is to see that the format is professional, for an attractive format will enhance the content by making the information easier to approach. Thus, you can see that the memo in Figure 10.2 has more chance of success than the one in Figure 10.1.

ASPECTS OF FORMATTING

To write an effective formal report, follow the guidelines of your workplace. If a format is not specified, review several reports written

Figure 10.3 *A poorly formatted letter is unattractive and difficult to read.*

by others in your organization to determine general expectations, then follow the guidelines listed below.

Alignment

When listing items in a table, align words at the left; align columns of numbers (including page numbers in the table of contents) at the right or by decimal points. Centre the headings over such columns.

Figure 10.4 *A well-formatted letter is easy to read.*

Monthly Utility Charges	Average Costs
Gas	$27.34
Water	10.30
Telephone	57.25
Electric	195.00
Cable TV	25.80

Binding

Reports are typically submitted in a cover or binder. Place reports within covers appropriate to their size. Use a ring binder for very long reports (more than about 20 pages); use a clear plastic cover with a plastic spine for shorter reports. Some photocopy shops will bind your reports at a reasonable charge and offer you a variety of covers. Do not use staples or paper clips in long formal reports, and never turn down the page corners of any report.

Bullets

Bullets vertically align indented elements in a series and visually separate them from the text. Essentially a list without numbers, bulleted material stands out from the text and is easy to read. Bulleting is illustrated below and throughout this textbook.

◆ Use a word-processing program (such as WordPerfect 6.1 for Windows) to create bullets like the ones in this text.

◆ Indent bulleted material.

◆ Keep bulleted items in parallel structure. (Notice that all the sentences following the bullets in this list start with a command verb.)

◆ Be consistent when capitalizing and punctuating bulleted items. Capitalize the first letter of all bulleted items, and use punctuation at the end of each if any of the items in the list is a complete sentence.

Any word processor will offer a variety of characters or typographic symbols to choose from. Be consistent in your use of symbols.

Citations

Citations within the text may indicate that you are giving credit for material (data, direct quotes, or ideas) to an outside source. They may also indicate (by means of a number, symbol, or small letter) that further explanation of a point can be found at the bottom of the page. Whatever their function, citations should be consistent and clearly understood.

In general, traditional footnotes (the kind that indicate credit for material by means of a raised number — or superscript — at the end of the citation in the text, and the source at the bottom of the page) are not used in technical reports. Nevertheless, you may occasionally be expected to use these kinds of footnotes, especially in an academic assignment. If so, you should observe these rules and/or consult a reputable style guide:

- Raise the number half a space above the line of type at the appropriate place where credit is due.
- Provide the source at the bottom of the page.

> TEXT: Recognizing the significant growth of home-based businesses, manufacturers are producing more and improved technologies for the home office.[4]

FOOTNOTE: [4] Kevin Yarr, "Inner Space: Creating Your Own Home Office," *Atlantic Progress Special Supplement* (September 1995), 2.

Instead of traditional footnotes, parenthetical (or in-text) references are more frequently used in technical reports. When you use this system for citing your sources, follow these guidelines:

- Alphabetize the List of References (following the body of the report) and number each reference in sequence.
- Indicate the reference in the text by placing the reference number and page number(s) of the source — if applicable — inside parentheses. Insert a colon between the reference number and the page number(s).
- Insert a space before and after the parentheses (unless the parentheses are followed by a period).

TEXT: In response to the surge of home-based business (4.2), manufacturers are producing improved technologies for the home office.

Colour

Since word-processed reports are now standard, your printout will be black and white. If you wish to incorporate colour graphics (and if you have access to a computer and/or printer that can produce coloured type or graphics), you should adhere to the following guidelines:

- Keep black as the basic text colour.
- Use black ink for signing your name. (Pencil and vivid colours such as green and purple are not acceptable.)
- Supplement graphics with colour to add emphasis, clarity, and readability — but do not use colour excessively or without a good reason.

Corrections

All corrections should be made before your final submission of the report. Using the editing and spell-check functions of your word processor and proofreading carefully several times before submission should result in a report that does not require last-minute corrections. You should always have your disk at hand so that you can easily correct any errors.

Graphics (Figures)

Graphics contribute a great deal to the quality of technical reports: They clarify, they supplement, they emphasize, and they make your words memorable. To use them effectively, follow these guidelines:

◆ Integrate visual illustrations into the page of text whenever possible, with triple-spacing above and below.

◆ Draw a box around a visual aid to separate it from the text.

◆ Choose an appropriate size for your visual. A simple drawing, for example, does not usually require an entire page.

◆ Place the visuals as close as possible to their first reference in the text.

◆ Precede the placement of a figure with a comment, discussion, or reference to it in the text. Never show a visual before you have directed the readers' attention to it. Refer to a figure within a sentence or in parentheses, as shown below.

EXAMPLE: As Figure 12 shows, costs have tripled for branch offices in the past five years.

EXAMPLE: Costs at branch offices have tripled in the past five years. (See Figure 12 on page 5.)

Each aspect of a report's format makes an impression on the reader and reflects the writer's professionalism and competence. The key to effective formatting is to recognize your audience's need to read a report rapidly and easily. Good formatting means an effective report presentation.

Headings

Meaningful headings in a report help readers move quickly from point to point. They help readers identify the hierarchy of information and they help writers prepare the executive summary or abstract.

There are two kinds of headings: those which label the main parts of a report (discussed in Chapter Nine) and those which categorize the content of a section in the body of a report.

Guidelines for Report Part Headings

◆ Type headings in all capital letters (for example, ABSTRACT, EXECUTIVE SUMMARY, TABLE OF CONTENTS, APPENDIX, etc.).

◆ Place these headings flush with the left margin or centre them as illustrated in Figure 10.5.

Guidelines for Section Headings

◆ Type the main heading in ALL CAPITAL LETTERS and underline subsequent subheadings.

◆ Centre all main headings, or place them flush with the left margin.

◆ Place first subheads flush with the left margin and underline or bold.

◆ Place second subheads five spaces (same as for paragraphing) from the left margin, underline or bold, and end the second subhead with a period. (A page of text without headings and a page with headings are shown in Figure 10.6.)

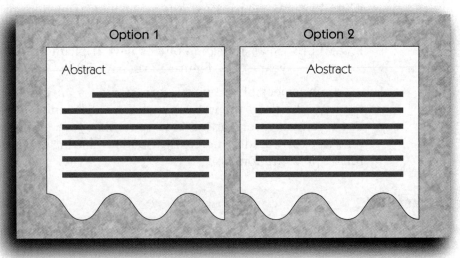

Figure 10.5 *Headings for parts of the report may be placed flush with the left margin or centred.*

◆ Number the headings for certain kinds of reports, such as scientific reports. (You will not need to number the headings for more general kinds of reports.)

◆ Number report headings consistently:

I, II, III or 1, 2, 3	MAIN HEADINGS
A, B, C or 1.1, 1.2, 1.3	First-Level Subheads
1, 2, 3 or 1.1.1, 1.1.2, 1.1.3	Second-Level Subheads

◆ Give the most important headings the most pronounced attention (boldface type or a box, for example).

◆ Make certain that headings are parallel in structure (that is, worded in similar grammatical form). Notice the poor and good examples of headings below:

POOR: 1. Satisfaction of employees paid by the hour

      1.1 With working conditions

      1.2 Supervision

      1.3 Their benefits

   2. Salaried Employee Satisfaction

      2.1 With conditions at work

      2.2 Top management

      2.3 With package of benefits

GOOD: 1. Hourly Employee Satisfaction

      1.1 With working conditions

      1.2 With supervisory personnel

      1.3 With benefits package

   2. Salaried Employee Satisfaction

      2.1 With working conditions

      2.2 With management strategies

      2.3 With benefits package

◆ Place at least one heading on each page of text.

◆ Include at least two lines of type under any heading that starts near the bottom of a page.

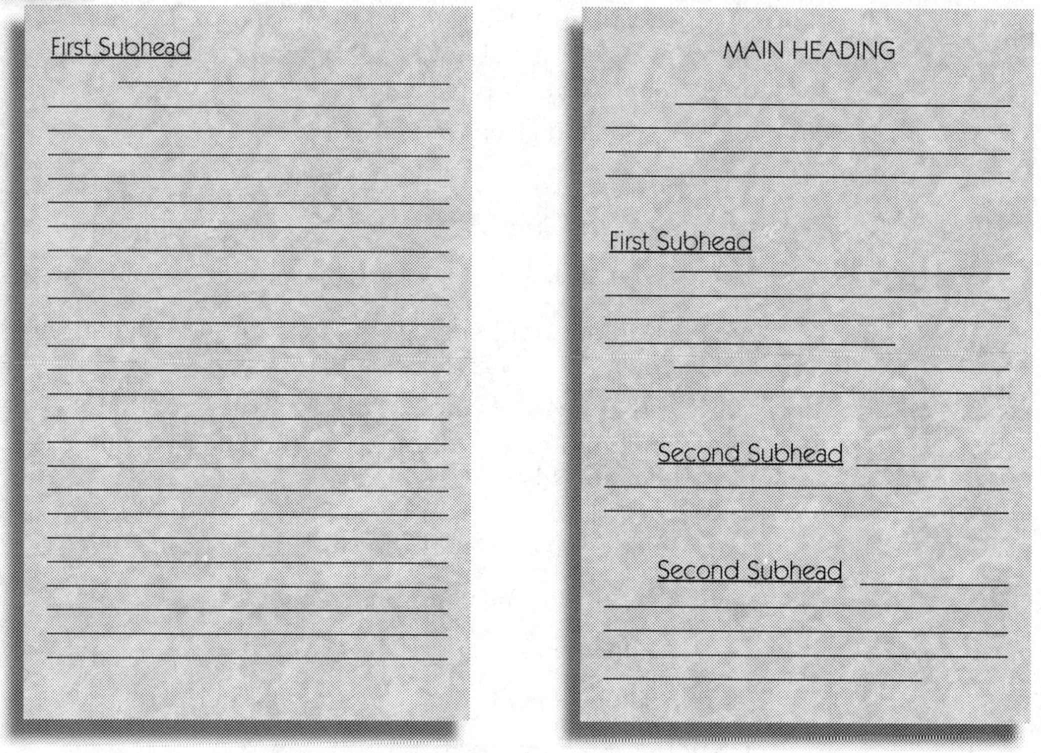

Figure 10.6 *Headings enhance the readability of a page of text.*

Margins

A well-formatted document includes adequate margins around the printed text. Your readers will find it difficult to read a report with narrow or nonexistent margins.

- Include margins that are at least 1 inch wide on all four sides of your text. For reports in binders, insert a $1\frac{1}{2}$-inch margin between the left side of the page and the text.

- Place all typed lines evenly flush ("justified") against the left margin for single-spaced text. "Left justify" double-spaced text as well, but also indent five spaces at the start of each paragraph.

- Leave the right margin "ragged." Justify the right margin only if you are using a word-processing program with proportional-spacing capabilities. Right justification without proportional spacing can create uneven spacing within the text.

- Place all visual illustrations within the margins.

Neatness

A report's appearance gives readers the first impression of its quality. In other words, readers *do* "judge a report by its cover" and format. Therefore, you should take great care to submit only absolutely clean copy — stainless and uncrumpled.

Numbering

For most reports, you will need to number both the pages and the visual illustrations.

◆ Number the pages in the body of the report with Arabic numerals, starting with page 2. Number the pages preceding the body with lowercase Roman numerals, starting with ii (following the title page) or iii (following the title page and transmittal letter). By convention, the title page and letter of transmittal are not numbered, but they are counted.

◆ Place page numbers at the top centre, the top right margin, or the bottom centre of the page. Whichever placement you choose, be consistent.

◆ Do not punctuate page numbers (no periods, no parentheses, no brackets, no dashes).

◆ Use Arabic numbers for figures (illustrations), number them in the sequence in which they appear throughout a report, and insert the word *Figure* (Figure 1, Figure 2). For very long reports (30 pages or more), indicate in which section a particular figure appears by inserting both the section number and the figure number. (Figure 1.1, for example, would be the first figure in the first section of the report.)

◆ Number the List of References pages as a continuation of the body.

◆ Label Appendices with capital letters, starting with A: Appendix A, Appendix B, and so forth. Number pages within each Appendix: A-1, A-2, A-3, B-1, B-2, B-3, and so forth.

Paper

The kind of paper you use will make a difference in the overall appearance of your report. Readers do notice, so use high-quality paper: white, unlined twenty-pound bond (no onionskin, very thin, or coated paper). Use standard-sized paper ($8\frac{1}{2} \times 11$) printed on one side only.

Paragraphing

The paragraphs in a report should adhere to the general expectations for good paragraph development: They should include a main point, a topic sentence, and specific details to support the main point. The following guidelines apply to format:

◆ Keep paragraphs to less than 8–10 lines of type (about half a page of double-spaced material). Every page should have at least two paragraphs (including headings).

◆ Set off lists in paragraphs with numbers or bullets.

Figure 10.7 illustrates a poor and a proper way to format paragraphs in a report.

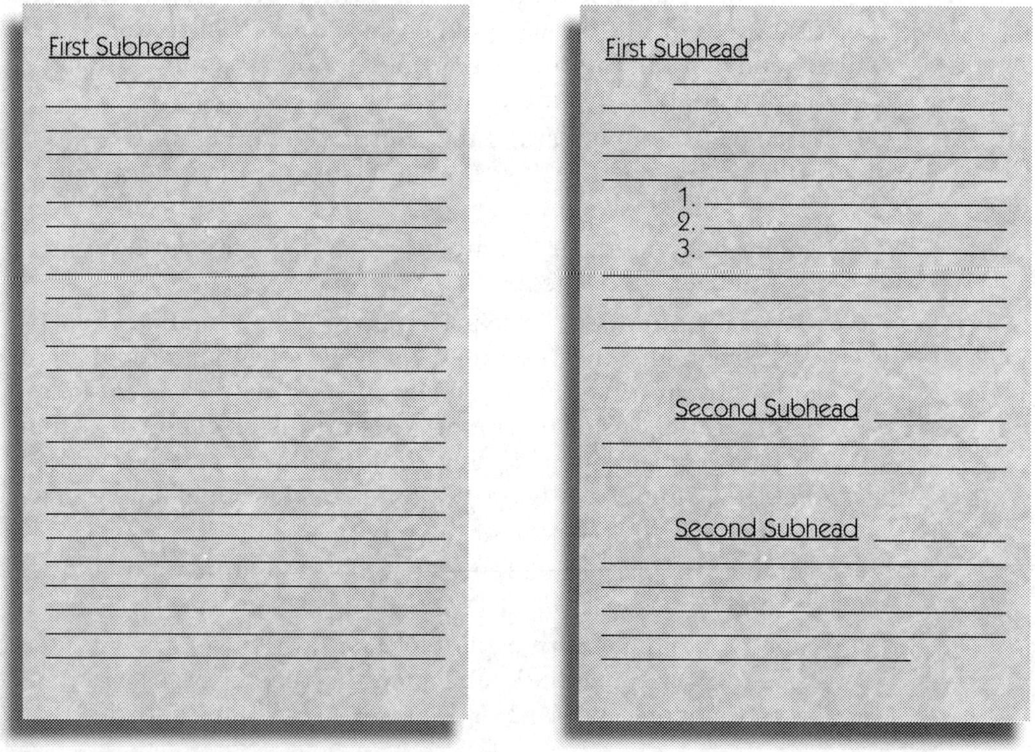

Figure 10.7 *Break the report pages into appropriate paragraphs with headings.*

Photocopying

You may be required to submit more than one copy of a major report to your instructors (in a college course), or to your coworkers (in your business). When you reproduce multiple copies, remember to do the following:

- Prepare a clean copy for photocopying.
- Align the pages correctly on the copier to avoid slanted text.
- Realize that colour used in visual material will show up on copies as black or shades of grey (unless you have access to a colour copier).
- Ensure that all copies look professional. If a machine is not working properly, find another one.

Print

The quality of the typing or printing is a key factor in your report's appearance. To ensure both quality and consistency, remember to do the following:

- Use the same typeface throughout.
- Avoid script type and dot matrix printing. (Both are difficult to read.)
- Use a letter quality, near letter quality, or laser printer for word processing.
- Make sure the typing or printing is clean, free of smudges, and consistently dark throughout. If the type is light, replace your typewriter ribbon or printer cartridge.

Quotations

Directly quoted information or opinions should be integrated smoothly into your text, as follows:

- Incorporate directly quoted material of four or fewer typed lines into a sentence and enclose the quoted words in double quotation marks.
- Indent directly quoted material of more than four lines 10 spaces from the left margin (MLA style); double-space the quotation and omit the quotation marks. Do, however, cite the source. (See "Citations" in this chapter, pp. 271–272.)
- Give credit for directly quoted material, whether incorporated or indented.

INCORPORATED: The result of the merger has been an upsurge in domestic sales as well as, according to M. C. Accordi, "a dramatic increase in potential overseas markets, especially in European cities." (3)

INDENTED: For almost fifty years, a "new" process of generating electricity, magnetohydrodynamics

(MHD) has been in the development stage. Today, because of the interest in space technology programs, MHD's potential is being reexamined. According to one source:

> Magnetohydrodynamics (MHD) can make better use of coal resources and can reduce pollution. When combined with a conventional coal-fired powerplant, it can produce electricity with maximum efficiency (5:17).

Spacing

Unlike those of many novels and short stories, pages of a technical report are not crowded. For easy readability, space the text in your report according to these guidelines:

- Double-space the body of a formal report. Single-space memos and letters.
- Space the text on the page to enhance your report's readability; do not use excessive space simply to give a false impression of length.
- Separate figures and tables from the text by triple-spacing.

Underlining

Do not overuse underlining to emphasize words in a technical document; instead, use precisely chosen words to achieve the same effect. However, there are certain occasions when underlining is appropriate:

- For titles of books, magazines, and long printed works
- For headings
- For an unusual use of a word or for a foreign term

Computer Tips

Desktop publishing (DTP) is an exciting state-of-the-art computer aid for the technical writer. It gives you the ability to format a report and then make changes onscreen. Although mastering DTP's full capabilities requires perseverance, most users find that within a short time they can produce reports with significantly improved visual quality. The brief overview which follows is aimed at encouraging you to examine DTP and try some of its format-enhancing features.

Text Formatting

Text formatting refers to the type fonts used, the size of the print, the use of special effects, and a number of other typographical elements.

Sample type fonts: Times Roman, Helvetica

Sample type sizes: 12-point, 14-point

Sample special effects: *Italic* **boldface**

- This is a round bullet
- This is a square bullet
- This is a dashed bullet

These elements emphasize the various parts of your document. For example, section titles, headings, and subheadings can be set in type fonts and sizes different from the ones used in the body of the report; key words and phrases can be emphasized with italic or boldface; pertinent lists can be presented with attention-getting bullets. DTP gives you significant control over the appearance of the text in your report.

Page Formatting

Page formatting refers to the appearance of the individual page. With DTP, you can easily control the margin settings, the number of columns, the page orientation (vertical, or "portrait"; horizontal, or "landscape"), the headers and footers, and the placement of graphics on a page. DTP is a particularly useful tool when you wish to determine the size or position of a table or a figure. Many of the graphics programs mentioned in Chapter Eight can be easily integrated into your text documents with DTP.

Advantages and Precautions

Among the numerous advantages of DTP are its time-saving efficiency, its ability to improve a document's visual quality, and, some DTP users suggest, the extinction of scissors and paste!

On the other hand, DTP will only improve the *appearance* of your report, not its content. Once you have polished the content, DTP can help you make the final product shine.

QUESTIONS FOR DISCUSSION

1. Why is formatting so important in technical writing?
2. What characteristics distinguish informal and formal reports?
3. What are the advantages of bulleting items?
4. What advice about paragraphing in technical reports would you give to a beginning writer?
5. What advice would you give to a new technical writer about the placement of visual materials?

EXERCISE 1

Find a technical document (ask an instructor, ask at work, ask an administrator or manager) and evaluate it solely on the quality of its formatting. State your comments in an effectively formatted memo to your technical writing instructor.

EXERCISE 2

Read the following short selections. Rewrite and bullet the listed items to emphasize them for readers.

a. Computer operators have at their command several different standard design and documentation techniques. There is the HIPO Method. The Flowcharting, Pseudocode, and Procedure Manuals are also available, as is the Folklore method.

b. Each field of the record structure is specified with a field name; the type of data (character, numeric, or date) needed; the number of characters in width; and, if numeric, the number of decimal places to be displayed.

WRITING ASSIGNMENTS

1. Obtain from your library a copy of an old textbook, magazine, journal, company brochure or report, or catalogue. These could be publications from between 1950 and 1975. Write a short report comparing and contrasting the formatting of the older publication with a similar text from the 1990s. Include aspects such as use of white space, headings, colour, visual materials, and any others which are especially effective or ineffective. In your report, demonstrate effective use of listing or bulleting, paragraphing, headings, and spacing — and, in fact, of all the elements which constitute good formatting.

2. In a short informal report (three to five pages) analyze the formatting of a publication from your college or workplace. You might evaluate the college catalogue, the weekly newsletter, service booklets from the library, the company's monthly bulletin or annual report, or printed statements of company policy on safety, fringe benefits, hiring, or health care. (You may want to review evaluation reports in Chapter Fifteen.) In your report, be sure to demonstrate — as well as discuss — effective formatting.

3. From a magazine, newspaper, or journal, choose a full-page or half-page advertisement. Analyze its format. Then write a brief critique in which you comment on the relationship between content and structure.

Chapter ELEVEN

Technical Style: Writing and Editing

The technical writer's progress from blank page to rough draft is often difficult. Even with plenty of data, with note cards all over your desk, with a reasonably comprehensive outline, and with several free hours, you may find yourself experiencing "writer's block." All your notes must now become a totally new product (perhaps a one-page memo, perhaps a 20-page report), a product with *your* name on it. Hesitation and uncertainty are natural.

Once you have collected your data, the writing process has two different stages: creating and editing. In the creating stage, you concentrate on *writing* — getting content on paper. In the editing stage, you concentrate on *rewriting* — revising the content for clarity, conciseness, and correctness. Although writing is a learned skill, there are different ways to go about it. Some people laboriously pull each word from head to hand; others seem literally to pour their ideas onto the page. *There is no one "correct" way to write.* However, a systematic approach to the process of writing — as presented in this chapter — will help you move through the two stages of the writing process efficiently.

WRITING: STEP-BY-STEP

When you must begin writing but just can't seem to get started, follow these steps and refer to the flowchart in Figure 11.1 for an overview of the process.

Step 1: Assemble Your Notes

In addition to your outline, you probably want to have some of the actual published sources at hand for easy reference. For a long formal report, you may have accumulated dozens of note cards. However, do not let your desk become cluttered, for too many books or magazines may well bury an important source or note card.

Step 2: Review and Sort Your Note Cards

With your outline as a guide, separate your note cards according to the sections of the report in which they belong. Sort first by main headings (all cards relating to I or 1, all those for 2, all for 3, and so forth). Then further subdivide, depending on the number of cards you have and the complexity of the sections.

As you organize the actual material into stacks, you should begin to feel a sense of satisfaction and control. You may also realize that certain stacks are short (limited material), so you may have to do more research. However, do not stop to search for additional information now. That is a stalling tactic. Just work with the information you have at this point.

Step 3: Decide Where to Start

You do not have to start by writing the first sentence that the reader will see. Instead, start with the section you are most interested in or most comfortable with, or the section for which all the material is available. Read the cards for that section. If you find cards with duplicate information, select the most recent source or the most valid authority.

Step 4: Rough Out a Paragraph Based on Your Notes

Start with the main point of the paragraph. The heading of the section should give you the basis of a topic sentence. If you wrote a sentence outline, its entries should likewise give you possible topic sentences. Fill in the details: why, when, what, how, where — whatever supports the main point of the paragraph.

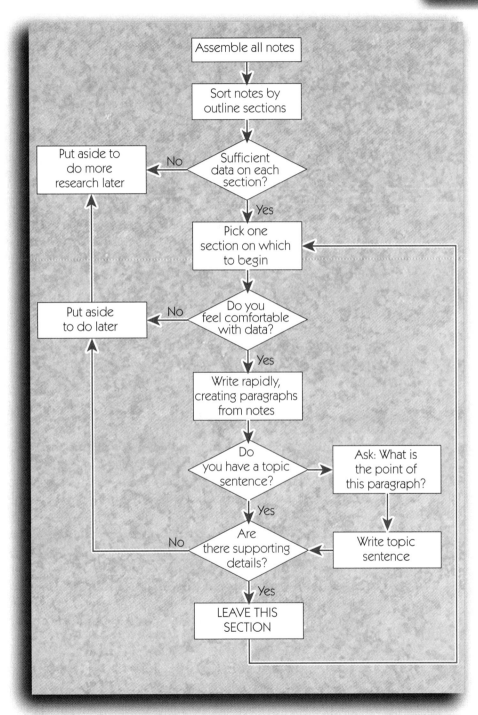

Figure 11.1 *A flowchart shows the writing process: stage 1, creating/writing.*

Step 5: Start Writing

If you're still thinking about the information on your note cards, stop thinking and get something down on paper. Press the keyboard or push your pencil. Put the material down in your own words.

Do not stop to clean up or polish your writing at this point. This is the time to create, not clean. You lose momentum when you pause to fret, erase, look up a word, or worry about subject–verb agreement. Just write.

Use the same five-step approach for all the sections of your outline, but remember to take a break when you're tired. There is no real virtue in working six hours at one sitting. Whether you are working with a computer, a typewriter, or a pencil, the biggest hurdle is getting started. When you treat writing as a manageable step-by-step process, however, you should clear this hurdle much more successfully.

It may also help you to focus on an imagined reader, sitting in front of you, quietly listening to what you have to say. Alternatively, talk to a real audience — a friend, colleague, or instructor. They will be glad to ask you questions to get you started. They may say, "Tell me about what you've done or what you're doing." Write down your replies, and you have your introduction in place.

EDITING: AN ESSENTIAL INGREDIENT

Allow some time to pass (at least a day, if possible) between your first creative efforts and the cleaning-up process. Once you have the content down in rough draft form, you can then work on improving what you've written. When you edit, you must put on a different "hat" and look objectively and critically at your work. You should expect to write several drafts of the entire report (or of different sections) and then revise and edit each one.

A word of advice: Type your report before you begin serious editing. Somehow, as long as it's handwritten, most writers do not view their work objectively. In fact, you will probably be composing your report at a terminal and can see immediately what should be edited.

The editing stage — like the creating stage — can be divided into five steps, although you do not have to follow these steps in sequence:

♦ *Step 1: Edit for clarity.* Check your choice of words. Is each as specific as possible? Does each contribute to content, not merely to cloudy prose? Are all expressions appropriate for formal communication?

◆ *Step 2: Edit for conciseness.* Check each sentence to be sure you have written exactly what you mean and no more. Are your paragraphs free of wordy phrases and clauses?

◆ *Step 3: Edit for coherence.* Check the flow of your ideas. If sentences have two or more points, are they connected with logical transitions? Can the reader follow the logic through each paragraph and the entire report?

◆ *Step 4: Edit for conventions of standard English.* Check your spelling and punctuation. Are pronouns and verbs used correctly? Are sentences complete and properly punctuated?

◆ *Step 5: Edit for consistency and accuracy.* Check all abbreviations, capital letters, and hyphens for consistency. Review your math. Are all numbers (including dates) correct? Have you conformed to expectations of formal usage? In fact, is everything correct? If you are still unsure about any usage after reading this chapter, find a handbook and use it diligently.

In the editing stage, use whatever resources will help: computer software, textbooks and grammar handbooks, and other people. Asking a friend (or classmate) to read your report will really pay off, particularly if he or she is not familiar with the technical aspects of your work. Ask this reader to tell you whether the draft makes sense and to point out any areas that do not. These comments can then help you pinpoint problems with organization, logic, style, or terminology. Also, spelling and punctuation errors that have escaped your spell checker and proofreading are likely to surface for another reader — remember that you are so close to your work that you will often see what you expect to see, and therefore you may not detect simple errors.

You will also benefit from asking a colleague to read your report, particularly if he or she works in your department or studies the same specialty or technology. This reader can tell you whether you have accomplished your technical objectives, used appropriate tone, and presented your information accurately and completely. Your colleague may also check your calculations and graphics.

Having colleagues check reports is a common practice in industry, since successful business depends on exchanging accurate and complete information. For example, some law enforcement agencies employ professional readers to scrutinize police officers' reports for accuracy, tone, and terminology.

If you do ask other people to read through your draft, remember to give them enough time. It is, however, essential that *you* edit your document *first* by completing the five steps.

Step 1: Edit for Clarity

Clarity is the single most important aspect of good technical writing. If your writing is clear, your reader will never have to say "I don't understand. What do you mean?"

The opposite of clarity is cloudiness — vague and general writing that leads to misinterpretation and misunderstanding. Clear writing keeps readers grounded in specifics, not lost in the clouds. Readers need facts, not hazy or imprecise terms, to make decisions. They need to know, not wonder.

As you revise and edit for clarity, keep the following guidelines in mind:

◆ Use concrete words.

◆ Use appropriate verbs.

◆ Use standard expressions.

Use Concrete Terms

Concrete terms are exact enough to create a specific image in your reader's mind. Test the concreteness of a term by asking, "Could my readers draw a picture of this?" For example, most people could draw a "shrub" but they might have difficulty drawing "vegetation"; they could draw a "shovel" or a "box" but would be less sure of "appropriate instrument for digging" or "a packaging container suitable for mailing."

Many times, abstract or general words (those naming a concept, function, or attitude) are necessary. Words such as *potential*, *development*, *personnel*, and *function* can be made perfectly clear if you include concrete examples and terms. For example, the terms in the lists below refer to the same thing (in the writer's mind). At what point will the reader actually "see" the object and activity?

1. Means of transportation
   a. wheeled vehicle
   b. motorized vehicle
   c. cycle
   d. moped

2. Activity
   a. physical exercise
   b. water-based exercise
   c. surfing

Activity 1

Read the following pairs of sentences or phrases. Place a check mark next to the one that is more concrete. Then circle the word(s) that provides specific information.

_____ a. Appropriate attire required.

_____ a. Men must wear coats and ties.

_____ b. Slow.

_____ b. Speed Limit: 50 km/h

_____ c. Low monthly fee.

_____ c. 12.5 percent monthly fee.

_____ d. Bring appropriate identification.

_____ d. Bring your birth certificate, Social Insurance card, and one other piece of identification such as a driver's licence or credit card.

_____ e. Operate this machine at reasonable speeds for short periods.

_____ e. Operate this machine at speeds of 5–8 rpm for periods of less than one hour.

The second sentence or phrase in each pair tells readers exactly what to do or expect. The first contains vague terms which contribute to different interpretations.

Activity 2

For each of the following abstract terms, list four concrete terms. The first one has been completed for you.

Printed material

1. book

2. textbook

3. technical communication textbook

4. *Some Assembly Required: A Complete Guide to Technical Communications*

a. Lending institution

1. _____

2. _____

3. _____

4. _____

b. Communication device

1. _____

2. _____

3. _____

4. _____

c. Personnel

1. _____

2. _____

3. _____

4. _____

d. Obstacle

1. _____

2. _____

3. _____

4. _____

Use Appropriate Verbs

Verbs are key elements in most sentences. Your writing will be more exact if you are consistently aware of the difference between action and linking verbs and between active and passive voice.

For direct and less wordy prose, use action verbs. They show something happening — mental or physical action. Linking verbs (often forms of "to be"), on the other hand, show a static situation: They are followed by words that describe or identify the subject of the sentence. These sentences illustrate the difference:

ACTION VERB: Our local office requires a monthly payment.

LINKING VERB: A requirement of our local office is a monthly payment.

Action verbs produce strong sentences; they have more visual impact. Linking verbs ("to be" verbs, plus their attendant modifiers) produce weak sentences. These examples illustrate the difference:

WEAK/LINKING VERB: The company is in the process of determining the full extent of its responsibilities at the Monroe site.

STRONG/ACTION VERB: The company will determine the full extent of its responsibilities at the Monroe site.

WEAK/LINKING VERB: There are many factors that contribute to good writing.

STRONG/ACTION VERB: Many factors contribute to good writing.

WEAK/LINKING VERB: The solution was under consideration by the supervising engineers.

STRONG/ACTION VERB: Supervising engineers considered the solution.

Notice that the "to be" verb forms are often used as helping verbs — they assist the main verb by indicating time or other conditions.

In addition to checking for active verbs, you should pay attention to the *voice* of your verbs. Use the active or passive voice by choice — not by accident. Choose the verb voice appropriate to the tone and content of the sentence.

In the active voice, the subject of the sentence does the acting. More direct and forceful (and far more common in speech), the active voice is generally a better choice than the passive. In the passive voice, the subject of the sentence is acted upon or receives the action; the actor is either unnamed or included in a prepositional phrase. These sentences show active and passive voice:

ACTIVE: During November, park in Lot A.

PASSIVE: During November, employees' cars should be parked in Lot A.

ACTIVE: Two machines can service the Y-2 lines at 20–45-second cycles.

PASSIVE: The Y-2 lines can be serviced by two machines at 20–45-second cycles.

ACTIVE: Nordane Corporation improved its cash flow by 27 percent in the fourth quarter.

PASSIVE: The cash flow at Nordane Corporation was improved by 27 percent in the fourth quarter.

ACTIVE: Nordane Corporation employees expect an appropriate raise for their efforts.

PASSIVE: An appropriate raise is expected by Nordane Corporation employees for their efforts.

The passive voice is useful when you don't know or don't want to name the doer/actor in the sentence or when you want to soften the message. The following sentences use passive voice appropriately:

EXAMPLE: The company's computer system has been infected. (You don't know the cause.)

EXAMPLE: Your account will be closed unless full payment is received within 10 days. (You do not want to be too direct and forceful.)

Activity 3

Change the passive-voice verbs in the following sentences to active voice:

a. A higher quality is added to the process by the use of machine vision.

_____

_____

b. The image is taken from its memory and is compared to known objects by the computer.

_____

_____

c. The system has been found to be successful by many companies.

_____

_____

d. Lasers that produce a single beam are used by the system.

_____

_____

Change the active-voice verbs in the following sentences to passive voice:

e. The board members re-elected incumbent chairperson Lassiter for a third term.

_____

_____

f. Nordane's Federated Union will deny affiliation to any subsidiary that does not comply with mandated waste treatment guidelines.

_____

Use Standard Expressions

Your choice of words should not distract the reader from the meaning of the content. Be careful to avoid the following pitfalls when you want to write clearly.

Clichés   Also called trite expressions, clichés are phrases so familiar that they require no thought from you or the reader. They have been used so often that they may flow naturally from your fingertips to the paper in certain situations. They may also flow through the reader's mind without leaving any impression.

Check your writing; when you come across phrases you've seen or heard many times before, put them into different, more specific words. Here are a few clichés:

First and foremost
In this day and age
New and improved
When in doubt
Last but not least
At this point in time
Straight from the shoulder/hip
Get to the heart of the matter
Each and every

Colloquialisms   Colloquialisms are informal expressions that are perfectly acceptable in conversations among peers, at the cafeteria or in the hall, but are not acceptable in formal technical documents. They create a conversational (informal) tone. You might say to your supervisor, "We're in a tight spot with this deadline," but in a report you would write, "The company will have difficulty meeting this deadline." In a conversation, the company may be "in A-1 shape," but in a report, the company "meets production schedules and turns a profit."

Notice the differences in the tone of the colloquial expression as compared to the formal version:

COLLOQUIAL: The top brass nixed the decision.
     FORMAL: Top management vetoed the decision.

COLLOQUIAL: The company can squeeze through another quarter
               and play for time.
     FORMAL: The company can survive for another quarter and
               request more time.

COLLOQUIAL: The insurance company plays hardball but comes
               through in a pinch.
     FORMAL: The insurance company requires satisfactory
               accounting but also produces results.

Slang   Like colloquialisms, slang expressions have no place in a formal report. Besides becoming outdated very quickly, their casual tone adds too much informality to a report. A report using terms such as "turkey," "beef up," "brill," "rad," and "shell out" will not receive much respect from current or future readers. (Don't these terms seem dated to you?)

For those of you who are English as a Second Language (ESL) students, distinguishing between acceptable idiomatic language and that which is unacceptable (clichés, colloquialisms, slang) will be a challenge. Your instructors will be able to direct you to books about idioms, and your fellow students, coworkers, and friends will be a constant resource for you. Other resources include your textbooks, scientific and business sections in your newspapers, and radio and television programs on science, technology, and business.

Technical Jargon   Technical jargon is the specialized vocabulary of a profession or particular group of workers. Because it is precise (a kind of professional shorthand), jargon is often useful, expected, and necessary within a group. The problem occurs when the reader is not a member of a specialized group. For example, this product description is probably clear to a reader familiar with plastics technology: "Single-end, zero-catenary fibreglass rovings for filament winding are now available. Designated 660 RO99, the new rovings offer high-burst physical properties for applications such as high-pressure RP pipe." Likewise, an emergency medical technician would have no trouble deciphering this message: "PT DX COPD; CYANOTIC W/PRODUCTIVE COUGH; RX: 2 LPM O @ 28%." Use jargon in a technical report only when you're absolutely certain that your readers — *all* your readers — will understand the specialized language.

Step 2: Edit for Conciseness

Conciseness means that every word counts; anything that can be omitted without loss of clarity should be cut. When you can say all you need to say in 6 pages, don't attempt to pad the information to fill up a 10-page report.

Use these checkpoints to produce a concise report:

◆ Select short, simple words.
◆ Reduce wordy phrases.
◆ Eliminate unnecessary words.

Use Short, Simple Words

When a short and simple word expresses the same thing as a multi-syllabic (a big word for "big") word, choose the short and simple one. Your report will not sound simplistic when you choose to be concise rather than pompous. For example:

Rather Than	Use
Aggregate	Total
Interrogate	Question
Utilize	Use
Demonstrate	Show
Ascertain	Find out
Endeavour	Try
Prioritize	Rank

Of course, experts in every technical field use plenty of big words, and big words may be necessary to express your meaning precisely, but don't toss them in merely to impress the reader.

Activity 4

Find a shorter, simpler word for the following words:

Emanates	_____	Conflagration	_____
Corpulence	_____	Verdant	_____
Proximity	_____	Phraseology	_____
Verisimilitude	_____	Plethora	_____

Reduce Wordy Phrases

Using an excessive number of unnecessary phrases (groups of words) may slow the reading. When possible, reduce prepositional and verb phrases to words. The following list presents some alternatives:

Rather Than	Use
As a whole	All
With reference to	About
In its entirety	Entire
Give consideration to	Consider
In view of the fact that	Because/since
Would appreciate it if	Please
Prior to	Before
Is in operation	Operates
Comes in conflict with	Conflicts with
In spite of	Despite
In order to	To
At this point in time	Now/currently
In the event that	If

Notice in the following sentences how easily wordiness can be reduced without changing the meaning:

WORDY: When a company is engaged in international sales, it typically employs multilingual accountants. (13 words)

LESS WORDY: When engaged in international sales, a company typically employs multilingual accountants. (11 words)

EVEN LESS WORDY: A company engaged in international sales typically employs multilingual accountants. (10 words)

Activity 5

a. Edit this sentence for wordiness: "I would appreciate it if you would give consideration to word choice as a whole prior to sending in a report in its entirety in view of the fact that I am busy."

b. Make the following sentences more concise by editing the wordy phrases (in italic):

1. Birchco *made application* to the city for a building permit.

_____

2. A building permit *involves the necessity of* greater resources.

_____

3. Birchco has limited resources *at the present time; in the event that* its finances improve, a new contract will be issued.

_____

4. Birchco applied *with the object of* building new bus stops.

_____

5. Birchco's plants *are in operation* 24 hours a day.

_____

c. Reduce the following sentences to no more than the number of words indicated in parentheses:

1. The warehouse that was recently purchased by Birchco is in a condition which is structurally unsound. (7)

_____

_____

2. After Birchco made the purchase of Zebedee's warehouse, the company decided that it would sell the land. (10)

_____

_____

Eliminate Unnecessary Words

Learn to recognize words that simply clutter a sentence without adding substance. "Clutter words" weaken meaning and sometimes obscure it. Watch for (1) redundant words, (2) timid, ambiguous openers, (3) introductory "it" and "there" constructions, and (4) weak modifiers. Although you may use any words which come to your mind during the creating stage, during the editing stage you will need to cut any redundant words.

CLUTTERED: We want you to know that we appreciate your help and assistance with our project.
CONCISE: We appreciate your assistance with our project.

CLUTTERED: The project in the province of Quebec which was initiated and begun with the approval of Deschênes's management as well as the employees is expected to terminate and conclude in the month of May.
CONCISE: The project in Quebec, initiated with the approval of Deschênes's management and employees, will conclude in May.

When you are uncertain about the content or style of your writing, you tend to write sentence openers cluttered with weak, ambiguous terms such as the following:

As has been suggested
For the most part
As has been noted
Generally speaking
I would have to say that

Such openers leave the impression of a writer hiding timidly behind vague, nonspecific words or apologizing for an opinion.

In addition, avoid the introductory pronoun "it" when it has no clear referent. Almost always you can be more concise — and emphatic — by putting the main idea into a main clause. In the following "It" sentences, notice that the main point (italicized) is relegated to a subordinate clause:

WORDY/WEAK: It is obvious that *Birchco cannot meet its obligations*.
CONCISE: Birchco cannot meet its obligations.

WORDY/WEAK: It should be remembered that *Birchco defaulted on its debts only two years ago*.
CONCISE: Birchco defaulted on its debts only two years ago.

WORDY/WEAK: It has been demonstrated that *Birchco is financially incapable of managing its subsidiaries*.
CONCISE: Birchco is financially incapable of managing its subsidiaries.

Also avoid sentences beginning with "there." Omit "there" and place the true subject (italicized in the examples below) at the beginning of the sentence, preceding the verb.

WORDY: There were *two meetings* held with Birchco's executives.
CONCISE: Two meetings were held with Birchco's executives.

WORDY: There was a *misunderstanding* between Birchco's tax lawyers and Revenue Canada which resulted in heavy fines.
CONCISE: A misunderstanding between Birchco's tax lawyers and Revenue Canada resulted in heavy fines.

Activity 6

Make these sentences more concise:

a. Regarding the matter of the Deschênes contract, please get in touch with and contact the accounting department for a review and consideration of the estimated anticipated costs.

b. Full remuneration and payment was put in the postal service mail today and should reach your office immediately without delay.

c. Never under any circumstances disengage the monitoring system which monitors the voltage between Number 1 and 2 machines which are numbered as such and are clearly labelled.

d. There were 40 members of the national accounting staff who attended the seminar which was held the morning of May 11 at 10:30 a.m.

e. Here are the brief reports attached which you requested when we met and talked about the construction sites available to Fluharrie's Fast Foods.

Lastly, eliminate weak modifiers that add nothing factual or substantial to a sentence. Use specific words or follow general modifiers with concrete details. Notice the examples below:

POOR: The merger was successful.
BETTER: The merger gave Birchco 47 percent of outstanding
            stock and the Zwicker family controlling interest.

POOR: The new management is efficient.
BETTER: The new management is efficient. In two months, losses
            have been reduced by 35 percent and income has risen
            11 percent.

Step 3: Edit for Coherence

Coherence is the smooth flow of ideas and data. Readers can move rapidly through a coherent report — not plod through it. Appropriate headings, one aid to coherence, are discussed in Chapter Ten. Edit your writing to ensure appropriate transitional words and other transitional devices.

Use Transitions

Transitional words are like highway and street signs: They prepare readers for the next point or for a change in direction.

Transitions indicate that a sentence is continuing the same thought as the previous one or that readers should mentally prepare for a comparison or contrast, a conditional idea, a time or spatial relationship, a result, or an emphasis.

Ideally, when transitions are incorporated smoothly, they are hardly noticeable. Transitions tie thoughts and points together; they do not replace data.

Make sure that transitions are appropriate to the meaning of the sentences they link. A list of typical transitions is shown in Figure 11.2. In addition, notice the following sentences and their transitions:

INAPPROPRIATE: The recent shipment of precast trusses arrived
                with several missing sections, *but* the shipment
                was rain-damaged.

APPROPRIATE: The recent shipment of precast trusses arrived
                with several missing sections; *moreover*, the
                shipment was rain-damaged.

INAPPROPRIATE: The company will reimburse the homeowner for
                costs incurred in repairing electrical circuits.
                Therefore, it will replace outdated plumbing
                fixtures as necessary.

APPROPRIATE: The company will reimburse the homeowner for costs incurred in repairing electrical circuits. *In addition*, it will replace outdated plumbing fixtures as necessary.

TIME
  a year/quarter later
  after/afterwards
  before
  during
  finally
  next
  soon
  subsequently

COMPARISON
  in the same way/manner
  similarly
  in comparison

CONDITION/CONCESSION
  although
  if
  unless
  in the circumstances

ADDITION
  also
  in addition to
  moreover
  furthermore

EXAMPLES/ILLUSTRATION
  for example
  to illustrate
  for instance

SPACE
  above
  beyond
  behind
  directly in front/back
  forward
  to the right/left

CONTRAST
  but
  however
  in contrast
  on the other hand

RESULT
  as a result
  consequently
  therefore
  thus

CONCLUSION
  in conclusion
  in summary
  on the whole
  to summarize

CAUSE
  because
  for that reason
  since

Figure 11.2 *Common transitional words and phrases.*

Activity 7

Fill in the blanks below with the appropriate transitions:

a. Jameson Tool and Die has fulfilled all contractual agreements made by its former CEO; _____, it will not be responsible for contracts made after June 1, 1995, unless they are cosigned by the company's attorney.

b. Jameson Tool and Die has acquired all rights to the patents held by Carl James; _____, it expects to purchase patents currently held by Carlett Industries.

c. Specialty bottling might be a logical next step for the company. _____, Jameson is not planning expansion into the bottling market at this time.

Use Other Transitional Devices

Pronouns, repeated words, and synonyms also aid in coherence.

Within paragraphs, *pronouns* are effective coherence devices. Once specific nouns at the beginning of each paragraph announce the topic, pronouns tie the material together without unnecessary repetition. In the following paragraph, notice how the pronouns (in roman type) help the reader move quickly and smoothly through the material.

> *Computers save school office personnel much time. Computers keep records accurate enough to validate statistics for an auditor.* They *allow entire reports to be edited without retyping all the text before a hard copy is printed.* Their *editing function allows for corrections, additions, deletions, and rearrangement of portions of the text.* They *sort through a database on command to retrieve only the desired data.* They *quickly compile the information into a usable form.* They *can generate a graphic display which allows trends, needs, and problems to be studied in detail.*

In long paragraphs especially, the transitional device of *repeating the topic word* unifies and adds coherence. Notice the repeated topic words in this paragraph:

The next element to be considered is physical growth patterns. *There is a characteristic* human pattern of physical growth *which applies to most of the body; in brief it is a* pattern *in which* growth *is very rapid at the beginning (prenatal, post-natal, and infancy) then slows down during the years from two to six or seven. After this initial slowing down in early childhood, a period of four or five years of smooth, even* growth *occurs. This plateau is followed by a period of more rapid and variable* growth *during the years of puberty.*

If repeating the same word appears monotonous, you can use *synonyms* (words that mean the same thing) as another kind of transitional device to tie the paragraph together. The following paragraph illustrates the use of synonyms:

Computer hardware includes the processor, the monitor, and the keyboard. This basic setup *enables you to operate the* equipment *and to perform all software functions installed on it. To get a hard copy of any output performed on the* system, *you need to add a peripheral printing device to the* basic hardware.

Be careful, however, of using too many synonyms and falling into the trap of "elegant variation." The following passage illustrates the overuse of synonyms:

Mr. Harawitz, CEO of Brooklyn North Software, received the visiting team *from Gould Distributors in his Bedford office. After a short welcoming speech, he took them on a tour of the facility. The* visitors *were most impressed with the labs and the multimedia equipment. The* tourists *were amazed to see the basement room in which the ingenious Harawitz had written his first winning program.* Tour participants *then joined Harawitz for lunch.*

The unnecessary use of synonyms can be misleading and absurd.

Step 4: Edit for Conventions of Standard English

When you edit, be especially careful about correct sentence structure. Readers are quick to notice these three common sentence errors: sentence fragments, comma splices, and run-on (fused) sentences.

Avoid Sentence Fragments

Sentence fragments are pieces of sentences capitalized and punctuated as if they were grammatically complete. They often occur in the creating stage and in the copying stage. Sentence fragments are unacceptable in formal reports. Notice the following italicized examples of fragments.

FRAGMENTED: Place the base against the wall outlet box. *Allowing the screw heads to protrude through the keyhole slots.*

FRAGMENTED: The differences in growth patterns are, however, most noticeable after the period of late childhood. *When the pubertal growth cycle may begin in one child at age 7 or 8 and in another at age 14 or 15.*

Checking for sentence fragments requires close reading. Between each capital letter starting a sentence and the terminal punctuation, be sure each sentence has a clear subject and verb relationship. In particular, two kinds of sentence beginnings tend to create sentence fragments:

◆ Present-participle (verbs ending in "ing") beginnings following a complete sentence (Example: "The cost of the construction site predisposed Cobbett to move elsewhere. *Causing a loss of expected revenue for Murrary County.*")

◆ Subordinate conjunction beginnings (Example: "Murrary voted to solicit the aid of Merchants Marketing Concepts to review its position. *Because it has suffered major loss of service jobs.*")

Read your report slowly, sentence by sentence, to find fragments.

Avoid Comma Splices

Comma splices occur when two independent clauses are connected *only* by a comma. A comma *alone* is not sufficient punctuation to terminate a complete thought.

EXAMPLE: The Environment Canada feasibility study revealed that Beaver Lake could sustain its current wildfowl population indefinitely, it is not contaminated by oil leaks or municipal sewage.

Once you spot a comma splice, you can easily correct it. Revise comma splices in the following ways:

◆ Add a coordinating conjunction (*and, but, or, for, yet, so, nor*) if the conjunction clearly relates the two ideas.

EXAMPLE: "… wildfowl population indefinitely, for it is not …"

◆ Change the comma to a semicolon (a punctuation mark that is strong enough to separate main clauses), or a semicolon with a conjunctive adverb (such as *moreover, consequently, therefore, however*).

EXAMPLE: "... wildfowl population indefinitely; it is not ..."

◆ Connect one clause to the other with a subordinate conjunction such as *because, since, if, after,* or *although*.

EXAMPLE: "... wildfowl population indefinitely because it is not ..."

◆ Change the comma to a period to make two separate sentences.

EXAMPLE: "... wildfowl population indefinitely. It is not ..."

Avoid Run-On or Fused Sentences

The absence of any terminal punctuation between two complete sentences creates run-on (or fused) sentences. This error is easily corrected by adding appropriate end punctuation (a period or a semicolon), using a comma plus a coordinate conjunction, or subordinating one clause to the other. Notice the following example of a run-on sentence and the possible alternatives for editing.

EXAMPLE: The citizens of the Beaver Lake community were dissatisfied with the Environment Canada report they voted to fund a separate investigation.

CORRECTIONS: ... with the Environment Canada report. They voted to ...

... with the Environment Canada report; they voted to ...

... with the Environment Canada report, and they voted to ...

Because the citizens ... with the Environment Canada report, they voted to ...

Activity 8

Edit the following for sentence fragments, comma splices, and run-on sentences:

a. Beaver Lake residents supported an environmental impact study in 1994 the study has been postponed until further notice.

b. The creation of a new multipurpose recreational facility meant destruction of a 60-metre protective hedge. Which, in turn, caused water spilloff following each heavy rain.

c. The newly formed advisory committee has met with local leaders and state congressmen, they have been given no reassurances that money or engineering assistance is forthcoming.

   d. Expecting to gain support from the production of a video showing the dozens of species of wildfowl. The advisory committee has contracted a well-known wildfowl writer to direct the project.

   e. A setup fee of $30,000 is required, after that is paid, production will begin.

Use Commas Constructively

Even if you are familiar with punctuation basics, you may still find the use of commas confusing. This section should clarify for you some uses of the comma, particularly in technical writing. Commas are important to your sentence structure. Used carefully, they enable your reader to understand your ideas. By acting as separators, commas can prevent the collision of words, phrases, and sentences.

Commas separate items in a series of nouns.

EXAMPLE: Compost enriches the soil to make healthier trees, shrubs, flowers, and vegetables.
Note: While the final comma (after *flowers*) was once optional, most handbooks recommend its inclusion to prevent ambiguity.

AMBIGUOUS: Send invitations to Chengapa Industries, Bear Mills Products, Alice Automotive, PK Designs and Superior Drafting Ltd.

CLEAR: Send invitations to Chengapa Industries, Bear Mills Products, Alice Automotive, PK Designs, and Superior Drafting Ltd.

However, do not use a comma between a verb and its object:

WRONG: Applicants should be able to test, characterize, evaluate, and document, new products.

CORRECT: Applicants should be able to test, characterize, evaluate, and document new products.

Commas can also separate a series of adjectives.

EXAMPLE: Erica is a reliable, intelligent, motivated employee.

But do not use a comma to separate adjectives that belong together.

EXAMPLE: The dusty old machine shop

Here the adjectives "dusty" and "old" modify "machine shop" but obviously belong together. Use commas to *clarify*, not to *clutter*.

Commas are also used to separate a series of phrases.

EXAMPLE: Mahmood meets with clients, works on proposals, coordinates projects, and approves designs.

Use commas to set off the items in an address or in dates.

EXAMPLE: Write to me at 42 Grove Crescent, Kingston, Ontario K7K 2Y2. (No comma is used between the province and the postal code.)

EXAMPLE: Please respond by July 1997. (Do not use a comma between month and year.)

EXAMPLE: He left the premises on July 6, 199x, and went abroad. (Use a comma after the date in mid-sentence.)

Use a comma to set off an introductory phrase.

EXAMPLE: Using his experience in project management, Jean completed the assignment on time and within budget.

Use a comma to prevent misreading.

EXAMPLE: While we were checking, the power failed.

Use commas to set off nonrestrictive clauses.

EXAMPLE: Visitors to the site must wear safety clothing, which is available at the security desk. (While the clause "which . . . desk" contains useful information, it does not limit the visitors to the clothing available at the security desk.)

Do not use commas to set off restrictive or limiting clauses.

EXAMPLE: Visitors to the site must wear the safety clothing that is available at the security desk. (Here the clause "that ... desk" restricts the visitors to the clothing at the security desk. They cannot wear their own or obtain safety clothing from another area.)

Activity 9

Use commas where necessary to clarify the following sentences:

a. Qualified applicants should send a detailed résumé to the Personnel Manager Lai Engineering 3233 Falmouth Road Windsor Ontario N8W 4E8.

b. The meeting will be held on Thursday October 14 at the Town Hall.

c. Let's break John before we run the final test.

d. Having carefully retraced the steps in the process Greg eventually found the error.

e. Those of you who are going to the Trade Show should gather in the foyer now.

f. Mike Lo and Sue O'Neill who are going to the Trade Show will meet us in the foyer.

Use Semicolons Appropriately

If it is used appropriately, the semicolon can effectively order the flow of your sentences. You have seen how the semicolon avoids fragments by separating two independent clauses (p. 307). Do not *overuse* the semicolon, but use it to

♦   connect two independent clauses related in meaning

EXAMPLE: He ordered the tests to be conducted immediately; the results were surprising.

♦   precede a transition between two independent clauses

EXAMPLE: He ordered the tests to be conducted immediately; however, the technicians were working on another project.

EXAMPLE: He ordered the tests to be conducted immediately; moreover, he personally supervised the procedures.

♦   control items in a series that contain internal punctuation

EXAMPLE: The following officers were elected to the Board: Paul LaFleur, president; Duncan Watt, vice-president; Laura Ferguson, treasurer; Adam Blinn, secretary; and Roxanne Rogers, Colleen McIntyre, and Lara Redmond, members-at-large. (Note how the semicolons work with the colon and commas to control the structure of this long sentence.)

Use the Colon Powerfully

Used properly, the colon can streamline and strengthen your sentences.

Employ it to

♦   announce information to follow

EXAMPLE: Before starting to design her résumé, Tu Pham considered the following: details of her education and experience, special skills she had acquired during training, and names of people who would give her a reference.

♦   expand or explain a statement

EXAMPLE: We usually get our audio in a digital format: compact discs, laser discs, and soon radio.

♦   show contrast

EXAMPLE: Like forces repel: Unlike forces attract.

Avoid misusing the colon. Do not place a colon between a verb and its objects.

WRONG: He went to the computer show to learn about: innovative multimedia systems, new applications, and software developments.

IMPROVED: He went to the computer show to learn about innovative multimedia ... developments.

IMPROVED: He went to the computer show to learn about the following: innovative multimedia ... developments.

Remember, the colon functions somewhat like the period: It follows a complete thought.

Activity 10

Insert the necessary semicolons, colons, and commas in the following passages:

a. Representatives from the following departments attended the meeting Sales Engineering Customer Service Quality Assurance and Repair and Maintenance.

b. Chris Fielding completed the Emergency Medical Technician Course he is now working in Bridgewater.

c. Our company flourishes through strong employee enthusiasm innovation and commitment to customer satisfaction.

d. Give us the tools we will do the job.

e. Talkers are many listeners are few.

Use Pronouns Correctly

Be careful how you use pronouns in a technical report. First-person pronouns (*I, me, my, mine, we, us, our*) and second-person pronouns (*you, your, yours*) create an informal tone. Although they may be appropriate in letters and memos and in many short informal reports, they should be avoided (or at least limited) in longer formal reports. Unless you are writing instructions, you usually do not need to make any reference to yourself or to the reader in a formal report. Notice the difference that first- and second-person pronouns make in the degree of formality in the following examples:

FORMAL: Observations at Leemore Tracking Station revealed no infractions of safety policies.

INFORMAL: My colleagues and I observed Leemore Tracking Station over a three-day period, and we saw no infractions of safety policies.

FORMAL: Leemore Station will report all trespassers and unauthorized visitors to the appropriate office.

INFORMAL: You can be sure that we will report all trespassers and unauthorized visitors we see here at Leemore Station.

FORMAL: For each possible total number of stocking centres, the minimum total distribution cost for that number of centres is determined and plotted as illustrated in Figure 4. As can be seen in Figure 4, the best overall configuration is six stocking centres. The locations for these centres are shown in Chart 1.

INFORMAL: For each possible total number of stocking centres, we calculated the minimum total distribution cost and plotted that number of centres as illustrated in Figure 4. As you can see, the best overall configuration is six stocking centres. We show these locations in Chart 1.

Although personal pronouns do indeed create a more informal tone, you should not try so hard to avoid them completely that you construct awkward sentences. In the following examples, since the student writers clearly conducted the survey, they should not write about themselves in the third person.

POOR: In October 1994 a dental survey was conducted at Owenby High School by two Dental Hygiene students at Carlyle Technical College. The students interviewed cafeteria and office staff, completed an analysis of health care of forty students, and made recommendations for improving oral hygiene through school programs.

BETTER: In October 1994 we conducted a dental survey at Owenby High School. We interviewed.... (These sentences assume that the report includes a title page with the students' names.)

In addition to their impact on a report's formal or informal tone, pronouns (particularly the third-person singular pronouns — *he, she, him, her, his, hers*) may reflect a sexual bias. To avoid even the appearance of bias, follow these guidelines:

◆ When you know a position is held by a man, use the masculine pronoun; for a position held by a woman, use the feminine. In these sentences, the writer knows that the contractor is a man and the builder is a woman:

EXAMPLE: The contractor called two meetings with the board. He will send the plans within a week.

EXAMPLE: The builder, however, intends to foreclose unless a payment is forthcoming. She has a March 21 deadline.

◆ When you refer to a group that includes both men and women, use a plural term and plural pronouns.

POOR: Each staff member must sign his revised W-2 form before he is paid.

BETTER: All staff members must sign their revised W-2 forms before they are paid.

◆ When you want to refer to the singular form of a noun which could refer to either sex, then use the pronouns *his/her*, *he/she*, *his or her*, or *he or she*. This double form illustrates a lack of bias, but its overuse can create awkward sentences.

POOR: Every engineer should check with his supervisor about current road conditions.

BETTER: Every engineer should check with his or her supervisor about current road conditions.

AWKWARD: Every engineer should check with his or her supervisor if he or she is unsure of his or her assignment.

To avoid the problem of sexism in pronoun reference, use the appropriate gender pronoun when you know it, and use plural constructions the rest of the time.

Activity 11

a. Rewrite the following sentences to avoid unnecessary personal pronouns and to give the sentences a more formal tone. The first one has been done for you.

Our annual sales exceed $22 million with more than 19,000 lines being filled on a daily basis. Our simple line fill rates are 93 percent and we have an average inventory investment of approximately $4.8 million.

Annual sales exceed $22 million with more than 19,000 lines being filled on a daily basis. Simple line fill rates are 93 percent with an average inventory investment of approximately $4.8 million.

1. I found that the Number 7 machine was damaged by the storm which we experienced on November 27.

   _____

   _____

2. Our report concerns the evaluation we (the Safety Committee) made in the three weeks we used the proposed version of safety goggles and gloves at our workstations.

   _____

   _____

3. In my opinion, we (the company) should reveal our position on the disposal of hazardous waste products near our water treatment facility on Sardess Road.

   _____

   _____

b. Revise the following sentences to avoid gender bias in pronoun choices.

1. Each employee at Nordane gets his choice of insurance plans, but he can change plans each fiscal year.

   _____

   _____

2. Any new plant manager at Nordane is expected to complete his probationary period within six months.

   _____

   _____

Step 5: Edit for Consistency and Accuracy

Edit carefully for consistency in your use of abbreviations, capital letters, numbers, and hyphens. Be sure to check all mathematical statements and dates. Although many general rules prevail, you will need to make some decisions based on common sense. Follow this advice for any specific use not covered in this section:

◆ Use the form found in published works in your field.

◆ Use a recent and reputable handbook or dictionary; usage conventions are typically discussed in a separate section or appendix.

◆ Be consistent in whatever choice you make.

Use Abbreviations Correctly

Because technical readers are usually familiar with the topic about which they are reading, they will probably understand the abbreviations. However, you should not abbreviate simply to save space, since excessive abbreviations slow down reading. Here are guidelines for abbreviations:

◆ Abbreviate well-known agencies with all capital letters and no punctuation: RCMP, NASA, CEC, CSIS, CBC.

◆ Spell out less well known abbreviations the first time you use them, then include the abbreviation itself in parentheses. You may then abbreviate all subsequent references.

EXAMPLE: The Canadian Cable Television Association (CCTA) invites nominations for two vacancies on the Board. The CCTA was founded....

◆ For units of measurement, generally use words rather than abbreviations (*centimetres*, *litres*, *millimetres*, or *cubic*, for example). When the same measurement is mentioned several times in a report, place the accepted abbreviation after the word the first time; then use the abbreviation (*cm., l., mm, gal.,* or *cu*) throughout the rest of your report.

◆ Some titles are always abbreviated; others are not. Use the abbreviations *Dr.*, *Mr.*, and *Ms.* when they precede a name, but never abbreviate them when they stand alone. Do not abbreviate position titles such as *Professor*, *President*, *Superintendent*, *Manager*, or *Director*.

Here are some miscellaneous abbreviations; notice that a few are followed by a period, but most are not.

ac	alternating current	m	metre
C.	Celsius	ms.	manuscript
cd	candela	p., pp.	page, pages
dc	direct current	Pa	pascal
Fig.	Figure	psi	pounds per square inch
K	kelvin	RFP	Request for Proposal
km	kilometre	T	tesla

Do not abbreviate the following:

Days of the week	Tuesday — not Tues.
Months	February — not Feb.
Names of streets	Beston Avenue — not Beston Ave.
Cities or provinces	Halifax, Nova Scotia — not H'fax, NS (in addresses the two-letter designation for provinces is correct: Halifax, NS).
Countries	England — not Engl. (some exceptions exist, such as U.S.S.R. and U.K.).
Chapter	Spell the entire word when used in a complete sentence. ("Chapter 10 is long.")
Page	Spell the entire word when used in a sentence. ("The figure on page 10 reproduced poorly.")
Section	Spell the entire word when used in a sentence. ("Section 2 deals with cost.")
Foreign Words	that is — not i.e.
	for example — not e.g.
	and others — not et al.

A Note About SI Units   The International Metric System, or Système International d'Unites (SI), is the standard currently accepted in most industrial nations (except the United States, which uses the imperial system). However, many of your technical textbooks (and even diaries, gardening books, or cookbooks) will contain methods of conversion from customary imperial measures to metric, and vice versa.

Although SI is the accepted system in Canada, some of our industries (for example, construction and horticulture) still use a mixture of SI and the imperial system. If you examine many product data sheets or instruction manuals, you will find that measurements are often given in both metric and imperial. It is important that you use SI, but you should also be able to convert if you are doing business with the United States.

Use Capital Letters Correctly

Use the following checklist for general capitalization guidelines and examples. (For any words not covered below, use a dictionary.) Capitalize the first letter of the following:

◆ The first word of a sentence

Recent market fluctuations affected the grain market.

- The first word of a quotation which is a complete sentence

     According to researchers at Hanley, "The value of animal research has diminished in the past four years."

- The first word in a table entry or a stub or column head
- Trade names (but not common nouns which may follow them)

     Nottingham paper products, Electra mobile telephones, Swingline staples

- The first word and all important words in second- and third-level headings (sections) of reports and outlines

     1. MAIN HEADING

        1.1 Dwellings in Substandard Condition

           1.1.1 Built before Zoning Act

           1.1.2 Built after Zoning Act

        1.2 Rental Units in Substandard Condition

     Unless they are the first words in a title, prepositions (such as *of*, *in*, *to*) and articles (*a*, *an*, *the*) are not capitalized.

- The first word in each item in a list when the list is displayed vertically; do not capitalize the first word when the list is incorporated into a sentence.

     The equipment damaged in Operation Breakthrough included the following:

        One city-owned bulldozer

        One city-owned backloader

        Nine leased heavy-duty chainsaws

        Nine portable fire extinguishers

     The company will replace the following outdated equipment: (1) one 1974 alarm system, (2) three medium-grade electric security carts, (3) twelve manual typewriters, and (4) twelve Somler copiers.

- The words *Figure*, *Section*, *Table*, and *Chapter* when they are followed by a specific number

     See Figure 3 in Chapter 10.

     The figures are cleverly done, and each chapter is well documented.

- Compound words with single-letter prefixes

     T-square, U-turn, I-beam

Use all capital letters for the following:

- Abbreviations of words that would commonly be capitalized

> BCIT (British Columbia Institute of Technology)
> IBEW (International Brotherhood of Electrical Workers)

◆ Computer languages, codes, and equipment panel designations

> Before he learned COBOL, he learned BASIC.
> Check each SETPOINT switch.

◆ The report title and primary headings (section titles)

> SUBSIDIZED HOUSING: WATBOROUGH, ONTARIO
>> 1. DWELLINGS IN ZONE A
>> 2. DWELLINGS IN ZONE B

Use Hyphens Correctly

The use of hyphens varies considerably. Hyphens often divide words that have been created from two or more words, such as *time-saver*, *self-starter*, and *money-maker*. They also indicate breaks in words at the end of a line of type. Use the following guidelines and examples (or refer to an up-to-date dictionary):

◆ Compound words preceding nouns (although they often are not hyphenated when they stand alone)

> The lead chromate–based pigments are not soluble in body fluids.
> The pigments which are chromate based do not dissolve in body fluids.

◆ Prefixed capitalized words

> pan-Pacific, sub-Arctic, trans-Atlantic

◆ Combinations of prefixes and suffixes that could be misread if not hyphenated

> re-creation (not "recreation"), tie-in, un-ionized (not "unionized")

◆ Words beginning with *self* and *ex* (when *ex* means *previously*)

> self-starter, ex-CEO, self-propelling

◆ Fractions used as adjectives (but not when used as nouns)

> two-thirds majority, two thirds of the voters
> one-half cup, one half of the book

◆ Numbers and words used as adjectives

> a 30-hp motor, a 3-inch blade, the 20-litre bottles

◆ Compound numbers between 21 and 99 written as words

> Fifty-four errors were found. More than thirty-five…

◆ Phrasal adjectives preceding a noun

> Our state-of-the-art equipment, a beside-the-press machine

Use Numbers Correctly

Especially in technical writing, numbers must be expressed clearly. As with hyphens, the rules for numbers vary greatly. Use the following quick reference:

For	Use	Such As
Ages	Numerals	a 20-year mortgage
Centuries	Words	the twenty-first century
	Numerals	the 1900s, the 1970s
Consecutive numbers	Numerals and words	buy eight 3-inch dowels 115 two-edged rulers
Fractions	Numerals and words	$\frac{1}{4}$ inch or $\frac{1}{4}$ of a hectare two thirds of the workforce
Pages	Numerals	The answer is on page 26.
Time (specific)	Numerals	2:10 a.m. or 2:10 A.M. 2 a.m. or 2 P.M. (no zeros)
Numbers beginning a sentence	Words	Twelve machine operators quit.
Exact units of measurement	Numerals	10 litres, $47, 31 kilograms, a diameter of 40 centimetres
Less than 10	Words	More than five persons...
10 or more	Numerals	Approximately 15 persons...
Electronic/ electrical uses	Numerals	42 megawatts, 640 volts

Activity 12

Edit the following sentences for errors in abbreviations, hyphens, capitalization, and numbers.

a. The nineteen nineties should produce a two thirds increase in demand for out patient clinics.

b. The soon to be ex president of City manufacturing company intends to complain to the Canadian Manufacturers' Association.

c. Refer to p. 54, figure twelve, in CARLYLE INDUSTRIES: A feasibility study.

d. Doctor Smythe consistently abbrev. words which should not be abbrev., e.g. "Prof." and "Dir."

e. 88 of the trees in downtown Carlyle were damaged in nineteen hundred and eighty nine.

Good editing is an essential ingredient of good report writing. With diligent attention to the five steps discussed here, you can edit your work effectively and turn in perfect reports.

Use the checklist shown in Figure 11.3 for every technical document you create.

CHECKLIST FOR EDITING

Clarity

Are my words

   specific? ❑

   necessary? ❑

   appropriate? ❑

Conciseness

Are my sentences

   concise? ❑

   meaningful? ❑

   economic? ❑

Coherence

Is my message

   clear? ❑

   logical? ❑

   easy to follow? ❑

Conventions of Standard English

Is my writing accurate in the following areas?

   spelling ❑

   punctuation ❑

pronoun–verb agreement ❑

subject–verb agreement ❑

complete sentences ❑

   no fragments ❑

   no run-ons ❑

Consistency and Accuracy

Is my document consistent and accurate in the following areas?

   abbreviations ❑

   capitalization ❑

   hyphens ❑

   numbers ❑

All boxes checked? ❑

Send or submit ❑

Figure 11.3 *A checklist for the writing process: stage 2, editing/rewriting.*

QUESTIONS FOR DISCUSSION

1. After you have gathered your information, how do you begin the writing process?
2. How does the process of writing differ from the process of editing?
3. What are the five steps of the editing process?
4. What are "concrete" terms?
5. Which kind of verbs and which verb voice are typically preferred in technical writing?
6. What three kinds of expressions should you avoid in formal technical writing? Give an example of each.
7. What is meant by conciseness? How is it achieved?
8. What is meant by coherence?
9. What devices should be used to achieve coherence?
10. How are sentence fragments corrected?
11. How are comma splices corrected?
12. What are fused (run-on) sentences and how are they corrected?
13. How do first- and second-person pronouns affect the tone of a technical report?
14. How can you avoid gender bias in a report?
15. How can you determine the conventional use of abbreviations, capitalization, and numbers?

EXERCISE

Practise your editing skills by revising the following writing samples (taken from an accident report) to make them clear and concise. You may also find an occasional grammatical mistake to correct.

a. There has been no failures to date of this machinery since it was installed in 1989.
b. It was reported that in 1992 the motors were modified by Zebulon to conform to federal Occupational Safety and Health regulations.
c. On Friday, October 11, 1989, at about 11:00 a.m. the #17 boiler circulating pump tripped off the unit was immediately shut down.
d. An investigation was made and it was determined that there was water in the stator windings.
e. Temporary repairs that were initiated to achieve full output of the boiler since this was the second pump on this boiler to fail.

f. In view of the fact that the motor assembly was removed from the premises, positive identification of parts could not be established.

g. Sludge or foreign particles could have worn through the liner. Thereby allowing water to enter the stator windings.

h. Generally speaking, the remaining pumps should be dismantled sometime in the future by the appropriate personnel.

i. There was a 14 day period between October 11 and October 25 that the #17 boiler had to be operated at a reduced capacity.

j. The #17 pump has not been dismantled since 1977, this could have contributed to the incident.

WRITING ASSIGNMENTS

1. Apply the editing principles in this chapter to a report or paper which you completed at least two weeks ago.

2. Apply these editing principles to a report you are currently working on.

3. Exchange reports with a colleague and edit each other's work.

4. Proofread two or three sections of a national or local newspaper. Bring your findings to your class for editing.

Part FOUR

WRITING INFORMATIONAL REPORTS

Objectives

When you finish Part Four — Chapters Twelve through Fourteen — you should be able to do the following:

- Recognize the role and characteristics of informational reports in the workplace.
- Write the following types of informational reports:

Progress reports
Project reports
Situation reports
Site visit reports
Process descriptions
Instructions

Progress and Project Reports

Information that is accurate, objective, and timely is the foundation on which many organizations base their business operations. As shown in Figure 12.1, information is also the foundation on which all technical reports are written — information which gives readers the facts they need to operate their businesses effectively.

Managers in all types of organizations — large or small — must stay informed of employees' work activities and major projects. As an effective way of getting this information, most managers depend on progress and project reports (sometimes generically referred to as "status reports"), which may be filed weekly, monthly, quarterly, annually, or at other designated intervals. The following summary lists differences between these two types of reports:

◆ Progress reports

are primarily time-related.

deal with one individual's work efforts.

deal with more than one project.

◆ Project reports

are primarily task-related.

often deal with more than one individual's work efforts.

deal only with the tasks related to one specific project.

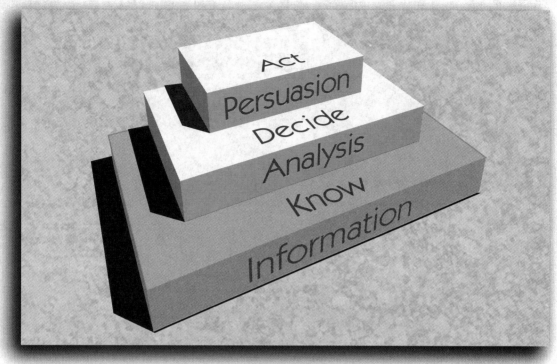

Figure 12.1 *Information provides a solid basis for all technical reports.*

As a computer programmer for ABC Software, for example, you might file a project report on the database software product you are developing along with several coworkers — as well as a progress report on the general status of all your projects.

The following sections present the general types of information expected in each of these reports and their standard formats.

PROGRESS REPORTS

A progress report is a compilation of all your current projects and the specific tasks you undertook during the past week, month, quarter, or year. Most progress reports are written for a specific supervisor and are prepared routinely at regular intervals.

Reasons for Writing Progress Reports

Essentially, progress reports are a method for keeping track of how you spent your time. You could think of them as "Your Week/Month/Quarter/Year in Review," and they are written as much for *your* benefit as for your organization's or supervisor's benefit. Progress reports, in fact, have several important functions:

◆ They document your work volume for review.

◆ They detail your job performance — responsibilities, abilities, and expertise.

◆ They confirm that your assigned work is being prepared for or is in progress.

◆ They demonstrate that your schedule and time management are meeting predetermined deadlines.

◆ They help your supervisor plan work assignments effectively for you and for the department.

Knowing how to prepare concise and informative progress reports is an asset in the workplace. After graduation, you could find yourself in one of the following job situations where you will be expected to write regular progress reports:

Health care: Your head nurse expects you, a caregiver at a small nursing centre for the elderly, to prepare a weekly report that summarizes all the cases you worked on and the major services you performed.

Business and marketing: As a sales representative for a computer hardware firm, you must prepare a monthly report that lists all your business development activities, including follow-up efforts for previous contacts and plans for new sales contacts.

Engineering and science: As a research assistant at a mammal rehabilitation centre, you must prepare quarterly reports that summarize the specific projects that you worked on and your major accomplishments.

Law enforcement: As a security officer at a government building, you must prepare a report at the end of the year that lists, in descending order of importance, the number and type of incidents you encountered during the past year.

In almost every field, writing progress reports is a routine and integral part of the job.

Activity 1

Picture yourself working in a challenging job in your chosen field, review your contact training experience, or consider a project that you are working on for one of your courses. List two reasons in the blanks below for keeping a supervisor regularly informed of your specific job activities. (If you have difficulty imagining this scenario, ask someone working in your field what information needs to be conveyed regularly to his or her supervisor.) Then check the appropriate blank(s) to indicate how often you would expect to routinely write your progress reports.

Reason 1: _____

_____

Reason 2: _____

_____

_____ Weekly   _____ Monthly   _____ Quarterly   _____ Annually

Other (explain): _____

Compare your responses with those of others in your class. No doubt you will see that the reasons and frequencies vary, while the need to inform remains constant.

Content in Progress Reports

Progress reports focus on the work you did this past week, month, quarter, or year. Generally, your audience will want to know the following:

◆ Which projects did you work on?
◆ What progress did you make?
◆ What continuing efforts are you making?
◆ Were any projects completed?
◆ Were there any problems?

Include this basic information in all your progress reports. The length and detail of each point may vary, depending on the form and style of the report. However, one characteristic of a progress report will not vary: the inclusion of *specific* information. Your audience wants to know the specific work done on each project — not such generalities as "I worked on developing new sales contacts. Several persons seem interested." The following kind of information will be far more meaningful to your audience:

I contacted three potential customers for our new thermoplastic resins:

    1. Williams Sports Co. in Bridgewater, Nova Scotia
    2. Midway Manufacturing in Hamilton, Ontario
    3. Superior Sporting Goods in Burnaby, British Columbia

The manufacturing managers at Williams and Superior expressed their need for a strong resin, and I sent them com-

plete marketing information on our new product offerings. I will follow up on these possibilities next week.

When giving information in a progress report, use facts, numbers, names, and titles (whenever possible.) The model outline shown in Figure 12.2 will help you identify the specific information to include in a report. Use this model as a starting point for a report, but don't hesitate to modify it to fit your specific situation or the standards set by your employer.

As shown in the model outline, some additional report components (for example, a table of contents or an executive summary) may be necessary if your supervisor requires a long, formal document. The following briefly indicates what to include in these sections of a progress report. (Chapter Nine discusses the detailed "how to's" of composing each part in a report.)

Table of Contents

Include a table of contents when the report is more than five or six pages long.

Executive Summary

An executive summary is also necessary when the report is longer than five or six pages. Often, quarterly or annual progress reports are more lengthy and formal than reports written at frequent intervals; executive summaries must thus be added to these lengthy reports.

Briefly state your major projects and tasks, the specific activities accomplished during the reporting period, and a general overview of your progress. Be sure to mention that further details are included in the body of the report.

Overview/Introduction

When a short report does not include a formal executive summary, you should provide a brief overview that summarizes your most significant activities during the reporting period.

Write an introduction for long, formal progress reports to identify your major projects and activities and present any necessary background data concerning your projects and activities. Your readers will probably not remember everything that you did last month or last quarter, so you should use the introduction to help reacquaint them with your current projects.

Recommendations

This optional section is necessary when you want to suggest changes regarding your workload. For example, when you need additional resources (personnel, supplies, equipment) to accommodate your

MODEL OUTLINE: PROGRESS REPORTS

Title or Title Page
Table of Contents*
Executive Summary*
1. Introduction/Overview
   1.1 Major projects
   1.2 Summary of significant activities
2. Specific tasks undertaken (use priority or chronological order)
   2.1 Actions initiated or in progress
       2.1.1 Dates initiated
       2.1.2 Interactions with other involved personnel
       2.1.3 Comments on status
   2.2 Projects/activities completed
       2.2.1 Date completed
       2.2.2 Comments on results
   2.3 Activities planned
       2.3.1 Anticipated start dates
       2.3.2 Anticipated problems
       2.3.3 Forecast for completion
3. Recommendations (when appropriate)
   3.1 Scheduling changes needed
   3.2 Personnel/resource changes needed
   3.3 Budget changes needed
4. Conclusion*
   4.1 General status
   4.2 Comments

---

*Indicates parts required for formal reports.

Figure 12.2 *A model outline shows the organization of topics in a progress report.*

current workload, designate *what* you need and *why* in this section. Be sure your rationale and requests are clear to your audience. Be specific about what you need (clerical assistance to help with correspondence, a deadline extension for one of your projects) and why you need it (to ensure that customer follow-up letters are sent promptly, to allow adequate time for a more pressing project).

Conclusion

Include this section when a long, formal report describes many activities and many projects, primarily in quarterly or annual progress reports. The audience will want to know, briefly, the status of your major projects and the general impact of your activities and accomplishments on your job, department, and organization.

Writing Style

Progress reports are essential to effective business management. Write in a direct, plain style, particularly if you need to alert your reader to a problem. For example, maintenance technician Giuma Madi has found that the routine method of checking a receiver system is too time-consuming, and he says so in his weekly progress report to his supervisor. In his conclusion, he writes:

> *This preventive maintenance routine took 20–30 minutes to perform for each service. However, in most cases, there were service disruptions for longer periods because corrective maintenance was needed.*
>
> *Although receiver system checks are a good idea, perhaps someone can suggest a more practical and less disruptive maintenance routine.*

Madi expresses his concern about time management and service disruption in appropriate terms, allowing his supervisor to acknowledge and address a recurring problem that may have important implications for quality assurance and customer satisfaction.

Note, too, how Madi presents the problem. He uses positive terms ("a good idea") but tactfully suggests that there is a better way of proceeding. However, he does not overstep the responsibilities of his position and leaves the important decisions to his supervisor. A competent supervisor would, in this case, invite Madi's input.

Form in Progress Reports

Progress reports can be written in several different forms and styles. They can be written as brief memos or letters, or as longer informal or formal reports. Some companies have their own prepared forms for progress reports. This variety of forms and styles offers you some choices in writing reports (summarized in Table 12.1). Choose a format for your report based on your specific audience, on the amount and detail of information you wish to include, and on any existing policies at your workplace.

Some companies have standardized, preprinted forms or specify a format to be followed. These forms reinforce the need for compre-

TABLE 12.1

GUIDELINES FOR CHOOSING THE APPROPRIATE FORM FOR YOUR PROGRESS REPORTS

Form	Frequency	Audience	Content
Memo or Letter	Frequent intervals (weekly or monthly)	Your immediate supervisor	Brief lists of your projects and activities during the work period. (Limited detail or commentary included.)
Informal Report	Whenever brief comments about tasks performed are required	Your immediate supervisor or upper management	Overview or summary of major projects and activities for the work period. (Report components such as title page and introduction not usually included.)
Formal Report	Quarterly or annually	Upper management	Detailed discussions of your projects and accomplishments. (Report components are included: table of contents, executive summary, etc.)

hensive yet concise reporting. In many job situations, you will be on your own to document your work activities effectively. When this is the case, design your own document using Table 12.1 as a guide.

Order in Progress Reports

Even though the content of all progress reports must relate to a specific reporting period, you have two choices for organizing the details of the tasks that you undertook: priority order (you list your most significant projects and tasks first, then the rest of your activities in descending order) and chronological order (you list the specific tasks you performed in that reporting period in the order that you worked on them).

The method you choose will depend on the nature of your job and on the criteria established by your employer. Employers may prefer a specific order for progress reports; if so, organize the body of your report accordingly. Below are two workplace situations where the writers chose the priority order for very specific reasons:

As an engineer who works on several major projects, Robert Lopez chooses the priority order for his monthly progress reports. He first writes in detail about the work he performed on his major projects, then briefly mentions routine activities (staff meetings, for example). Robert chooses the priority order because he knows that his supervisor is more interested in learning how near to completion his projects are than in what work he did when. Because his reports require a brief commentary on each of his major work assignments, Robert prepares informal reports for his manager.

Nancy Hamawski is manager of the Information Systems Department at Midway Manufacturing in Hamilton, Ontario. Over the past year, her department made great strides in implementing new computer systems throughout the company. Her supervisor, the vice president of operations, has asked her for a report that details the significant progress her department made last year. Nancy chooses the priority order because she knows this progress report will be lengthy, and she wants to mention the department's most significant accomplishments first. Because the report's primary reader is a member of the organization's senior management — and because the document will be lengthy — she prepares a formal report.

Figure 12.3 shows the final report that Nancy presented to her supervisor. Read through the report carefully.

Activity 2

Answer the following questions about the progress report shown in Figure 12.3.

a. In what section of the report are you first made aware of the main points the writer will discuss?

_____

_____

b. What is the purpose of the "Scope" section in the introduction?

_____

_____

c. Where do you find the main sections restated?

_____

d. Where does Nancy "personalize" the report by thanking specific individuals?

_____

e. The writer requests an increased budget of _____ in

order to buy _____ and _____ .

f. These figures are presented in the _____ section.

**THE YEAR
IN REVIEW
19--**

Submitted to:
Albert Ahmeden, Vice President
Operations

Submitted by:
Nancy Hamawski, Manager
Information Systems Department

MIDWAY MANUFACTURING CO.
October 30, 19--

Figure 12.3 *A formal progress report uses priority order to emphasize important milestones.*

TABLE OF CONTENTS

EXECUTIVE SUMMARY 1

I.   INTRODUCTION 2
      Purpose 2
      Scope 2
      Acknowledgments 2

II.   MAJOR ACHIEVEMENTS 2
      Personnel Enhancements 2
      Department Security 3
      Technical Support 3
      Personal Computer Technology 3

III. RECOMMENDATIONS 4
      Equipment 4
      Personnel 4
      Budget 4

IV.   CONCLUSION 4

Figure 12.3 *continued*

EXECUTIVE SUMMARY

The past fiscal year was a period of significant growth and change for the Information Systems (IS) Department. The following paragraphs summarize the major accomplishments of 19--. The main portion of this report includes further details and additional information on each area in this Executive Summary.

Personnel Enhancements

Even though the number of full-time employees did not increase, the work volume and quality grew significantly. A better technical mix of IS personnel made this growth possible. As resignations occurred, replacements with a broader range of experience eliminated any "gaps" in the department. IS now has a full complement of competent technical personnel.

Department Security

We implemented tighter controls to ensure system safety and security. Offsite storage of backup tapes became a routine procedure to protect against loss of valuable data.

Technical Support

Effective and efficient technical support of computer hardware and communications links to all areas within the organization reached optimal levels. The regular addition of hardware and software kept technical support and users on the leading edge of computer technology.

Personal Computer Technology

More than 50 new personal computers were installed throughout user departments at Midway Manufacturing (MM). Many employees took advantage of the employee personal computer purchase plan offered and thus could extend their workdays.

The IS Department worked as a team to accomplish set goals and objectives and to improve systems throughout MM. This report addresses only its major accomplishments.

1

Figure 12.3 *continued*

I. INTRODUCTION

Purpose

This report documents the organizational and departmental advancements of the Information Systems Department during the fiscal year 19--. Major achievements in the areas of personnel, department security, technical support, and personal computer technology are specifically detailed.

While reflecting on the past year, we can see clearly what our goals and objectives must be for the coming year.

Scope

Of the many projects and activities accomplished, this report discusses only the major areas that affect a large part of the organization.

Acknowledgments

The contributions of many individuals were essential to these successes. I wish to applaud the entire IS Department for its competent, high-quality work efforts, but especially the following employees:

- Jane Knockwood, Assistant Director
- Byron Johnson, Security Coordinator
- Jacob Smicer, Support Technician

II. MAJOR ACHIEVEMENTS

The following sections detail the four areas of most significant change in the IS Department.

Personnel Enhancements

The most notable personnel changes in the IS Department were the additions of a PC hardware specialist, a systems analyst, and a technical support specialist. These positions were added without increasing the number of department personnel when the database administrator resigned for a position with another firm, when a computer operator resigned to join a family business, and when a senior programmer retired.

These resignations provided the opportunity to reevaluate the requirements for the changing demands on the IS Department. These new employees have strengthened the quality of support the department can now offer and have fit in well with the department's "team" attitude.

2

Figure 12.3 *continued*

Department Security

In the past, security was one of the weakest areas within the IS Department. We addressed many facets of security during the past fiscal year, including controlled system access, controlled data centre access, and equipment protection.

Working in collaboration with the Internal Audit Department, IS has implemented tighter controls for system access.

Offsite storage (that is separate and apart from the organization's main building facility) of critical backup tapes became a routine procedure.

Security and contingency plans for the data centre are ongoing processes. These measures become even more important as additional systems and multi-accessible computers are added to the organization's computer network. IS continues to work with Internal Audit to ensure a safe and secure environment for the organization's equipment and employees.

Technical Support

Technical Support is a vital part of IS. This area expanded its physical space during the past fiscal year to provide for more effective and efficient support of the computer hardware and communication links to all areas of Midway Manufacturing.

Due to expanding financial and customer files, physical disk space had to be increased. A budgeted disk drive was installed in the first quarter of this year. An additional disk drive was purchased in the fourth quarter. These drives allowed storage expansion of 5 billion characters of information for a current storage capacity of 16 gigabytes (16 billion characters). The disk space is routinely monitored for optimal utilization, and files are condensed regularly.

Personal Computer Technology

Many departments throughout the organization use personal computer technology as a means of better accomplishing their jobs. This technology includes productivity tools such as word processing, spreadsheets, and databases — and timesaving functions like telephone messaging and meeting scheduling.

The IS Department set hardware and software standards during the past fiscal year. These standards allow us to improve the quality of support provided to new users and to troubleshoot effectively.

In the first quarter, a task force was organized to develop a plan to allow Midway employees to purchase personal computers at a discounted rate through payroll deduction. This purchase plan allows some employees to extend their workday, and reinforces the value of personal computers to our employees.

3

Figure 12.3 *continued*

III. RECOMMENDATIONS

The following suggestions will, I believe, help the Information Systems Department work even more effectively in the coming fiscal year.

Equipment

During the coming year, 50 additional personal computers and one additional disk drive will be required to maintain data integrity and ensure increasing employee productivity throughout the organization.

Personnel

Because of the significant increase in users throughout the organization and the anticipated growth of the system, the addition of two hardware technicians and one programmer is mandatory for continued, effective IS operation.

Budget

Additional personal computers and mainframe disk drives will be required. I am requesting a supplement of $30,000 to cover the cost of this necessary equipment.

IV. CONCLUSION

The 19-- fiscal year was a year of significant growth and change for Midway's computing technology. Spearheading this effort, IS has experienced a year of exceptional progress in these areas:

- Personnel
- Department Security
- Technical Support
- Personal Computer Technology

The IS Department worked as a team to accomplish its goals and objectives and to improve systems throughout the organization.

This report has addressed only the major accomplishments. We will continue to maintain excellent computer support and service to Midway as we move into another exciting and prosperous fiscal year.

4

Figure 12.3 *continued*

Even though Nancy's report is lengthy, the specific information you looked for was relatively accessible. Good organization and a good format will help any reader find information easily.

Below is another job situation that could be similar to your own experience. In this case, the writer chose to use chronological order:

> Marjorie Lester works in her company's storeroom facility, where she must keep track of the daily, weekly, or monthly demands on supplies. She chooses the chronological order for her progress reports because this method shows how her workload increases during certain times of the week or month.

Figure 12.4 shows one of Marjorie's weekly progress reports, written as a memo for her supervisor.

If, as a student, you are asked to report on the progress you have made so far toward completing work required for graduation, you might also choose chronological order — as Simon Petitpas did on his progress report. (See Figure 12.5.)

Progress reports are key elements in an organization's success: They relay information that helps the organization plan tasks effectively, and they help employees organize their time efficiently.

PROJECT REPORTS

Some projects in the workplace require a significant amount of work and several months or more to complete. Such major, complex projects may consume most of your work schedule and typically require an initial master plan (or schedule of work). Your employer (or your customer — whoever contracted you to complete the project) will expect regular reports on your progress; the most effective way to communicate this information is to write a project report. When you write a project report you are, in effect, comparing your work performance with the master plan.

Most project reports are written regularly throughout the various phases of a project. Often, a final report that summarizes the major tasks performed and their successful execution will be required when the project is completed.

Reasons for Writing Project Reports

A project report tells interested readers how the work is coming along. Your readers will usually be quite interested in what you have to say. Frequently, they have a financial or other interest in the project, perhaps as a customer who has contacted you directly or as a supervisor who must answer to the customer.

MEMORANDUM

TO: Stella Doiron, Supervisor
FROM: Marjorie Lester, Storeroom Coordinator
DATE: October 3, 19--
SUBJECT: Progress Report for the Week of September 27, 19--

OVERVIEW

A large portion of the week was devoted to reorganizing the control switch storage areas of the warehouse, due to the new control switch product line absorbed recently by our plant from the Moncton facility.

SPECIFIC TASKS UNDERTAKEN

Monday

- Attended weekly departmental staff meeting.
- Answered request from Cell 7 for silastic fluid.
- Filled out purchase orders to refill supplies of O-rings and lubricant for CNC lathes.

Tuesday

- Directed installation of new storage shelves in Area D of the warehouse.
- Began inventory of current control switch (CS) components.

Wednesday

- Completed inventory of CS components.
- Installed new parts numbers to shelves and boxes of CS components.
- Began relocating the CS components that are not in the same series as the Moncton components.

Thursday

- Finished CS component move to new storage area.
- Entered into computer system location and parts numbers of all CS components.

Friday

- Attended meeting on new employee insurance benefits.
- Filled and distributed supply orders for Cells 2 and 4.

Figure 12.4 *In this progress report, the writer uses chronological order to record daily variations in her work activities.*

To: Mr. Sheldon Mercer, Electronics Technology Instructor
From: Simon Petitpas, Student, Electronics Technology 2
Subject: Progress toward graduation
Date: April 25, 19--

In conjunction with Technical Communication 502, I am required to submit a report to you on my progress toward graduation. This report includes work completed, work in progress, and a schedule of work to be completed.

Work Completed: I have completed the contact training requirement and 90 percent of the course work for graduation, maintaining an 88 percent average grade.

My winter work term report was completed and submitted on March 1 to Mr. Alan Thistle, Engineering Department Head, and to Mr. Thomas Abriel, Director of Engineering at Crescent Electronics. A rough draft of the technical report on my major project, "Designing a Force Measurement System for a Sailboat Application," is ready for revision.

I have been employed as a tutor and clerk for the College's Write Program since September, and I have worked for the Extension Department two evenings per week. In November, I was a volunteer worker for the Quality Forum hosted by the local chapter of ASQC (the American Society of Quality Control) at the World Trade and Convention Centre.

Work in Progress: I am currently
- editing the body of my technical report and constructing materials required for the front matter and figures.
- preparing my project for demonstration at the College Showcase on May 20.
- finishing a power supply for Mr. O'Hara.
- studying for finals in Industrial Control Systems, Microwave Techniques, and Mathematics.
- preparing a team presentation (a Powerpoint slideshow) with Craig Russell on "Entrepreneurship and Technology."
- preparing targeted résumés for nine electronics firms (three in province, six out of province).

Schedule: I will
- complete my technical report and project demonstration material by May 15, 19--.
- give the "Entrepreneurship and Technology" presentation to instructors, colleagues, and guests in the College lecture Theatre on May 10.
- present my project at Showcase on May 20.

My curriculum requirements will be met by June 2 when I write finals.

I expect to graduate with a Diploma In Electronics Engineering Technology (June 12, 19--).

Conclusion: There have been no problems in completing my work for graduation.

Figure 12.5 *This report arranges items chronologically to show progress made to date.*
Adapted with permission of Simon P. Petitpas, Electronics Engineering Technology Graduate.

Project reports (like progress reports) benefit you (the project specialist, project member, or project leader) as well as your audience:

◆ They document the project tasks you have performed to date and they forecast what will happen next.

◆ They detail your performance by showing your supervisor or customer the significant milestones and progress you are making on the project.

◆ They assure your readers that the project is being worked on and that the tasks are being accomplished.

◆ They demonstrate that you have organized your time to meet a predetermined schedule.

◆ They enable you to request any necessary adjustments as soon as possible.

Depending on your specific job title and the nature of the work, you may be required to write several reports during a major project: an initial project report at three months, an interim report at six months, and a final report at completion, for example.

Content in Project Reports

Project reports focus on the work done during the specific report period and on the work that still needs to be done to complete the project. Generally, the audience wants to know:

◆ Is the project on schedule and within budget?

◆ Which tasks were accomplished?

◆ What work is currently being done?

◆ How much work is yet to be done?

◆ Are there any anticipated problems or delays?

Readers expect this basic information to be included in the body of all your project reports, whether you write them in memo, letter, or informal or formal report form. As discussed in the "Writing Style" section below, they also expect *specific* information — numbers, percentages, dates, and names.

The model outline shown in Figure 12.6 will help you organize the specific information to include in a project report. As always, you may modify the model to suit a specific project and audience. (See Chapter Nine for a detailed discussion of any additional components such as the table of contents, executive summary, and introduction.)

MODEL OUTLINE: PROJECT REPORTS

Title or Title Page
Table of Contents*
Executive Summary*
1. Introduction/Overview
    1.1 Project and objectives
    1.2 Summary of current status and work completed
2. Work completed during this project phase
    2.1 Tasks
    2.2 Dates
    2.3 Comments on results
3. Work in progress
    3.1 Tasks
    3.2 Dates
    3.3 Comments on status
4. Work left to do
    4.1 Tasks
    4.2 Anticipated completion
5. Anticipated problems
6. Forecast for completion
7. Recommendations*
    7.1 Scheduling changes needed
    7.2 Personnel/resource changes needed
    7.3 Budget changes needed
8. Conclusion*
    8.1 Current schedule
    8.2 Current budget

---

*Indicates parts required for formal reports.

Figure 12.6 *Effective project reports include the areas listed on this model outline.*

Writing Style

Project reports document stages of a project from start to completion and require *specific* information on scheduling, budget, and any problems that cause delay. Specific terms and clear, coherent sentence structure are essential.

POOR: Terrible weather has put the project behind schedule somewhat, and this will be expensive.

IMPROVED: Heavy rains from Hurricane Bertha have delayed project completion by two days. August 1 is now the estimated completion date. Budget overrun is estimated at $5,000.

Giving specific information means including numbers, percentages, dates, and names. Generalities ("The work should be done soon") not only give the audience vague information, but they could undermine the confidence that supervisors/customers have in you. They may think that you are reluctant to provide specifics because there are problems — or because you are not in control of the project. Pertinent and specific information allays these fears and confirms that the project is being worked on competently.

Form in Project Reports

Project reports (like progress reports) can be written as brief memos or letters, short informal reports, or long formal reports. Table 12.2 lists some general guidelines for selecting the form and style of your various project reports.

TABLE 12.2

GUIDELINES FOR CHOOSING THE APPROPRIATE FORM FOR YOUR PROJECT REPORTS

Form	Frequency	Audience	Content
Memo or Letter	Frequent intervals (weekly or monthly)	Your immediate supervisor or your customer	Brief lists of the tasks accomplished during the work period and any associated costs. (Limited comments included.)
Informal Report	Whenever some discussion of the project and tasks undertaken during the work period is required	Your supervisor or your customer	Overview of the current status of the project. (Normally, formal report components are not required.)
Formal Report	At the completion of a major project	Upper management or your customer's management	Detailed discussions of work completed and undertaken, any problems encountered, and the general outcome of the project. (Formal report components and headings included.)

On different occasions you will probably use all three forms for project reports in the workplace. The length and formality of these reports may vary as your projects near completion. Since each form serves a different informational purpose, choose a form based on the complexity of the project, the amount of information you need to communicate, and the expectations of your audience. (Remember your audience analysis in Chapter Four.)

Order in Project Reports

Even though most project reports are related to a specific work period, they all focus on the work — or tasks — involved with the project. Therefore, the most effective order for project reports is task-related. As shown in Figure 12.7, the tasks involved in a project may be arranged in one of two ways:

◆ By the status of the work (work completed, work in progress, work remaining)

◆ By the individual task (task 1, task 2, task 3, etc.)

STATUS ORDER
2. Work completed
(Task 1, Task 2, Task 3, etc.)
3. Work in progress
(Task 1, Task 2, Task 3, etc.)
4. Work left to do
(Task 1, Task 2, Task 3, etc.)

TASK ORDER
2. Task 1
(Work completed, work in progress, work left to do)
3. Task 2
(Work completed, work in progress, work left to do)
4. Task 3
(Work completed, work in progress, work left to do)

Figure 12.7 *Two ways of ordering project reports: by status or by task.*

Either arrangement is acceptable; choose between these orders by considering the complexity of the tasks involved in the specific project. For example, you might choose the order shown in the model outline (status order) when the tasks are not complex and can be accomplished in one or two steps. (Status order in an informal project report is shown in Chapter Three, Figure 3.4.)

The other choice for ordering information in a project report is task order. This method is preferable when the individual tasks are fairly complex, and each involves several steps before completion. In the workplace, a project similar to the one described below would require a report arranged in task order:

> John Oster works for A&J Agricultural Solutions, a company that evaluates and solves crop and livestock problems for private farmers and ranchers. John is the leader for a large project that A&J undertook a month ago. The customer, Westvale Cattle Company, wants to know how much work John has accomplished so far and whether everything is going according to schedule.

Figure 12.8 shows the project report, written in letter form, that John sent to his customer. Since each task involved a number of complex steps, John used task order to assure his customer that the project was going well.

Project reports are an important part of business operations. Your audience's main concern is the successful completion of the project. If a situation develops to jeopardize the project, your project report becomes an effective vehicle for communicating the problems and solving them. (Of course, it is equally important to be straightforward and realistic when relaying specific information in your reports.)

Whether you write about a scientific research project, a building construction project, a software development project, or a project to implement new methods of pest control, the information you include in your project report will help your organization — or your customer — make important decisions.

Activity 3

Choose two projects that you are involved with at school (writing a term paper, completing an experiment) or at home (building a bookcase, redecorating or remodelling a room). In the blanks below labelled "Project," briefly describe each project. Then, in the following skeleton outlines, show how you might write about one project

AGRICULTURAL SOLUTIONS
A & J

June 12, 19--

Mr. Kenneth Houseman
Westvale Valley Cattle Company
1220 Longridge
Westvale   AB   T7X 3V5

Dear Mr. Houseman:

The following information on the project to control pests (poisonous plants and insects) in your cattle-grazing land and your herd documents the progress being made. Overall, the work is going well; it is on schedule and well within the costs estimated at the onset of this project.

TASK 1: Eliminating current and preventing future growth of poisonous ragwort plants.

<u>Work Completed</u>

The purchase order has been sent to the Saskatchewan Centre for Agricultural Development for 1,000 Cinnabar moths, which will help control future plant growth. The order is due to be received on July 1.

<u>Work in Progress</u>

Sixteen acres of grazing land are being cleared of current plant growth. This acreage is now safe for cattle grazing.

<u>Work Left to Do</u>

Fourteen additional acres need to be cleared of ragwort. Anticipated completion is August 1.

Figure 12.8 *This letter documents the status of a project for a customer.*

Mr. Houseman
-2-
June 12, 19--

TASK 2: Installing sensing devices on a 50 percent sampling of cattle to detect insect infestation.

<u>Work Completed</u>

Electronic sensors have been attached to 22 percent of the herd to date.

<u>Work in Progress</u>

The remaining 28 percent of the sampling herd is currently being fitted with sensors.

<u>Work Left to Do</u>

After all sensors have been attached to the herd, we will install monitors in Roy Hensen's office to detect insect swarms. Anticipated completion is August 25.

ANTICIPATED PROBLEMS: We anticipate no problems at this time. However, the timely (August 1) delivery of the sensing monitors is critical to successfully completing this project.

FORECAST FOR COMPLETION: August 30

If you have any questions on the current status of the project, do not hesitate to call me.

Sincerely,

John Oster
Project Leader

Figure 12.8 *continued*

using *status order* and how you might write about the other project using *task order*.

Project: _____   Project: _____

_____   _____

Status Order   Task Order

Work completed: _____   Task 1: _____

_____   _____

_____   _____

_____   _____

Work in progress: _____   Task 2: _____

_____   _____

_____   _____

Work left to do: _____   Task 3: _____

_____   _____

_____   _____

_____   _____

Did you choose the order for each project by first considering the complexity of the tasks involved? Since the complexity of your projects will vary in the workplace, you should order your project reports accordingly.

QUESTIONS FOR DISCUSSION

1. What are the main differences between progress reports and project reports?
2. Why do progress reports contribute to workplace operations?
3. Which questions do audiences want answered in progress reports?

4. Which factors help determine the order of information included in progress reports?

5. When would you most likely be required to provide project reports for an employer or for a customer?

6. What is the focus of project reports and what do readers want to know?

7. What are the two ways of ordering the information in project reports, and how would you decide which to use?

EXERCISE

Read the brief work situation described below. Some key terms discussed in this chapter are listed, and following them are definitions, situations, or descriptions. Match this material by number to the term it most closely fits.

> Lindstrom Construction Company, of which Burnside Lindstrom is a local branch, has been contracted to construct a two-mile fitness trail at Burnside's Industrial Park. The construction of the trail, along with more than 50 fitness stations, is expected to take three months.

1. Progress report
2. Project report
3. Memo form
4. Letter form
5. Informal report
6. Priority order (progress report)
7. Chronological order (progress report)
8. Executive summary
9. Introduction (formal progress report)
10. Task order (project report)

_____ a. Each week the three crew chiefs send a brief review of their work to Mr. Ferguson, Burnside Lindstrom's Managing Director, detailing what each crew has accomplished that week.

_____ b. The crew chiefs use this form:

TO: Mr. Bill Ferguson, Managing Director
FROM: Lorenz Crawford, Crew Chief
SUBJECT: Burnside Industrial Park Trail: July 1–7, 19--
DATE: July 7, 19--

_____ c. The crew chiefs list the work their crews completed on each workday. Mr. Ferguson prefers to see a five-part report based on their five-day week.

_____ d. Mr. Ferguson compiles the weekly reports and every 21 days sends a report to the head office. This report summarizes the status of the overall work during that time. The report is usually between four and five pages long.

_____ e. For any construction job which extends beyond the fiscal year, Mr. Ferguson sends a report to the head office which details the major accomplishments up to that point. This report contains his forecast for completing the job and recommendations for budgeting the following year.

_____ f. On one page, Mr. Ferguson highlights the accomplishments of Burnside Lindstrom during the past year; this is the one section of his report which he is sure Mr. Noel Julian, the chief executive officer, will read.

_____ g. As the fitness trail nears completion, Mr. Ferguson sends a project report to the Burnside Industrial Park management; in this report he lists what has been done and what remains to be completed before the grand opening of the trail: railings at steep sections, caution signs and crosswalks, painting of all signs.

_____ h. At one point in the fitness trail project, Mr. Ferguson finds it necessary to report to the employees at the industrial park on the status of the construction. He uses this form:

Ms. Vicki Moriarty
Director Employee Health Club
Burnside Industrial Park
Burnside, NB E2M 5P9

Dear Ms. Moriarty:

_____ i. Twice yearly, Mr. Ferguson must send a formal report to Burnside's vice president of operations. At the beginning of this report, he includes a brief overview of his activities, emphasizing the major projects for which he is responsible.

_____ j. When Burnside Lindstrom's crew chiefs are supervising several projects (as is often the case), Mr. Ferguson requires monthly reports in which they document those jobs which have taken up most of their time.

WRITING ASSIGNMENTS

1. Write an informal progress report (250 to 500 words) for your instructor, describing what you have accomplished so far in your technical writing course. Discuss your activities and accomplishments in terms of what you now know about writing technical reports — the different categories and specific kinds of technical reports, the methods for gathering and documenting information — and the various writing assignments you have done so far. Write your report in either chronological or priority order.

2. Write a one-page letter or memo report to your technical advisor or instructor describing the progress you have made so far on your major technical project.

3. Since you have already developed two partial outlines in Activity 3, continue the process and write a formal project report (at least five pages in length) for your technical writing instructor on one of the outlined projects.

5. Write a project report in letter form (one to two pages) to your technical writing instructor on the status of one of your class assignments.

6. Investigate any ongoing project at your college or workplace — preferably one in which you are involved. Select the order you think is most appropriate, and write a formal project report (five pages or more) detailing the activities to date, the past successes and failures, any anticipated problems, and a forecast for completion. You might consider the following projects:

   ◆ Organizing a showcase, open house, or quality forum
   ◆ Recycling efforts for paper, glass, aluminum
   ◆ Blood donor clinics
   ◆ Cleanup or antilitter campaigns
   ◆ Car pooling
   ◆ Promoting the cafeteria
   ◆ Food Bank or other community activities

THIRTEEN
Chapter

Situation and Site Visit Reports

I nformation is a valuable commodity in the workplace. Organizations that gain and manage pertinent information also gain a competitive edge. Realizing this, many organizations require their employees to report routinely on all incidents, situations, or conditions that may affect business operations. They also require employees who visit other sites (such visits are sometimes referred to as "field trips") to report — in detail — on what they did or observed. These situation and site visit reports provide the organization's decision makers with firsthand information.

Vivid and accurate descriptions are an important part of these reports. The writer's objectivity is also essential to ensure that these informative reports are effective.

SITUATION REPORTS

A situation report documents an event that occurred in the workplace — an event that affects or could potentially affect business operations. Situation reports (also referred to as incident reports, accident reports, or occurrence reports) are a mandatory part of the job.

Reasons for Writing Situation Reports

Essentially, a situation report documents an occurrence such as an accident, malfunctioning or inoperative equipment, a deviation from normal procedures, a variance in expected actions or responses, or the loss or theft of an item. Effective informational vehicles for organizations, as well as for yourself, situation reports function in these ways:

♦ They document the circumstances of an unusual event so that supervisors can take precautions to prevent a similar occurrence.

♦ They serve as a permanent record to refer to if a question ever arises about any detail of the incident.

♦ They provide valuable statistics on the reliability of machinery or on the safety of work conditions.

♦ They help protect employees and organizations from possible liabilities.

As you can see from these functions, writing clear, precise situation reports is extremely important, as they describe incidents to people who were not present and who have to rely on the document for decision and action.

In most jobs, you can expect to write detailed reports explaining any event that may raise questions about causes, effects, or consequences. Persons working in fields like those described below write situation reports frequently:

Health care: Caregivers of all levels (at hospitals, medical centres, or facilities for the aged or physically impaired) must document incidents that involve patients and visitors.

Engineering technology: Engineers and technicians involved in any type of manufacturing or machine-related environment often must use their technical knowledge to describe accidents that affect employees or conditions that affect equipment and production.

Law enforcement: Persons involved with security or criminal justice must document the details of any occurrence that requires their assistance or attention.

As an informational (and sometimes legal) aid to effective business operations, situation reports are an important part of the workplace.

Content in Situation Reports

Situation reports focus primarily on the facts: the who, when, what, where, and why or how of the event. Whatever the specifics of the situation, your audience wants only objective and factual information.

Writing Style

The content in most situation reports is presented primarily as a narrative — a discussion and a description, in as much detail as possible, of exactly what happened. Since your main objective is to include just the facts, you should write narratives that are crisp, to the point, and, above all else, totally objective. Avoid words that may convey your personal reactions to a situation or that may evoke an emotional response from the reader. Use facts, not feelings, when writing descriptions:

◆ *Tall* is feeling; *6 feet 2 inches* is fact.
◆ *An oily mess* is feeling; *a quart of spilled lubricant* is fact.
◆ *Hardly noticeable* is feeling; *one millimetre* is fact.

You can write situation reports objectively and still include descriptive words. Use adjectives and adverbs whenever possible; however, select these words carefully to ensure that they state facts — not personal feelings.

Activity 1

Read the brief description below of an incident that occurred at a health-care facility in Timmins, Ontario, and fill in the blanks that follow.

> *The patient, Daniel Wiggins, was admitted to the hospital because of complications resulting from diabetes. (He is on a 1,500 calorie CDA diet.) The patient, who has complained since he got here about everything and who never pays any attention to the nurses' instructions, once again refused to follow medical advice. On July 2 at approximately 2:45 p.m., he sneaked off the floor and went to the hospital's*

cafeteria where he bought an egg salad sandwich, a huge piece of chocolate cake, and a cola. When Dr. Winters saw the patient hiding in the back of the cafeteria, eating the food as fast as he could, she asked him if he was aware of his restricted diet. The patient snapped, "Yeah, and I don't care."

a. Do you get a definite impression of how the writer feels about the patient or the incident?

_____ Yes _____ No _____ Not sure

b. Do you think this situation report contains more than just the facts?

_____ Yes _____ No _____ Not sure

c. List at least five words or phrases which seem inappropriate for a totally objective description.

_____

_____

_____

_____

_____

While this brief description contains adequate details concerning the incident, it goes beyond (far beyond!) the boundaries of objective writing. The writer has charged the description emotionally, so that the report no longer states just the facts.

Readers expect facts in response to questions like these:

- What was the situation?
- Who (if anyone) was involved?
- When did the situation happen?
- Where did it happen?
- What exactly happened?
- Why did the situation happen (how was it caused)?
- What was done by responsible personnel?
- What were the consequences?

Include the answers to these questions in the body of all situation reports; the length and detail will vary depending on the complexity of the situation being described.

When you relate this information to the persons who need first-hand observations or experiences, refer to the model outline presented in Figure 13.1. This model includes all sections required for a lengthy situation report and will serve as a helpful guide for the basic content. (Section numbers are optional.) You may modify this model outline as each particular situation merits. The following paragraphs describe briefly each section listed on the model. Refer to Chapter Nine for more details about the "how to's" of writing effective report parts.

MODEL OUTLINE: SITUATION REPORTS

Title or Title Page
Table of Contents*
Executive Summary*
1. Background/Summary
    1.1 Situation or event
    1.2 Relevant conditions prior or leading to situation
    1.3 Summary of effects
2. Discussion/Description
    2.1 Who or what was involved
    2.2 When and where the event took place
    2.3 Causes
    2.4 Details of what happened
    2.5 What was done in response to the event
3. Outcome/Effects
    3.1 Resulting injuries
    3.2 Resulting impact on continuing business operations
4. Conclusion
    4.1 Suggestions for follow-up actions
    4.2 Other persons/departments who were (or need to be) informed

---

*Indicates parts required for formal reports.

Figure 13.1 *This model outline lists the areas covered in effective situation reports.*

Table of Contents

You need a table of contents to guide your audience through reports of more than five or six pages. The table of contents lists the report's parts and subsections so your readers can see at a glance the material that you cover.

Executive Summary

An executive summary is also required if your report is longer than five or six pages. Usually reports of this length are situation reports that deal with major incidents or conditions that significantly affect many people or overall business operations. Include only brief statements concerning the who, what, where, when, why, and how of the situation. (Include details in the body of the report.)

Background/Summary

This section sets the scene for the audience. Include any relevant information that helps familiarize the audience with the onset of the situation. Summarize, in a sentence or two, the effects or outcome of the situation. (See the sample reports included later in this chapter for ideas about the type of information to include.) If your report includes an executive summary, you may omit this section.

You will notice that the *background* needed here is brief; that is why it is considered a summary statement. Do not confuse it with the background information required in a longer formal report such as a feasibility report. If you look at Section 2 of the report shown in Figure 15.6, you will see the heading *Overview/Background*. The background information in this instance needs to be more substantial for the reader to understand the situation.

Discussion/Description

This part in a situation report includes the important details of the event. Be specific and descriptive. Identify people by name, identify equipment or vehicles, and give exact locations. Include specific times for the hour, minute, and date of the event, as well as for its duration. Use numbers whenever possible to describe relevant measurements, times, and quantities. Include step-by-step details of any actions that took place before, during, or after the event. Help the readers "see" the situation for themselves.

Outcome/Effects

This important part in a situation report describes the impact of the event. Again, specific details are essential. Readers want to know the extent or seriousness of any injuries or damages that occurred, as well as any continuing effects or consequences. If no significant or continuing effects are likely, state that as well.

Conclusion

If you think or know that your audience will want them, include suggestions for appropriate follow-up actions to be taken. (Refer to your audience analysis in Chapter Four.) If this information is appropriate (if you have been asked to present evaluations or analyses as well as the facts), remember to provide specific actions or measures, detailed with as much information as possible. Broad sweeping solutions are of little value to readers. You may also identify any other persons or departments that may be affected by the event and state whether you will notify or have already notified them — or whether your readers should notify them.

Form in Situation Reports

Situation reports can be written in memo, letter, or informal report form. They may also be written in a standard form that an organization has developed for this specific purpose. Situation reports are seldom prepared as formal reports.

After graduation, you may work for an organization that requires a standard form similar to the illustration shown in Figure 13.2. In this case, your task will involve little more than understanding the terminology and marking the appropriate choices on the standard form. In other cases, a standard form will look similar to the one shown in Figure 13.3, which requires that several descriptive and narrative paragraphs be written.

Most often, however, you will be on your own to write effective situation reports. Table 13.1 presents some brief guidelines to help you select the appropriate form for each report you write.

For your situation report, choose a form based on the circumstances of the event, the quantity and detail required, the audience, and any criteria established by your employer.

Order in Situation Reports

The most effective choice for ordering the narrative section of a situation report is chronological order — presenting the information in the exact sequence in which it occurred. Your audience will understand the situation better when you describe chronologically what happened first, second, third, next, and so forth.

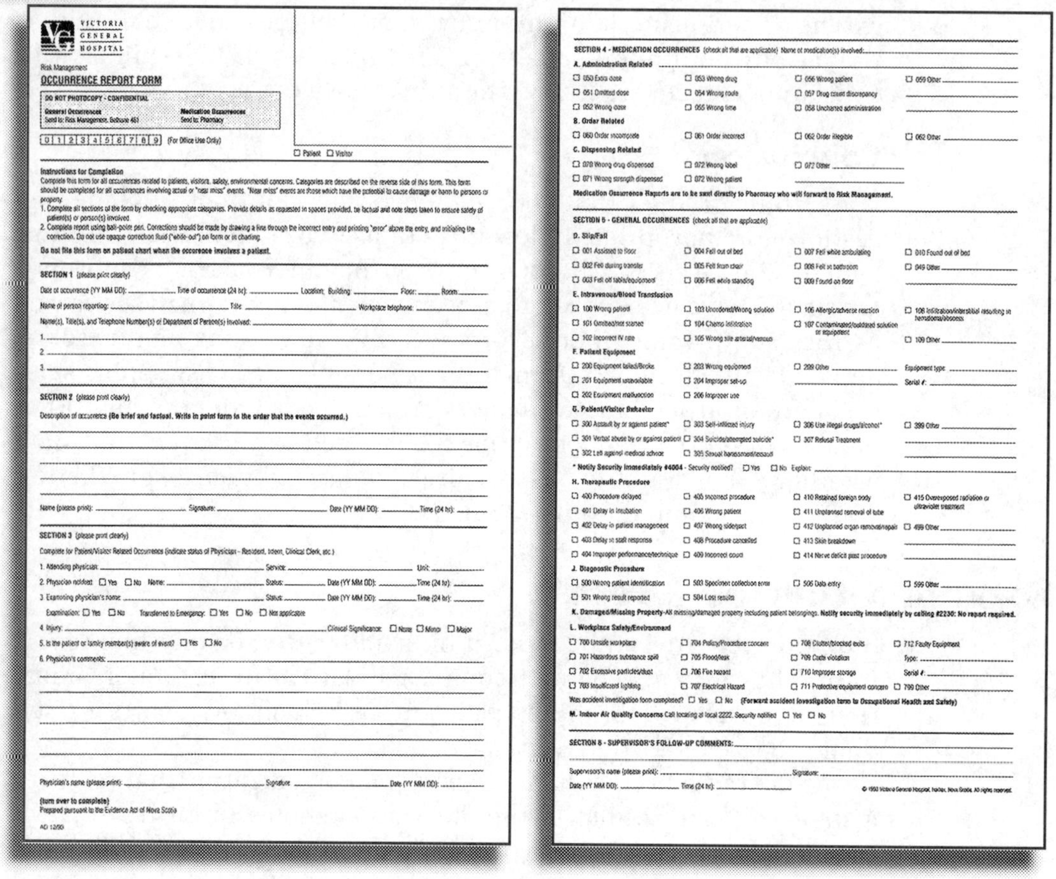

VICTORIA GENERAL HOSPITAL

Risk Management

OCCURRENCE REPORT FORM

DO NOT PHOTOCOPY - CONFIDENTIAL

Instructions for Completion

SECTION 1 (please print clearly)

SECTION 2 (please print clearly)

SECTION 3 (please print clearly)

(turn over to complete)

SECTION 4 - MEDICATION OCCURRENCES

SECTION 5 - GENERAL OCCURRENCES

SECTION 6 - SUPERVISOR'S FOLLOW-UP COMMENTS:

Figure 13.2 *Some businesses use standard forms for situation/incident reports*

Occurrence Report form. Copyright 1993, Queen Elizabeth II Health Sciences Centre. Reprinted with permission.

Below are several situations similar to those you may encounter on the job. The writers in these situations chose different forms for their reports (a memo, a letter, an informal report) because of their differing audiences and purposes, yet they used the chronological order effectively in each report.

A group of visitors was touring the new Robotics Centre being showcased as part of Technology Week in Basinview, Nova Scotia. Two members of the group strayed away from the tour guide and entered a restricted area where high-voltage controls were housed. Jack Edwards, the security officer for the area, was notified that two persons were missing from the group, and he found them taking notes on

QUEEN ELIZABETH II HEALTH SCIENCES CENTRE
HUMAN RESOURCES, ALLIED HEALTH PROGRAMS
PERFORMANCE INCIDENT

STUDENT NAME: ______________________
DATE OF INCIDENT: __________ TIME OF INCIDENT: __________
DIDACTIC: ________ CLINICAL: ________ OTHER ________

I. SIGNIFICANT BACKGROUND INFORMATION:

II. DESCRIPTION OF INCIDENT:

III. ACTION TAKEN:

IV. RESULTS:

SIGNATURE OF REPORTER: ______________ DATE: ________
SIGNATURE OF STUDENT: ______________ DATE: ________

.../2

-2-

STUDENT COMMENTS:

STUDENT SIGNATURE: ______________ DATE: ________

MBB/hp
96 03 26

\usr\ahp\perform.inc

Figure 13.3 *This standard form for a situation report requires descriptive paragraphs.*
Performance Incident form. Copyright Queen Elizabeth II Health Sciences Centre, 1996. Reprinted with permission.

> what they saw. He also saw a 35 mm camera in one person's tote bag. Jack immediately escorted them to the security office where he phoned authorities.

Jack must now follow the standard procedure for all unusual situations at the centre and write a detailed situation report for permanent filing with the centre's director and Corps of Commissionaires. Jack's informal report is shown in Figure 13.4.

> While making his usual rounds to his patients on 3 West, Ronnie Poss found a patient lying on the floor of his hospital room, beside his bed. The patient was disoriented and was unable to relate what happened. Ronnie immediately called another nurse for assistance and noticed that the bedrails were locked securely in the "up" position. The patient was then taken to Radiology for X-rays. It was discovered that he had suffered a cracked rib from the fall.

TABLE 13.1

GUIDELINES FOR CHOOSING THE APPROPRIATE FORM FOR SITUATION REPORTS

Form	Audience	Content
Memo	Immediate supervisor	Brief facts, and descriptions concerning each aspect of the incident or condition. (Formal headings are optional, but always helpful to a reader.)
Letter	External audiences (outside the organization)	Brief descriptions and some background information, since the reader presumably is not completely familiar with the incident or condition. (Formal headings are optional, but always helpful to a reader.)
Informal Report	External audiences	Sections that include a brief summary, background, a lengthy discussion of details, a discussion of the incident's or condition's outcome or consequences, and (perhaps) specific recommendations to remedy the situation. (Formal headings for the specific sections are required.)

Hospital policy requires that Ronnie write a detailed account of the incident and send it to the hospital attorney within 24 hours. Figure 13.5 shows the situation report, written in letter form, that Ronnie sent. Ronnie chose not to include formal headings in his letter. Do you think the information would be easier to follow if he had?

Joyce VanMeer is a manufacturing engineer at Barrie Tool & Die Co. While assisting the machine operator with the maintenance check on the cut and balance machine, Joyce noticed that the LED screen was not registering their test figures. She began checking the main electrical source to the monitor and discovered that the cable was singed in several places. She then discovered that the power surge protector was inoperative. Joyce determined that the machine was unsafe to use and had it taken off the production line until these critical factors could be repaired and replaced. Joyce's manager now wants a report that explains why this expensive machine is not working.

REPORT ON THE VISITOR INCIDENT AT BASINVIEW ROBOTICS CENTRE
MARCH 3, 19--

Background/Summary

An incident occurred on March 3, 19-- that involved unauthorized entry by two persons into a restricted area of our facility. I was notified by Gina Valardo, tour guide, that two persons from her group were unaccounted for and were last seen in the vicinity of Hangar B on the ground floor of our control building. No apparent damage or tampering was done to any of the equipment at the facilities.

Description

A 10-person group from InfoNational in Sussex, New Brunswick, visited our facilities on March 3, 19-- for the special technical tour of our control building. Ten minutes after the tour began, I received a page on my beeper from Gina Valardo, the group's tour guide. Gina informed me that two persons from the tour group were missing. She said that other members of the group did not know where they went, but they were last seen touring Hangar B.

I started my search of the hangar and searched each section in sequence. I then proceeded to Control Room A on the second floor, a clearly marked "restricted entry" area, where I heard soft voices in the room. I unlocked the door and entered the room. I saw a man later identified as Cyril Brown writing down notes on a small tablet that he held in his left hand. His companion, Arthur Purcell, was telling him what to write. I requested that the men accompany me to the security office, and I radioed security for assistance. The men did not resist. While waiting for my backup, I saw a 35 mm camera in Purcell's tote bag. I did not witness him actually taking photos in the room. After my backup arrived, I confiscated the film from the camera and have since turned it over to my supervisor, Sgt. Morgan. We then escorted the men to security. The Basinview Police were phoned, and the men accompanied them to the station for further questioning.

Outcome/Effects

No apparent damage occurred to any equipment in Control Room A. The chief engineer has inspected the area thoroughly and all operations seem to be normal.

Conclusion

Since stray visitors have been a problem in the past, I would like to suggest these modifications to our touring procedures: (1) reduce the number of people in the group to five so the tour guide can more easily account for each one as the tours proceed, (2) assign an assistant guide to tail each group as it travels through the facility, or (3) increase the number of guides on special Showcase occasions.

Figure 13.4 *This informal report includes headings to help readers understand the situation.*

HILLCREST HOSPITAL

October 25, 19__

Mr. Anthony Waters
McMaster Associates
1221 The Wharf
Fairview, AB T2C 3R5

Dear Mr. Waters:

I am writing this letter to provide you with an accurate account of a patient fall that I assisted with after the incident occurred. Before the incident, the patient was recovering from an incision to the perirectal area due to an abscess. Since the surgery, the patient had been disoriented and needed aid to get up from bed. As a result of the fall, the patient has one cracked rib.

The patient involved is Grant Williams, a 64-year-old male. The fall occurred in the patient's room (317) on October 25, 19-- at 1600 hrs. on the third floor, west wing. The patient apparently climbed over the left side rail of his bed in an attempt to get out, then slipped and fell to the floor. When I arrived in the patient's room for a routine bed check, I found the patient lying on the floor on the left side of the bed. I then saw that all four rails were up and locked on his bed.

I called for assistance immediately and Nurse Mulcahy arrived within seconds. Since the patient was obviously in great discomfort, we kept him on the floor covered with a blanket until the doctor on duty arrived. I paged Dr. Carter via my beeper and he arrived within three minutes of the call. After checking Mr. Williams, Dr. Carter asked me to contact Radiology to take X-rays because he suspected injured ribs. The three of us moved Mr. Williams onto a stretcher on the floor, then the Radiology aides lifted him onto a mobile bed that they wheeled to X-ray.

I received Mr. Williams's X-rays at 1800 hrs. the same day and presented them to Dr. Carter. The film confirmed that the third rib on the left side of the patient's chest had a hairline crack. He has been returned to my nursing station for recovery, where he is now kept securely in bed with cloth straps. Dr. Carter expects that Mr. Williams will remain a patient here for six more days.

If you need further clarification or information on this incident, please contact me at the 3-West Nursing Station (extension 3005).

Sincerely,

Ronnie Poss

Ronnie Poss, RN

Figure 13.5 *This letter effectively documents the chronological events of a situation.*

TO: Melvin Donaldson, Engineering Manager
FROM: Joyce VanMeer, Manufacturing Engineer
DATE: July 14, 19--
SUBJECT: Situation Report on Inoperative Cut and Balance Machine

Background/Summary

The cut and balance machine in Cell 7 has an inoperative surge protector that apparently allowed a power surge through the power cord to the LED monitor. The protective rubber coating on the cord has been burned. The problem was discovered July 13 during a routine weekly maintenance check on all machines in Cell 7. The machine is unsafe to use until a new surge protector is installed; therefore, the cut and balance portion of the production process in Cell 7 is temporarily interrupted until Wednesday, July 17, when the new part is scheduled to arrive.

Description

At 8:30 a.m. on July 13, 19--, I began my routine maintenance check of all machines in Cell 7. Frank Murphy, the machine operator, was assisting me with the cut and balance machine maintenance check. As we entered our test figures for display on the LED monitor, we saw that the screen remained blank. I first checked the main power cable to ensure that it was attached to the machine and to the plant's power source. That is when I saw the protective rubber coating on the 2-foot coaxial cable burned through to expose the wiring in one area, and singed on the surface in two other locations.

As a preliminary safety precaution, I next reached to remove the main power source from the machine to prevent any sparks or a fire hazard. I then noticed that the "on" light on the power surge protector was not lighted. I pressed the switch several times to activate the device, but it did not respond. I removed the main power cable from the plant's power source to disable the machine completely.

I notified our maintenance department that the cable and surge protector needed to be replaced. They informed me that the protector was a special order item. I next instructed Purchasing to rush order the device. The quickest delivery will take two days.

Outcome/Effect

From my follow-up testing, I believe that no other damage to the machine was caused by this apparent power surge through the monitor's cable. Both the Purchasing and Maintenance Departments have been alerted to the need for immediate response when the replacement surge device arrives at our plant.

Conclusion

Because of the two-day downtime of this machine, the operators may have to work overtime on July 16 after the machine is repaired to meet the order deadline for RVR Electric. The cell foreman has been alerted to this possibility.

Figure 13.6 *This situation report is written in interoffice memo form.*

Joyce's situation report, written in memo form, is shown in Figure 13.6. Joyce chose to organize her information with formal headings. Do you think she made the right choice?

Situation reports are important vehicles for relaying information that may affect many aspects of business operations. They document information with factual descriptions, and they assure all persons involved that the event did not go unnoticed.

SITE VISIT REPORTS

A site visit report documents the actions and observations of an employee who visits another location. These reports are sometimes referred to as *field trip reports* because they often involve a person leaving his or her usual place of employment and travelling into the field.

Reasons for Writing Site Visit Reports

Essentially, you write site visit reports to describe why you went to another location, what you did, and what you saw. An employer may ask you to travel to another site for reasons similar to these:

Agriculture and science: Breadbasket Farms has given your proposal for insect sensing devices a favourable review. They do, however, have some questions that they want clarified. Your manager asks you to visit Breadbasket Farms and address the questions in person.

Business and marketing: Because of employee resignations, the Lethbridge branch of your savings and loan institution has been left critically short-handed. Your manager asks you to go there for four days to help out.

Health care and computer science: The hospital where you work is considering a new computer system that tracks and documents nursing acuity. The director of nursing asks you to visit a nearby hospital to observe firsthand how a similar system works there.

As part of your job you may be required to travel to another location for a number of different reasons: to attend a seminar or conference, to inspect equipment or property damage, to check on policies or procedures at another plant, or to develop a work estimate for a proposed project. When you return from a trip, your employer will probably expect a report on what you saw or what you did.

Sharing information in the workplace is a critical aspect of good business operations, and technical reports are important tools for ensuring that effective communication takes place.

Content in Site Visit Reports

Site visit reports focus on the facts of a trip: the who, when, what, where, and why of the visit. In some cases, you may also want (or be asked) to present some brief recommendations — perhaps for scheduling a follow-up trip.

Include the following facts, with varying amounts of detail, in a site visit report:

- The name and location of the site visited
- The date and duration of the visit
- The names and titles of individuals travelling
- The names and titles of individuals contacted at the site
- The purpose of the visit
- The details of what you saw or did
- The outcome of the visit (what specifically was gained or accomplished)

Include this information in the body of all site visit reports. To ensure that you have addressed all these points, use the model outline illustrated in Figure 13.7 for each site visit report you write. As with all model outlines in this text, do not hesitate to modify the model to suit your specific report situation.

Remember that the purpose of a site visit report is to relay the facts. Your readers will analyze the information for themselves.

Frequently, if you are required to make extended visits to a site (those that last several weeks or months), your employer or customer may request that you formally evaluate the data you acquired, the actions you took, or the observations you made. In these cases, you will need to write an evaluation report or a feasibility study, depending on the situation. These kinds of reports are discussed in Chapter Fifteen.

Be precise, but also be concise. Readers want details, but they do not want unnecessary or extraneous details. You must select the important aspects of the trip and detail only those activities. Of course, it is also possible to be too concise and to leave the audience with many unanswered questions, as this supposed "site visit report" of a trip to the Pacific during World War II shows:

Saw sub. Sank same.

MODEL OUTLINE: SITE VISIT REPORTS

Title or Title Page
Table of Contents*
Executive Summary*

1. Background/Summary
   1.1 Date of trip
   1.2 Who went on trip
   1.3 Summary of overall results
2. Discussion/Description (use priority or chronological order)
   2.1 Purpose of trip
   2.2 Who authorized trip
   2.3 Locations and people visited
   2.4 Details of what took place
       2.4.1 Actions taken
       2.4.2 Observations made
       2.4.3 Information/data gathered
3. Outcome/Effects
   3.1 Benefits gained
   3.2 Impact of trip on organization
4. Conclusion
   4.1 Suggestions for follow-up trips
   4.2 Suggestions for follow-up contacts (phone or written)

---

*Indicates parts required for formal reports.

Figure 13.7 *This model outline shows the organization of topics in a site visit report.*

Know your audience — specifically, their purpose for reading and/or requesting the report, and their technical level. You can then decide effectively how much detail, or how little, to include.

For many site visits, your assignment will be simply to visit and document what you learned, saw, or did. In these cases, you should objectively report only the who, when, where, and what of your trip. Reserve your opinions ("I thought the trip was worthwhile") for those assignments in which you have been specifically asked for them. Even then, however, immediately support and follow these judgmental statements with facts that explain why. ("I thought the trip was worthwhile because I learned to operate our new threading machine more efficiently.")

Writing Style

Like situation reports, site visit reports require a crisp and concise narrative writing style. Short paragraphs are the norm for these reports; numbered or bulleted lists also help readers focus on important information.

When presenting the facts of a site visit, give the audience specific information. Use figures to relate measurement or time; avoid vague terms like *very large* or *fairly quick* or *many*. Tell the audience, instead, the exact size, the exact span of time, or the exact quantity.

Activity 2
....

In the appropriate blank, check "Yes" if the writer gives objective and specific information; check "No" if the information is subjective and general.

a. After visiting the ConTech plant in Drummondville and observing the capabilities of its new Impact Ripper, I have decided that this piece of equipment is a fantastic machine and that we should order three of them.

_____ Yes _____ No

b. At a demonstration of the Impact Ripper at ConTech's Drummondville plant, I saw the machine develop enough drawbar strength to forcibly pull its ripper tip through intact rock and sustain this ripping force for 20 minutes.

_____ Yes _____ No

c. While on a temporary four-day assignment to our Summerside branch, I spent three days interviewing prospective customers for various loans (home improvement, automobile, education) and one day helping at the drive-through window.

_____ Yes _____ No

d. While at our Summerside branch, because they were short-handed, I took care of customers and helped with many daily operations.

_____ Yes _____ No

In the site visits reported in a. and d., the writers neglected to state the facts objectively and specifically. In a. the writer let feelings override fact; the writer in d. was so vague about his/her activities that the report was virtually worthless to his/her manager.

Form in Site Visit Reports

Site visit reports usually are written in memo, letter, or informal report form. Unless you travelled for an extended time (several weeks or months), or your trip involved complex actions or observations, you will not need to give your site visit reports formal report treatment.

Choose a form for your site visit reports based on your readers and the complexity and amount of the information they need. Table 13.2 presents some guidelines to help you make the appropriate choices.

Some organizations require standard forms for site visit reports. A few high-tech companies even integrate site visit forms into their computer mainframe systems for ease in completing and filing. In most cases, however, you will be expected to write and organize these reports on your own.

Order in Site Visit Reports

Similar to situation reports, site visit reports present facts and descriptions in a narrative style. You can choose, however, to present the information in chronological order (the details are presented in the sequence they were observed or performed) or priority order (the details of the most important feature/action are presented first, followed by the rest in descending order of importance).

In most cases, priority order is the more effective method of organizing site visit reports. But at times, depending on the nature of the trip and the purpose of the assignment, chronological order may be useful. Below are two situations that prompted site visit reports. They demonstrate the typical reasons a writer might choose a specific report form and order.

> Scott Best's company gave him the opportunity to attend a technology conference in New Orleans. The three-day conference included many activities: workshops, presentations, exhibits, demonstrations. After his return to the office, Scott begins telling his manager of all the new products and methods he learned about at the conference. His

TABLE 13.2

GUIDELINES FOR CHOOSING THE APPROPRIATE FORM FOR SITE VISIT REPORTS

Form	Audience	Content
Memo	Immediate supervisor	Concise facts about the who, when, where, and what of a short trip. (Formal headings are optional, but always helpful to your reader.)
Letter	External audiences	Details concerning the facts of a trip. (Formal headings are optional, but always helpful to a reader.)
Informal Report	Upper management	Detailed information about a long or complex visit, including formal sections (an introduction and conclusion, and an executive summary if the report is longer than five pages).

manager suggests Scott write a trip report on the conference and circulate it throughout the department so everyone can benefit.

Figure 13.8 shows Scott's report, written in interoffice memo form. Because he did not learn new or relevant information from every activity, Scott chose the priority order, listing only the most significant activities of the conference.

One of the Elmhurst Corporation's robotic installations at a customer's site is malfunctioning. Stacy Young is asked to visit the plant, and identify and repair the problem. After six hours of troubleshooting, she discovers the problem and repairs it. Her manager wants a step-by-step report that proves to the customer that no other problems are present.

Figure 13.9 shows the report Stacy submitted. Because her information is complex, and because she has been asked to show methodical steps, Stacy wrote an informal report (with formal headings), using chronological order.

In the workplace, site visit reports may be required for a variety of different offsite assignments. Your employer will depend on you providing accurate, objective, and concise accounts to share and document important firsthand information.

MEMO

TO: Members of the Fibre Optics Department
FROM: Scott Best, Design Technician
DATE: April 30, 19--
SUBJECT: Trip to Louisiana Symposium & Exhibit

Background/Summary

The Louisiana Symposium & Exhibition conference was held April 25, 26, 27, 19-- in the New Orleans Convention Center. The three days of technical sessions included information on new and improved products and on advances in fibre optics technology.

Description

At the suggestion of Matt Cooke and with the approval of Frank Clare (our new vice president), I attended this conference as a representative of our department to learn about the latest applications of fibre optic components and any new products in the field.

The most informative technical session I attended was held the second day of the conference (April 26) on Fibre Optics Test Equipment. The speaker, Toshio Kaneta from Adtest America, spoke on the special equipment now available for taking optical measurements. The new optical fibre Reflectometer has some capabilities that I think we can use when we perform in-service tests for our customers. The product brochure is attached to this memo.

Another session held the next day (April 27) demonstrated the advantages of using fibre optics over present cable systems. The speaker was Dave Pallodino, a systems manager from ADK. The versatility and durability that fibre optic components now have over twisted pair and coax make them worth considering when we redesign the ECE Mountables in June.

Also attached is a bar chart that Pallodino handed out which gives an overview of the ideal characteristics of fibre optics compared to what we're using now. This new technology may be an effective way for us to improve our applications.

One other technical session (held the first day) netted some valuable information on a product called "Zip-Meshing." The manufacturer's rep gave an impressive demonstration of its uses. Briefly, it is a zipper tubing used for hard-to-reach areas. It may work well for our wire and harness branchouts — particularly those in the OTDR stations. (Matt Cooke is reviewing the product brochures.)

Outcome

This trip was most worthwhile because the workshops, presentations, exhibits, and demonstrations allowed me to obtain the latest information on the latest technologies. Matt Cooke is now reviewing some of the products introduced, particularly those mentioned in this report.

Conclusion

I have recommended to Matt and to Mr. Clare that at least three representatives from our department be sent to the conference next year. Concurrent sessions made it difficult for me to attend all presentations of possible interest to our department.

Figure 13.8 *The priority order in this site visit report addresses the most important aspects of a trip first, and then briefly mentions minor activities.*

ELMHURST CORPORATION

SITE VISIT REPORT
AT THE DONALDSON ROBOTIC INSTALLATION

Background/Summary

On November 2, 19--, I spent nine hours troubleshooting and repairing the Donaldson Co.'s robotic installation in Mississauga. The malfunction was caused by a broken support ring in the cylinder.

Description/Actions Performed

I visited the Donaldson site after a phone call from its plant supervisor reporting inaccurate vertical movement of the robotic arm. Our department head, B. R. Lipton, authorized the trip when analysis over the phone netted no significant results.

In Mississauga, I first checked the pressure rate of the rodless cylinder; it registered a satisfactory 42 Pa. I then inspected all seven cushion screws to verify that they were tightened correctly; all were in place and secure. Next, I removed the dust shield and cleaned it. The shield needed maintenance but was not the main cause of the malfunction. The inner band around the piston was flexible and free from cracks and wear.

I then began my inspection of the piston and piston mount. I moved the piston cylinder manually in varying stroke lengths from 2.54 cm to 6 m and verified that movement was unimpeded. Visual inspection of the piston did not show any problems. However, as an extra test measure, I decided to use a proximity sensor to determine the positioning control on the robotic arm. To attach this sensor, I had to remove the outside casing around the piston.

When I removed the outside casing, I saw immediately that the support ring on the right side of the piston was broken in half. I replaced it and finished my check of the left support ring and lubrication fluid.

I restarted the robotic arm and verified the accuracy of the vertical arm movement.

Effects

Donaldson's textile production of nylon fibres resumed before the second shift began work. The plant supervisor was relieved and grateful to have the machine back online.

Conclusion

I suggest that Donaldson's maintenance supervisor check the support rings (right and left) in two weeks to ensure that they are still in good condition.

Figure 13.9 *The chronological order in this site visit report documents the exact sequence of actions performed.*

QUESTIONS FOR DISCUSSION

1. How do situation reports help communications in the workplace?
2. What kind of writing style is appropriate for situation reports?
3. Which questions do readers expect situation reports to answer?
4. What is the main focus of a site visit report?
5. What is the purpose of a site visit report?

EXERCISE

Read the following report written by a dental hygienist, and then answer the questions that follow.

TO: Watborough Dental Health Technicians Association
FROM: Lanna Merino, DH
SUBJECT: Accident
DATE: August 12, 19--

Summary
A child left in the dental chair at Dr. Gupta's office was hurt slightly. And the mother, too.

Description
One day in August a kid came to Dr. Gupta's office for a routine checkup and cleaning of teeth. Somehow this brat — big for its age — got some equipment from the tray next to the chair. I don't know where the mother was when she should have been right next to the kid. Anyway, when I returned to the room from taking an emergency call about my dog, the kid was bleeding a little and screaming a lot.

I dashed out to get another hygienist and the dentist, while I was gone, the mother came in and grabbed the kid. She slipped on a damp patch of floor and hurt her back. She is now threatening to sue us for negligence!

Outcome
I have been suspended from my job pending your investigation. I want you to know that I was not negligent and do not consider myself responsible for a mother who leaves her kid and then hurts herself just because of a couple of small cuts which didn't even require stitches.

Conclusion
I expect you to recommend that I be reinstated with back pay for the days I've been out of work. Then I recommend

that the association draw up guidelines for the behaviour of mothers in the dental office.

a. Here are some questions normally addressed in a situation report. Indicate, with a check to the left, those questions that Lanna's report addresses adequately.

_____ 1. What was the situation?

_____ 2. Who was involved?

_____ 3. When did the situation happen?

_____ 4. Where did it happen?

_____ 5. What exactly happened?

_____ 6. Why did the situation happen (how was it caused)?

_____ 7. What was done by responsible personnel?

_____ 8. What were the consequences?

b. Give Lanna *one* piece of advice about writing memos:

_____

c. Give Lanna *one* piece of advice to help her improve her choice of words:

_____

d. Give Lanna *one* piece of advice to help her improve her sentence structure:

_____

e. On a separate sheet of paper, rewrite and improve the memo, adding any details that you think the writer should have included.

WRITING ASSIGNMENTS

1. Write a situation report in letter form, describing an event that could or did happen at your school. Prepare the report for the

proper administrative personnel at your school (department head, division director, dean, vice president, or president). You may describe an actual situation or event that you observed or participated in, or you may choose a scenario from the list below (supplying any specific details).

a. A bomb threat to a crowded area (classroom, lab, gymnasium, dormitory, or cafeteria) resulted in confusion, damage to some property, and a few injuries.

b. A large oak tree, the pride of the campus, is being or has been damaged by construction crews working nearby.

c. A three-car accident at a busy, poorly marked campus intersection resulted in property damage and bodily injuries.

d. An accident occurred in an improperly supervised work area (kitchen, carpentry shop, machine shop, automotive shop, chemistry lab); two students were hurt and the facility sustained some smoke and water damage.

2. Write a situation report in memo form for an event that could or did happen on the job. Prepare the report for your immediate supervisor. Choose an actual event, or choose from one of the following (supplying specific details):

a. A fight occurred between two new employees at your workstation. A machine was damaged, one employee was hospitalized, and the other suffered a broken arm.

b. Immediately following a break period in which several workers bought drinks from vending machines, some employees complained of nausea, dizziness, and excessive fatigue. In the interim before an ambulance was called, one person collapsed and hit her head on a sharp-edged bench.

c. Within weeks after new monitors were installed in your computing section, employees complained of stiff necks and blurred vision — several took sick leave. The company which installed the equipment refused a request to review the installation and quality of the monitors; now some employees are preparing a petition documenting their health problems.

d. Newly paved parking lots and redesigned routes to the main gate seem to have caused several "fender benders" in the company's one-hectare parking lot; employees blame the change, while the company blames the employees.

3. Write a situation report (use any form) based on an event or situation which actually occurred at your home, or select an incident from the possibilities listed below (supplying specific

details). Prepare the report for any audience that should know what happened in order to take action.

a. Lightning struck a tree near your house and caused more than $2,000 worth of damage. Electrical outlets near the furniture burned holes in your sofas, chairs, and beds, and the surge destroyed the software programs and data on your personal computer. Your insurance company wants a complete report on the exact cause of the damage and the costs involved.

b. You and your neighbour disagree on the placement of a fence between your properties. When you insist on the fence being moved back half a metre, your neighbour refuses. One day you find the fence gone entirely and much damage done to your shrubbery. You did not see the actual removal and your neighbour is now on vacation. Your lawyer wants a report in writing.

c. A five-year-old child wandered uninvited into your backyard and turned over and smashed a bird bath. Fortunately, the child is uninjured, but the parents refuse to take responsibility for replacement of the bird bath. Having failed to negotiate some recompense, which is under $200, you decide to take them to Small Claims Court. As you will be presenting your case to the judge, you must prepare a detailed report, which should include diagrams or photographic evidence.

4. Write a site visit report in memo form based on a trip to a local site of your choice. Here are two suggestions:

a. Visit a local manufacturing company, construction site, hospital, or any workplace that is relevant to your major field of study. Write a report to students currently enrolled in your program. Detail what you saw in terms of working conditions, employee morale, and any other factors that you think prospective employees would like to know.

b. Visit a health club or fitness and recreation centre in your community. Write a brief report to your classmates or to your fellow employees who are interested in taking advantage of group membership rates, providing the centre meets their needs.

5. Write a report in letter form based on observations at your college. Here are two possibilities:

a. "Visit" another program on campus, spending at least two hours observing its activities, classes, and students. Write to a friend in another city who has expressed interest in that program.

b. Observe a specific place on campus (the library or learning resources centre, a computer writing centre, a tutoring centre, a vocational assessment centre, for example) for at least two hours. Write to your advisor about what you saw and did.

Chapter FOURTEEN

Process Descriptions and Instructions

We live in an age where information surrounds us. At home, school, or work, information is available (and often essential) for learning and doing almost everything: using a new food processor, learning to use a desktop publishing program, understanding how roof trusses are made. Whatever we try to learn or do, we want appropriate explanations and directions so that we can easily understand the information we need.

Clearly written process descriptions and instructions are important vehicles for conveying this information to us. In the workplace, they play prominent roles. Professionals in all fields must not only use and refer to countless process descriptions and instructions, they must also write many of them.

Although similar in some ways, process descriptions and instructions differ in several fundamental aspects: (1) the purpose for writing them, (2) the specific need(s) of the audience, (3) the style in which they are written, and (4) the way they are presented visually to the audience. Essentially, process descriptions are informative, narrative accounts of what is required to achieve a result. They do not expect the readers to take any action. Instructions, on the other hand, are step-by-step accounts of all actions required to do or operate something. They do expect hands-on involvement from the reader.

Put even more succinctly, process descriptions describe the "what" of a process; step-by-step instructions describe the "how." For example, a process description tells the reader *what* major stages are involved when an automated threading machine produces a slotted pipe; instructions tell the reader *how* to operate the threading machine.

To decide whether your audience needs a process description (a general understanding) or instructions (specific directions), ask these questions:

QUESTION: Does the audience need to *understand* this process? (If yes, write a process description.)

QUESTION: Does the audience need to *do* this process? (If yes, write instructions.)

PROCESS DESCRIPTIONS

A process description gives the audience an overall understanding of the process used to reach a result. You could think of it as a narrative that says to the audience, "Here is the way it happens" or "Here is the way it went."

Reasons for Writing Process Descriptions

In the workplace, a process description often covers *what* was involved when you did or do something:

◆ What areas you considered when you estimated auto repairs (labour, parts and materials, overhead)

◆ What major steps you take when reviewing an employment application (check for completeness, verify previous experience, confirm references)

Process descriptions may also explain *what* is involved overall when something is done:

◆ The overall process for packaging materials

◆ The major operations of the new telephone system

Process descriptions, then, are written when reader action is not directly involved (when, for example, the reader will not actually perform the estimating or material handling) and when the reader wants or needs to learn only the major sequences used.

Content in Process Descriptions

Readers of a process description will want some basic information. For example, they will want answers to questions like these:

◆ What is this process used for?

◆ What underlying or general principle is used to reach the end result?

◆ What level of expertise is required?

◆ What resources are needed to carry out this process?

◆ What major sequences should be followed?

◆ Is this process effective?

Include this information in all process descriptions, whether you write them as stand-alone reports or as parts of longer documents. The model outline shown in Figure 14.1 contains all elements needed for a longer, stand-alone report. Modify this model to suit your specific audience's needs and your supervisor's requirements.

Writing Style

Use the narrative style in a process description — write paragraphs that *describe* major sequences or areas involved to reach an end result. Do not confuse descriptive narrations with rambling explanations, however. Write crisply and concisely; every word counts. If you can say something clearly in five words instead of eight, do so; the shorter version will probably be more understandable to your audience.

Title Page and Executive Summary

Detailed information about developing effective title pages and executive summaries is included in Chapter Nine of this text. Review this material and include these items when you write a stand-alone process description of more than five or six pages.

Introduction

This part varies in process descriptions; the amount of information included depends on the purpose of the description and the needs of your readers. Several basic elements, however, do not vary. First, identify the process for the readers with a careful sentence definition.

EXAMPLE: Online scheduling is the process of assigning paramedic personnel to all Avalon County emergency medical vehicles (EMVs) via the DataMed computer system.

Also, always clearly state the purpose of the process (what it is used for or why it is used).

EXAMPLE: Staff scheduling done on the DataMed system helps ensure that no conflicts or vacancies in staffing hours occur because personnel are unavailable.

Depending on the type of process you are describing and the technical level and needs of your specific audience, adapt the explanation of any general principles or basic concepts involved.

MODEL OUTLINE: PROCESS DESCRIPTIONS

Title or title page
Executive Summary*
1. Introduction
   1.1 Define the process
   1.2 Explain why the process is used
   1.3 State any general or basic principles (as needed)
   1.4 Mention the level of expertise required
   1.5 Include definitions of specialty terms (as needed)
2. Required Resources
   2.1 List equipment/instruments needed to do the process
   2.2 List materials needed
   2.3 List tools needed
   2.4 List personnel needed
3. Major Sequences in Process (organized from start to finish)
   3.1 Identify sequence 1
      3.1.1 Explain why you perform this sequence
      3.1.2 Describe briefly what is involved
   3.2 Identify sequence 2
      3.2.1 Explain why you perform this sequence
      3.2.2 Describe briefly what is involved
   3.3 Etc.
4. Outcome/Results (Conclusion)
   4.1 Summarize the complete cycle of the process
   4.2 Evaluate the effectiveness of the process

---

*Component needed only if description is a stand-alone report and longer than five pages.

Figure 14.1 *This model outline lists the elements in an effective process description.*

EXAMPLE: The scheduling process is based on a spreadsheet sorting program that reads data entered in two separate 28-day calendars, which is the maximum capacity in the computer memory (1 megabyte).

You may expand on any general principles if your reader needs to understand more. Using the previous example, you could briefly discuss the basic principles in electronic spreadsheets or data sorts or explain why only two 28-day calendars are active on the system.

You may also omit any general principles if, as in the previous example, the reader is your immediate supervisor and he or she was involved in selecting the system. You can assume your supervisor is aware of these basic principles. The county manager, however, may not have a clear idea of the principles involved in electronic spread-sheeting or sorting. To understand the process, the manager will need you to explain these principles *as they apply to the process.* Avoid complex or in-depth explanations; remember, your reader needs only a general understanding.

Sometimes your audience will include technical and nontechnical readers: Some will understand the principles involved and some will not. You may then omit the general principles in the introduction, but include a statement similar to this:

EXAMPLE: To understand the scheduling process described next, the reader should have a general understanding of how electronic spreadsheets and data sorts function in a computer.

If the process description contains a number of specialty terms that a reader may not know, you can include a concise "Definitions" subsection in the introduction. See Chapter Seven for information on writing appropriate definitions.

Required Resources

In any process, specific resources are required to reach a result. List these resources so that your audience will know in advance what is going to be used. List such resources as these:

◆ *Equipment:* personal computers, lab trays, monitors, gauges, beakers
◆ *Materials:* distilled water, litmus paper, lint-free cloths, wiring
◆ *Tools:* Phillips screwdriver, 8-bit drill
◆ *Personnel:* technologist, courier, engineer

Major Sequences in a Process

This part contains descriptions of the specific major stages involved in beginning, continuing, and ending the process. Remember, your readers want to know *what* sequence is included in the process; they do not want to know all the details of *how* to do it themselves.

WRONG: First, I press the ENTER key until the Master Menu appears, then I select option 2 (PERSONNEL ROSTER). In the SELECTION field, I key in the…

RIGHT: First, I access the personnel roster for a current list of active paramedics and vehicle drivers. This list contains pertinent information about each employee, such as date and times of availability, phone number, and whether this person has already declined a request to work on a specific shift.

Always prepare an outline *before* you write a process description An outline helps you focus on the major sequences involved in the process, rather than on the individual steps. Be aware, however, that although your readers want a general understanding, they do not want information that is too general and vague. Suppose the writer attempting to describe the process for scheduling paramedics were to write, "First, I check to see who is available." You undoubtedly would ask, "Check what? Why? How can you tell who's available?"

Activity 1
. . . .

_____ a. I make sure my body is warmed up before I play tennis.

_____ b. I do five minutes of stretching exercises for the muscles in my neck, arms, legs, and feet before I begin playing tennis.

_____ c. I test the overall balance of the finished fan assembly by first checking the digital reading on the cut and balance machine to see if any registered imbalance is off by more than 0.15 oz/in. and where the imbalance is located.

_____ d. If the cut and balance machine indicates, I correct any imbalance on the finished fan assemblies.

Do the descriptions in statements a. and d. leave you with many unanswered questions? Are you inclined to ask the writer of a., "Which muscles do you exercise? For how long?" You would not expect, however, to receive in a *major sequence* exact details of the exercises. These belong in the *Describe briefly what is involved* section. Would you like to ask the writer of d., "How does the machine indicate? With a digital readout? With bells or whistles?" When you compare a. and d. with the sentences in b. and c., which give more detailed information, you immediately see the value of using specific words.

As you narrate each sequence in a process, explain clearly and concisely why the sequence is performed: for example, to evaluate operability or to determine the extent of infection. Then give a brief overview of what is involved when you perform this sequence.

Outcome/Results

Essentially, this brief section in a process description is your conclusion. For your readers' convenience, summarize the complete cycle of the process: List succinctly the major sequences you described earlier. You may also give a brief assessment of the effectiveness of the process. Answer these questions about the process:

◆ Does it work well?

◆ Is it relatively easy to do?

◆ Is it time-consuming or complicated?

Graphics

Simple illustrations, especially flow diagrams, can help explain process descriptions for all levels of readers.

> After writing a process description for his general manager on preparing new business proposals, Frank Faulkner also included a flow diagram using key words that depicted the major sequences in the process. Frank prepared this pictorial reference and summary because the task is rather complex and the process description, out of necessity, is somewhat lengthy.

The flow diagram in Figure 14.2 is not detailed enough to be understood fully without the narrative explanation in the main document. It does provide, however, a quick reference to and summary of the process *after* Frank's manager reads the description. Always consider including some pictorial support to help the audience understand a process description even more clearly.

Form in Process Descriptions

Process descriptions can be prepared as interoffice memos, letters to customers, or parts of informal or formal reports. Choose the form for your process description based on how much detail your audience needs and whether the description will be a stand-alone report or integrated within a larger report. Unless your organization is highly specialized and deals mostly with one primary end product or process (an accounting software company, perhaps), it is unlikely that you will have access to a standard form for process descriptions.

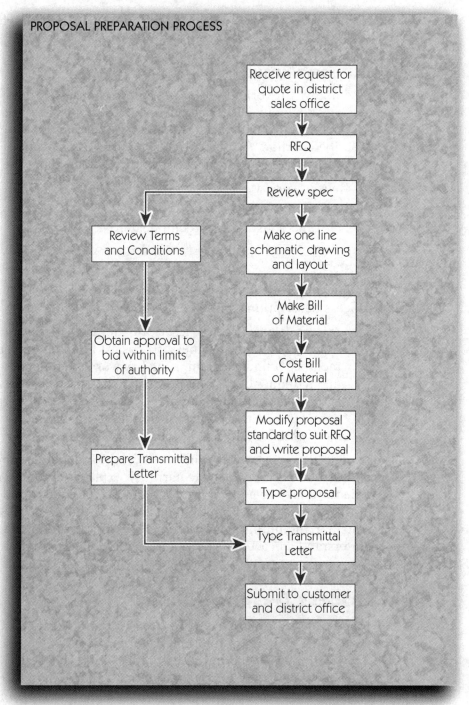

PROPOSAL PREPARATION PROCESS

Figure 14.2 *This flowchart helps readers visualize the major sequences in a complex process.*

Table 14.1 presents guidelines to help you select the appropriate form for process descriptions.

TABLE 14.1

GUIDELINES FOR SELECTING THE APPROPRIATE FORM FOR PROCESS DESCRIPTIONS

Form	Audience	Content
Memo	Immediate supervisor	Narrative focusing on the major sequences in a process, with minimal background information because of the reader's familiarity with this material. (Formal headings are optional, but always helpful to a reader.)
Letter	External audiences	Narrative explanations of what the process accomplishes and materials or equipment needed to achieve the desired results. (Formal headings are optional, but always helpful to a reader.)
Informal or Formal Report	Upper management (yours or your customer's) or external audiences	In-depth narratives on introductory information, resources required, descriptions of major sequences in the process, and often evaluations of the effectiveness of the process; frequently, process descriptions are only one part within longer reports: manuals, proposals, evaluation reports. (Formal headings are always included.)

Order in Process Descriptions

A chronological order (items listed in the sequence in which they naturally occur) is often the most effective arrangement for process descriptions. This order frequently includes word signals like *first, second, next, then, last*, or *finally* to help readers move easily from one major sequence to another. They also provide smooth transitions from the first sequence of the process to the last.

Use your outline to guide you logically from one sequence to the next. Start at the beginning of the process, then move methodically through each sequence until you reach the end of the process. In the workplace situation described on page 392, the writer has prepared a clear process description (shown in Figure 14.3) as a business courtesy to his customers. (This business courtesy also resulted in good customer relations!)

CARING FOR NEW TREES

Introduction

Caring properly for new trees is the process of preparing a favourable growing environment to ensure their survival. Correct care involves planting, fertilizing, watering, mulching, pruning, and protecting the tree from insects and diseases. A new tree must be cared for until it has a chance to become established.

Required Resources

The first essential item is a carefully selected tree — one that is reliably hardy in the environment that it must grow in. Other items needed are a spaded shovel for digging, good soil, water, support stakes with hose-covered wires, burlap or creped kraft paper, mulch, and pruning tools.

Planting

The key to good tree planting is generosity: in digging a planting hole, in replacing poor soil with good, in expending energy to do the job right. The right way to do the job depends on how good the soil is on the planting site.

In good soil, planting holes should be large enough to receive the tree roots when they are spread in a natural position. The holes also should be deep enough that you can set the trees at the same level at which they grew in the nursery.

In poor soil, holes should be as wide and deep as you can conveniently make them. Poor soil from the hole must be replaced with good soil when filled in around the newly set tree.

Essential to any tree's survival is setting it in the hole at the same level at which it grew in the nursery.

Staking and guying the tree next to the rootball before the hole is backfilled ensures that it grows straight. Thorough watering settles the soil around the roots. Burlap or creped kraft paper wrapped around the new tree trunk protects it from sunscald.

Fertilizing

Newly planted trees backfilled with plenty of good soil are not likely to need fertilizer for the first year after planting. However, if the leaves are paler than normal and if growth is slower than normal, fertilizer may be applied in the spring.

Watering

Water trees for the first two seasons after planting them. Water about once a week and let the water run for several hours. If the soil in your area is tight clay or underlain with hardpan, be careful not to overwater. Excess water kills some kinds of trees faster than drought.

Figure 14.3 *This process description provides the overall steps involved in reaching an end result.*

Mulching

Mulching beneath the tree conserves natural moisture, tempers summer's heat and winter's cold, and adds organic matter to the soil. Pine bark, ground corncobs, or peanut hulls are attractive mulches. Rotted leaves also supply the soil around the tree with needed organic matter, but may not be as desirable in the landscaping. Keep the area beneath the tree mulched to prevent the soil from becoming depleted.

Pruning

Pruning improves the tree's appearance, guards its health, and makes it stronger. Corrective pruning should be done as soon as the need becomes apparent on dead, dying, or unsightly parts of the tree; sprouts growing at or near the base of the tree trunk; branches that grow toward the centre of the tree; crossed branches; and "V" crotches.

Small pruning cuts heal quickly. Large cuts — more than 2.5 centimetres in diameter — should be treated with antiseptic tree dressing to prevent entrance of decay or disease while the wound is healing.

Protecting from Insects and Diseases

Most insects and diseases can be controlled by spraying. Your landscape specialist can tell you what spray schedules to follow to protect your trees from insects and diseases that are inherent in your area.

Outcome

Success in growing trees depends on how well the trees are prepared for survival. Correct planting, fertilizing, watering, mulching, pruning, and protecting from insects and diseases are essential steps to give a new tree a chance to become established — and to ensure a beautiful addition to your landscaping.

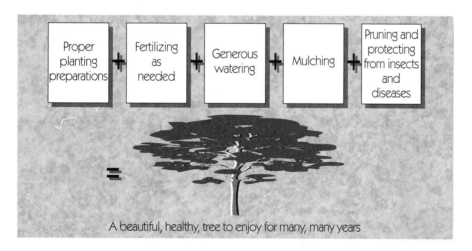

A beautiful, healthy, tree to enjoy for many, many years

Figure 14.3 *continued*

Because Outdoor Designs & Nursery receives frequent inquiries from its customers asking how to ensure strong, healthy trees in their yards, owner Jim Alexander sent them a description of the overall process for planting and caring for new trees. His customers were delighted to receive the information, and Jim has seen an increase in referral business.

Jim knows that his customers need a general understanding of good tree care, not step-by-step directions on every sequence in the process. Note that the process description he sent to them explains chronologically the major sequences involved, from planting the tree to protecting it from insects and disease.

Process descriptions play an important role in the workplace. In business and industry, employees involved in quality assurance must document the processes they follow — or want others to follow — to guarantee the consistent high quality of their companies' products. Many institutions, like your college, document processes (curriculum or course development, for example) because of frequent external reviews and audits. Government agencies like the one described below often write and distribute various process descriptions as a public service.

One of the main missions of the Medford County Home Extension Office (MCHEO) is to provide residents with timely and useful information that helps improve the quality of their home life. Because of the growing interest in nutritious foods, Dietitian Jane Stewart wrote a description of the process involved in making homemade yogurt to encourage people to try it.

Figure 14.4 shows Jane's process description of what is involved in making yogurt at home. Note that her information does not provide step-by-step instructions; rather, it familiarizes the reader with the overall yogurt-making process.

A Note on Terminology: Process and Procedure

These two terms are often used interchangeably, as they both describe a course of action.

Dictionaries define *process* as (1) a course or method of operations in the production of something, and (2) a series or course of actions that bring about a particular result.

A *procedure* is defined as (1) a manner of proceeding in any course of action, and (2) the methods or forms of conducting a business, etc.

You may find it useful to think of a *procedure* as part of the documentation of a larger *process*. For example, if you are hired by a company that has applied to become ISO 9000 registered, you may well be involved in documenting the procedures necessary for that registration. ISO 9000 is an international standard for a basic management system for quality assurance, and companies that apply for registration have to scrutinize and document their procedures: management, purchasing, design, control, production, etc.

Whatever your writing tasks may be, however, the key point to remember is that clear descriptions result from careful analysis of purpose, situation, and audience; effective organization of sequence; and the appropriate amount of detail.

MAKING A BATCH OF YOGURT

Introduction

Yogurt, sometimes spelled yoghurt, yoghourt, yogourt, or yohourt, is a custard-like preparation made by fermenting concentrated whole milk. It is snow white in appearance and differs from other fermented milks in that it is consumed as a custard rather than as a liquid. The process for making a small batch of yogurt (which differs from making it in large-scale bulk quantities) involves obtaining and propagating a bacterial culture, and preparing the yogurt.

The following general process can be performed by an individual to make a small batch of nutritious and tasty yogurt at home.

Basic Principle

A yogurt culture is a living mixture of at least three kinds of bacteria that are kept under conditions which permit their normal growth (propagation) for a limited time and that are protected from outside contamination.

This yogurt or "mother" culture is the main ingredient used in the fermentation process. It creates the custard-like consistency and the flavour of the mixture.

Required Resources

The materials and equipment needed for preparing yogurt are as follows: a mother culture of known purity which contains all the essential bacteria in active

---

Figure 14.4 *A primary function of process descriptions is to help readers understand the overall process.* *(Continued on page 394.)*

form; a supply of concentrated milk or suitable equipment for concentrating whole milk; equipment for sterilizing the milk and for maintaining constant fermentation conditions at 44 to 46 degrees Celsius; and refrigeration space for holding the finished product at 10 degrees Celsius or below.

Obtaining the Culture

Yogurt culture starters may be obtained from commercial laboratories.

Propagating (Growing) the Culture

After the culture is obtained, maintaining it in its original form is usually possible for several months. However, care in the use of sterile equipment may prolong its usefulness for a considerable time. Using a small quantity of yogurt as the starter for the next batch is convenient, but the practice is rarely satisfactory for perpetuating a useful culture. The mother culture, then, should be carried in a separate series. Make transfers every other day into milk which is as nearly sterile as possible, and incubate the new culture at a temperature of 29 to 32°C.

In handling cultures, both in maintaining the mother culture and in preparing the batch of yogurt, take every precaution to prevent contamination. Clean all equipment carefully before each use. After the sterilization process, ensure that fingers or other parts of the body do not touch the surfaces of the equipment that come in contact with the milk.

Preparing the Yogurt

Successful home yogurt preparation is achieved by following this simple process:

- Add the correct ratio of culture to whole milk.
- Condense the mixture to two-thirds its original volume.
- Heat the mixture to boiling and then cool it immediately.
- Bottle and cover the mixture in sterile containers.
- Incubate the mixture in warm water until it coagulates (usually about three hours).
- Refrigerate the containers until they are cool.

Results

The yogurt may be eaten as soon as it is cool enough — usually in about five to eight hours. Yogurt keeps for a week or longer if it is held at 10 degrees or lower. Enjoy — and proudly share with your family and friends — the tasty, nutritious goodness of your home-made yogurt!

Figure 14.4 *continued*

INSTRUCTIONS

Clear and concise step-by-step instructions tell readers *how* to get a job done — whether the job is at home (how to assemble and operate a snowblower), or at school (how to install software into your network account), or at work (how to administer an intravenous injection).

Reasons for Writing Instructions

You will frequently have to use instructions — and, in the workplace, you will often have to write them. All the reasons for writing instructions are tied primarily to performance: getting the job done right and safely. Instructions benefit both you and the organization for which you work:

◆ They ensure that no actions are misunderstood or performed incorrectly.

◆ They encourage productivity, efficiency, and safety.

◆ They provide ready access (and quick reference) to accurate instructions, particularly when a trainer is unavailable.

◆ They contribute to the sharing of important information throughout an organization so that business operations can continue without interruption.

Instructions are written whenever an operator is involved — when the writer *expects* active participation from the reader in performing the process being described. For example, you would need to write instructions when your supervisor gives you assignments such as the following:

◆ Describe how to assemble the swing sets that your company manufactures.

◆ Explain to everyone in the office how to use the new photocopier correctly.

◆ Detail the steps necessary to assess accurately a patient's dental condition.

The readers of these instructions need more than an overview of these tasks. They need to know each step and action involved so they can accurately perform these processes themselves.

Content in Instructions

Clearly written instructions focus on the detailed steps required to complete a process, with a writing style that makes it easy for the reader to understand. As you write each set of instructions, continually remind yourself of the importance of clarity.

Writing Style

Instructions should be written in a style that is somewhat different from the style of other technical reports. Although all reports should be written concisely — every word should count — instructions make great use of "word economy." Since instructions are action-related directions, you can economize on words by using the *command form of the verb* (also called the imperative mood). If, for example, you need to instruct readers on how to clean paintbrushes correctly, tell them concisely, "*Scrape* the brush on the side of the paint can and *press* lightly to squeeze out excess paint." If you use too many unnecessary words ("By scraping the brush on the side of the paint can and by pressing lightly, excess paint can be squeezed out of the brush") you will probably confuse them.

Active *command* verbs (*scrape* and *press*) make instructions concise and understandable. They evoke "action" from readers rather than just passive understanding.

When you use command verbs, you streamline the number of words in instructions by avoiding repetitive or awkward subject pronouns. With command verbs, the subject of the action — you — is implied or understood: "(you) close the window tightly," "(you) cut a piece of stripping," "(you) inspect the surface." Most of the time, it is not necessary to address readers directly because of this implied pronoun. When you address the reader, however, continue with the "you" implied in the commands rather than "the operator" or "the assembler." This can help you avoid writing a weak and passive sentence like the first example shown here.

WRONG: The operator should read all safety and operating
instructions before the equipment is operated.

RIGHT: Read all safety and operating instructions before you use
the equipment.

Activity 2

Read the following set of instructions on how to install a peephole in a door. Economize where possible, and, in the blanks provided, rewrite these instructions to make them more concise, more action-related, and more direct.

Step 1. A mark should be made at eye level on the door.

Step 2. *Check the back of these instructions for the correct drill bit size for your door and insert it into your drill.*

Step 3. *To avoid splintering the door when drilling, it is a good idea to place a 5-cm wood strip over the site to be drilled on the front and inside of the door. The installer can secure the strips with a C-clamp.*

Step 4. *The installer may now drill through the door and the two wood strips.*

Step 5. *The hollow tube portion of the peephole should be inserted into the hole from the outside of the door.*

Step 6. *The threaded eyepiece can now be inserted into the hole from the inside of the door and turned until it is tight.*

Step 1. _____

_____

Step 2. _____

_____

Step 3. _____

_____

Step 4. _____

_____

Step 5. _____

_____

Step 6. _____

_____

You should have been able to improve the clarity and reduce the number of words considerably in all of these steps — except one. Ask a friend or colleague which set of instructions he or she prefers — the first set, or yours.

You also achieve clarity by the *thoroughness* of your instructions — by not assuming that, if an action is obvious to you, then it must also be obvious to your reader. In Step 2 of the previous activity, for example, the writer did not assume that the reader (someone who has never installed a peephole before) knows what to do with the drill bit after checking for the right size; the writer, instead, says "insert it into your drill." The extent to which you detail every action in the instructions, of course, varies with the knowledge level of your readers. A reader analysis (see Chapter Four) can help you identify that level clearly.

Activity 3

Read the everyday processes listed in the first column. Compare the way the first step is written for an inexperienced reader with the way it is written for a more experienced reader. Fill in the appropriate blanks for the remaining two processes.

Process	Inexperienced Reader	Experienced Reader
Washing laundry	Step 1: Sort all laundry into stacks according to kinds of fabrics and lightness and darkness of colours.	Step 1: Sort the laundry.
Driving a car	Step 1: Insert the key into the ignition and turn it clockwise.	Step 1: Start the car engine.
Boiling water	Step 1: _____	Step 1: _____
Using a payphone	Step 1: _____	Step 1: _____

Your audience's technical or experience level plays a key role in determining the amount of detail you include in your instructions.

Nothing clouds clarity in writing more than incorrect or incomplete information. After writing instructions, follow these three rules to ensure they are accurate:

1. Test them.
2. Test them again.
3. Have someone else test them.

The credibility of an entire set of instructions is seriously diminished when even one step is incorrect, out of sequence, or incomplete. As a knowledgeable person who probably has completed a process dozens of times, you may overlook or forget an action that an inexperienced person may need to know. Careful testing of all written instructions reveals any problems. Therefore, *follow your own instructions yourself to see if all steps are correct.*

Regardless of your readers' knowledge level, they all want some basic information in your instructions. Essentially, your readers will expect answers to these questions:

◆ What are these instructions used for?
◆ Are there any specialty words that I will need to know to understand these instructions?
◆ What level of expertise will I need?
◆ Is there anything I need to be careful of?
◆ What equipment, materials, and tools will I need?
◆ What is the first, second, third, … step I will take?
◆ How can I tell whether I did it right?
◆ How can I fix it if I did something wrong?
◆ What should my project look like or be like when I am done?

Include this information in all sets of instructions (with some variations as needed). Use the model outline shown in Figure 14.5 as a guide. Since this model contains every element needed for a lengthy set of complex instructions, modify it to suit each specific instructional purpose and audience.

Title or Title Page

Begin your instructions with a clear, limiting, yet inclusive title. See Chapter Nine for detailed information on writing titles and on developing well-balanced title pages.

Introduction

The introduction is important in instructions because it states what the instructions are used for; it gives readers a brief overview of the

MODEL OUTLINE: INSTRUCTIONS

Title or title page
1. Introduction
   1.1 Explain briefly what these instructions are used for
   1.2 Describe the general areas covered
   1.3 State the level of expertise required
   1.4 Include a glossary of specialty terms
   1.5 State any safety warnings or cautions
2. List all equipment/materials/tools needed
3. Give a step-by-step account of all basic operating instructions
   3.1 Step 1
      3.1.1 State the specific action required
      3.1.2 Describe the expected result(s) (if appropriate)
   3.2 Step 2
      3.2.1 State the specific action required
      3.2.2 Describe the expected result(s) (if appropriate)
   3.3 Etc.
4. Give a step-by-step account of all optional or sophisticated options (as needed)
   4.1 Step 1
      4.1.1 State how and where this option fits in with the basic operations/process
      4.1.2 State the specific action required
      4.1.3 Describe the expected result(s) of this action (if needed)
   4.2 Etc.
5. Explain what to do when things go wrong (troubleshooting)
   5.1 State the potential problem
   5.2 Give the cause of the problem
   5.3 Give the response required to correct it
6. Outcome/results (as needed)
   6.1 Describe briefly what the finished product/process should look/be like
   6.2 Describe briefly what happens now to the finished product or what happens next in the process

Figure 14.5 *Effective instructions include the topics shown in this model outline.*

entire process; it tells them what (if anything) they need to know before following the instructions; it defines all specialty terms; and it states any safety warnings or cautions readers need to be aware of as they perform the actions stated. Of course, not every set of instructions will need all these elements. *After* you have carefully identified the purpose of the instructions and the knowledge level of your readers, you may omit any parts you think unnecessary.

In general, begin instructions with a concise purpose statement similar to this:

EXAMPLE: These instructions give the steps required to process the 220 Series Fan Assemblies through the water bath.

Next, tell the readers what general procedures they will complete as they follow the step-by-step directions. You could think of this part of the introduction as an abbreviated process description.

EXAMPLE: To complete the water bath process, you will perform the following procedures:

1. Use process sheets to verify correct components and temperatures.
2. Inspect the cover for damaged grooves.
3. Correctly set the reservoir plate.
4. Correctly stake the reservoir plate.

If readers need to know other processes before they will be able to follow your instructions, state clearly what their technical/experience level should be.

EXAMPLE: Before performing the water bath procedure, you should be completely familiar with the clip weld and coil installation procedures so you can accurately inspect the condition of the assembly as it arrives at the water bath station.

Warn readers about any safety precautions *before* you present the operating or process instructions. For longer sets of instructions, include warnings or cautions in the introduction ("Keep your hands away from the cutting mechanism whenever it is operating"), then repeat the warning or caution in the operating instructions, just before the appropriate step.

If readers need to know any terms in order to understand your instructions, define them in the introduction. For example, readers may not have any idea what a reservoir plate is, does, or looks like. Define the term clearly before telling them to do something with it. See Chapter Seven for information on writing definitions.

List of Equipment Needed

List all the supplies the reader will need to complete each step given in the instructions: equipment, materials, tools. Be specific. Tell readers they need "a Phillips screwdriver," not just "a screwdriver"; tell them they need "a $3\frac{1}{2}$-inch diskette," not just "a diskette."

Step-by-Step Directions

Specific directions give readers a well-marked road map to help them travel through the process until they reach their final destination (a job done right). Make this section as detailed as your readers need it to be. It is better to include *too much* detail than to omit a step. Use action-related statements, not lengthy explanations.

To show the correct sequence of actions clearly, use one of these two methods for presenting instructions:

◆ *Enumeration.* Numbering steps 1, 2, 3, … , or Step 1, Step 2, Step 3, …

◆ *Dialogue.* Numbering steps and telling the reader what the results of each action should be

Enumerated (numbered) instructions are much easier to read and follow than paragraphs. Number and state each specific action required in a list like the following:

1. Wrap adhesive tape around the nut.

2. Put a wrench on it and turn it counterclockwise.

3. Remove the old shower head.

Whenever possible, divide the steps so that only one action is included in each step.

Additionally, you should add "dialogue" to enumerated steps if the process is one where each action shows visible results. When you include dialogue, you show the reader what specific results to expect from each step in the process. For example:

Action	**Screen Response**
Step 1: Key in your user ID and confidential password, then press the ENTER key.	The Master Menu appears on your screen.

Dialogue instructions are frequently used for computer-related directions. This method for writing instructions confirms results so that your readers will know when they acted correctly.

Additional/Sophisticated Options

Show your readers the basic steps first. Do not clutter the path that readers must travel with "signs" pointing in other directions. After you provide the basic instructions, then you may include any additional or sophisticated options in a separate section. Be sure to tell the reader where these options occur in the sequence of basic steps:

EXAMPLE: After completing Step 4 in the basic operating instructions, you have the option to....

Troubleshooting

If appropriate, give your readers any help you can to correct inadvertent errors that they may make while following your instructions. Try to anticipate potential difficulties. (Perhaps you can remember some specific problems you had while you were learning the process!) At the very least, you should always test and troubleshoot what you have just written. Follow the instructions yourself; intentionally press the wrong key or attach a component incorrectly; consider and solve the typical problems or difficulties your reader might have.

   To present troubleshooting information clearly, state the potential problem ("nut and bolt won't turn"), tell what probably caused the problem ("sulphur has built up in threads"), then describe the actions required to fix the problem ("clean the surface with a mild solvent and soft cloth"). Listing this information (as shown below) often provides a clear and quick solution for frustrated readers:

Error Message	Cause	Response
FILE NOT FOUND	The filename keyed is not contained on the current diskette inserted in your computer.	Check the directory of your diskette files to confirm that the file is listed, and then rekey the filename exactly as it appears on the list.

Outcome/Results

Include this optional section when appropriate. For example, if the process is long or complex, tell the audience what to look for to confirm that the finished product/process is correct. If the process continues with a subsequent set of instructions, tell the audience what to expect in the next part of the process, especially if someone else will perform the next part.

Graphics

Use graphics whenever possible to add even more clarity to instructions. Examine your step-by-step directions to see if a supporting graphic may help readers perform the task even more accurately. In effective instructions, visuals *support* or reinforce the written directions given first; they should never replace a step or a description. Simple line drawings, clear photographs, and pictograms often help the audience see what the finished product should look like, how one part should be aligned with another, where the cursor on a computer screen should be positioned, or what important safety message should be noted. See Chapter Eight for more information on developing clear graphics to help your readers accomplish their tasks more successfully.

Form in Instructions

Instructions may be written as informal reports or formal reports. In informal reports, the instructions and related sections compose the entire report. In longer formal instructional reports (frequently called manuals), the basic operating instructions compose only a portion of the entire report. (Other parts may include a detailed product/mechanism description, details on specific controls and switches involved, and maintenance instructions.) Instructions are rarely written as memos or letters.

As described earlier, instructions may be written in either a dialogue or simple enumerated format. Either form can be used in a formal or informal instructional report. Table 14.2 provides a quick reference for choosing the best form for each set of instructions you write.

Both formats — dialogue and enumerated — are important aids in producing clear instructional reports. Unlike lengthy paragraphs which are sometimes difficult to follow, these formats help readers focus on what is important.

TABLE 14.2

GUIDELINES FOR CHOOSING THE BEST FORM FOR INSTRUCTIONS

Form	Used When	Content
Dialogue	Direct and immediate results of each action are visible	Numbered steps of action-related directions and corresponding results of each action
Enumerated	Results of actions are not evident (essentially) until process is complete	Numbered steps of action-related directions only

Order in Instructions

The most effective order for all sets of instructions is sequential and chronological (from beginning to end). In the workplace situations described below, the writers chose different instructional forms because of the specific nature of the processes being explained, yet both used an effective sequential, chronological order.

> Sandy Glassman is a head nurse in the Family Medicine Centre. The patients admitted to her floor often have just undergone surgery. Intravenous feedings are a common occurrence, but only on occasion do the physicians order potassium chloride added to the patient's IV solution. Correct infusion of this drug into the IV is essential to guarantee that the patient does not suffer from an accidental skin lump.

As part of her involvement in the Centre's quality initiative, Sandy suggested that a set of instructions be written for the registered nurses on her unit, detailing the exact steps necessary to ensure correct infusion into the IVs. The administration asked Sandy to write them and accepted her instructions as part of the documenting procedure (See Figure 14.6.) The numbered steps emphasize the correct sequence of each action and ensure that no step is omitted.

> Jason Kehoe, the cut and balance machine technician at Power Manufacturing, is going on vacation next week. Linda O'Reilly will be replacing him until he returns. Since Linda has never used the cut and balance machine with a digital display monitor, Jason must tell Linda exactly how to operate the machine by giving her detailed step-by-step instructions.

Figure 14.7 shows the set of instructions Jason prepared for Linda. Since each step produces a specific response on the screen, he used the dialogue instructional form. Again, the correct sequence of actions is essential and the enumerated steps emphasize the importance of following them in order. Note also the "warnings" of general concern, which Jason included in the introduction, and the need for "caution" he noted before he described the specific steps.

> Louise Santini recently bought a digital clock radio/cassette recorder. As a frequent traveller, she had often been confused by the variety of clock radios she had encountered in

HOW TO INFUSE POTASSIUM CHLORIDE CORRECTLY INTO AN INTRAVENOUS SOLUTION

Purpose

These instructions detail the steps required to infuse potassium chloride correctly into an intravenous (IV) solution. The insertion, injection, and inversion steps detailed next ensure that your patient is safe from the risks of concentrated potassium that result from incorrect infusion.

Expertise Needed

Before proceeding with these instructions, you must have an understanding of the proper procedures for handling and preparing any IV admixture.

Materials Needed

You will need a 4 cm additive needle, a flexible plastic IV container filled with D_5W, rubber IV tubing, and the prescribed dosage of potassium chloride.

Directions

Step 1: Fill the syringe with the drug.

Step 2: Insert the additive needle fully (up to its hub) into the rubber injection port tubing.

Step 3: Inject the potassium quickly to create a turbulent flow around the top of the needle and to distribute the drug into the solution.

Step 4: Invert the container four to six times to mix the potassium thoroughly into the IV solution.

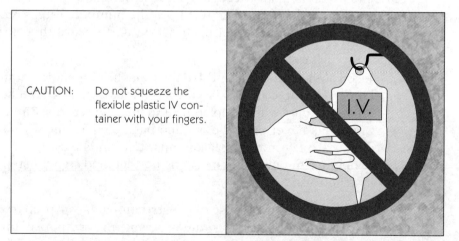

CAUTION: Do not squeeze the flexible plastic IV container with your fingers.

Outcome

This careful technique of infusing potassium chloride into an IV container creates a powerful mixing force that prevents pooling of the drug in the bottom of the container. It virtually guarantees that your patient will be safe from the risks of burning pain and an accidental skin lump at the injection site and from tissue damage.

Figure 14.6 *These instructions enumerate steps to emphasize the correct sequence.*

OPERATING INSTRUCTIONS FOR THE DIGITAL CUT AND BALANCE MACHINE

Purpose

Follow the directions given below to locate any imbalances on the fan assembly covers. This process includes inserting the covers correctly on the machine, pressing the correct keypad sequences to get an accurate reading on the display, and marking the imbalances with the correct colour code.

Expertise Needed

You must know the names of all specific locations on the fan assembly covers to identify accurately any imbalances indicated on the machine's digital display.

Definitions

An imbalance is a variance in the equilibrium of the fan cover that affects the stability of the entire assembly when mounted in an automobile. A cover variance of plus or minus 0.15 oz/in. requires correction.

Warnings

To reduce the risk of electric shock, make sure all covers are free from any moisture before inserting on the balance wheel.

Operating Instructions

STEP	SCREEN RESPONSE
1. Insert cover onto balance wheel and press ENTER on the keypad.	Three zeros (000) appear on the screen display.
2. Press ENTER again.	FIRST READING DONE message appears.
3. Press NEXT LINE button on keypad.	TURN PART CLOCKWISE message appears.
4. Press SET UP button on keypad.	DO TOOLING COMP message appears.
5. Press IMBALANCE button on keypad.	AMT OK or specific digital imbalance message appears.

Figure 14.7 *These instructions use dialogue form so that readers can confirm correct actions immediately. (Continued on page 408.)*

CAUTION: The colour-coding procedure given next is essential to ensure that the covers are corrected as needed.

6. If imbalance is >0.15 oz/in., mark location in red as displayed on the screen. If imbalance is <0.15 oz/in., mark location in orange as displayed on screen. If no imbalance is indicated, mark the centre of the cover in green.

Digital imbalance reading flashes until you perform the next step.

7. Remove the cover from the balance wheel and press the RESET button on the keypad.

ALL READINGS RESET message appears.

8. Place cover in appropriate colour-coded basket and start again with Step 1 and a new cover.

Outcome

A materials handling operator picks up your colour-coded baskets and distributes them to the appropriate areas for correction (if required) or for insertion of the hex shaft (if no correction is required).

Figure 14.7 *continued*

hotel rooms. They all seemed to have different methods of setting the time and alarm, and no instruction booklets were provided. Therefore, when she bought her own clock, she was careful to buy from a company that provided with its product complete, accurate, and easy-to-follow instructions on how to set all the functions. Louise said the clear instructions were one reason she bought the product.

Figure 14.8 shows an excerpt from the step-by-step instructions Louise followed. The instructions include helpful hints and optional features sections. The *Setting the Correct Time* procedure is well organized and illustrated; Louise can easily match the three boxes with the written instructions, and she can also see the results of each step she takes.

To Set the Correct Time

To set the correct time on the clock display, use the following procedure.

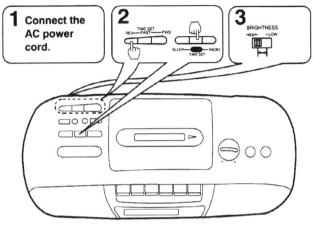

1 Connect the AC power cord to your household AC power outlet.
The clock display will begin to flash continuously.

2 While pressing the off/time set button, press and hold the time set buttons until the correct time appears on the clock display.
The digits should stop flashing.

To forward or reverse the displayed time rapidly, press and hold the FAST button with the FWD or REV button.

To forward or reverse the displayed time minute by minute, press the FWD or REV button repeatedly.

The seconds are automatically set to "0" when the FWD or REV button is pressed.

Observe the PM indicator. A green dot (PM indicator) indicates "PM" and no dot indicates "AM".

3 Set the brightness selector on the back of the unit to "HIGH" or "LOW".

To increase the brightness of the time display, set this selector to HIGH"; to decrease it, set to "LOW".

The correct time can usually be obtained by listening for time checks on the radio or from telephone time services.

The time set (REV-FAST-FWD) buttons can only activate when the off/time set button is pressed.

Figure 14.8 *Illustrations, well-divided directions, and the inclusion of helpful information make these instructions easy to follow.*
Copyright Matsushita Electric Industrial Co., Ltd. Reprinted with permission.

QUESTIONS FOR DISCUSSION

1. When is a process description written? Why?
2. Which questions do readers want answered in process descriptions?
3 When is a set of instructions written? Why?
4. How does the writing style of instructions differ from that of process descriptions?
5. What are the two forms for listing instructions? Describe when to use each and how each appears on the page.

EXERCISES

a. Assume you are writing a *process description* on how to register for classes at your college or local recreation centre. Read the parts of a process description listed below; then, in the blanks provided, write what information you would include in your report.

1. Definition of the process

   _____

   _____

2. Explanation of why the process is used

   _____

   _____

3. Sequence 1 in the process

   _____

   _____

4. Sequence 2 in the process

   _____

   _____

5. Outcome/results of the process

   _____

   _____

b. Assume you are writing *instructions* for first-time registrants at your college or local recreation centre. Read the parts of a set of instructions listed next; then, in the blanks provided, write the appropriate information as specified.

1. Brief explanation of what these instructions are used for

2. Description of the general areas covered

3. Step 1

4. Step 2

5. Explanation of what to do if something goes wrong

WRITING ASSIGNMENTS

1. Find a process description in a printed source (such as trade magazines, library books, journals, or your textbooks). Make a photocopy of the description. Using the model outline shown in Figure 14.1, underline the major parts and the major sequences and label them in the margins of the description.

2. Write a short process description (250 words) about a simple process. Here are some possible topics:

- Reducing the risk of breakage in the mail
- Ordering/selecting office supplies

◆ Checking your workstation for fire hazards
◆ Ensuring proper care of computer diskettes

3. Write a longer process description (500 words or more) on one of the following topics:

◆ Closing out a cash register
◆ Installing a CD player in your car
◆ Inspecting a house for termites
◆ Getting a loan approved
◆ Preparing for a job interview
◆ Setting up and/or conducting a lab experiment
◆ Leaving a workplace (such as a fast-food restaurant) or workstation in order
◆ Protecting a house from severe storms
◆ Conducting a computer-based search for information

4. Write a short set of instructions (no more than seven steps) for a very simple process. Write these instructions for a reader who is familiar with similar processes. Include tools and materials and even drawings, as you wish. Below are some suggested topics:

◆ How to drive a nail
◆ How to use a handsaw
◆ How to install toggle bolts
◆ How to clean a paintbrush

5. Write an informal set of instructions to explain to the students at your college the steps involved in locating a book on the library's computer. Assume that most of these students are unfamiliar with computers and the data bank. Include all necessary introductory and concluding material, and use visual aids (depictions of the screen menus, perhaps) as you wish. If your library does not have a computerized database, detail the steps required to locate material through the card catalogue (Dewey decimal system, Library of Congress), through various printed directories, and so forth. Follow the same writing guidelines given above.

6. Write a complete set of instructions for something you know how to do quite well. Be sure your topic is narrowed sufficiently. Write these instructions for another student who knows little or nothing about how to do the process. (Determine your intended reader's knowledge/experience level before you write.) Include the appropriate amount of detail, as well as all necessary introductory, troubleshooting, and concluding material. Below are some suggestions for topics:

- How to groom a horse
- How to ride a motorcycle
- How to use telephone etiquette for business success
- How to change the spark plugs in your car
- How to develop film
- How to operate a sewing machine
- How to format a diskette on the computer lab's computers
- How to use dental floss correctly
- How to install a laser printer for a personal computer
- How to tie a fly or bait a hook

Part FIVE

WRITING ANALYTICAL AND PERSUASIVE REPORTS

Objectives

When you finish Part Five — Chapters Fifteen and Sixteen — you should be able to do the following:

- ◆ Analyze data.
- ◆ Organize and write well-researched evaluation reports.
- ◆ Organize and write effective feasibility reports.
- ◆ Identify the purposes of and audience for various persuasive reports.
- ◆ Organize and write winning proposals.
- ◆ Write appropriate responses to requests for proposals.

Chapter FIFTEEN

Analytical Reports

Analytical reports do more than just present information: They *interpret* the meaning of that information for the readers. (See Figure 15.1.) After your readers have read the "what" and "why" of a report, they might next ask, *"So what?"* An analytical report responds to this question with answers like these: "So ... a CompTech computer meets our needs better than does a MicroTech computer," or "So ... redirecting drug distribution duties in the pharmacy is a reasonable and possible action."

Individuals in all job fields — engineering and technology, health and medicine, business and marketing — frequently must separate and examine (analyze) information for others. Their expertise qualifies them to evaluate, compare, interpret, diagnose, and recommend with judgment.

Depending on their main objectives, analytical reports may interpret information in the following ways:

◆ *Evaluate.* Is a specific product/process effective?

◆ *Compare.* Is Brand X better than Brand Y?

◆ *Interpret.* What do test/survey results mean?

◆ *Diagnose.* What is the cause of a problem?

◆ *Conclude.* Does a project/process meet objectives?

◆ *Recommend.* What is the solution to a problem? Should a project be developed or not?

Analytical reports are effective vehicles for communicating the data's meaning in the workplace. Two kinds of analytical reports frequently written are evaluation reports and feasibility reports. Though both analyze data, their objectives and focuses differ: The evaluation report analyzes data concerning an unchanging, static situation and then draws specific conclusions; the feasibility report analyzes data to determine whether a change in a situation is possible and reasonable and then recommends action.

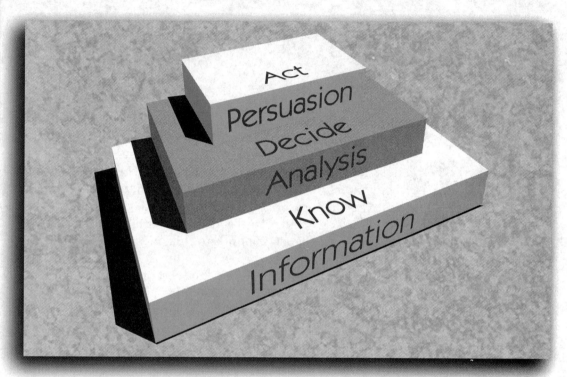

Figure 15.1 *Analyses and decisions are based on solid knowledge and information.*

Both reports interpret information, and both reports draw conclusions based on their findings. A feasibility report, however, focuses strongly on action. Sometimes it expands on an evaluation or analysis presented in a previous report.

For example, you would write an evaluation report when your readers want to know whether their workplace environment is contributing to a drastic increase in employee absenteeism through sickness. You would write a feasibility report when readers want to know whether there is a reasonable or urgent need to renovate the building or to rent new office space, and whether sufficient resources are available to make the decision workable.

You would write an evaluation report when readers want to know whether "just-in-time" manufacturing is an effective production system. You write a feasibility report when readers want to know whether implementing "just-in-time" manufacturing at Palmer Industries is a practical idea and whether the resources are available to do so.

With some variations, these two kinds of technical reports cover many analytical assignments on the job. Below are some guidelines and considerations for writing them.

PREPARING TO WRITE AN ANALYTICAL REPORT

You must begin to work on a successful analytical report long before you begin to write — even before you begin to analyze the information. When you prepare either an evaluation or a feasibility report, follow the three steps below to ensure that your efforts result in a competent analysis.

Step 1: Identify the Objectives

First, clearly define the purpose of the analysis. You cannot do a good job until you know exactly what the job is. Be sure to complete an objectives and audience worksheet. (See Chapter Four.)

Step 2: Find Useful Information

Use the library only as a starting point for gathering information. For many analytical reports, library sources cannot adequately address the important questions that readers need answered. You can also gather useful information for analytical reports from a variety of other sources. If you are employed, many of these sources will be easily accessible in company files and records or from the personnel department. If you are not employed, check with community resource persons or personnel directors at local organizations. For the most part, you will find cooperative assistance in locating useful information for your report.

Depending on the specific nature of your analytical report, look into these research possibilities:

◆ Resources for technology/methodology
  Regional and industrial directories
  Inquiries and requests to all possible technology sources
  Interviews with other organizations which have evaluated similar situations and similar actions
  Laboratory tests
  Firsthand observations

◆ Resources for finances/costs
  Your company's annual report
  Financial reports and fiscal budgets
  Other related reports

       Interviews with key personnel in your company's financial
department

       Questionnaires and surveys

◆ Resources for personnel/operations

       Organization charts

       Operating unit profiles

       Company staff profiles

       Company job descriptions

       Personnel data

       Interviews with other organizations attempting similar
actions

       Interviews with persons who might be affected

       Questionnaires and surveys

Refer to Chapter Six ("Collecting and Documenting Information")
for other possibilities for finding information and for guidelines
about conducting interviews and developing questionnaires.
Nonlibrary sources are often the best places to acquire data for a
valid and valuable analysis.

Step 3: Place Raw Data in Outline Order

Frequently, you collect a large stack of potentially usable information as you prepare to write an analytical report. An outline is a
valuable tool to help you sort through the data. Take the raw information you have collected — charts, reports, budgets, tables, note
cards — and place each item in order according to your outline. This
step helps you see any gaps in your information where you may need
to gather more data.

INTERPRETING AND ANALYZING THE INFORMATION

After collecting and organizing the data for your analytical report,
allow yourself enough time to examine and separate each piece of
information. Effective analysis is the result of careful scrutiny.

Examine All Data Objectively

As you begin to examine the data closely, remember the importance
of objectivity. To make certain that your interpretation and analysis
are unbiased, you must review *all* the data, not just the part that
helps you reach the conclusion or recommendation you want or

expect. As an example, look at these statements found in an informational report on current methods of pest control:

a. The potato beetle is becoming increasingly resistant to chemical insecticides. The "Beetle Eater" vacuum machine works effectively to rid plants of beetles.

b. The "Beetle Eater" has a weak drive system causing frequent downtime.

A writer preparing an analytical report for Breadbasket Farms on whether these vacuum machines are a reasonable and possible alternative to chemical pest control must consider both statements. If you include only Statement a., you may lead the reader to conclude that a vacuum machine is necessary because soon chemicals will no longer work at all, and to accept the recommendation that the Beetle Eater is the best alternative. Statement b., however, may cause you and the reader to draw a different conclusion about the Beetle Eater's potential problems: probable malfunctions and possible costly repairs.

Assess the Data's Relevance

When you review your information, always look closely at each item and ask "Is this information important and relevant?" or "What does this information *mean?*" You will know that the information belongs in your report when your answers are similar to these: "It may mean this product is effective"; "It may mean this action is reasonable"; "It may mean these survey results are invalid"; or "It may mean this solution is not possible."

PLANNING GRAPHICS

Analytical reports usually contain significant amounts of data — relevant facts, numbers, and percentages which lead the writer (and the reader) to sound conclusions and, frequently, to reasonable recommendations. Clear presentation of all data is an important mission for every writer of technical reports. This mission frequently is accomplished (particularly in analytical reports) by giving statistics, test results, financial forecasts, and so forth in clear, visual representations: tables or charts; line, bar, or pie graphs; clear photographs or line drawings.

As you gather useful information for your analytical report, keep a sharp eye out for any graphics that have already been developed. If none are readily available, consider developing a table or graph yourself, rather than "burying" pertinent data in your text.

Plan to incorporate into your report as many graphics as possible to help clarify the analysis. Gather and develop these visual aids before you start to write; then make sure they supplement your verbal discussions adequately and appropriately.

WRITING STYLE

To be convincing, evaluation reports and feasibility reports need a style that inspires faith in the writer's technical competence. In presenting the facts, your interpretation of the facts, and your recommendations, you should choose words that reflect a careful and objective evaluation of the problem or situation, as the following examples illustrate.

> POOR: Unless you buy new welding equipment soon, the business will go under.

> IMPROVED: To prevent further equipment downtime and ensuing loss of revenue, we recommend that you purchase the TriumphArc Welder, which our analysis has shown to be the best option.

Your language must show that you have approached the problem, conducted the evaluation, and made the final recommendation in the best interests of your customers. Extreme or threatening statements will not encourage your readers' trust.

WRITING AN EVALUATION REPORT

Evaluation reports supply both data and the interpretation of that data for a decision maker. The writer reviews a situation, a product, a service, or a procedure with the clear intention of judging its value to the organization.

Reasons for Writing Evaluation Reports

Evaluation is an ongoing process in all professional areas; a report that evaluates something essentially answers the general question "How good is it?"

Materials are constantly tested; institutions are reviewed (your college program, for example, undergoes periodic self-studies and reviews by its provincial or national accrediting association); social and health programs are evaluated by companies and agencies; governmental task forces evaluate programs; consumer advocate groups evaluate products; businesses evaluate their services, personnel, and equipment; total quality management or continuous quality improvement organizations constantly evaluate and document processes and procedures. Only when something is evaluated objectively and found to be effective, useful, safe, or workable can valid decisions be made for the next move. Thus, the general label *evaluation* applies to many kinds of reports.

Effective evaluation reports answer specific questions about quality and/or quantity. The writer should not waste time researching general or irrelevant points, and the reader should not have to waste time reading them.

Evaluation reports may answer questions relating to past actions, current status, or potential outcomes. They often start with questions such as the following:

◆ *Past performance.* Was the drug prevention program instituted last year at Yardley High School effective? Did the no-smoking regulation at Tremont Mall result in a healthier staff?

◆ *Present status.* How well is the automated assembly line working compared to the nonautomated lines? Are employees at IMT adequately protected from noise, air, and chemical pollution? How cost-effective is the current mainframe system at IMT? How knowledgeable are Jones Elementary School children in the use of computers?

◆ *Potential outcomes.* Will a specific piece of equipment improve our output? Will a mandatory wellness program increase productivity and improve attendance at Cuvett's Distribution? To what extent?

Activity 1

Reread the questions in the preceding bulleted material. Find eight words or phrases (nouns, verbs, modifiers) which indicate that the intent of the reports based on the questions is *judgmental* and *evaluative*. Then, in the blanks below, write the words or phrases that you found.

_____   _____

_____   _____

_____   _____

_____   _____

The main purpose of an evaluation report is to judge something. When you identify the objectives for an evaluation report, be sure to include words that clearly indicate your judgmental, evaluative purpose.

Evaluative Areas and Criteria

To analyze a fairly large or general subject, you must subdivide it into specific areas to be covered, and then apply specific criteria to measure or evaluate those areas.

For example, you might evaluate a new car by analyzing these areas: appearance, fuel economy, and ease of handling. You might further subdivide an area such as "appearance" into these specific parts: interior and exterior, paint and upholstery, or accessories. When your college program is undergoing its evaluation for reaccreditation, reviewers study areas such as faculty, facilities, and courses, subdividing each area into more specific parts.

In the workplace, you might evaluate a policy by looking at these areas: impact on salaried employees, impact on hourly employees, and impact on management. You might further subdivide the area "impact on hourly employees" into these parts: full-time employees and part-time employees. Similarly, you might evaluate a CNC machine lathe by interpreting data in these major operating areas: loader arm, tooling bits, keyboard, and digital display Typically, an evaluation report investigates at least three areas and, when possible, subdivides each area into at least two parts.

Activity 2
....

Subdivide the following general topics into at least three evaluative areas as the bases for analysis:

a. Your watch

_____

_____

_____

b. Your textbook for this or another course

_____

_____

_____

c. The registration procedure at your college

_____

_____

_____

The next step is to look at each area to see if it might be examined in even more specific ways. Select one of the topics from the list above along with one of its areas. Then subdivide it further into two specific parts.

Topic: _____

    Area 1: _____

        Part 1: _____

        Part 2: _____

The *criteria* you select to evaluate these areas and parts will be an essential component of your analysis. Criteria are the specific standards by which areas/parts can be judged. For example, the criteria you select to evaluate your car's appearance might include durability, upkeep or maintenance, and resale value. The criteria for evaluating a policy might include time saved, money saved, and quality added. All evaluative areas and parts must be measured against clearly defined criteria to ensure a valid analysis.

Appropriate Evaluative Strategies

You must determine the various ways to proceed with an investigation and the best strategies to gather data for the subject. The methodology you use to collect the data and subsequently to arrive at a conclusion is important. If your research methods appear invalid or superficial, your analysis and conclusions will be suspect.

Effective investigative strategies include citing published or unpublished works; using questionnaires, surveys, or interviews; performing tests; and documenting firsthand observations. Use methods appropriate for your subject.

Consider the case of a manufacturing company that wants to choose the best colour for a new appliance. To evaluate customer appeal, the company asks potential customers to view different colours and report their preferences. To determine which paint will best withstand the heat generated by the appliance, the company also conducts scientific laboratory tests.

When you choose a strategy, be mindful of the goal you want to achieve. To determine whether pedestrians would use a bridge across downtown streets, you would choose one strategy; to determine whether a certain grade of steel is sufficient for building such pedestrian bridges, you would need quite a different strategy. Readers expect you to tell them how you gathered the data supporting your conclusions, and they expect you to use appropriate strategies for your subject.

Valid and Logical Conclusions

An effective evaluation requires more than just an accumulation of facts and information, and it demands more than mere opinion. Valid conclusions (the purpose of an evaluation report) are always clearly supported by data. A logical analysis of test results, survey and questionnaire tabulations, testimonials, or secondary resources should produce conclusions which the reader will accept as plausible and reasonable.

If in a report on ABC Industries' equipment, you conclude that "The present machine lathe equipment is outdated and inefficient," the reasonable question is "How do you know?" When you respond, "Based on ..." and supply sufficient data to support your conclusion, the reader can use your information and conclusion to make a decision about whether or not to purchase new equipment.

Include recommendations in your evaluation reports only if you are specifically requested to do so. For example, your supervisor might ask you to draw a conclusion *and* to recommend whether ABC Industries should replace its present equipment with computerized equipment.

Activity 3
....

Assume that your research has produced the following data for each of the subjects below. Write a valid conclusion about each.

a. The reliability of your watch
   1. In two years, it has not lost even a minute.
   2. Fourteen friends have the same brand and they report accurate timekeeping over a period of one to seven years.
   3. In water and sub-zero weather, your watch has continued to run.

   Conclusion: _____

b. The usefulness of the textbook in NOCOURSE 108
   1. One hundred and twenty students ranked it poor to fair in coverage.
   2. Three instructors found more than 20 factual errors in the first five chapters.
   3. No exercises and no objectives are included.

Conclusion: _____

c. The feasibility of requiring all students enrolling at Camborne College to buy their own notebook computers

1. A recent survey shows that the four existing labs cannot accommodate the 500 students who need computer time.
2. In the last two years, students have not been able to submit assignments (business and CAD in particular) on time.
3. Levels of frustration among students in high-tech courses are increasing because of computer assignment workload.
4. Despite computer labs staying open 24 hours a day, students still cannot get enough computer time.
5. Many students cannot afford to buy notebook computers.
6. The college has a policy of accessibility and affordability.
7. Students who cannot afford to buy a computer can make arrangements to lease-to-buy.
8. Students will not comply with the new requirement.
9. Fewer students will drop out if they invest more in their education by buying a computer.
10. Fewer students will enrol and more students will leave if the new requirement is implemented.

Conclusion: _____

_____

You will have noticed that c. requires you to examine positives and negatives and to draw your own conclusion. Discuss the conclusion in class or with your colleagues.

Content in Evaluation Reports

Since the purpose of an evaluation report is to judge how good something is, your readers will focus on the conclusion(s) you draw. The bulk of your report, however, will be the analysis which leads to those conclusions.

A model outline for evaluation reports is shown in Figure 15.2. Depending on the reports you write, modify the outline accordingly. The short report in memo form in Figure 15.3 illustrates the typical content of an evaluation report. Many evaluation reports are much longer than this example and require the components of a formal report. Chapter Nine provides detailed information about these formal report components; the following discussion explains how you adapt these components for an evaluation report.

Title Page

The title of an evaluation report should specifically indicate the subject being evaluated. Notice the sample titles below:

POOR: Evaluation Report on Tempero Watch

IMPROVED: An Evaluation of Tempero Watch: Its Cost, Durability, and Reliability

The title page also includes the writer's name and position, the date, and the name and position of the report's recipient. Other elements are optional, depending on the company's policy.

Table of Contents

This quick guide to the topics being covered and methods of assessment gives your readers their first overview of the report's contents. Make it easy to read at a glance by indenting, spacing, and capitalizing appropriately.

Abstract or Executive Summary

An abstract tells your readers whether the report meets their needs by summarizing exactly what the report covers and concludes. For managers, the executive summary highlights the main points of the report. Your report should include one or the other, not both.

Conclusions

Conclusions may be placed preceding the body of the evaluation report to save readers time (assuming they do not need to read the body of the report carefully) or they may be placed following the analysis in the body of the report (when readers will be more prepared for them). Wherever you decide to place your conclusions, be sure they are logically and objectively derived from the data presented in the body of the report. Avoid any excessive terminology, any comment which sounds like a sales pitch, or any unwarranted praise. Look at the conclusion statements below:

POOR: The working conditions at the Newtown branch are terrible.

IMPROVED: The working conditions at the Newtown branch are poor compared to those at the head office in Oldborough.

Any extreme statement — positive or negative — is likely to make your reader suspect your impartiality and objectivity.

Recommendations

Include recommendations in an evaluation report when they have been requested. While conclusions are *supported* judgments, recommendations are the writer's ideas about what should be done as a result. The key word in a recommendation is *should*. State your

---

MODEL OUTLINE: EVALUATION REPORTS

Title or Title Page
Table of Contents
Abstract or Executive Summary* with Conclusions (and Recommendations)

1. State conclusions based on analyses in 6.0**
   1.1 Conclusion 1
   1.2 Conclusion 2
   1.3 Conclusion 3
2. Make recommendation(s) if needed or requested**
3. Introduction
4. Overview/Background
   4.1 Describe the situation, product, or service
   4.2 Tell what areas are to be evaluated
   4.3 Tell what criteria will be used
5. Describe the methodology or assessment strategies used
   5.1 Printed primary sources (surveys, questionnaires)
   5.2 Personal observation
   5.3 Published (secondary) sources
   5.4 Other means of collecting data
        5.4.1 Tests
        5.4.2 Interviews
6. Discuss the findings
   6.1 Analysis of first area (and its parts)
   6.2 Analysis of second area (and its parts)
   6.3 Analysis of third area (and its parts)

---

*Include only one of these items.
**This item has optional placement.

Figure 15.2 *This model outline shows the organization of topics in an evaluation report.*

TO: Johannes R. Schoonover, Engineering Manager
FROM: William Singleton, Administrative Assistant
SUBJECT: Evaluation of Flexible Machining Centres
DATE: June 28, 19--

Introduction

In 19-- ABC purchased (after an initial six-month loan period) two Leblond Makino Flexible Machining Centres to replace 20-year old equipment which could not keep up with increased orders and with a new product line introduced last year.

On June 18, you requested a brief evaluation of the specific impact of the two Centres on ABC operations. The three areas reviewed were (1) overall production, (2) quality of parts produced, and (3) lead time and downtime.

Assessment Strategies

Plant personnel were interviewed; company records of employment, downtime, customer correspondence, and production schedules were reviewed; and personal observations were conducted of the revised floor plan.

Production

The Flex Cell is an automated manufacturing system designed specifically to increase productivity by making a wide variety of components as quickly as possible. Parts positioning and automatic tool changing are numerically controlled. A display screen on a control panel quickly detects potential problems. Thus, fewer operators are required and less training is necessary for new employees.

The Flex Cells are scheduled 24 hours per day, five days per week for 9,216 available machining hours per year at an 80 percent utilization rate. The remaining 3,180 hours were used to combine the operations from 47 other machines.

Thus floor space was better used and fork truck moves were reduced from 1,400 to 280 moves per month — an 80 percent improvement. This combination of operations reduced distance travelled by forklift moves from 3,575 to 750 metres per month, a 79 percent improvement. Improved forklift efficiency meant that 5 out of 15 employees could be placed elsewhere in the company.

Time

Lead time has been reduced from eight weeks to two weeks. The Flex Cells are programmed to produce the required number of parts on a weekly or monthly basis and to signal when the required number is completed. The setups on the Flex Cells are much less complex and require less operator time.

Figure 15.3 *This evaluation report presents its analysis in memo form.*

Downtime has also been significantly reduced since the new machines were introduced. In many cases, parts were unavailable for older machines and improvised repairs at the site could not be relied on. The plant foreman estimates downtime as less than 2 percent of that of previous years, although specific percentages cannot be determined. In the current year, fewer than 10 hours of downtime have occurred.

Improved Quality

Since the machines adjust themselves with the aid of an automatic measuring system (AMS), no scrap has been generated.

Conclusions

The installation of the Leblond Makino Flexible Machining Centres produced three major results:

1. Increased production
2. Reduced lead time and downtime
3. Improved quality of parts

Figure 15.3 *continued*

recommendations as actions and make them as specific as possible. Notice the following examples:

POOR: Something should be done about the working conditions at the Newtown branch.

IMPROVED: Oldborough head office should seriously consider implementing the list of improvements requested by Newtown branch management.

You may present your recommendations at the beginning or at the end of your report.

Introduction

For longer reports, the introduction reorients the reader who requested the report to a subject which he or she may have assigned weeks or months earlier. It states the purpose of the report and identifies specifically what is being evaluated and why. The introduction may also include definitions of special terms, statements about the scope and authorization, and any other information that the reader might need before starting the body of the report.

The Body of the Report

An evaluation report usually includes four main sections:

1. Background (What is the situation?)
2. Methodology (How is it assessed?)
3. Analysis (What is specifically revealed?)
4. Conclusions (What has been found or learned?)

In the background section, briefly orient the reader to the subject. Indicate what is being evaluated, where, and when, and in what circumstances the study is being done. You might also describe the product, situation, or service. The background section leads into the other main sections of the report and prepares the reader for the in-depth analysis.

The methodology section tells the reader how you went about gathering data. Here you state very clearly your strategies: the number of questionnaires you sent, the way you conducted tests, the circumstances in which you observed the situation, and so forth. Notice the sample statements below which could appear in a methodology section:

POOR: Questionnaires were distributed to employees at Newtown.

IMPROVED: On March 15, 19--, questionnaires containing 25 multiple-choice questions were distributed to 35 employees (3 management and 32 office workers); 31 questionnaires were returned.

In the analysis section (the major portion of your report), state what you found in your research. In well-constructed paragraphs supported by visual material, supply the data and information that led to your conclusions. Notice the following samples. One is very general; the other gives the specifics that the reader needs.

POOR: Some of the employees complained about the lack of proper ventilation.

IMPROVED: Sixty percent of the employees complained about the lack of ventilation in second-floor offices.

Selected pages of a student report are shown in Figure 15.4. The pages include the title page, transmittal letter, table of contents, abstract, conclusions, and introduction, along with the list of references. Two pages of the body are also shown so that you can see how the writers handle headings, use references, and integrate visuals. A look at the table of contents shows that the students evaluated four areas (heating loads, domestic hot water, domestic and public lighting, and equipment and appliances) and then described four energy conservation options.

AN ENERGY STUDY AND DESIGN

FOR AN 84-UNIT CONDOMINIUM

Prepared for
The Halifax County Condominium Corporation #15
and
The Nova Scotia Community College, Institute of Technology
Department of Mechanical Engineering Technology

Prepared by
Liling Tang and Mark MacLeod
Senior Mechanical Engineering Technology Students

June 8, 19--

Figure 15.4 *These selected pages from a student paper show some of the parts included in an evaluation report.*
Adapted with permission of Liling Tang, Mark MacLeod, and Stefan Dromlewicz.

Nova Scotia Community College, Institute of Technology
P.O. Box 2210
Halifax, Nova Scotia   B3J 3C4
June 8, 19--

Mr. S. Dromlewicz
Board member, HCCC#15
RR #2
Oceanside, Nova Scotia   BOK 2Z2

Dear Mr. Dromlewicz

The enclosed report titled "Energy Study and Design for an 84-Unit Condominium" is submitted in accordance with your request of November 30, 19--.

The purpose of this report is to evaluate the existing energy management of the building and to identify options for reducing energy costs.

We would like to thank the following people for their help and information:
Mr. R. Moulton, P.Eng., Design Engineer, Moulton Engineering;
Mr. David G. Lea, P.Eng.; the engineers at Whitman Benn Consulting; and
Ms. C. Rogers, P.Eng., our technical advisor at the Institute of Technology.

We would like to give special thanks to you for giving us this opportunity to complete and document an energy study as our major project, a requirement for graduation. This study has a practical significance as its results will, we trust, be used for the future energy management of the building.

Sincerely yours

Liling Tang and Mark MacLeod
Enclosure

Figure 15.4 *continued*

TABLE OF CONTENTS

Transmittal Letter   ii

Table of Contents   iii

Abstract   iv

Conclusions   v

1.   Introduction   1
    1.1 Background   1
    1.2 Objective   1
    1.3 Methodology   1
2.   Energy Usage Calculation   3
    2.1 Heating Loads   3
    2.2 Domestic Hot Water   8
    2.3 Public and Domestic Lighting   9
    2.4 Equipment and Appliances   11
3.   Energy Balance   14
4.   Energy Conservation Options   22
    4.1 Lighting Systems and Operation Control   22
    4.2 Alternative Energy Sources   24
    4.3 Domestic Hot Water Control   26
    4.4 Demand Meter   27
5.   Estimation of Energy Reduction and Financial Analysis   28
    5.1 Lighting   28
    5.2 Alternative Energy Sources   30
    5.3 Domestic Hot Water   33
References   35
Appendix A   Floor Plans
Appendix B   Detailed Calculations

Figure 15.4 *continued*

ABSTRACT

This report identifies the work required to meet the objectives of reducing energy costs of an 84-unit condominium in Dartmouth. The study focuses on the heating, lighting, domestic hot water, and other relevant systems. We evaluated these systems, calculated the energy consumption, identified cost-saving measures, and considered and recommended design options. We also investigated the usefulness of a public awareness campaign.

iv

CONCLUSIONS

Most energy consumed by the building is used in the heating system. According to the analysis, the following conservation options have been assessed and recommended. See Table 5.1, which summarizes the various cost-saving options.

1. Lighting System: The incandescent lamps can be replaced by energy-efficient fluorescent lamps for domestic and inside hallway lighting systems. If possible, automatic lighting control systems should be used.
2. Energy Sources: The solar-powered heating system is not a practical cost-saving option. Converting to oil domestic hot water heating is an option which should be considered. The upgrade costs are substantial ($40,000), but if conversion was used with other cost-saving measures, the payback would be approximately 15 years.
3. Domestic Hot Water Control: Low-flow shower heads can replace the present shower heads as a cheap effective option for cost savings. Payback takes less than a year. Low-flow shower heads used in combination with an oil domestic heating system is a cost-saving option, for which the payback is 16 years.
4. Public Awareness Campaign: A public awareness campaign should be considered. Features could include flyers on energy conservation, stickers above light switches reminding people to turn off the lights, and signs above clothes washers urging people to use cold water.

v

Figure 15.4 *continued*

1. INTRODUCTION

Energy conservation, one of the major components of energy management, can be defined as the more efficient or effective use of energy. The Halifax County Condominium Corporation #15 (HCCC#15) has concerns about one of its condominiums in Dartmouth. The electricity bills are high and the corporation is looking for short-term and long-term cost-containment measures. This report describes an energy audit. We completed an energy balance by comparing the heating loads of the system components to the energy input. From an analysis of the energy balance results, we were able to propose various energy conservation options.

1.1 Background

The condominium has three storeys. The entire building's space heating and hot water is electric. Space heating for all 84 apartments is controlled by individual room thermostats; hot water is provided from a central hot water tank. The building's electrical consumption is supplied through one metered supply. The cost of providing heat and hot water services to individual apartments is levied through the condominium fee. The current annual expenditure for electricity is in the range of $90,000 to $100,000.

Floor layout drawings for the building are given in Appendix A.

1.2 Objective

The overall objective for this report is to examine, recommend, and plan long-term and short-term cost-containment measures for the building. This objective is achieved first by calculating the energy usages within the building: energy used for heating the building, energy to heat water for domestic use, energy used for domestic lighting and equipment, and energy used for public lighting. With these theoretical energy usage calculations, we then make an energy balance by comparing theoretical energy usage to actual energy usage. From the results of the energy balance, we then propose energy conservation options.

1.3 Methodology

We obtained the information presented in this report by reviewing existing drawings, specifications, and operating manuals. We followed up with detailed site inspections to confirm building construction, mechanical and electrical installations system performance, occupancy, and operating procedures.

Figure 15.4 *continued*

2.3 Public and Domestic Lighting

(1) The energy usage for public lighting such as hall lighting, which is on 24 hours a day, and for outside lighting, which is on 14 hours a day, was calculated by the following formula supplied by Nova Scotia Power's *Energy Guide*:[11]

$$E = \frac{(N)(W)(h)(d)}{1,000}$$

E = energy consumed for the estimated time period
N = number of lights
W = power rating for the lights (watts)
h = number of hours per day the lights are on (hr/day)
d = number of days per month (day/month)
1,000 = conversion factor to convert watts to kilowatts (w/kw)

Table 2.6 summarizes the results of the public lighting energy usage calculations. For more detailed information on these calculations, see Appendix B.

9

Figure 15.4 *continued*

The results of the energy balance show that our theoretical energy consumption figures are accurate to within 7 percent of the actual energy consumption of the building. Figure 3.1 shows the distribution of energy throughout the building and the distribution of the power bill.

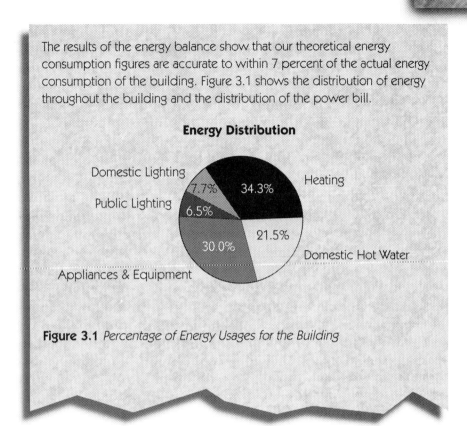

Figure 3.1 *Percentage of Energy Usages for the Building*

19

Figure 15.4 *continued*

REFERENCES

1. American Society of Heating, Ventilating, and Air-Conditioning Engineers. 1991. *HVAC Applications Handbook.* Atlanta: ASHRAE.

2. ASHRAE. 1981. *Handbook of Fundamentals.* Atlanta: ASHRAE.

3. ASHRAE. 1976. *Product Directory Systems.* Atlanta: ASHRAE.

4. Clifford, George. 1990. *Modern Heating, Ventilating, and Air-Conditioning.* Englewood Cliffs, N.J.: Prentice Hall.

5. Howell, R. H., and H. J. Sauer. 1985. *Environmental Control Principles—A Textbook Supplement to the* ASHRAE *Handbook Fundamentals Volume.* Atlanta: ASHRAE.

6. Dankert, Paul A. 1990. "Lighting Control Considerations," *Energy Engineering* 87:1.

7. Gershon, Meckler. 1994. "New Directions in HVAC Systems," *Energy Engineering* 91:2.

8. Rabl, A., and L. K. Norford. 1991. "Peak Load Reduction by Preconditioning at Night." *International Journal of Energy Research* 15.

9. Harris, R. 1991. *Modern Air Conditioning Practice.* Englewood Cliffs, N.J.: Prentice Hall.

10. McQuiston, Faye C., and J. D. Parker. 1988. *Heating, Ventilating and Air Conditioning Analysis,* 3rd edition. New York: Wiley.

11. Nova Scotia Power, Customer Relations Department. 1995. *Energy Guide.* Halifax, NS: NSP.

35

Figure 15.4 *continued*

FEASIBILITY REPORTS

A feasibility report looks closely at an alternative to a situation or at a potential solution to a problem, and then recommends whether such action is possible and reasonable. Since recommendations for appropriate actions are its essence, a feasibility report is often referred to as a *recommendation report*. This kind of report involves considerable data gathering and analysis.

Reasons for Writing Feasibility Reports

Feasibility reports help the reader determine whether an action should be pursued or whether a project should be judged "go" or "no go." As an entry-level professional (a project specialist, for example), you may have few occasions to write a feasibility report on your own. You may be asked, however, to participate on a team to analyze and recommend potential actions or solutions for your organization. As your career progresses, you will probably become more involved in writing feasibility reports.

All the information you collect and organize for your report should answer the following specific questions about the action being considered:

◆ *Technical feasibility.* Are the technical resources (equipment, materials, designs) available to accomplish the action being considered?

◆ *Economic feasibility.* Is money available for implementing this action? What are the characteristics of the overall market area? Are the costs reasonable compared to the projected benefits?

◆ *Operational feasibility.* Are appropriate personnel available to implement the action being considered?

◆ *Environmental feasibility.* Will this action create an environmental hazard? Will we be creating a new environmental hazard in our haste to remove an old one?

◆ *Social feasibility.* Will the community approve of this idea? Will this project have special benefits for this area? What can this project contribute to the life of the community?

These questions help your readers answer the bottom-line question that all companies pose when considering a major endeavour: Does proceeding with this action make sense?

Questions are important in feasibility reports. The topics of most feasibility reports are often first conceived as questions. In the workplace, a feasibility report might be written to answer questions such as these:

♦ *Health care/administration.* Should Greenfields Hospital open an extended care facility?

♦ *Engineering/construction.* Is passive solar heating practical in Swift Current?

♦ *Science/technology.* Should a marine biology centre be built in Charlottetown?

♦ *Business/marketing.* Is Sydney a good location for a new automotive plant?

♦ *Environmental technology.* Should Wheatsheaf Farms consider giant vacuum machines as a reasonable alternative to chemicals for pest control?

Activity 4

In the blanks provided below, write two questions relevant to your major field of study that would be appropriate for a feasibility report.

Question 1: _____

_____

_____

Question 2: _____

_____

_____

Be prepared to discuss these possible topics in class.

Key Assumptions and Constraints

In feasibility reports, senior managers frequently suggest potential actions or solutions that contain certain assumptions and that have certain constraints. These key considerations often alter significantly how viable any action or proposed solution might be. An assumption is anything taken for granted as fact; it is generally accepted as true and requires no proof. A constraint is anything that sets the parameters of an action; it restricts what can be done.

ASSUMPTION: A new automotive plant is needed.

CONSTRAINT: The plant must be built for no more than $15 million.

ASSUMPTION: Insecticides are harmful to people and to the environment.

CONSTRAINT: The alternative to chemical pesticides must not add more than 15 percent to operating costs.

When you write a feasibility report, establish any assumptions or constraints. These key considerations may greatly affect your final recommendation.

Activity 5
....

Read the following statements. Identify each assumption-related statement by placing an *A* in the blank next to it. Identify each constraint-related statement by placing a *C* in the blank next to it.

_____ a. Laser beams can accurately guide farm drainage machines.

_____ b. New dyes for colouring paper pulp may be toxic to fish and plants.

_____ c. To accommodate new technologies, no additional full-time employees may be added to Palmer Industries' employee roster.

_____ d. There is a growing market for small engine repairs.

_____ e. As "baby boomers" age, the national percentage of people over 65 also increases.

Be prepared to explain in class why you labelled each statement as you did.

Content in Feasibility Reports

The primary focus of a feasibility report is to identify favourable or unfavourable solutions or alternatives to an existing situation and to recommend appropriate action. The proof of a recommendation's validity lies in the analysis. Other basic report components are also necessary for the readers' total understanding of the topic, but the analysis is critical. All information included in your analysis should build toward logical conclusions and reasonable recommendations.

The model outline shown in Figure 15.5 serves as the basic framework for all feasibility reports. Use and modify this outline for each feasibility report you write. The following information, as well as a review of relevant sections in Chapter Nine, will help you prepare the final report.

MODEL OUTLINE: FEASIBILITY REPORTS

Title Page
Table of Contents
Abstract or Executive Summary* (with Recommendations)
1. Introduction
2. Overview/Background
   2.1 Review the problem/situation
      2.1.1 Current conditions
      2.1.2 Need for an alternative
   2.2 Identify major issues
      2.2.1 Assumptions
      2.2.2 Constraints
3. Analysis of the alternative
   3.1 Explain methodology used
      3.1.1 Market analysis
      3.1.2 Cost analysis
      3.1.3 Other analysis (tests, etc.)
   3.2 Describe technical feasibility of alternative
      3.2.1 Technology needed
      3.2.2 Availability of technology
      3.2.3 Specific sources of technology
   3.3 Describe economic feasibility of alternative
      3.3.1 Costs involved
      3.3.2 Availability of capital required
      3.3.3 Related market data (if appropriate)
   3.4 Describe operational feasibility of alternative
      3.4.1 Administrative personnel required
      3.4.2 Personnel required for ongoing success
      3.4.3 Time required to implement
4. Conclusions
   4.1 Identify any risks or uncertainties
      4.1.1 Environmental
      4.1.2 Personnel
      4.1.3 Capital
   4.2 Identify the benefits
      4.2.1 Organizational benefits
      4.2.2 Environmental benefits
5. Recommendations
   5.1 Specify the action to be taken
   5.2 Recap the benefits of the recommendation

---

*Report usually contains only one of these components.

Figure 15.5 *Effective feasibility reports include the sections listed on this model outline.*

Title Page

Because feasibility reports are frequently lengthy, they require a separate title page.

Table of Contents

Include a table of contents to help readers quickly understand all the areas included. The table of contents also directs them to the location of specific information.

Abstract/Executive Summary with Recommendations

If your feasibility report focuses on science, health, or technology, include a formal abstract in the front of the report. If your report focuses on business or marketing, include an executive summary. Since the recommendations are the primary reason for preparing a feasibility report, they must be included in a well-written abstract or executive summary.

Introduction

State the main purpose of your report in the introduction and include appropriate subsections for these areas: the scope of the report, your sources for information, the authorization, appropriate product or mechanism descriptions, and a list of specialized terms and definitions.

Analysis of the Alternative(s)

The analysis is the body of your report: It includes facts, figures, and details, all of which are essential to the effectiveness of your analysis.

First, explain to your readers the specific methods you used in the analysis. You may, for example, have conducted a market analysis to determine the current size and potential growth of a product (or you may have conducted the analysis for an earlier evaluation report, the results of which you are now using in your feasibility report). State when and how you conducted these studies, and how you determined the results.

Perhaps you performed specific tests and your feasibility analysis includes, in part, a comparison of test results. Or perhaps you used questionnaires to gather data. In your analysis, state how you obtained answers or tallied results and whether you used actual numbers or percentages.

Next, tell the readers what information you are analyzing. Focus specifically on the technical, economic, and operational feasibility of the alternative you are considering. The model outline (Figure 15.5) suggests some important aspects (with some variations depending on the topic) that you should address.

Conclusions

In this important section, tell readers what the analysis *means*. Using sound logical reasoning based on the facts established in the analysis, state the strengths and limitations of the alternative you are considering. For example, the analysis may point to conclusions like these:

♦ The necessary technology is still being developed and may not be available for two years.

♦ Sufficient capital is required before the new fiscal budget is implemented.

♦ Personnel currently employed have the capabilities and qualifications needed to implement the alternative action being considered.

You should state any risks or uncertainties concerning the alternative: technology is not completely reliable, personnel may resist additional responsibilities, and so forth. Readers also want your conclusions regarding the advantages or benefits of proceeding with the alternative: potential revenue increase of 15 percent, greater use of personnel talents and skills, and the like.

Recommendations

Many readers view this part in a feasibility report as the "bottom line" because it recommends a specific action (a "go" or "no go" with project development, for example). Logical and reasonable recommendations are based solely on the information presented in the body of the report. By the time your readers finish reading the conclusion, they should know exactly what you are going to recommend. If your recommendation surprises them, your analysis has not been very convincing. To reaffirm the validity of the recommendation, you should recap the benefits that you detailed in the conclusions.

Form in Feasibility Reports

Because a thorough analysis with sufficient supporting data is essential, most feasibility reports are lengthy. When you include a separate title page, table of contents, or other necessary components, you help your audience absorb and review the information in the report. Look at the following situation, which prompted a feasibility report.

Jean Curtis, Pharmacy Coordinator at Greenfields Hospital, received this request from her supervisor: "The vice president of operations wants us to determine the feasibility of assigning drug distribution duties to the pharmacy technicians instead of the pharmacist."

Jean took three preliminary steps that helped her to prepare an effective and well-received feasibility report: (1) she clearly defined her purpose; (2) she gathered all the useful data possible; and (3) she organized her information according to her outline (based on the model outline in Figure 15.5) before beginning to write the report. Figure 15.6 shows how Jean modified the outline slightly to suit her specific writing purpose. She addressed all areas and submitted a comprehensive and successful report.

**FEASIBILITY REPORT ON
REASSIGNING DRUG DISTRIBUTION SERVICES
AT GREENFIELDS HOSPITAL**

Submitted to
Daniel Garrison, Pharmacy Director

Submitted by
Jean Curtis, Pharmacy Coordinator

September 19--

Figure 15.6 *This feasibility report thoroughly analyzes an alternative and then recommends an action.*

TABLE OF CONTENTS

Section	Title	Page
	ABSTRACT	1
1.	INTRODUCTION	2
1.1	Scope	2
1.2	Sources	2
1.3	Authorization	2
1.4	Definitions	2
2.	OVERVIEW/BACKGROUND	3
2.1	Current Situation	3
2.1.1	Current Job Conditions	3
2.1.2	Need for Clinical Information	3
2.2	Major Assumptions and Contingencies	3
3.	ANALYSIS OF REDIRECTING DRUG DISTRIBUTION DUTIES	4
3.1	Technical Analysis	4
3.2	Economic Analysis	5
3.2.1	Availability of Capital	5
3.2.2	Anticipated Savings in Operating Expenses	5
3.3	Operational Analysis	6
3.3.1	Personnel	6
3.3.2	Implementation Schedule	6
4.	CONCLUSIONS	6
4.1	Risks and Uncertainties	7
4.2	Benefits of the Alternative	7
5.	RECOMMENDATION	8
	REFERENCES	9

LIST OF FIGURES

Figure 1. Allocation of Registered Pharmacist Work Time   7

Figure 15.6 *continued*

ABSTRACT

This report determines the feasibility of reassigning drug distribution duties in the Greenfields Hospital Pharmacy Department from the registered pharmacists to an alternative means (human or automated). This alternative will increase the time available to the pharmacists to deliver more clinical information services to Greenfields' medical staff and to the medical staff of Foothills Hospital and Withington Centre in the upcoming rationalization of medical services. The report concludes that the required automated drug dispensing technology is available to reassign these duties and that existing pharmacy personnel can implement and operate the new system.

Based on the technical, economic, and operational analysis presented, this report recommends implementing the Harper Fail-Safe system and reassigning drug distribution duties from the registered pharmacists to the pharmacy technicians.

1

Figure 15.6 *continued*

1. INTRODUCTION

The purpose of this report is to determine the feasibility of using means (human or automated) other than registered pharmacists to dispense drugs in the Greenfields Hospital Pharmacy Department.

1.1 Scope

This report identifies the specific considerations involved in reassigning the current drug dispensing duties from the registered pharmacists to another source. It does not evaluate or recommend the need for this change, but rather analyzes the technical, economic, and operational feasibility of the action.

1.2 Sources

Information used in this feasibility analysis was obtained from the Human Resources, the Risk Management, and the Business Services Departments, and from a presentation by the major technology provider.

1.3 Authorization

The Vice President of Operations, George DeVault, requested this feasibility report on August 12, 19--. Mr. DeVault issued this assignment after his review of the Evaluation Report on Expanding Pharmacy Clinical Services (prepared by the Pharmacy Director and submitted on August 4, 19--). The Evaluation Report determines the need for and assesses the value of expanded clinical services.

1.4 Definitions

The term *clinical information services* as used in this report means the following: nutritional support services, patient medication counselling, kinetic drug dosing service, nursing inservice programs, community education programs, formulary development, and targeted drug use review services (in conjunction with the medical staff).

Figure 15.6 *continued*

2. OVERVIEW/BACKGROUND

The following sections present a brief overview of the need to expand clinical services through the pharmacy.

2.1 Current Situation

Efficient drug distribution is a primary service of the Pharmacy Department at Greenfields Hospital, and the registered pharmacists currently dispense the drugs.

2.1.1 Current Job Conditions. Pharmacists spend 40 percent of their time dispensing drugs, and their expertise is needed to provide clinical information to the medical staff. Currently, they can do this only 5 percent of the time.

2.1.2 Need for Clinical Information. Questionnaires and surveys done with Greenfields' medical staff clearly indicate the need and desire for more clinical information. The physicians unanimously requested greater availability of the pharmacists to help enlighten them about new developments in the field and documented results of existing drugs. Community organizations surveyed also expressed a strong interest in having presentations and literature on a variety of drug-related areas. The previously mentioned Evaluation Report documents all statistics and analyses on these issues.

Two other hospitals in the region—Foothills Hospital and Withington Centre—also expressed interest in collaborating with Greenfields in this initiative.

2.2 Major Assumptions and Contingencies

The proposed change in drug distribution duties is based on the assumption that accurate and efficient drug dispensing can be performed by means (human or automated devices) other than registered pharmacists. This alternative is contingent upon the following condition: No additional full-time employees (FTEs) may be added to the Pharmacy Department to accomplish a change in work duties.

Figure 15.6 *continued*

3. ANALYSIS OF REASSIGNING DRUG DISTRIBUTION DUTIES

An alternative method of drug distribution was compared with the current dispensing method. The criteria of availability, reliability, and cost-effectiveness were applied in determining the feasibility of the alternative method.

3.1 Technical Analysis

By federal law (12345.67), only a registered pharmacist may assume the responsibility of personally filling physician drug requests. The law, however, does allow the use of an approved automated drug dispensing system and stipulates that the system be operated by trained pharmacy technicians. All federally approved automated systems operate via a mainframe computer system.

These restrictions narrow the technical feasibility of the proposed action to the choices listed next in Table 1. This table also briefly describes the technological availability of each system.

TABLE 1
TECHNICAL FEASIBILITY/AVAILABILITY OF IMPLEMENTING AN AUTOMATED DRUG DISPENSER

Technology	Vendor	Availability
Fail-Safe Dispensing System	Harper Technologies, Montreal, Quebec	Currently on market; 3 weeks required to implement
PharmCare Dispensing System	Medical Systems, Inc., Toronto, Ontario	Still under development; to be released in 6 months
Accu-Measure	K. Liddard Co., Saint John, New Brunswick	Still under development; targeted for mid-year 19--

Figure 15.6 *continued*

The Fail-Safe system not only is the most readily available system, but it also has a proven track record at 18 other pharmaceutical facilities across the nation. Documented statistics (see vendor literature in Appendix A) show that the system has a high reliability rate for both accuracy and performance.

3.2 Economic Analysis

The following capital investments (shown in Table 2) will enable the full implementation of an alternate automated drug distribution system.

TABLE 2
RELATED EXPENSES FOR A NEW DRUG DISTRIBUTION SYSTEM

Item	Cost
Programming charges from Information System Dept	$3,000 (approx.)
Fail-Safe Dispensing System (Harper)	$25,000 (includes training)
Maintenance contract (Harper)	$1,200 (five-year contract)
TOTAL	$29,200

3.2.1 Availability of Capital. The 19-- fiscal budget for the Pharmacy Department contains a 10 percent increase in operating expenses ($40,000), which adequately covers the additional costs involved for the new system. Other than the expected employee salary increases, no other significant increases in operating expenses are anticipated.

3.2.2 Anticipated Savings in Operating Expenses. With the increase of valid and needed clinical information from department pharmacists to area physicians, Greenfields' implementation of the automated system would (a) free up the pharmacists needed at Greenfields and (b) implement cooperation and shared expenses with the region's other two referral hospitals. (Data extracted from previously referenced Evaluation Report.) This savings is estimated at $175,000.

Figure 15.6 *continued*

As the medical staff realizes the value of clinical information, the assistance of Greenfields' pharmacists will become increasingly important in helping deliver high-quality health care.

3.3 Operational Analysis

The initial implementation of the computerized drug dispensing system can be done under the direction of Daniel Garrison, Pharmacy Director, with the collaboration of Thomas Handley, Information System Director.

3.3.1 Personnel. The system requires additional department employees to operate or to increase the amount of time available for pharmacists to assume more clinical information activities. Specifically, the duties of second- and third-shift pharmacy technicians increase to include automated drug distribution activities. The automated system is a straightforward distribution program, and complete training is provided by Harper.

Additionally, the department's pharmacy technicians have a high level of competence, and their educational and experience levels far exceed the minimum organizational and federal requirements for persons holding these positions. Thorough checks by pharmacy coordinators and reviews by pharmacists ensure the accuracy of all orders.

3.3.2 Implementation Schedule. Full implementation takes approximately six weeks: three weeks to install the system, and three weeks for operator training and apprenticeship.

4. CONCLUSIONS

Because of federal restrictions, reassigning drug dispensing activities at Greenfields Hospital must be done with an automated system. A reliable and cost-effective automated system is available and can be implemented effectively. This reassignment of drug distribution duties will result in the changed work allocations for pharmacists shown on the following pie graphs (Figure 1). As these graphs illustrate, the pharmacists will acquire a substantial increase in their time available to administer clinical information to Greenfields' physicians.

Figure 15.6 *continued*

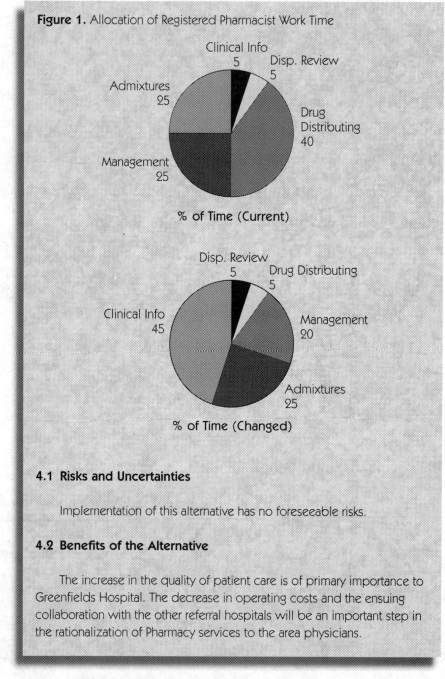

Figure 1. Allocation of Registered Pharmacist Work Time

% of Time (Current)

% of Time (Changed)

4.1 Risks and Uncertainties

Implementation of this alternative has no foreseeable risks.

4.2 Benefits of the Alternative

The increase in the quality of patient care is of primary importance to Greenfields Hospital. The decrease in operating costs and the ensuing collaboration with the other referral hospitals will be an important step in the rationalization of Pharmacy services to the area physicians.

Figure 15.6 *continued*

5.　RECOMMENDATION

The data and evidence in this feasibility report clearly point to implementing a changed drug distribution system. With a reliable, automated drug dispensing system and with the department's competent pharmacy technicians, the time-consuming tasks of filling medication orders in the pharmacy not only can, but should, be reassigned. Therefore, this report recommends reassigning drug distribution duties from registered pharmacists to pharmacist technicians via the Harper Fail-Safe dispensing system.

Compared to the current method of requiring the registered pharmacist to dispense all drugs, the automated method has several significant benefits to the organization. Compared to the capital outlay involved, the new system promises considerable returns on the investment.

8

REFERENCES

1.　"Evaluation Report on Expanding Pharmacy Clinical Services." Greenfields Hospital, Peach Lake, British Columbia. 4 August, 19--.

2.　Miller, Wayne. Vendor presentation, 15 August, 19--, at Harper Technologies, Montreal, Quebec.

3.　Rinehart, Bryan. The Automated Pharmacy. Columbus, Ohio: Glencoe/McGraw-Hill, 1990.

9

Figure 15.6 *continued*

QUESTIONS FOR DISCUSSION

1. In what ways might analytical reports interpret information?
2. What are the major differences between evaluation and feasibility reports?
3. How should a writer analyze a fairly large or general subject?
4. What is the primary consideration when choosing an appropriate evaluative strategy?
5. What is the main function of a feasibility report?
6. Explain the importance of identifying any key assumptions or constraints when preparing a feasibility report.
7. What kind of information do readers expect to see in the "Conclusions" section of a feasibility report?

EXERCISES

a. List three appropriate evaluative strategies for gathering information (excluding library research) for each of the three topics below:

1. Your community's literacy program

2. Computer services at your college

3. Emergency policies or procedures where you work or study

b. Indicate whether the following statements are conclusions (*C*) or recommendations (*R*).

_____ 1. Increased workloads of church personnel have caused late reports and a loss of revenue.

_____ 2. Signal Automated Church System (ACS) software should be purchased for central office use.

_____ 3. Selecting larger carbide inserts will produce higher production rates.

_____ 4. Union Manufacturing should conduct a formal tool research evaluation program.

_____ 5. Implementing a quality circle program at the Mistover Corp. will increase productivity and lessen the high turnover rate among hourly paid employees.

_____ 6. The Forward Five Committee recommends that the Mistover Corp. fund a three-week training program for quality circle facilitators.

c. Indicate whether the following statements describe an evaluation (*E*) or a feasibility (*F*) report.

_____ 1. A report that compares the capabilities of MicroTech and Comptronics computers

_____ 2. A report that assesses the quality level of the Deluxe Compact Disc Player

_____ 3. A report that recommends building an Interpretation Centre for Labrador

_____ 4. A report that diagnoses the causes of increased dental cavities at Gladstone Elementary School

_____ 5. A report that recommends adding foreign-car repair services at Burke's Automotive Shop

WRITING ASSIGNMENTS

1. Write a short (two- or three-page) memo report evaluating a policy, a procedure, equipment, or a situation. Possible topics relating to college, work, and community are listed below.

College

a. Emergency procedures for fire, lab accidents, toxic fumes, and bomb threats

b. The availability of computer facilities (hours, assistance, software)

c. The library or other service facility (hours, services, personnel)

Work

a. Policy/procedure for reporting equipment malfunctions for downtime

b. Emergency procedures for bomb threats, fire, accidents

c. Any piece of equipment

d. Any services provided by the company (cafeteria, child care)

Community

a. Literacy programs

b. The policy or procedure for student participation in extra-curricular activities

c. Environmental projects or policies

d. Housing issues

2. Write a long, formal evaluation report on one of the topics above or on a similar topic. Include all necessary front matter such as title page, table of contents, and abstract.

Persuasive Reports

A persuasive report goes beyond informing the reader of the facts — and beyond interpreting those facts. A persuasive report builds on facts and on interpretation; *then it convinces the reader to take a specific action* (see Figure 16.1). Unlike a feasibility report, which deals objectively with an action in which the writer has no vested interest, a persuasive report deals with an action from which the writer usually has a great deal to gain: a contract, an improved sales staff, or a new piece of equipment.

A persuasive report first deals with the essential *what* or *why* of a topic, then it addresses the analytical *so what*. Finally, the persuasive report gives a clear, direct response to the question *what next?* The responses to this question are always aimed at influencing the reader to agree with and act on the statements presented: "CompTech computers are best ... Palmer Industries should buy them." "Our customers deserve better service than they are getting ... this bank should expand its hours."

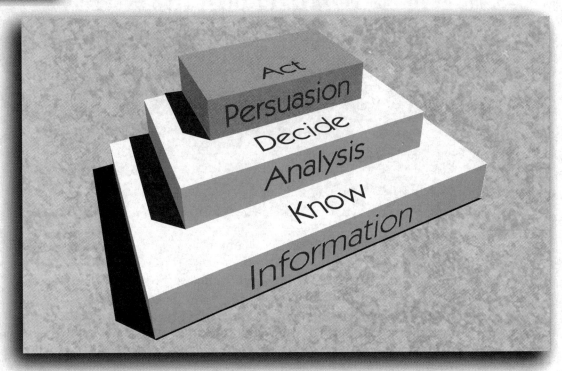

Figure 16.1 *Persuasive reports build on information and analysis to convince readers to act.*

PROPOSALS AND RESPONSES TO RFPs

Whether your report is aimed at persuading your audience to accept and act on your ideas or to buy your products or services, its main purpose is to convince your audience to agree with you. Essentially, there are two main types of persuasive reports: (1) *proposals* and (2) *responses to requests for proposals* (RFPs). A *proposal* is a persuasive report that uses well-chosen words, data, and graphics to convince a reader, who may or may not be aware of a situation, to take action. A *response to an RFP* is a persuasive report in which the writer responds to a direct invitation to propose a specific action.

These two types of persuasive reports may be similar in content, but different circumstances motivate the preparation of each. RFPs are fairly straightforward: They request — or *solicit* — specific information on a specific, predetermined need. In the workplace, the persons requesting a response to an RFP are always from an *external* source — a government agency or another business — and are always well aware of the need to act on some problem or need.

The circumstances prompting a proposal, however, may vary somewhat. A proposal can also be requested or solicited by the reader — but the writer may prepare an *unsolicited* proposal to initiate an action without invitation. The readers of proposals (solicited and unsolicited) can be *external* (outside the writer's organization) or *internal* (senior management, for example).

As a quick reference, Table 16.1 lists these types of persuasive reports, their audiences, and the circumstances that initiate their preparation.

Identifying these aspects of a persuasive report is a key planning step in its effective preparation. The type of report and its readers directly influence the content and form of the document. For example, a solicited persuasive report does not need to contain as much convincing material as an unsolicited one. The readers of a solicited report already know their needs; your task is to convince them that *you* can meet those needs. On the other hand, an external persuasive report requires more formal treatment than an internal report, since its readers may not be familiar with you or your organization. Always review the circumstances and analyze your readers before you begin writing a persuasive report.

TABLE 16.1

TYPES OF PERSUASIVE REPORTS

Type	Audience	Typical Circumstances for Writing
Response to RFP, Solicited	External	A formal, written "invitation" to propose action for a specific need
Proposal, Solicited	Internal	An assignment from upper management
Proposal, Solicited	External	A verbal or informal request from the prospective customer
Proposal, Unsolicited	Internal	Writer's knowledge of a need for action
Proposal, Unsolicited	External	An indication from a secondary source of a need for action

Activity 1
. . . .

Read the brief circumstances described below that would motivate someone to write a persuasive report. With a check mark, indicate whether the document is *solicited* or *unsolicited*. Indicate also whether the reader of the document is *internal* or *external* to the writer's organization.

a. A tool and die maker has a suggestion for his vice president of operations on how to reduce hazardous dust particles when making graphite moulds.

_____ Solicited _____ Unsolicited _____ Internal _____ External

b. A marketing representative from VIPwear Industries hears that the buyer at Gould's Department Store is looking for a new line of men's casual clothes.

_____ Solicited _____ Unsolicited _____ Internal _____ External

c. The Government of Newfoundland and Labrador advertises a request for proposals for planning and designing a Labrador Regional Interpretation Centre.

_____ Solicited _____ Unsolicited _____ Internal _____ External

d. Pierre Benoît, an employee at Palmer Industries, tells CEO June Polquick that opening a fitness trail to the surrounding community would be good public relations. She asks him to write a proposal for getting the job done.

_____ Solicited _____ Unsolicited _____ Internal _____ External

e. The Purchasing Manager at the Skyland Metropolitan Authority advertises a request for tenders (proposals) for providing daily cover material at the Highway 66 landfill site (tender no. 95-83).

_____ Solicited _____ Unsolicited _____ Internal _____ External

PROPOSALS

In many environments (the workplace, your community, your college), a proposal is an effective means of connecting people who know how to do a job with people who have a job that needs to be done. A proposal is, in a strong sense, a sales vehicle. Whether its topic is an idea, a product, or a service, a proposal's primary purpose is to persuade the reader to buy the ideas or items offered. Closure on the sale is made when the buyer (the person with the authority to say yes) and the supplier (the person proposing the idea, product, or service) agree on the job — and on the actions required to get it done.

Proposals in the Workplace

Regardless of your major field, you are likely to be involved in some way in proposal writing after you enter the workplace. Proposals may be written by and for people in technical fields, people in business and industry, people in public administration and government, or for the public consumer. Frequently, a proposal is reviewed by more than one reader (for example, someone in engineering and someone in marketing). Proposals are written for a variety of reasons:

Funding a project. A private foundation grant to establish a health education project in your community, provincial funding to build a new highway, federal funding to support a literacy program.

Approving a plan. Extending late-night shopping to include Tuesdays, a community-supported annual boat race, a corporate-wide computer training program, a plan to streamline company purchasing procedures.

Making a sale or winning a contract. A one-year agreement to provide home care to seniors in the village of Waterford, a new CNC machine lathe for Palmer Industries, a new heating system in Oxford Condominiums, all masonry work in the hydrostone housing development.

This list of reasons is certainly not all-inclusive; the possibilities are numerous. A proposal's basic purpose, however, is to persuade the reader to say yes to the action proposed.

Activity 2

Imagine yourself employed in a position in your major field of study. In the blanks provided below, speculate on three circumstances that would probably motivate you to write a proposal. Using the reasons listed earlier *(funding a project, approving a plan, making a sale or winning a contract)*, indicate your primary reason for writing the document.

Circumstance	Reason
a.	
b.	
c.	

Be prepared to discuss your responses in class.

Persuasive Writing

A proposal should be objective and unemotional, yet positive in tone. A well-written proposal also includes and honestly describes *all* information.

An overly enthusiastic writer may tend to colour the language and content in a persuasive report and exaggerate the merits of an idea or product. While superlatives (*best, fastest, most advanced*) certainly can be used in proposals, use them only when you are prepared to state factually *why:* "Our tool and die makers are the best because…" "Our delivery system is the fastest anywhere because…" "Our computers have the most advanced technology, including…." Good proposal writing qualifies all claims with *specific* information rather than broad, sweeping statements.

Rather Than Writing	Write
ABC Co. has many years of experience.	ABC Co. has been in the heating and ventilating business for 20 years.
This software has tremendous capabilities.	This software's capabilities range from simple addition to advanced calculus.
Our company has a long list of customers who are extremely satisfied with our product.	Among our many satisfied customers are Adams Office Supplies, Business Machines Inc., and Fox's Office Technologies.

Even when you are eager to make a certain impression or convince someone to do something, you must maintain the highest level of integrity. You build integrity into your proposal by reporting the facts and using honest language, not by decrying all other points of view, products, or services. A negative persuasive approach is rarely successful. It is far more effective to emphasize the positive aspects of *your* idea, product, or service.

Activity 3

Read the statements below. Write *yes* or *no* in the blank beside each statement to indicate whether it reflects good proposal writing style.

_____ a. Palmer Industries has extensive experience in installing numerous generators for extremely satisfied customers everywhere.

_____ b. Palmer Industries has a proven track record with more than 20 generators installed at customer sites in five provinces.

_____ c. All our technicians have two-year diplomas and a minimum of three years' on-the-job experience.

_____ d. Our technicians are the best-qualified persons found anywhere.

_____ e. XYZ Sportswear sold poorly at your store last year because it did not keep up with the changing lifestyles of your male customers; VIPwear does.

Accent the Benefits

A well-written proposal always emphasizes the benefits of the action being proposed. It should convince the reader of the advantages resulting from a positive decision. Knowing your audience (internal or external positions, technical and knowledge levels) and the type of proposal (solicited or unsolicited) helps you determine which specific benefits to emphasize. Usually, benefits fall into four areas: technical, performance, economics, and safety. A superb idea, product, or service will offer substantial benefits in all these areas. Your idea, product, or service must offer advantages in at least one of these areas to convince your reader to make a positive decision.

Technical Benefits

Technical benefits result from any improved or innovative technology that has not been previously used by (or available to) your reader (for example, an innovative adhesive compound, an improved stain-resistant fabric, a new removable components drawer). Consider the technical level of your reader when determining how strongly to emphasize this benefit. When you write for engineers, scientists, or health personnel, you should discuss technical benefits more thoroughly than when you write for business executives, purchasing agents, or other nontechnical personnel.

Performance Benefits

Performance benefits are related to the operation, usability, or achievement of the idea, product, or service. The proposed action may make operating equipment less complex, more efficient, or more reliable. Or the action may help to streamline an assembly process or to enhance productivity. Performance benefits usually interest persons at all technical and organizational levels.

Economic Benefits

Economic benefits are the cost-saving aspects of the proposed action and are particularly impressive to readers in management positions. Economic benefits may be tangible or intangible. Tangible cost savings are usually easy to present (for example, the new equipment price is lower than the repair costs; the volume of manufactured parts will double; expensive downtime will be reduced). Intangible economic benefits, however, should be discussed carefully. Usually, you cannot guarantee that "sales will increase," or that "workers will be more productive," or predict by how much. The organization may certainly realize economic benefits — but your proposal can only *encourage* these results, not promise them. Thus, you must use caution when stating economic benefits and make only rational and realistic claims.

Safety Benefits

Safety benefits have to do with the protection of employees or equipment. If you know, for example, that your reader's current machine lathe has caused eye or hand injuries, you should stress your equipment's splash guards and blade protectors. Discuss all features of your idea, product, or service that help guard the health and safety of employees or that protect the mechanism from damage: improved ergonomics, grounded wiring, posted safety labels, an easily accessible stop button, or thermostatic shut-off valves, for example. When you write for senior management, also consider mentioning the reduced risk of liability because of these safety features.

An effective proposal — one that gets favourable results — strongly and honestly emphasizes the advantages of the action proposed in the body of the report. Determine the areas of greatest benefit to your reader and develop a persuasive strategy based on these aspects.

Difficult Issues

Omitting important information in an attempt to gloss over or ignore a difficult fact only distorts the information presented — and usually fools no one. Instead, consider explaining any possible problems: for example, timely delivery of the goods may be affected by a possible dockworkers' strike, meeting the deadline is dependent on the availability of your technicians, the costs quoted are based on bulk quantity and any reduction in quantity may affect the price. Tell your readers all the "good" news you can honestly impart, but also be honest about other serious considerations (perhaps you could call them "challenges").

Graphics

You can define new ideas by illustrating them with line drawings and photos. You can stress important benefits by illustrating them with pie charts and bar and line graphs. You can also suggest action and movement by including flow diagrams and graphic elements. Figure 16.2 shows an illustration from an environmental group's proposal to

Figure 16.2 *This visual emphasizes an important point made in a proposal.*

their local council. Group members want support for a public awareness campaign aimed at reducing waste and creating a greener environment. The writers have included a page from their publicity brochure to convince the councillors that "greener environments grow people." Visuals can effectively reinforce a significant point — without saying it twice.

You can also transform technical information into easily readable data when you illustrate the information in tables. Readers often expect proposals dealing with complex projects or systems to contain detailed diagrams or blueprints. Be sure these illustrations are legible and error-free; readers do examine visuals carefully.

Proposal Organization

A good writing style and clear visual aids help illuminate the contents of your proposal. When the content convinces your readers that the actions you are proposing are better than any other alternative available, they will buy your idea, product, or service.

Although proposals vary in content, certain components are common to nearly all of them. The model outline shown in Figure 16.3

guides you through the process of organizing information for a comprehensive, formal proposal. Rearrange, expand, or omit sections to fit the specific purpose and audience of each proposal you write.

For the most part, the components listed in the model outline (discussed in detail in Chapter Nine and briefly below) require only minor changes to suit the proposals you write.

Transmittal Letter

Proposals are usually submitted to someone with authority over the writer: a supervisor, a senior manager, a customer, or an approval board. Therefore, a transmittal letter should accompany the document. This letter explains briefly what the proposal is about and what prompted its preparation. A proposal in memo form omits the transmittal letter but includes similar information at the beginning of the memo.

Title Page

Include a separate title page for a lengthy proposal. Include the words "Proposal for [the action that is being proposed]" so that your reader knows immediately the nature of the document and its topic.

Table of Contents

Include a table of contents in a lengthy proposal to give your readers a quick overview of all areas discussed. Be sure also to include a complete list of figures when the document contains many illustrations.

Executive Summary

Since a proposal is, in effect, a sales tool, an executive summary is more appropriate than an abstract. Most readers (especially busy executives) expect this component to precede a lengthy proposal, and some foundations and institutions that grant research funds require a summary at the front of each proposal. The heading for this report section may be shortened to "Summary."

Problem/Situation

Begin the body of your proposal by first describing the current situation or problem. Be objective, open, and honest about your assessment, but be careful not to make the current situation sound like a terrible mess. Overly negative descriptions serve little persuasive purpose in a proposal (or anywhere else). If your proposal is prepared for senior managers, you do not want them to think that the current situation is so bad that a competent job cannot possibly be done — only that it could be done better with your proposed actions. (Your proposal may not be approved, and you may have to continue

MODEL OUTLINE: PROPOSALS

Letter of Transmittal
Title Page
Table of Contents
Executive Summary
1. Introduction
   1.1 Purpose of proposal
   1.2 Scope of proposal
   1.3 Authorization (if needed)
   1.4 Sources of information
2. Problem/situation
   2.1 Current conditions
   2.2 Need for action/change
       2.2.1 Effects on personnel
       2.2.2 Effects on equipment
       2.2.3 Effects on cost
       2.2.4 Effects on quality
3. Solution
   3.1 Action to be taken
   3.2 Methods to be used
   3.3 Materials/equipment/supplies to be used
   3.4 Requirements/limitations (facilities, resources)
   3.5 Expected results
4. Benefits
   4.1 Technical
   4.2 Performance
   4.3 Economic
   4.4 Safety
5. Implementation
   5.1 Steps to be taken
   5.2 Personnel who will take action
   5.3 Timetable
6. Costs
7. Conclusion
   7.1 Restate the action recommended
   7.2 Recap the benefits
   7.3 Make a request for action

Figure 16.3 *This model outline shows the organization of topics in a proposal.*

working under the current conditions.) Likewise, if your proposal is prepared for a customer, a dark and gloomy description may put him or her on the defensive. When necessary, use *facts*, not feelings, to describe a situation that you believe needs to be improved. Even when the proposal has been solicited by someone who is aware of the current situation, you should describe the problem so that the reader knows that *you* also clearly understand it.

After describing the current situation, state the need for action or change. Describe the current situation and its effects on personnel, equipment, cost, quality, or any other relevant aspect. In a solicited document, state these effects briefly.

EXAMPLE: Frequent "help" calls to the Computer Services Department about malfunctioning equipment and lost data indicate that users have inadequate knowledge of hardware and software. The substantial time used by the computer technicians to correct these problems seriously affects their abilities to perform their regular job duties.

The effects pointed out clearly here lay the groundwork for the benefits discussed later in the proposal.

Solution

In a proposal, "solution" is synonymous with "recommendation." State and describe, in specific terms, the exact action(s) you are proposing to meet your reader's need. When appropriate, describe the methods that will accomplish the action and the materials, equipment, and supplies that will be used. If you must address any difficult issues (as discussed earlier in this chapter), present them as tactfully as possible here. End this section on a positive note by describing the expected results (or purpose) of your proposed action.

Benefits/Advantages

This important persuasive component describes the effectiveness of the proposed action. This section is your prime opportunity to "sell" your idea, product, or service to your audience. Use numbers, statistics, case histories, quotations from experts — anything that substantiates the advantages of the action. Focus on the technical, performance, economic, and safety benefits that will result from the reader's positive decision.

Disadvantages of Inaction   In some cases, it is important to advise your reader of the serious implications of not adopting the proposed solution. The problem for which you are proposing a solution may need urgent attention if the situation you are proposing to change is deteriorating fast. If, for example, you are proposing an improved delivery procedure, you need to advise your reader of the implications of not taking action: continued decrease in sales and loss of competitive edge.

Implementation

The length and scope of this important section will vary, depending on the complexity of the proposed action(s). Outline the steps necessary to accomplish the recommended solution, and include the names and/or positions of the people who will take action, along with their responsibilities. When appropriate, include their individual qualifications in condensed résumés that focus on work experience relating to the proposed job. Also include a timetable with specific tasks and dates.

Costs

Always place costs in a separate section, regardless of how long or short the proposal is. Costs are a significant factor, so never bury these figures in other sections of the text. Include all costs relevant to the recommended solution. You can present these items in a vertical list because you are featuring numbers, not words.

Conclusion

Briefly restate the solution and its benefits, based on the situational need. Note the word "restate." Do not repeat the same words you used earlier. If appropriate, include brief explanations about how you derived each conclusion. Finally, make a clear and direct request for action.

Proposal Formatting

A proposal may be as simple as a 2-page memo which an engineering manager might write to the engineering vice president, proposing the purchase of a new machine. Or a proposal may be as complex as a 30-page document written to a prospective customer, proposing that a new generator be purchased by a utility plant. The complexity and length depend on your proposal's purpose and audience. The type of proposal (solicited or unsolicited) determines how much information you should include; the audience (internal or external) determines how formal or informal the format should be.

Figure 16.4 shows a formal proposal written by a member of the Computer Services Department at Midway Manufacturing to persuade the vice president of operations to approve a computer training program for company employees. After making minor revisions to the model outline, the writer prepares a convincing report that receives a nod of approval from the reader.

**PROPOSAL FOR
PERSONAL COMPUTER TRAINING CLASSES**

Submitted to
Jack E. Menedis, Vice President of Operations

Submitted by
Megan Pillar, Computer Services Department

May 25, 19--

Figure 16.4 *A sample formal proposal makes a convincing case for action.*

TABLE OF CONTENTS

EXECUTIVE SUMMARY 1

INTRODUCTION 1
    Purpose 1
    Sources of Information 2

CURRENT SITUATION 2
    Current Conditions 2
    Need for Change 2

SOLUTION 3
    Methods for Development 3
    Resources for Instructors 3
    Equipment and Facilities Needed 4

BENEFITS OF PC TRAINING 5
    Technical Benefits 5
    Performance Benefits 5
    Economic Benefits 5

IMPLEMENTATION 6
    Class Rosters and Offerings 6
    Teaching Resources 6
    Timetable for Completion 6

ESTIMATED TRAINING COSTS 7

CONCLUSION 7

LIST OF ILLUSTRATIONS
Figure 1 — Proposed Equipment Layout for Personal Computer
Training Classes (Midway Conference Room 303) 4

Figure 16.4 *continued*

EXECUTIVE SUMMARY

The proposal on the following pages presents a cost–benefit analysis for implementing formal computer training classes at Midway Manufacturing. The following factors identify the need for formal training classes:

- Nonuse, underuse, and misuse of equipment
- Training requests by users
- Established fixed assets

Computer training classes will bring numerous benefits to Midway. These benefits may be categorized into three major areas:

1. <u>Technical benefits</u>: Implementation and use of the latest computer technologies which allow cost-effective operations
2. <u>Performance benefits</u>: Development of good, efficient habits; increased assertive problem solving; efficient exchange of data
3. <u>Economic benefits</u>: Correct use of equipment; reduction of equipment repair and replacement costs; reduction of costly wait time

The recommended plan for implementing formal training classes involves using the resources and personnel already available in the Human Resource Development (HRD) and Computer Services departments. This arrangement allows for onsite training on Midway's equipment, which ensures direct application.

Classes will be implemented in three phases: Phase 1 — Senior Management; Phase 2 — Professional; Phase 3 — Clerical. A list of all Phase 1 (Senior Management) computer users who will receive training is included in the body of this proposal.

The total cost based on this proposal is approximately $9,000. This estimate covers training equipment and classroom material and one new computer setup to complete the proposed six-person training forum.

INTRODUCTION

This proposal establishes the need for increasing the level of computer knowledge among Midway Manufacturing users and recommends a plan to achieve that objective.

Purpose

The purpose of this report is to recommend a reasonable solution that substantially increases competency among Midway's computer users and that reduces the number of "help" calls received by Computer Services from troubled users. These calls detract significantly from the time available for computer personnel to complete their regular duties.

1

Figure 16.4 *continued*

Sources of Information

The Computer Services Helpline Log and a questionnaire surveying employee educational needs provided pertinent data for this report. The Human Resources Development Department assisted in preparing this report.

CURRENT SITUATION

When the Computer Services Department established the "Helpline" (extension 809) last year, Midway Manufacturing had fewer than 12 computer users, and the department received only a few phone calls each week.

Current Conditions

In keeping with Midway's strategic plan to computerize every department over the next three years, more than 25 new personal computers have been installed in key departments during the past four months. The number of active users increased proportionately. Many of these users, sitting down at the keyboard for the first time, lack even basic computing skills. They have great difficulty with equipment and the sophisticated software installed on the systems.

During the past two months, the "Helpline" received an average of eight calls per day. (The department keeps a log of all requests for assistance.) Computer Services personnel answered some questions easily over the phone, but many required personal visits where technicians sometimes found problems so serious that the computer vendor had to be contacted. This often time-consuming assistance demands a significant part of the computer technicians' work time.

New installations during the next six months will increase the number of active users to nearly 75. Undoubtedly, the number of inexperienced users — and trouble calls — also will increase.

Need for Change

The statistics gathered from "Helpline" calls are only one indication of the educational gaps in Midway's computer users' backgrounds. HRD surveyed 20 Midway department heads in March 19-- to learn of the various perceived educational needs among company employees. Of the employees receiving the 15-question survey sheet, 87 percent responded. Two questions on the survey reveal an urgent need for personal computer training in a wide cross-section of company departments.

2

Figure 16.4 *continued*

One question asked for a pointed response: "What assistance do you need to use your computer effectively?" More than two-thirds of the respondents specified the need for some type of PC class. Some typical comments were: "Though I have taught myself some DOS basics and I am fairly comfortable with Word and WordPerfect for Windows, I'd like some formal classes to help me become more competent," "We need classes in word processing, spreadsheets, databases," and "We need a better understanding of our PCs — it takes so long to figure out the problems." The remaining respondents commented that they did not yet have a computer in their departments.

Another question asked more generically about their needs for education: "What do you perceive as your priority educational needs?" Twenty-eight percent of the respondents focused again on PC education.

With a projected total of nearly 75 personal computers to be in use within the next six months, Midway Senior Management has already made the commitment to computer technology. This commitment reflects an investment of approximately $250,000. Capitalizing on this significant dollar investment requires informed and productive PC users.

SOLUTION

Based on the evidence presented earlier, this report recommends instituting a formal program of onsite computer training classes for all current and projected Midway personal computer users. The following paragraphs present the details of this proposed action.

Methods for Development

The Computer Services Department, in collaboration with HRD, recommends developing this formal program by first assessing users to determine (1) current skill levels and (2) projected skill levels needed. Based on these evaluations, an assessment then can be done to determine the specific class offerings needed in the program. Effective class schedules and rosters then can be developed.

Resources for Instructors

Midway's own teaching resources should be tapped for instructors. Both the Computer Services and HRD departments offer competent personnel who could create the ideal situation: one in which classes are conducted by a qualified teaching team with knowledge and experience in both computer technology and education.

3

Figure 16.4 *continued*

Equipment and Facilities Needed

According to research done by Human Resources Development, computer training classes are most effective when limited to six participants. Four computer setups from Computer Services and one setup from HRD may be made available for the classes, which necessitates the purchase of only one additional processor, monitor and keyboard, and dot matrix printer. These classes should be conducted in Computer Services conference room 303 on the third floor. This conference room contains all adequate wiring outlets to install these setups. Figure 1 shows the proposed classroom layout.

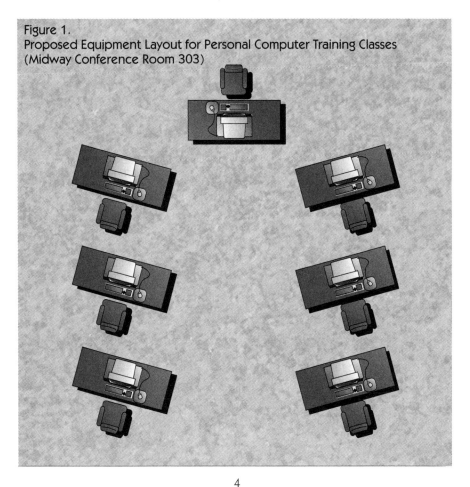

Figure 1.
Proposed Equipment Layout for Personal Computer Training Classes
(Midway Conference Room 303)

4

Figure 16.4 *continued*

Onsite training classes taught by Midway's own employees on company-owned equipment ensure that all class participants receive computer skills that are carried back directly to their jobs. Correct and efficient use of equipment and software will reduce the need to go to others for assistance, and Computer Services personnel will be able to spend their time accomplishing their own job assignments.

BENEFITS OF PC TRAINING

Computer training classes bring numerous benefits to Midway. These benefits may be divided into three major areas.

Technical Benefits

With increased and improved employee use of computer technology, Midway ensures that its business operations are conducted in the most cost-effective and time-efficient ways available. As new technologies emerge, Midway will be able to implement new equipment and methods effectively because its employees will have gained the knowledge and confidence required to welcome improvements.

Performance Benefits

Formal computer training classes help improve time management skills by:

- Developing good, efficient computer habits at the outset or eliminating time-consuming, data-endangering habits
- Promoting assertive, effective problem-solving actions because of increased knowledge levels
- Encouraging and enabling efficient exchange of data

Economic Benefits

Formal computer training classes enable Midway to use its resources well by:

- Ensuring correct use of computer equipment
- Reducing computer repair and replacement costs
- Eliminating overdependence on Computer Service personnel and reducing costly wait time

The benefits listed here will be realized many times over, thereby affirming an investment in formal computer training classes as a sound and far-sighted approach to successful business operations.

5

Figure 16.4 *continued*

IMPLEMENTATION

The following paragraphs list the practical elements in planning Midway computer training classes and the recommended actions for effectively implementing them.

Class Rosters and Offerings

This proposal recommends implementing classes in three phases: Phase 1 — Senior Management; Phase 2 — Professional; Phase 3 — Clerical. All phases will include classes in these computer applications: basics of DOS, word processing, spreadsheets, and databases. Participants will receive the classes appropriate to their specific business-related needs. A sample class roster of senior managers with the specific classes each will receive (marked with an X) is shown in Table 1. After the employees in Table 1 complete their classes, the next phase of classes will begin.

TABLE 1
SAMPLE CLASS ROSTER AND CLASSES
(Phase 1 — Senior Management)

Name	Basics of DOS	Word Processing	Spreadsheets	Databases
Alvarez, James	X	—	X	—
Becker, Allan	—	—	X	X
Brendle, Donna	X	—	—	X
Byrd, Roberta	X	—	—	X
Caldwell, Leroy	—	X	X	X

Teaching Resources

This report recommends Carla LeMoyne, Computer Technician, and Jaspal Sodhi, Education Coordinator, as the teaching team conducting all classes. These employees have technological knowledge and teaching experience, and both express an enthusiasm to meet this new challenge.

Timetable for Completion

A time period of six to nine months should be sufficient to complete all training proposed in this document. If classes begin in July, all would probably be completed between January to March 19--.

Figure 16.4 *continued*

This training period is dependent on the following factors:

- Availability of all proposed participants
- Compliance of scheduled participants to attend classes when notified

ESTIMATED TRAINING COSTS

The following cost estimates are based on current vendor prices which include taxes:

```
1 personal computer processor, monitor, keyboard, and laser printer . .$3,800.00
1 computer overhead projector with display panel (colour) . . . . . . . .3,060.00
1 MagiOffice Deluxe software package . . . . . . . . . . . . . . . . . . . . . .500.00
1 Electronic Math software package . . . . . . . . . . . . . . . . . . . . . . .400.00
21 cartons of computer printout paper @ $27.50 per box . . . . . . . . . .577.50
6 toner cartridges @ $60.00 each . . . . . . . . . . . . . . . . . . . . . . . . .360.00
Miscellaneous classroom supplies (transparencies, name tags, etc.) . . .200.00
   Total . . . . . . . . . . . . . . . . . . . . . . . . . . . . . . . . . . . . . . . .$8,897.50
```

CONCLUSION

A growing and ongoing need for personal computer training classes at Midway Manufacturing mandates the support of senior management. Midway users have pointedly asked for help in acquiring the computer skills needed to do their jobs with the technology made available to them. A natural extension of Midway's commitment to computer technology is its additional commitment to employee computer training; the time to take action is now.

Formal computer training classes have a positive impact throughout the organization:

- Users in management gain enhanced planning skills and tools.
- Improved job performance through time-efficient computer applications results in an improved business environment.
- Shared knowledge enables existing computer personnel to perform in their own areas of expertise.

When Midway Manufacturing invests in its employees by providing effective and productive computer skills, it is making an investment today to ensure better business operations tomorrow.

7

Figure 16.4 *continued*

Activity 4

Read the proposal shown in Figure 16.4 and answer the following questions.

a. Is the proposal a solicited or unsolicited document?

_____

b. Is the reader internal or external to the writer's organization?

_____

c. In what part of the proposal (excluding the table of contents and executive summary) does the writer first state the specific action being proposed?

_____

d. What specific benefits does the writer emphasize as a result of taking the action proposed?

_____

_____

_____

e. What "difficult" issues does the writer address in the proposal?

_____

_____

_____

RESPONSES TO REQUESTS FOR PROPOSALS

A request for proposal (RFP) is a document sent from one business or government agency (the customer) that needs a specific product or service to another business (the supplier, vendor, or contractor) that supplies the product or service. The business or government agency may also publish its RFP in a special section of a newspaper or in the classified advertisements. The RFP describes the job that the requester needs done and asks (solicits) the companies or individuals receiving the RFP to propose how they would do the job. The response to the RFP is always an externally solicited proposal. In the workplace, these originating documents also may be called Requests for Quotes (RFQs) or Requests for Tenders, especially when the primary purpose of the document is to obtain costs for a specific need or product.

Early in your career, you will be more likely to *respond* to an RFP than to write the originating RFP. In an entry-level position, you may not be required to write the proposal, but you would be asked to get quotations, inspect a site, write estimates, and participate in appropriate data gathering and information meetings. However, once you have become familiar with the processes involved, you may be expected to write the proposal or parts of it. The following section deals primarily with the "how to's" of writing an effective *response* that meets the requester's requirements and that gets you and your company winning results.

Reasons for Responding to a Request for Proposal

When a company needs a product or service, an RFP is frequently the most effective vehicle for communicating that need to someone who can satisfy it. In many fields, RFPs are sent to suppliers of products and services when organizations have needs such as these:

Computer technology/health care. A mainframe computer system for a 500-bed hospital.

Engineering technology. An underwater actuator system for an oceanographic department.

Construction. An airport hotel.

Environmental technology. An electronically monitored drainage system.

Automotive mechanics. A three-year service contract on the city's emergency vehicles.

Some organizations view RFPs as their most important means for acquiring new work. In fact, their success often depends on the effectiveness of their responses to RFPs. Depending on the field you enter, responding to RFPs may be an important and integral part of your job.

RFPs usually are sent to suppliers (or advertised publicly) when the job that must be done involves many tasks or substantial capital investments or both. Because these projects may be large and complex, a potential supplier must determine in advance as many details as possible from the requester so the supplier can propose (and ultimately do) the specific job required. The RFP gives suppliers these details. Frequently, an RFP specifies *what* information is needed and *how* the requester wants it submitted.

Kinds of Responses Requested

Including accurate and sound information is, of course, of paramount importance in an effective response to an RFP. Also important, however, is including the specific information that the requester wants and, when specified, including it in the format that the requester expects (especially when the requester is a government agency).

An RFP requests either a nonnegotiable response or a negotiable response. These general labels may or may not be stated directly in the RFP, but a careful review of the document usually reveals terms and characteristics that identify which kind of response is being requested.

Nonnegotiable Responses

Some RFPs state exact specifications and, frequently, include strict rules for all responses. The requester wants a specific product or service with precise characteristics (size, capabilities, capacity, or time frame). Neither substitutes nor variations may be offered. Frequently, the requester also wants the information presented in a predetermined format: specific sections with specific points to be included, arranged in a specific sequence. These sorts of instructions are common to government-generated RFPs. Sometimes these requesters want responders to just "fill in the blanks" on specification and cost sheets.

These rules and standards allow the requesters to compare similar products, equipment, or services. For complex projects, when requesters know exactly what they want and need, this kind of RFP is an efficient way of sorting through dozens (and sometimes hundreds) of responses.

The submission process is common to many nonnegotiable responses: The responders enclose their proposals in sealed envelopes and then make certain that their documents arrive at the requester's office by a final submission date and time. These responses, many of which involve contracts for substantial amounts of money, are surrounded by highly competitive circumstances, since a number of other responders will usually be vying for the same contract. Sometimes the proposing supplier will have a chance to ask questions, for example at a bidders' conference, or to clarify information stated in the RFP, but frequently this opportunity is not granted. The responder will then have to rely solely on the RFP for directions concerning the response's preparation. After sometimes extensive reviews, the requester will then award the job to the supplier who best meets the technical and cost specifications.

Figure 16.5 shows an example of a request for tenders that might appear in the classified section of your local newspaper. Note that the advertisement distinctly tells all potential responders that specifications and drawings are available for examination. An efficient writer adheres completely to these instructions.

When construction companies read this announcement, they obtain the specifications and drawings, and put together proposals with estimated costs to meet the need specified. Then they mail, courier, or hand-deliver the sealed proposals, to ensure delivery before the specified deadline.

Negotiable Responses

Some RFPs offer the responders more leeway than nonnegotiable responses. The requester states in the RFP the specific need and gives adequate details of the job to be done, but does not necessarily provide firm instructions for exactly how the need or job should be satisfied. The responder is asked to propose a solution or an action. Based on the details given in the RFP (which also may include guidelines for acceptable solutions and for document formats), the responders present the action or solution that they determine best meets the requester's needs. The responder must thus *convince* the reader that the solution proposed in the response is the best. Negotiable responses, therefore, are similar to the proposals discussed earlier in this chapter. The negotiable response is useful to requesters who, for example, are not certain of the latest technologies or of all the possibilities available — and who want creative solutions or actions presented.

Figure 16.6 shows an RFP that a technical communications instructor may issue when he or she wishes to receive your selection of a major project, a requirement for your graduation. This request illustrates how proposal writing plays a role in technical training and education. As students, you may have to complete and document a major project in your discipline. Such a requirement prepares you for potential research and development tasks in the workplace, and perhaps for a research and development position in a company or government department.

HEAVENCAR REGIONAL MUNICIPALITY
REQUEST FOR TENDERS
POLICE FACILITY RENOVATIONS

SEALED TENDERS will be received by the undersigned up to 12:00 NOON, FRIDAY, FEBRUARY 14, 199- for the following:

POLICE FACILITY RENOVATIONS
BAYSIDE

Specifications and drawings may be obtained from the office of the Purchasing Manager, 77 Sunrise Strip, Adelaide, Any Province A1P 4A4, upon payment of a nonrefundable deposit of $25 per set; which deposit shall be in the form of a certified cheque, payable to the Heavencar Regional Municipality. Tenders must be sealed and designated Tender 16/9-.

Documents may be viewed at the offices of the architect, Icarus & Associates, 17 Wings Lake Road, Adelaide, AP; the Heavencar Builders' Exchange, The Parade, Adelaide; or the offices of the Construction Association of Any Province, Hadrian's Gap, Adelaide.

A Bid Bond or certified cheque in the amount of 10 percent of the contract price will be required with each tender.

The tender will be opened at a public meeting on Friday, February 14, 199-, at 2:00 p.m., at the Town Hall, Deanclose, Adelaide.

The Heavencar Regional Municipality reserves the right to reject any or all tenders or to accept any tender or part thereof considered to be in its best interest.

G. Bill DeMott
Purchasing Manager

Figure 16.5 *This request for tenders requires responders to adhere to specifications.*

REQUEST FOR PROPOSALS (RFP)
APPLIED RESEARCH TECHNIQUES 456/96

Summary

Applied Research Techniques 456 (ART456), a program in Technical Project Documentation at Joshua Slocum College, is designed to prepare students to write the kind of technical documents expected on the job. A major objective of the program is to give students the opportunity to produce a formal report (minimum 3,000 words) which documents the design, construction, and testing of a major project in their technical field. The project and report are the joint responsibility of the ART instructor and technical instructors in the Engineering Technology department. Proposals are now invited from those students interested in selecting projects in one of the engineering technologies.

The time for this project and its documentation is estimated at seven months. The time allotted following the receipt of proposals is approximately six months. Projects are to be completed and will be demonstrated at Spring Showcase, May 7, 199-, and final reports are to be submitted by May 18, 199-, at noon.

The deadline for receipt of proposals is 12:00 noon, October 15, 199-. Two (2) copies of the proposal should be sent or delivered to:

Dr. M. Gould
Technical Communications Instructor
Engineering Technology Department
Joshua Slocum College
Oceana, NS   B3J 3C2

State Ref: RFP # ART456/96

Who May Respond

Any student currently enrolled in Applied Research Techniques 456 and Engineering Technology (Electrical, Electronics, or Mechanical) may propose a project and request supervision by a technical instructor. Individual and small group projects will be considered. Students proposing to undertake projects with local industry will still need an internal supervisor. Each technical instructor will accept and authorize a maximum of six proposals. Proposals that are not accepted by the instructors to whom they are addressed will be forwarded to other instructors for consideration.

Figure 16.6 *This request for proposal (RFP) solicits creative solutions to a specified need.*

Proposal Scope

Each proposal should be limited to the project described in this RFP.

Technical Requirements to Be Addressed in This Proposal

Proposals must be for projects that require analytical and/or persuasive documentation. The reports must demonstrate engineering technologist level, technical and mathematical depth, and a clear understanding of the subject.

The subject may be a design, a test, or the selection or development of a process or significant piece of equipment. The final report should show an attempt to solve an engineering problem in a practical manner. The report should also contain reference to current technical literature to show an up-to-date understanding of the subject. The project should be displayed at Showcase and be accompanied by a preliminary report, a work log or research journal, and appropriate promotional material. The final report must be submitted by May 18, 199-.

Procedure for Application

Proposals must include the following information:

- a topic title
- an explanation of the problem or situation
- the need for a solution
- a clear statement of objectives
- a statement of investigation methods including a work plan (Gantt chart or similar)
- a list of resources
- approximate cost (if cost-sharing is requested)

Overall, the proposal must give evidence of the proposer's ability to produce the project and the final report on schedule.

Project Description

The report is to be addressed to the instructor with whom the student wishes to work. If the project is undertaken with a local industry, the report should also include the name of the external supervisor. Projects should involve the following tasks:

1. Identify the problem or question and the need for a solution or answer. Prepare — early in the project — a succinct statement of purpose to help give focus to the research.
2. Identify any assumptions about the situation, both the proposer's and the client's, and take those assumptions into account in the final report.

Figure 16.6 *continued*

3. Gather information from a variety of sources and keep a record of all relevant transactions and activities in a work log or research journal. Include a working bibliography. A minimum number of sources is seven, but use as many as needed. Secondary source material must have been published within the last five years.

4. Synthesize the information and write a literature survey, which may be summarized in the report's introduction.

5. Examine, analyze, and evaluate the information. Distinguish between fact and opinion.

6. Draw conclusions based on the evidence and formulate recommendations that address the client's problem or situation or question.

7. Write the report using the format to be specified following the acceptance of proposals.

8. Submit three progress reports at specified dates during the project, and schedule conferences every two weeks to review the work and to resolve any problems or conflicts. Bring the work log to each meeting.

Proposal Format

Proposals for the report should be no longer than five pages, including attachments. Address them to the intended reader(s) of the completed report but send them to the instructor at the address given above. Reference to the RFP number must be made in the subject line.

Method and Criteria for the Evaluation of Proposals

Each Engineering Technology instructor will supervise a maximum of six students, and will choose winning proposals. A proposal provides information in a persuasive manner, with the intent of demonstrating the writer's (and his or her organization's) ability to perform the job proposed. Thus the proposal will be evaluated primarily on the following points:

- Clarity of presentation
- Accuracy and specificity of details
- Appropriateness of tone and format
- Completeness

Students are encouraged to consult instructors early and informally to obtain information that may assist decisions on project choice or even win tentative verbal acceptance. However, all verbal acceptances must be confirmed in this formal proposal process.

Figure 16.6 *continued*

Content in Responses

The specific content you should include in a response depends on the kind of RFP you receive. Read the RFP carefully. First determine the kind of response expected, and then check for any instructions regarding the format of the response. Sections with labels such as "Proposal Preparation Instructions" or "Proposal Format" typically detail any page and size specifications. Lengthy government and military RFPs usually include these important preparation instructions.

When the RFP indicates a negotiable response (one that allows some flexibility in content and form), determine exactly how much leeway is being granted, and then develop an appropriate response. Refer to the "Proposals" section earlier in this chapter.

Next, determine your plan to meet the needs described in the RFP. All responses to RFPs require sound, appropriate solutions to the needs described by the requester. The success of your response will depend largely on how well your proposed action matches the need.

Because RFPs vary greatly and frequently offer their own unique requirements for responses (especially government or military RFPs), a model outline for RFPs would offer little guidance. Use the model outline for proposals shown earlier in Figure 16.3 as a general guide, modifying it to adhere to any requirements or restrictions stated in a specific RFP.

There are, however, some key aspects for preparing a successful response to any RFP. *A note of caution:* Read the specific RFP thoroughly to determine whether any of the following suggestions are clearly not acceptable. Even an otherwise good response may be rejected because you failed to comply with the stated requirements.

1. Include all information specified in the RFP (technical description, experience, features of the equipment, delivery date) in the order listed, and label the sections appropriately: for example, 1.0 Product Description; 2.3 Résumés of Qualified Personnel; 4.1.1 Solid State Circuitry. (If a heading numbering system is used in the RFP, match it consistently in your response.)

2. If "fill-in" forms (specification and cost sheets) are included with the RFP, use them. Do not invent your own format or modify the RFP's in any way.

3. Always respond within the acceptable page limit stipulated in the RFP.

4. Determine whether the front matter (title page, table of contents) and illustrations on separate pages will be included in the page count.

5. Prepare all text on the specified paper size with the required margins and lines of text.

6. Determine whether pages may be printed on one side only or on both sides.

An *effective* response to an RFP nets winning results: It persuades the readers to agree that your proposed action is just what they need.

Form in Responses

The responses to RFPs, which can range from a few pages up to several volumes of information, must follow the form specified in the RFP. They may be requested as letters or as informal or formal reports. Read the RFP carefully to determine whether a particular form is stipulated. When not stated, choose a form based on your audience analysis and on the amount and complexity of information to be included.

Figure 16.7 shows how one student responded to the RFP illustrated in Figure 16.6. Bill wrote a covering memo with his proposal, included attachments, and delivered the package as required to Dr. M. Gould by the deadline. Figure 16.7 shows the transmittal memorandum and technical proposal.

JOSHUA SLOCUM COLLEGE　　　**Mechanical Engineering Technology**

Memorandum

TO:	Tom Morehouse	DATE:	October 13 199-
FROM:	Bill Johnson	SUBJECT	Proposal for Project RFP #ART 456/96

For my ART 456 Project, I have taken on the responsibility of researching and designing an underwater actuator as designated by Mr. Paul Li, chief mechanical engineer at the Grandmer Department of Oceanography.

I require a technical supervisor to guide me during the research, design, and possibly the manufacturing of a prototype actuator. I know that this is one area of interest for you and that the project has many design parameters that are in your area of expertise.

With my background and interests as a commercial diver and a heavy equipment mechanic, I approached the Chief Mechanical Engineer, Mr. Paul Li, at Grandmer. The Department's underwater photography section has a problem of poor-quality photographs because of poor lighting. My solution to the problem is outlined in the attached proposal and supported by initial research summarized in the accompanying literature survey.

Would you please consider approving and supervising the project, in consultation with Mr. Li? I would appreciate your response in writing. I can be reached by E-mail at ETS32 on the college computer system and will be glad to provide any further details that may assist you in your decision.

Enc:　technical proposal
　　　literature survey

Figure 16.7 *Extracts from a student response to the RFP #ART456/96.*
Adapted with permission of Bill Johnson, Mechanical Technology Graduate.

**JOSHUA SLOCUM COLLEGE
MECHANICAL ENGINEERING TECHNOLOGY
PROPOSAL TO RESEARCH AND DESIGN
AN UNDERWATER ACTUATOR FOR
GRANDMER DEPARTMENT OF OCEANOGRAPHY
TO FULFIL THE REQUIREMENTS OF ART 456/96**

By: Bill Johnson
For: Mr. T. Morehouse, P.Eng.
    Mr. P. Li, P.Eng.

13 October 199-

Figure 16.7 *continued*

PROPOSAL TO RESEARCH AND DESIGN
AN UNDERWATER ACTUATOR SYSTEM FOR GRANDMER

Statement of the Problem

The underwater photography section of the Grandmer Department of Oceanography has for several years had a problem with photograph quality. The main cause of the poor-quality photographs is the placement of two strobe lights. With the existing camera sled, the strobes cannot be placed in a position to create optimum lighting. As a result, only about 60 percent of the photograph is of any use.

Statement of Objective

The objective is to design an actuator system that will meet the following criteria:

1. Be self-powered and self-actuating. The arm must deploy after the sled is in the water and be retracted before recovery by the support vessel, with no external power source.
2. Be suitable for underwater conditions at a maximum depth of 7,000 metres (corrosion resistant, pressure resistant, needing minimal lubrication).
3. Be able to be mounted on the existing camera sled.
4. Be able to deploy an arm that has a maximum of 5 kilograms of weight on it.
5. Have arms that stow within the camera sled superstructure and extend 1.5 metres when deployed.
6. Be as lightweight as possible.
7. Have minimal maintenance.

Procedure

The project will be approached and carried out as follows. I will

1. research and analyze the most efficient and practical source by using personal and suggested ideas and an iterative process
2. research and design the most efficient and practical configuration for the extendable arms by using kinematics, machine design, and other engineering techniques.
3. research and develop the actuator to meet the stated criteria by using personal experience, local designers and suppliers, and available technology.

Figure 16.7 *continued*

4. draft the final mechanism on AutoCAD and submit to Mr. Li at Grandmer for possible construction.

Resources

Joshua Slocum College technology instructors: A. Larevan, J. Flinn, G. Witherspoon.

Mr. Paul Li, Chief Mechanical Engineer, Grandmer Department of Oceanography.

Class colleagues.

Personal library.

Joshua Slocum College Library.

Oceana Regional Library.

Scientific and Engineering Library, University of Oceana.

Local material suppliers and designers.

Full details of material suppliers, designers, trade journals, engineering journals, and handbooks are available in the attached annotated, working bibliography.

Benefits

This project will provide me with the opportunity to work at Grandmer photography section during my contact training in February, and to develop a practicable solution to their problem. The project will also continue the valuable liaison between Joshua Slocum Engineering Technology Department and Grandmer.

Timeline

As the attached Gantt chart shows, the design will be ready for the Spring Showcase in May 199- together with a preliminary report, a work journal, and promotional material. The final report will be submitted to Mr. P. Li and you by May 18, 199-.

Conclusion

Working with Grandmer will provide me with valuable experience in research and development as well as in solving and documenting an engineering problem. I would much appreciate your approval and supervision.

Figure 16.7 *continued*

Activity 5
....

Read carefully the RFP in Figure 16.6 and the response in Figure 16.7.

List three ways in which Bill satisfied the requirements of the RFP.

_____

_____

_____

_____

Name two areas in which his response to the proposal could have been improved.

_____

_____

_____

Comment briefly on the tone and format of his response.

_____

_____

_____

Where does Bill demonstrate effective reader analysis? Comment on his persuasive technique.

_____

_____

_____

QUESTIONS FOR DISCUSSION

1. Explain the differences between solicited and unsolicited proposals and between internal and external readers.
2. What is the main purpose of all proposals?
3. In a proposal, why should costs always be placed in a separate section?
4. Why is careful reading of an originating RFP or RFQ essential?
5. Why would an RFP solicit a nonnegotiable response?
6. What is the main focus of any response to an RFP?

WRITING ASSIGNMENTS

1. Write a transmittal letter and an unsolicited proposal (1,000 to 2,000 words) to your technical writing instructor on one of the following possibilities — or develop your own topic:

   ◆ Solutions to student accommodation problems at your college
   ◆ Improvements in your major field curriculum
   ◆ Improvements in the class registration process at your school
   ◆ Suggestions for a guest lecturer series for your favourite course
   ◆ Improvements in the college bookstore
   ◆ Ways to attract more shoppers to your community's downtown area
   ◆ Ways to increase patronage at your favourite restaurant near campus
   ◆ Ways to improve attendance at 8:00 a.m. classes at your college.

2. Read the following requests for proposals that were advertised in the ABC Community College Newsletter. Choose one and write a response based on the needs described, inventing the details of your solutions as needed.

   Development of Solutions to Traffic Congestion at the Campus Main Entrance. *ABC-CC is seeking viable solutions to ease or eliminate traffic problems during peak hours at the Victoria Street entrance. Word-processed proposals of no more than 500 words should address these issues: effects on traffic flow along Victoria Street, safety to pedestrians, and traffic flow exiting the Engineering Building parking lot. The solution must not cost more than $1,500 to implement. The writer of the winning proposal will be awarded a guaranteed parking spot until the end of the academic year. Submit all* *responses within seven days of this announcement to your writing instructor.*

Request for Proposals for Making Computer Lab Equipment More Accessible to Students. *ABC-CC is seeking proposals for improving the accessibility of all computer lab equipment to its students. Responses may not propose new equipment purchases, must be sound technically, and must include specific details. Single-sided, word-processed proposals should contain three to four pages, 54 lines per page, and one-inch margins on all sides. Submit responses to the writing instructor within seven days of this announcement.*

Request for Proposals. *ABC-CC is seeking proposals from qualified suppliers of classroom furniture. The college has allocated $30,000 to furnish five new classrooms in its Language Arts Building with the following items as specified: student desks (washable surfaces only); instructor desks (a minimum of two lockable drawers); chalkboards (at least a five-year guarantee against permanent marking and peeling). Each classroom should accommodate a minimum of 23 students. Submit sealed responses within seven days of this announcement to the technical writing instructor.*

3. Reread the RFP shown in Figure 16.6, which was issued by a technical writing instructor to his or her students. Respond to this document as directed by your own technical writing instructor.

Part SIX

BUSINESS CORRESPONDENCE

Objectives

When you finish Part Six — Chapters Seventeen and Eighteen — you should be able to do the following:

- Recognize the circumstances that prompt business correspondence.
- Identify and effectively compose the parts of a business letter.
- Construct letters in these formats:

  Block
  Modified block
  Simplified

- Write letters in conventional form, appropriate tone, and clear style.
- Write the following specific types of letters:

  Inquiry and response
  Order
  Complaint and adjustment
  Transmittal
  Job application with résumé
  Follow-up

- Write memos in conventional form, appropriate tone, and clear style.

Chapter SEVENTEEN

Letters: Form and Tone

Correspondence relating to work situations, whether written to or originating from places of business, is a form of technical writing. Correspondence you write as a consumer or as an interested citizen is also technical writing, since letters perform many of the same functions as longer reports:

◆ They may request information or action.

◆ They may indicate what is right or wrong with a product or service.

◆ They may try to influence the reader to believe or act in a certain way.

◆ They may explain a policy or situation.

◆ They may indicate what has been done or left undone.

◆ They may justify what has been done.

Despite the widespread use of the telephone and fax machines and the increasing use of electronic mail, nothing has yet replaced the business letter as the essential means of communication. Even when a decision is made and communicated orally, it must usually be put in writing and signed before it is considered valid.

The professional world operates by means of letters, since anything communicated orally can be forgotten or misunderstood. A letter provides tangible proof of exactly what was said, and the content can be reviewed, if necessary, for clarification. If letters do not generate ideas, they support and record them. Thus, knowing how to write effective letters is a valuable asset in both your personal and your professional life.

There are three key ingredients in every letter:

◆ What you say (the content or message)
◆ How it looks (the appearance and form)
◆ How it sounds (the tone)

Chapter Eighteen discusses the first aspect: content. When you have something worthwhile to communicate at home or at work, something about which you take the time to write, that is the *content*. The basic premise of all business letter writing is straightforward: You or your company wants something from the recipient — information, action, goodwill, or a combination of all three. Chapter Eighteen shows how to compose specific types of messages: inquiries, orders, complaints, responses, report transmittals, and job applications. It also illustrates how to write résumés and memos. Before you study specific types of business correspondence, however, you should review appropriate form and tone.

Form is what the letter looks like. You may choose a form from the various accepted arrangements or formats of letters and their required and optional components. Although you have some leeway in form, your letters should contain certain conventional parts arranged in a specified order. These parts help you get your message across in the same way that conventional street signs and traffic signals move traffic along. A conventional form allows your reader to get to your message quickly. An inconsistent form hinders quick reading and distracts the reader from your message.

Tone is an important yet difficult element to define; it has to do with the way a document "comes across" to the reader, or the way a reader perceives the writer as a person. A pleasant and professional tone will do much to motivate your reader to respond as you wish. An unprofessional tone, regardless of the clarity of the content and the correctness of the form, may cause your reader to respond negatively or not respond at all.

Each element — form, tone, and content — is important if you want to write letters that get results.

BUSINESS LETTER FORMS

The generally acceptable forms for business correspondence include the following (with some variations):

◆ Full block
◆ Modified block
◆ Simplified

When you put your message in a standard format, your reader's attention is directed to your message's content; your reader will not be distracted by the unexpected.

Figures 17.1, 17.2, and 17.3 illustrate these three forms for business correspondence. These illustrations serve two purposes: They provide you with a model for proper format, and they display the specifics of that format within the body of the letter.

Each letter style has its advocates. The first two forms — full block and modified block — differ chiefly in their indention patterns and in the placement of the return address and the complimentary close. The modified block form, once typically preferred for personal and business letters, is now being superseded by the full block form. The latter lines up its components with the left margin, dispenses with indention, and takes less time to format. The simplified form, favoured by many business writers, omits both the salutation and the complimentary close, and gets straight to the message. You should use your company's preferred form or choose whichever form most appeals to you. Once you decide which form to use, remember to be consistent.

PARTS OF A BUSINESS LETTER

Business letters include the following components:

◆ Return address and date (heading)
◆ Inside address
◆ Attention line (optional)
◆ Salutation
◆ Subject line (optional)
◆ Body
◆ Complimentary close
◆ Writer's identification (including signature)

Depending on the need, letters may also include any of the following additional elements (following the writer's signature and typed name):

◆ Reference initials
◆ Enclosures
◆ Copy notations
◆ Postscripts

Each component is discussed in detail below.

123 Golden Road
Whitehorse, YT Y1A 3W7
January 2, 199-

Ms. M. Euloth
Supervisor, Communications
Career Services Centre
Northern College
Whitehorse, YT Y2B 5W4

Dear Ms. Euloth

As requested, I have examined several letter formats and recommend that Northern College Career Services Centre adopt the full block format. This letter is written in that format: Apart from the indented list, all the letter parts line up flush with the left margin.

As with all business letters, the full block style is single-spaced with double-spacing between paragraphs. It is attractively balanced on the page and has at least double-spacing between each of its parts.

Notice also that the paragraphs are short — with five or fewer lines. Paragraphs in business letters tend to be shorter than in essays or other expository writing. Short, easy-to-read paragraphs are appreciated by busy persons at work. However, avoid using too many one-sentence paragraphs. These produce a choppy effect, imply a lack of thought, and detract from a flowing style.

For assistance in this project, I surveyed six businesses from this region and six career services departments from colleges (three from Canada and three from the United States — see attached copies and responses). Four of our major employers use the full block format:

- ABC Electronics Inc.
- Wheeler Cable
- Greenacre Construction
- MechSwift Consulting

Employees at these companies say that the full block format is symmetrical, clean looking, uncluttered, easy to read, and simple to use. I strongly recommend it.

Erica Logan

Erica Logan
Project Assistant

Figure 17.1 *This letter of response to a request uses full block format.*

123 Golden Road
Whitehorse, YT Y1A 3W7
February 15, 199-

Dr. Alex T. MacDonald
Dean, Extension Division
ACC Technical College
North Viking, NF A1S 3C8

Dear Dr. MacDonald:

Subject: Business Writing Survey

As part of a project for the Career Services Centre, Northern College, Whitehorse, I am surveying the preferred letter formats in selected businesses and professional institutions. At this centre we wish to update our business writing practices and would much appreciate your assistance with this project. Please take the time or ask one of your faculty to

- Examine the attached business letter formats
- Name the preferred one
- State reasons for the preference

This letter illustrates the modified block style, which for many years has been the most commonly used of the letter formats.

The return address/date (heading) in this form is either centred or placed slightly to the right of the centre of the page. The inside address, salutation, and optional subject and attention lines begin at the left margin.

The return address, the complimentary close, and the signature line up with each other in the modified block format.

Paragraphs are indented, as shown here, or begin at the left margin. Whichever form of letter is chosen, spacing and indenting must be consistent throughout.

The postscript below is indented because the paragraphs are indented. If paragraphs start at the left margin, then the postscript would also line up with the left margin.

Please respond by March 1.

Sincerely yours,

Erica Logan

Erica Logan
Project Assistant

Enclosures (3)

Figure 17.2 *This letter of request for information uses modified block form.*

Engines Are US
4921-4926 Fourth Street   Bannerman   CA   93726   USA

199- 02 23

Ms. Erica Logan
123 Golden Road
Whitehorse, YT Y1A 3W7

SIMPLIFIED LETTER FORM

In response to your request (13 Feb), we use the simplified format illustrated in this letter, which varies slightly from the one you supplied.

As you can see, Ms. Logan, the customary salutation is omitted. It is replaced with an
announcement of the subject of the letter, usually in all capital letters. The writer often
uses the recipient's name in the body of the letter, as I have done in this paragraph.

This form also omits the complimentary close. These omissions are the essential difference between this and the more conventional styles.

The simplified form has been around for well over fifty years and is recommended by
the Administrative Management Society. We like it because it

*   emphasizes the content of the letter right away.
*   wastes neither time nor words.
*   dispenses with the salutation and complimentary close, which may be considered
    artificial and insincere, and which pose some problem when the addressee is
    unknown to the writer.

While some writers feel that omitting the salutation and complimentary close makes the
letter cold and discourteous, we can convey our messages through a warm and courteous tone and without using any outdated conventions. In fact, this style is being used
more often now, especially in order and sales letters. It helps avoid the problem of the
proper or appropriate salutation when the company or individual is unknown.

Even though there is no complimentary close, we leave sufficient space (usually four
lines) for the signature, and then put name and title in all capital letters on one line.

Monroe Scichen

MONROE SCICHEN — OFFICE MANAGER

Figure 17.3 *This letter or response to an inquiry uses simplified style.*

Return Address and Date

The return address and date (also called the heading) lets the reader know where to reach you and when you wrote the letter. When you write on plain paper, as an individual rather than as a representative of a company, this heading includes your mailing address, followed by the date.

Canada Post Corporation and the U.S. Postal Service prefer that two-letter abbreviations be used for all Canadian provinces and territories, and all states and U.S. territories. Figure 17.4 shows these accepted abbreviations for provinces, states, and territories.

Follow these guidelines for the return address and date section:

◆ Do not include your name in this section.

◆ Spell out words such as Street, Road, or Avenue.

◆ Spell out the name of the province or state or abbreviate (using Canada Post's preferred designation of two capital letters).

◆ Leave two spaces between province or state and postal or zip code but use no punctuation.

◆ Single-space between your home address and the date.

◆ Unless instructed otherwise, use the conventional form for dates (May 17, 19--, for example). If your company prefers, use the military form (17 May 19--, for example) or the numerical form (year, month, and day as shown in Figure 17.3). The numerical form is an international (SI) standard.

Here are return addresses with conventional and military dates:

32 Trevone Street	Apt. 2B Courtside
Cornwall, ON K6H 8X4	Bermuda Shoals, ME 04299
August 10, 19--	19 August 19--

Most workplaces use company stationery, with company name, address, and logo. When using this stationery, centre the date two spaces under the letterhead.

Activity 1

1. In the space below, write your *return address* (your home address) and today's *date* (conventional form).

_____

_____

_____

Canada		Louisiana	LA
Alberta	AB	Maine	ME
British Columbia	BC	Maryland	MD
Manitoba	MB	Massachusetts	MA
New Brunswick	NB	Michigan	MI
Newfoundland	NF	Minnesota	MN
Nova Scotia	NS	Mississippi	MS
Northwest Territories	NT	Missouri	MO
Ontario	ON	Montana	MT
Prince Edward Island	PE	Nebraska	NE
Quebec (Province de		Nevada	NV
Québec)	PQ	New Hampshire	NH
Saskatchewan	SK	New Jersey	NJ
Yukon Territory	YT	New Mexico	NM
		New York	NY
United States		North Carolina	NC
Alabama	AL	North Dakota	ND
Alaska	AK	Ohio	OH
Arizona	AZ	Oklahoma	OK
Arkansas	AR	Oregon	OR
American Samoa	AS	Pennsylvania	PA
California	CA	Puerto Rico	PR
Colorado	CO	Rhode Island	RI
Connecticut	CT	South Carolina	SC
Delaware	DE	South Dakota	SD
District of Columbia	DC	Tennessee	TN
Florida	FL	Trust Territories	TT
Georgia	GA	Texas	TX
Guam	GU	Utah	UT
Hawaii	HI	Vermont	VT
Idaho	ID	Virginia	VA
Illinois	IL	Virgin Islands	VI
Indiana	IN	Washington	WA
Iowa	IA	West Virginia	WV
Kansas	KS	Wisconsin	WI
Kentucky	KY	Wyoming	WY

Figure 17.4 *Postal abbreviations for provinces, states, and territories. From Canada Post Corporation and United States Postal Service.*

2. On the lines to the right, make any corrections necessary in the following return addresses:

   a. Mrs. Maretta Zappen
      15 Hazelmere Court
      Medicine Hat, Alta, T1B 6A7
      March 16, 19--

   b. Apt. 2-B Hillside Court
      Butte, MN 59701
      4/22/90

   c. 65 Bitten St.
      Delta, BC V4K 12S3
      Jan. 12 — '90

Inside Address

The inside address identifies the recipient of the letter and that person's (or the company's) address. You should name the specific reader, a position, or an organizational entity. Follow these guidelines for the inside address:

◆ Use the name of your intended reader, as long as you are sure of the correct spelling. If you are unsure, call the personnel director, check company files, or do whatever is necessary to find the correct spelling.

◆ Use a courtesy title such as *Mr.*, *Ms.*, or *Dr.* before the name. Place position titles such as *President* or *Administrator* after the name, separated by a comma, or on a separate line. Inside addresses should look like the following examples:

Dr. John N. Bowles, Vice President, Fiscal Services

Southampton Marine Technology Institute

222 Southampton Boulevard

Victoria, BC V8R 3C5

Mr. Barry Townson, Human Resources Director
General Catering and Cafeterias Company
234 34th Street
Chicago, Illinois 60640

Ms. S. Iswandi
Director of Accounting Services
McGlone, Smith, and Berman
989 Marine Drive
Charlottetown, PE C1A 3P9

◆ If you do not know the name of a particular person at a company or institution, you may address the position (as the following examples show):

Registrar   Hospital Administrator
Peabody Community College   University City Hospital
300 Old State Road   1776 Main Street
Lake City, GA 30553   Aurora, ON L4G 1Z8

◆ If you do not know which position to write to at a company, you can address the company itself. However, such a general address will slow down communication, since the staff person who opens your letter will have to determine to whom the letter should be routed. It is always more expedient to address a specific person or a specific position within a company. Here are examples of letters addressed to companies:

Freeway Bus Station   Nan's Factory Outlet
585 Almon Street   New Cut Road
Fredericton, NB E3A 4H7   Toronto, ON M2N 3P5

◆ Place the inside address from five to ten lines below the return address or date. (Placement may vary if you use a window envelope.)

The Attention Line

This optional item directs the letter to a specific person or department when the inside address and salutation are directed to a business or industry. Use the attention line sparingly and follow these guidelines:

◆ Place the attention line between the inside address and the salutation.

- Double-space between the inside address and the attention line and between the attention line and the salutation.
- Use this form: Attention: Ms. Jessica Smith.

Salutation

The salutation is a courtesy greeting preceding the body of the letter. The standard format is *Dear* followed by the recipient's title and last name. When you know the reader personally, you may use the informal first name. *Gentlemen* (when addressing a company) is seldom used since it implies that all executives are men. And *Dear Gentlemen* has never been correct.

Use the following guidelines for salutations:

- In a letter addressed to a person, use that person's last name along with the appropriate courtesy title.

    Dear Mr. Jones: Dear Dr. Smith: Dear Ms. Bateni:

- In a letter addressed to a position, the conventional salutations *Dear Sir* and *Dear Sir or Madam* have been replaced by the preferred alternative of addressing the position itself:

    Dear Personnel Director: Dear Librarian:

- In a letter addressed to a company, omit *Dear* and use the title of the department or position if known: *Attn. Engineering Division* or *Attn. Sales Manager.* The salutations *Gentlemen* and *Ladies* are used less often than they used to be, because they may be inaccurate and exclusionary and therefore offensive to both female and male recipients.
- Use *Dear Sirs* only when you address two or more men whose names you do not know and whose positions you do not wish to use (a rare situation).
- Even if you know a group is exclusively female, such as WITT (Women in Trades and Technology), do not use *Ladies* but address them as *Dear WITT Members.* You may also direct your letter to the organization secretary: *Dear WITT Secretary.* If the group is exclusively male, address the secretary or use *Dear Rotary Club—Metro*, for example. It is always better to find the name of the person, however.

Using terms that seem to include only males (even when that is not your intention) may offend readers, both men and women. When you receive letters, you may notice that the terminology is in a transitional state. The best choice, when possible, is to determine the *name* of the person you want to receive your letter and precede it with *Mr.* or *Ms.* or another appropriate title. Using a specific name personalizes your letter and avoids calling attention to your choice of salutation.

Activity 2

For each of the following *inside addresses*, write an appropriate *salutation* and punctuate accordingly. You may change to the simplified format if the occasion demands.

a. Registrar
Saint Martha's College
Grand Falls, NF A2A 2H9

_____

b. Ms. Clare Trahey
Ebb Tide Marketers
Norton, WI 53160

_____

c. Ebb Tide Marketers
Plumtree Mall
Norton, WI 53160

_____

d. Association of Women Business Owners
P.O. Box 636
Winnipeg, MB R3G 1V3

_____

The Subject Line

This line announces the topic of the letter immediately and briefly. It is convenient when you need to provide a policy number, for example, or address a specific problem, or reply to a specific question. Some guidelines govern the use of the subject line:

◆ Place the subject line (double-spaced) between the salutation and the first paragraph of the body.

◆ Use the subject line as a business courtesy. The subject line is an effective means of directing the reader straight to the point. Even in a letter of application, the subject line serves well to specify the position and job competition number. It focuses the reader immediately. Do not use the subject line on more personal occasions: letters of thanks or congratulation, etc.

◆ Write the subject line in upper and lowercase letters (Subject: Policy 314-B — Dental Coverage), or all caps (SUBJECT: CANCELLATION OF INSURANCE).

Body

The body of the letter contains your message, the point of your letter. Your message — as in any technical document — must be expressed clearly. The reader should never wonder "Why am I reading this? What exactly am I to do?" (The content of each kind of letter is fully discussed in Chapter Eighteen.) Besides the message itself, the appearance of the body is also important. Follow the guidelines below to be sure that the body of your letter is appropriate in appearance and is easy to read:

◆ Single-space the letter and double-space between paragraphs.

◆ Indent for paragraphs unless you choose the full block form.

◆ Keep the body to one page, if at all possible.

◆ If you must include a second page, put the recipient's name, the page number, and the date — usually in one line as shown here — at the top:

> Mr. Jake Abbott page 2 September 8, 19--

Letterhead is not used after the first page.

◆ Divide your text into short paragraphs rather than one or two long paragraphs.

◆ Adjust margins to avoid a short letter with only a few long lines.

Complimentary Close

The complimentary close (like the salutation) is a courtesy; it ends a letter much as a handshake concludes a business interview or meeting. Its absence may seem to indicate a lack of respect. The following are typical complimentary closes:

Sincerely,	Sincerely yours,
Yours truly,	Very truly yours,
Cordially,	Cordially yours,
Respectfully,	Respectfully yours,

Follow these guidelines for writing complimentary closes:

- ◆ Choose the complimentary close that reflects your relationship with the recipient or simply use your preference. *Cordially* is used when your relationship is friendly and you have established (or want to establish) a good working relationship. *Regards* and *Best wishes* are also used between colleagues and friends.
- ◆ Capitalize only the first word in the complimentary close.
- ◆ Follow the complimentary close with a comma (or omit punctuation if you did not punctuate the salutation).

Signature and Identification

The writer's identification includes your name and title, typed. The signature is the finishing touch to the letter. Do not sign a letter that you (or someone else) typed until you review it to see that it says exactly what you want to say and follows all the expected conventions of good letter writing. Your signature implies that you take full credit for the appropriateness of the elements, the tone, and the appearance, as well as the accuracy of the content. Follow these guidelines for the writer's identification and signature section of the letter.

Signature

- ◆ Allow at least four lines following the complimentary close for your signature.
- ◆ Sign your name as you are known in the business or professional world.
- ◆ Sign your name legibly in black ink — never in pencil.

Identification

- ◆ Type your name following the four line spaces allowed for your signature, using the name you wish to be addressed by in future correspondence.
- ◆ For full block and modified block forms, type your position or title on the line following your typed name. For simplified style letters, type your name and title in all capital letters on one line.

Here are examples of complimentary closes with signatures:

Sincerely yours,   Yours truly,

Talbot C. Squires   *Alisha Squires*

Talbot C. Squires   Alisha Squires, President
Membership Chairman   Scotia Air Conditioners

When you write as a representative of a company or when the company prefers that all correspondence go out under its name, use the following form:

Very truly yours,
WATBOROUGH MANUFACTURING, INC.

[signature: Richard L. Patroz]

Richard L. Patroz
Vice President, Consumer Services

Activity 3

a. Choose an appropriate complimentary close for each of the situations below and write it in the blank provided. Punctuate accordingly.

1. You are applying for a job.

_____

2. You are submitting a report with a transmittal letter to the president of your company.

_____

3. You are thanking a long-term business associate with whom you have corresponded for more than five years.

_____

b. You are asked to review the first three letters sent out over a new employee's signature. Below are three complimentary closes and signatures. Make any corrections in the blanks to the right.

1. Sincerely Yours, _____

   Phil Truesdale *[signature: Phil Truesdale]*

2. Sincerly _____

   Phil Truesdale *[signature: Phil Truesdale]*

3. Very Truely Yours;

Phil Truesdale: Manager   *Phil Truesdale*

Reference Initials

Initials included at the bottom of your letter indicate that someone else typed it for you. Although you, the originator, are ultimately responsible for any errors in content, form, or mechanics such as spelling and punctuation, the typist's initials (also called a stenographic notation) show who is physically responsible. Follow these guidelines:

◆ Use the initials alone or in conjunction with yours.

◆ Use lowercase or uppercase initials and separate them from the writer's initials by a slash or colon.

Below are examples of typist's initials when the letter's originator is Carla Hopkins Mueller and the typist is Krista Lebeau:

KL   CHM:KL   chm/kl

Enclosure or Enclosures

Include the word *enclosure* or *enclosures* at the bottom of your letter to indicate that you are sending other material with the letter. Follow these guidelines:

◆ Use the term only if you have also indicated in the body of the letter that you are enclosing other material.

◆ If you wish to indicate the kind of material you are enclosing, separate the kind of material with a colon, or omit the colon. (You may also abbreviate.)

◆ Use these forms:

Enclosure
Enclosure: Cheque 657
Encl. Accident Report

Copy Notation

This notation indicates that you have made a copy or copies for other persons or an extra copy.

◆ Name the person(s) to whom copies are being sent.

- Use these forms:

  > c: Service Manager
  > copy: George Smith
  > copies: George Smith
  >   Annabel Sleeman

  Note: The single c is preferred now that photocopies are far more common than carbon copies or circulation copies (cc).

P.S.

Originally, *P.S.* (postscript) meant that the writer had forgotten some information and was including it at this point. Now *P.S.* should be used only in sales letters to call attention to a final or important point. Use it *rarely*. Never use the P.S. in letters of application!

APPEARANCE: GENERAL GUIDELINES

A successful business letter is one that gets results.

> If you want a product, you get it.
> If you want a question answered, you get a response.
> If you want a job interview, you get one.
> If you want a problem corrected, you get it done.

Of course, your message must be clear and well stated, but a successful business letter "sells" more than just clear communication. Readers will react to the *appearance* and *tone* of your letters as well as to their *content*. Below are guidelines for ensuring that your letters look professional:

- Use good-quality paper.
- Use 21.5 cm by 28 cm ($8\frac{1}{2}$" by 11") white paper.
- Single-space within a paragraph and double-space between paragraphs.
- Balance the letter attractively on the page. Part of the body should always extend below the middle of the page.
- Use margins that enhance the letter's appearance (wider for short letters and narrower for long letters).
- Do not crowd the letter. Allow enough white space to make the letter easy to read and appealing to the eye.
- Compose short paragraphs. A paragraph of seven or more lines is too long. Several short paragraphs are more readable than two or three long ones.

◆ Do not mail a letter with noticeable corrections. Erasures, strikeovers, or visible correcting fluid will distract readers from your message. As you will probably be using your word processor, correcting a letter is easy and essential.

◆ Use a laser printer, if possible. Whatever printer or typewriter you use, make sure that the toner cartridge or ink ribbon is clear and not worn out. Your reader should not have to read pale print.

The appearance of your letter should enhance your message by creating a positive impression.

TONE

The right tone is far more difficult to achieve in a letter than the correct format or proper appearance. Think of your letter as conveying *your image on paper*. Since your reader will judge you and your employer by how you present yourself in writing, make sure that your letters always represent you at your personal and professional best.

Creating a positive tone or favourable impression is especially important in written communication because you have little immediate chance to rectify an initial poor impression. Assume, for example, that two supervisors send out the following policy statement:

STATEMENT 1: Blane Management reserves the prerogative of requiring its employees to extend working hours as necessary, subject, of course, to periodic review.

STATEMENT 2: We may ask employees to work overtime when necessary.

Although both say the same thing, the vocabulary of the first establishes a tone of excessive formality, while the second is far more positive. To create an appropriate tone in letters that get results, follow these guidelines:

◆ Be sincere.
◆ Be positive.
◆ Be concise.

Even the most formal correspondence should aim for a tone that conveys sincerity, warmth, and humanness — not mechanical assembly-line language. From the very first word, you want to sound like a pleasant and reasonable human being. Even if you are irritated with a poor product or poor service or are annoyed by delays and unfulfilled promises, you should sound approachable.

Activity 4

Read the short letter below and answer the questions that follow. Assume that the letter is correctly arranged and includes all appropriate parts.

> *Dear Student:*
>
> *You owe us $400 tuition and have owed it for three months. Send us the money now, or your file will be locked until you pay up.*
>
> *Cordially,*

* * * * *

a. Is the content clear? _____   _____

b. If you received the letter from your college, would you be properly motivated to send the money?

_____

c. What is your immediate reaction?

_____

d. Can you pinpoint the exact reason for your reaction?

_____

Write down how you would convey the same message to a student and discuss your opinion in class.

Sometimes when you want something very badly (a job, a response, your money back) you may choose words that do not sound sincere, even though you intend them to be. Avoid being "gushy" and excessive — regardless of the subject of the letter. Avoid seeming to extend false praise about a product, a situation, or a place. The best advice — in letter writing as in life — is "Don't fake it."

Activity 5

Evaluate the following sentences as sounding sincere *(S)* or not sincere *(NS)*. Be prepared to discuss your evaluations.

_____ a. Thank you for your help in filling out the enclosed questionnaire.

_____ b. It would be eternally appreciated if you will take your valuable time to complete the enclosed vital questionnaire.

_____ c. Ordering the Q-Zee Facial Kit will be the most important decision you ever make for your face. Don't deny your potential beauty by delaying. This offer will not be repeated.

_____ d. I have always wanted to work in your beautiful province, especially for such a forward-looking company, and I will consider any position available.

_____ e. For almost eighteen years, Servtron has serviced my car to my satisfaction. However, two hours after my tires were rotated on July 18, I noticed that the right rear tire began to wobble. Two of the lug nuts were missing.

Remember that a business letter is usually written when you want something, so you should always expect the reader to respond positively. After all, if you do not expect to get what you want, why write at all? A harsh and demanding attitude will usually put your reader on the defensive, while a pleasant and reasonable tone will usually elicit a positive response.

Activity 6
....

Evaluate the following sentences as positive *(P)* or not positive *(NP)* and be prepared to discuss your evaluation.

_____ a. I would welcome the opportunity of meeting you to discuss my qualifications and background in more detail.

_____ b. If my qualifications meet your approval, may I be considered for an interview?

_____ c. I am sure that Servtron will want to stand behind its reputation of high-quality service.

_____ d. You should certainly not quibble about replacing my right rear tire, but if you do, I will never deal with you again.

_____ e. Probably a big conglomerate like BestMart does not have time to listen to one small consumer voice, but every consumer is important and deserves to be heard.

A concise letter also communicates a favourable tone. A wordy letter which the reader must wade through to get to the point is usually irritating; a reader who is irritated is less likely to respond positively. An easy way to eliminate wordiness in your letters is to read them carefully and mark out any unnecessary words. State the facts, be courteous and pleasant, and do both with a minimum of clutter.

Activity 7

Evaluate the following examples as concise *(C)* or wordy *(W)*. Cross out any absolutely useless words.

_____ a. My electric bill for January was a shockingly high $589.00, an increase of $245.00 over December's bill.

_____ b. Can you imagine my surprise when I opened my electric bill for the month of January and found that it was shockingly high? It was $589.00, which amazed me since just the month before it was only $344.00 for the entire month of December.

_____ c. My work and class schedule allows me to be free to come for an interview any Monday, Wednesday, or Friday afternoon.

_____ d. I work every Tuesday and Thursday all day from 9 until 5, and I go to school every other weekday from 8 in the morning until lunchtime which is at 12 on Monday but a lab on the other days means I'm there until about 1 or 1:30.

_____ e. Last Monday, which was, as you know, a very snowy day, I was carefully driving my 1987 four-door Ford sedan down the ramp near the Municipal Building when I heard the rattle of what sounded like marbles in my right rear wheel and the wheel began to wobble crazily, causing me to pull off at once.

Remember that tone is a reflection of your personality — conveyed through your choice of words and sentence construction. To create a warm and personal tone, follow these guidelines:

◆ Use personal pronouns when possible rather than more distant and abstract terms.

When Referring to Yourself

Use: *I/me/my/mine*

Examples:

I would like a copy…

Please send me…

My last bank statement…

The mistake was mine…

Don't refer to yourself as

The customer

The undersigned

The user

The writer

When Referring to Your Company

Use: *we/us/our/ours*

Examples:

We can send samples…

Let us assist you…

Our policy allows…

The mistake was ours…

Don't refer repeatedly to

The corporation

The management

The institution

The company

◆ Use the active voice most of the time. When the subject of the sentence performs the action, the sentence is more direct and emphatic. In the passive voice, the "actor" (if named) is placed in a prepositional phrase, and the subject of the sentence receives the action. The passive voice is useful when you prefer indirectness.

Active

We can send our catalogue…

Blane's will reimburse…

I appreciate your help…

Prospective employees can apply…

Passive

Our catalogue can be sent…

You will be reimbursed by Blane's…

Your help is appreciated…

Application can be made by prospective employees…

◆ Use familiar words when possible rather than "big" words of four or more syllables.

Choose Words Such as These

Buying policy

Review

Questioning

Avoid Words Such as These

Procurement policy

Reappraise/reappraisal

Interrogation

The problem is not, of course, the use of *one* big word; it is the excessive utilization of multisyllabic terminology (like this) which leaves your reader cold.

◆ Choose your verbs carefully — avoid those that appear demanding, overly aggressive, and hostile. Use positive or, at the very least, neutral verbs.

Use Verbs Such as These	Avoid Verbs Such as These
Misunderstood	Cheated
Worked	Slaved
Compensate	Pay off
Suggest	Insinuate
Said	Claimed

Your readers will usually react immediately to the overall tone of your letter. They want to understand quickly what you are requesting and will respond to a sincere, positive approach. Appropriate form, appearance, and tone all contribute to effective, result-getting letters.

QUESTIONS FOR DISCUSSION

1. How can you avoid the gender issue in most salutations?
2. Why is the appearance of a letter important?
3. What is tone, and why is a positive tone important in letters?
4. How do you achieve a positive tone?

EXERCISE 1

Match each part of a letter with the sentence which best suits it.
 1. Return address/date
 2. Inside address
 3. Salutation
 4. Body
 5. Attention line
 6. Subject line
 7. Complimentary close
 8. P.S.
 9. Copy notation
10. Reference initials
11. Enclosure

_____ a. A money order accompanies your letter.

_____ b. You want to emphasize that the sale will end in two days.

_____ c. Your letter was typed by a secretary.

_____ d. You want Ms. Bloom — and your boss — to read the letter.

_____ e. You live in Mesa Verde, New Mexico.

_____ f. Your letter is to a Mr. Smith in Sussex, New Brunswick.

_____ g. You write your insurance company about a change in your policy, number 556-CV-19008.

_____ h. You write to the insurance company but want Ms. Bloom to get the letter.

_____ i. You explain carefully what you want done, how you will pay, and when the change should be effective, and you thank the company for its prompt consideration.

_____ j. You call the recipient of the letter "Dear."

EXERCISE 2

The following letter, in the block format, contains at least 15 mistakes in form and appearance, including punctuation and capitalization. Read the letter carefully.

M. K. Lester
Tutor Technical Writing 100
MNO Correspondence College
894 Raceway Circle
Sackville, Man, R3R2V5
4/12/90

George McLee
Distance Education Student #6198
Italy Cross, Nova Scotia

Attention: George McLee

Dear Sir;

The main reason for this letter is to see if you recognize and can correct serious errors in format and appearance. So don't worry about the message or lack of message; don't even worry about the tone. The letter will leave a very definite bad impression on any reader if it goes out with problems in form and appearance regardless of how clear the content might be. The parts of the letter are conventionally ordered. That means they appear in a certain arrangement and meet certain expectations on the part of the reader. If the reader doesn't have to pay attention to the format of a letter, he or she can devote more time and attention to the message it contains. Time taken away from the message means an irritated and annoyed reader who will be unlikely to do what the writer wishes.

Cordially Yours

M. K. Lester

M. K. Lester

Postscript. This line contains the final mistake.

a. In the blanks on the left, write any mistakes you find. In the blanks on the right, correct the errors or tell how to correct them.

b. Rewrite the letter if your instructor requests it.

Mistake	Correction/How to Correct
1. _____	_____
2. _____	_____
3. _____	_____
4. _____	_____
5. _____	_____
6. _____	_____
7. _____	_____
8. _____	_____
9. _____	_____
10. _____	_____
11. _____	_____
12. _____	_____

13. _____   _____

14. _____   _____

15. _____   _____

WRITING ASSIGNMENTS

1. Write a letter in *full block* style to your instructor, requesting his or her opinion of the use of the postscript (P.S.). Be sure to include all necessary parts of the letter. Use a subject line.

2. Write a letter in *simplified* form to a classmate, discussing the transitional status of salutations and titles in terms of gender and marital status. Indicate the salutations and terms you prefer and why, or what your company prefers (if you are employed).

Chapter EIGHTEEN

Letters, Memos, and Résumés

N ow that you have reviewed the format, conventions, and tone of effective business correspondence, this chapter examines the purpose and content of specific kinds of letters and memos: why they are written and what they contain. It discusses the types of letters you are most likely to write on the job or at home; for example, as a consumer you may send inquiry and complaint letters, and as an employee you may frequently write memos and transmittal letters for reports. You will write application letters and résumés in your job search. Communicating clearly in business correspondence is a skill each employee needs and all employers value.

INQUIRY LETTERS

An inquiry letter requests information, action, data, or assistance. It asks something of the reader. You might write inquiry letters for the following reasons:

◆ You want information about a product or service (such as the price, the quality, or the delivery date).

◆ You want to know about a company's or agency's policy or procedure.

◆ You want to know if an action is possible, and, if so, in what circumstances and to what extent.

◆ You want to know the when, where, how, or why of a situation.

◆ You want the reader to perform an action.

Inquiries may be fairly easy for your reader to answer if you simply ask for straightforward information such as the following:

◆ Are meals included in the budget vacation "getaway" advertised in a recent magazine?

◆ Will the materials designated for a specific project withstand extreme temperatures?

◆ What types of feed mixtures are recommended for certain domestic animals in certain locales?

Inquiries may call for more detailed responses if you ask questions such as these:

◆ Is a company taking adequate measures to ensure compliance with local pollution restrictions in its new location? If so, what are they?

◆ Can certain problems with mobile home heating systems be rectified by installing a newly advertised ventilating device?

Inquiries such as these call for more than a simple yes or no. They ask the reader for a fairly involved narrative or perhaps a prepared pamphlet or brochure.

Some inquiries request *more* than information; they anticipate some sort of action. For example, you may make requests such as these of your reader:

◆ Will you be able to speak at a special meeting of a group?

◆ Will your company join in a campaign for a cause?

◆ Will you fill out (or ask your employees to fill out) the enclosed questionnaire?

You may write two types of inquiry letter: solicited and unsolicited. A solicited inquiry letter, written in response to an advertisement, asks for information about a product or service. Since lengthy explanations are not required, this letter is typically very short and straightforward. You ask for what you want, indicate where you read about it, and include a "thank you." Here is the body of a solicited inquiry letter:

> *Please send me the free booklet, "Full Steam Ahead! A Guide to the Past," that was discussed in the July 1996 issue of Train Lovers' Newsletter.*
>
> *Thank you*

When you write unsolicited inquiry letters, keep in mind that you expect the recipient to supply you with something. To comply, your reader may have to spend time or money or both. Your letter certainly should not sound as if you are begging, but neither should it sound too demanding or arrogant. An effective letter states the following exactly:

◆ What you want
◆ Why you want it
◆ How you will use the information or make the reader's effort worthwhile
◆ When you want a response — if time is a factor

In addition, a result-getting letter always makes the request easy to answer and expresses sincere appreciation for your reader's effort.

Figure 18.1 illustrates an unsolicited inquiry letter written by a student to his former college registrar.

Activity 1

Read the letter in Figure 18.1 carefully and answer these questions:

a. What is a more appropriate salutation than "Dear Madam"?

_____

b. Does the letter include the four items usually found in an effective inquiry letter?

_____

c. Is the letter easy to answer? _____

d. Does the writer seem sincere? _____

42 Dunvegan Drive
Ottawa, ON K2L 3P9
March 17, 19--

Ms. L. Cooke, Registrar
Westfield Community College
Saskatoon, SK S7M 3L5

Dear Madam:

As a student in Westfield's Electrical Technology Program (1993–1995), I passed all courses except for the major technical project and report (Applied Research Techniques 300), a requirement for graduation. My student ID was 257-95-5626. I moved to Ottawa and have the opportunity to take Technical Writing 300, a similar course at Greenwich Park College. I am eager to obtain my diploma and would like to know if enrolling in the Greenwich Park course would enable me to complete requirements for graduation from Westfield.

I enclose a photocopy of the calendar description of Technical Writing 300, which is an evening course lasting six months. During this time, I will undertake an electrical design project with my present employer and submit a formal report to the company and to my technical supervisor. As you can see, the enclosed course description is almost identical to Westfield's. Would you please let me know if you will accept Technical Writing 300 toward the completion of my diploma in Electrical Technology.

If you need any further information, please call me at (613) 555-5555 (work) or write to the above address. The next section of Technical Writing 300 starts in May, so I would much appreciate hearing from you by April 4 so that I can apply to Greenwich Park.

I look forward to hearing from you.

Sincerely yours,

William Watton

William Watton
Enclosure

Figure 18.1 *Example of an unsolicited inquiry letter.*

The inquiry letter should state exactly what you want and usually why. Its pleasant tone should invite a response. Despite its "Dear Madam" salutation and some wordiness, William's letter will be easy to answer. The three *C's* help ensure a positive reader response:

◆ *Conciseness.* Omit all unnecessary details. Keep the inquiry brief but not abrupt.

◆ *Clarity.* Use specific words and clear sentences to help your reader understand your request.

◆ *Courtesy.* Always include a "please" or "thank you" or both. Make your reader want to reply.

Activity 2

Read the body of the following unsolicited letter. Answer the questions following it, and discuss your findings with your fellow students and instructor.

> *Gentlemen:*
>
> *Three months ago a letter was sent to you from Richard Penley, Director of our Technical Services, about a project comparing the use of safety goggles nationwide. We have not yet received your company's policy and we <u>need</u> it to finish the survey. <u>If needs be, we will pay for a copy</u>. Send the policy statement and an invoice, if you feel the expense will be too great in sending me a copy. If there are any problems, just let me know.*
>
> *This survey is under the direction of our CEO, Mr. W. T. Weirton. I hope I don't have to send another reminder regarding this matter. Send policy to: Mr. Herb Webster, Vice President, Spry Bay Welding Supplies, Shipton, BC V26 9C2.*
>
> *You will greatly assist our survey by your cooperation.*
>
> *Sincerely,*
>
> *H. Webster*
>
> *Herb Webster,*
> *Vice President*

a. Of the three *C's* in a good inquiry letter, which is *most* lacking in this letter:

_____ 1. clarity   _____ 2. conciseness   _____ 3. courtesy

b. Circle the three most offensive sentences in the letter.

c. Rewrite the offensive sentences to improve their tone.

_____

_____

_____

Sometimes companies combine an inquiry with a letter whose main purpose is to generate goodwill. In other words, the company wants to persuade the reader to do something, but it also wants to establish rapport with the reader. Figure 18.2 shows a good example of such a letter. As you read the letter, keep the three C's (conciseness, clarity, and courtesy) in mind. Although the writer's request is not made clear until the sixth paragraph, the pleasant, cordial tone and the simple request mean that most readers will respond positively.

Activity 3

a. Read the letter in Figure 18.2 as though you were a subscriber to the magazine. List five courteous words or phrases that contribute to the overall positive tone:

_____

_____

_____

_____

_____

b. Why do you think the writer includes the "P.S."?

_____

_____

STUDENT VOYAGEUR
Expanding Your Horizons
500 Matilda Street, Saint John, NB E2M 2V7
Phone (506) 555-6666

January 9, 19--

Dear *Student Voyageur* Subscriber:

Thank you for subscribing to *Student Voyageur* — the college student's "inside" guide to the awaiting world.

In the months to come, *Student Voyageur* will bring you the discoveries and perspectives of both student travellers and professional travellers who have found different and inexpensive ways of venturing through exotic areas of the world.

They'll share the kind of insight and information that tourists never get: where students — especially — want to go and where they don't; where their dollars go further; where to stay and what to do.

Issue after issue of *Student Voyageur* brings you a unique mix of travellers' wisdom, wit, and witness; the photography is award-winning and the "Exchange" section alone is worth the subscription price.

We would like you to share your opinions of our magazine. Please write us any time; we welcome your comments and suggestions.

For now, will you let us know if there is any error in the spelling of your name or in your address? Won't you please take a moment to check their accuracy on the enclosed acknowledgment? This way, you will be assured of prompt delivery each month of *Student Voyageur*.

Thanks for your help. Adventure beyond the classroom awaits you — to the bottom of the sea or across the top of the world, to that tiny pub or that dizzy disco!

Sincerely,

Jane Bunyan

Jane Bunyan
for *Student Voyageur*

P.S. If you have a question about your subscription, let us know by referring to your *File Number* which is shown on the enclosed Subscription Acknowledgment Form.

Figure 18.2 *Sample inquiry letter.*

RESPONSES TO INQUIRIES

For every inquiry in the business and professional world there should be a prompt response. A response gives a company or organization an opportunity to do more than just answer the questions asked — although that is the first objective of the response.

Effective responses to inquiries do the following:

◆ Answer the question(s) asked clearly and pleasantly.

◆ Create and leave a positive impression on the reader.

◆ Send additional information or give other sources of information.

◆ Motivate the reader to do business with the company again by doing more than merely answering the questions.

An effective response to an inquiry is shown in Figure 18.3.

Activity 4

Read the following response by a Chamber of Commerce employee to a writer's inquiry about available maps for the city. (This is an actual letter, all names have been changed, and the province is fictitious!)

> *Dear Sir:*
>
> *A more detailed city map is available, however there is a cost of $2.50. Kindly advise if you wish to receive and remit the above amount to:*
>
> *Slowton Chamber of Commerce*
> *Municipal Building — Drawer 796*
> *Slowton, GO D2R 2B1*
>
> *Sincerely,*

* * * * *

a. How could the salutation be improved?

_____

b. Do you see the grammatical error in the letter?

_____

APPLETOWN Chamber of Commerce
29 Bramley Street, Appletown, BC V36 5C4 Canada
Phone (604) 555-4444

March 1, 19--

Mr. Horace Chiarella
102 North Brunswick Street
Mapletown, GA 30052

Dear Mr. Chiarella:

Thank you for your interest in Appletown and the surrounding area. We are sure you will enjoy spending some time here. The pace is relaxing and the scenery is beautiful.

We do have available a detailed map which we are sending right away so that you may plan to attend the Festival of Blossoms.

I am enclosing a packet of brochures describing the many fine lodging and eating establishments in our area.

When you are next in our town, please stop in at our office, which is conveniently located on Bramley Street across from the Mountain Winery. We'll be glad to answer any questions about Appletown and its attractions.

Sincerely,

Vicki Moriarty

Vicki Moriarty

Enclosures

Figure 18.3 *Sample response to inquiry letter.*

How would you correct it?

_____

c. What words are better choices than "kindly advise"

_____

or "remit"?

_____

d. Does the writer create a good impression of his or her city?

_____

ORDER LETTERS

When you write an order letter, you ask for specific merchandise with the intention of paying for it. Usually you place your order by means of a form provided by a company or by a telephone call, but occasionally you may need to place an order without a form. An effective order letter includes the following elements:

- Item(s) desired and identifying catalogue number(s)
- Number of items desired and the price of each item
- Colour, size, product number (if available), and any descriptive elements that identify the item, usually including the page number of the catalogue from which the item is ordered (if known)
- Total price and the tax (if applicable)
- Means of payment and the means of delivery
- A "needed date" (if necessary)
- "Please" at the beginning or "thank you" at the end, or both

Since you want to get the merchandise as quickly as possible, you should arrange the ordering information so that it is easy to read.

Notice the arrangement, the courtesies, and the spacing in the letter in Figure 18.4. This simplified style is appropriate for order letters. The writer has supplied all necessary information and has followed the format of the catalogue order form.

45 Branston Avenue
Bathurst, NB E2A 3V9
July 23, 19--

Elgin Engraving Company
522 Stevens Street
Oshawa, ON L1J 6G9

SUBJECT: Order from 19-- Catalogue

Please send me the following items, engraved with the names shown in the third
column, from your most recent catalogue:

#405	1 Bikeplate	Sean Ryan	@ $5.00	$5.00
#102A	2 Bookmarks	Patrick Ryan	@ $5.00	$10.00
	(brass)	Mary A. Ryan		
#6	1 Pet Tag	J. Bond Ryan	@ $3.00	$3.00
			subtotal	$18.00
			postage	4.50
			subtotal	$22.50
			GST	1.58
			total	$24.08

My cheque for $24.08 is enclosed.

Thank you very much.

Sean Ryan

Sean Ryan

Figure 18.4 *Order letter in simplified form.*

COMPLAINT LETTERS

A letter that indicates dissatisfaction with a product, a service, or personnel and asks that something be done to correct the situation is difficult to write well. Since you are typically irate when you write a complaint letter, you may be excessively negative in your first version.

Remember, however, that the main purpose of a complaint (or claim) letter is not to vent your annoyance or to let off steam. The major reason to complain is to get some sort of adjustment:

- A refund on an unsatisfactory product
- A partial refund on a product that has not fulfilled its warranty
- A new product to replace a faulty one or a new part to replace a defective or damaged one
- An explanation or an apology for poor service or products

The best way to get results with a claim letter is to consider what you really want to see happen and to write the letter with that result in mind. Your calling attention to the problem could improve the situation for other consumers and perhaps prevent recurrences.

When you write a complaint letter, include the following elements in the order listed below:

1. State the nature of the problem as specifically as possible, detailing times, names, behaviours, faulty products, and circumstances, and indicating specifically how you were inconvenienced by the situation.

2. Assume that the recipient of the letter will react positively and will want to satisfy you, the consumer. If you are a previously satisfied and long-time customer, mention the fact.

3. State exactly what you expect from the company.

4. End firmly with a positive statement or a courteous "thank you."

Rather than emphasizing anger and disappointment, emphasize the facts. Avoid words that are belligerent or overly hostile, threaten legal action or the immediate loss of your business, or beg for what you think is rightfully yours. Avoid an apologetic tone.

Notice the firm, direct, and positive tone and the details included in the complaint letter in Figure 18.5.

P.O. Box 162
Kentville, NS B5N 4T9
September 21, 19--

S. J. Morgan, Manager
CarpetCharm Depot
42 Finnyscales Drive
Dartmouth, NS B2Y 3K9

Dear Mr. Morgan

The Dusty Rose carpeting which you installed in my residence on June 3 is not satisfactory. The living room carpet is rucked in four places, and the dining room carpet shows some different shading. I am requesting your prompt attention to this problem.

On May 25, I accepted your estimate of $3,735 for carpeting two rooms, hallway, and stairs in my residence, Briar Farm, Kentville (see attached receipt #2350). Your installers completed their work on June 3, and on July 5, I telephoned to advise you that ridges were appearing in the living room area. The installer you sent out on that same day told me that the carpet needed stretching and that he would be able to do it as soon as he received a work order from you. I also pointed out some discrepancies in the shading of carpet in the dining room, to which he replied, "This is a quality control problem. The manufacturer is looking into it. But it's hardly noticeable!" Sidney, it seems to me that it is far too early for ridging to occur, as there has been no time for contraction and expansion. As for the shading, that is a matter for you and Cresswell to solve.

On July 6, I left a message on your voice mail, requesting that you return my call as soon as you returned from vacation. As I haven't heard from you, I am formally requesting that you make an appointment to inspect the carpet installation to assess the ridging and shading problem, and to make the necessary adjustment by mid-October at the very latest.

As you know, I have done business with you for more than ten years, and I have come to expect high standards from CarpetCharm.

Please let me hear from you soon.

Sincerely,

Susan B. Rossignol

Susan B. Rossignol
c: B. Toulany, Sales Director, CarpetCharm Depot

Figure 18.5 *Sample complaint letter.*

Activity 5
....

In the two situations below, place a check mark in the blank next to the version of the complaint letter which — if you were the owner or manager of the business involved — would be more likely to elicit your positive response.

SITUATION A: In the first part of the letter, the writer explained that the sole of one of his new boots fell off the first time he wore them. Here are two versions of the rest of his letter:

_____ I don't understand why you can't make boots which stay together at least for one hike. If you don't send me my money back immediately, I intend to write the Better Business Bureau and certainly to tell all my friends in my hiking club never to buy Antler Boots again.

_____ I am enclosing a copy of my cancelled cheque and sales slip. I have shown the boot to the local store (Wampy's of Watborough) and although the manager will not refund my money, he will verify that the sole apparently had insufficient glue. Please send me a refund or a voucher for another purchase … before the hiking season is over.

SITUATION B: In the first part of the letter the writer explained that the patio furniture she ordered was not delivered on the scheduled date (causing some embarrassment at her party) and that a chair was damaged (which she discovered after the delivery truck had left). Here are two possible closing sentences for her letter.

_____ I'll never get over my embarrassment, but if you don't send your delivery truck with a new, unbroken chair within the next three days, the next letter about this matter will be from my attorney. He'll see that a single person gets proper treatment from your store.

_____ I'll expect a call from you to set up a date for delivering a new chair and picking up the damaged one within a few days. I am sure you want to do what is right in this matter.

ADJUSTMENT LETTERS

When you own a business or when you work for a company that offers a service or product, you can expect that not every customer will always be happy with everything. Thus, you will probably have to respond to letters of complaint such as the ones previously illustrated.

When you write to dissatisfied persons, you should try to keep the customers' business, if at all possible. You (or your supervisor) must also, however, judge the merits of the complaint and respond to it in a fair and just manner. Recipients should feel that they are being treated with respect and fairness. You thus have two responsibilities when you respond to a complaint: to keep the customer and to avoid losing money for the company.

A letter responding to a complaint does the following:

◆ It attempts to keep the customer's goodwill.

◆ It indicates what can be done about the situation.

◆ It states (when necessary) what cannot be done and explains why, or it explains to what extent something can be done and offers reasons for the adjustment.

◆ It almost always gives the customer something, if not all, that was requested.

◆ It ends on a positive note and expresses the expectation of future business with the customer.

The letters of adjustment in Figures 18.6 and 18.7 are good examples of how companies try to satisfy their customers by reacting to their claims in a fair and pleasant manner. In both instances, the company offers a substitute or partial settlement.

TRANSMITTAL LETTERS

A transmittal letter often accompanies a long formal report. Its basic purpose is to introduce the report and to remind the reader of the report's purpose. For a report that might have been assigned weeks or months earlier, a transmittal letter reminds the reader of exactly why he or she is getting the report and of the circumstances under which the report was researched and written.

The transmittal letter typically contains these elements:

◆ The title of the report and the date it was requested or authorized

◆ The reason it was written and the way it was researched

CarpetCharm Depot
a division of CarpetCharm Canada, Inc.
42 Finnyscales Drive, Dartmouth, NS B2Y 3K9
Phone: (902) 555-5555 Fax: (902) 555-3333

September 26, 19--

Ms. Susan B. Rossignol
P.O. Box 162
Kentville, NS B5N 4T9

Dear Ms. Rossignol

Thank you for writing to us about the problems with your carpet. Your letter to
Sidney Morgan has been passed to Ms. Sylvie Longard, who will be contacting
you immediately to make an appointment to visit your residence. She will also
bring with her Cresswell's quality representative to examine any defects in their
product. As soon as we have Ms. Longard's report, we will have our senior
installer replace the defective carpeting to your satisfaction.

We regret the inconvenience you have experienced. Mr. Morgan, who has had
the pleasure of serving you for several years, has unfortunately had to retire for
health reasons. We are confident that Ms. Longard will maintain CarpetCharm's
reputation for customer service.

Sincerely,

B. Toulany

B. Toulany
Sales Director

c: Sylvie Longard, Manager
bt/mrd

Figure 18.6 *Sample adjustment letter #1.*

Morehead Lites — Brighten Your Life
2370 Chippewa Road, Lethbridge AB T1K 6T9
Phone: (403) 555-2121 Fax: (403) 555-1212

February 20, 19--
Ms. Elizabeth Chaddock
32 Aston Park
Lethbridge, AB T2M 4X6

Dear Ms. Chaddock:

This is in response to your recent letter telling us of your Morehead Magic Lamp which did not operate properly. I am sorry to hear you had difficulty with our lamp but am grateful that you took the time to write us about it.

In our factories, we make every effort to produce a high-quality product, and we inspect each lamp as it leaves the production line. It is possible, of course, for our inspectors to overlook a problem; however, the lamp you returned to us has a shattered socket. Since the lamp was tested at Harold's Furniture Barn, where you purchased it, we cannot assume responsibility for the damage.

We are sending you a coupon good for a fifty (50) percent discount on any Morehead Magic Lamp which you purchase within the next six months. Your lamp is being returned by Express Mail. We are sure you will continue to see brightly with Morehead Magic Lamps.

We take pride in our lamps. Thank you for using our product and for contacting us.

Sincerely,

Catherine A. Storey

Catherine A. Storey
Product Services

Enclosure
CAS/mr

Figure 18.7 *Sample adjustment letter #2.*

◆ A review of highlights or main points

◆ A mention of any problems encountered

◆ A statement of appreciation for assistance

◆ A statement expressing willingness to discuss the contents and explain further, or expressing a desire for approval

You may also include any other comments that may be helpful to your audience. Since the letter introduces the report, mention any relevant information but keep the letter fairly short. Here are guidelines for effective tone and form in transmittal letters:

◆ Keep the letter to one page.

◆ Write short paragraphs rather than long ones.

◆ Maintain a friendly and professional tone.

◆ Use the first person (*I, me, my*) and second person pronouns (*you, your*) rather than a highly formal tone.

◆ Be positive and courteous.

Figure 18.8 shows a student's letter of transmittal illustrating these guidelines.

Activity 6

Read the letter in Figure 18.8. List four specific elements that contribute to the effectiveness of the letter.

a. _____

b. _____

c. _____

d. _____

JOB APPLICATION LETTERS

The letter that introduces you as a job seeker is one of the most important you will write. You can be sure you will write an application letter at some time in your professional life; if you have not already written such a letter, you probably will soon.

True, some people find their first jobs without a letter; they appear at personnel offices, fill out forms, meet their supervisors, and go to work ... usually at low-paying, entry-level jobs. However, even the "Assistants wanted — apply within" signs are appearing

102 Clearview Road
Gableton, PE C2C 3A4
September 20, 19--

Mr. M. Attia, CET
Coordinator, Building Technology
Gableton Community College
Gableton, PE C1C 2A8

Dear Mr. Attia:

The enclosed report, <u>A Study of Project Management at I. K. Brunel Construction Ltd.</u>, is submitted in accordance with your instructions of May 7, 19--.

The primary purpose of the report is to document what I observed during my work term with I. K. Brunel Construction Ltd., Gableton, from June 4 to August 24, 19--. During this period, I had the opportunity to observe several projects, ranging in price from $1,500 to repair a stone wall for a local resident to $1,000,000 to refurbish the Martello towers in Heaton Park, Gableton, for Parks Canada.

This report focuses on management aspects of two projects: the renovation of offices for Hazelbranch Walk-in Medical Clinic in Beechwood Mall, and the construction of Gabion cage walls on Heaton Park Road. The report includes my experiences in surveying, estimating, and drafting.

A large construction company, such as I. K. Brunel, owes a large part of its success to two factors: qualified and energetic project managers, and computerized project management tools.

I would like to thank Kenneth Brunel for the learning opportunity he afforded me, and Mona Salloum, senior project manager, for her information and assistance. I also thank you, Mr. Attia, for organizing this work term placement. I was able to see firsthand much of what we have learned during our program, including the use of Microsoft Project in the management of construction projects.

I sincerely hope this report meets with your approval. I will also make my work log available should you wish to see it.

Respectfully submitted,

Dennis Jeffries

Dennis Jeffries

Figure 18.8 *Sample transmittal letter.*

less frequently, and the skill levels expected for traditionally low-paying jobs are much higher than they used to be. Most employers for professional staff positions expect a letter and a résumé as the first steps in the job-hunting process.

Your first step, however, is to research the job market for which you are qualifying. You should not begin to compose any job search correspondence until you have identified and studied its recipient. Audience analysis, as you have learned, is key to effective communication. What is known as "the shotgun approach" — shooting off general letters and résumés in all directions — is almost always unproductive and frustrating. Therefore, whether you are writing a *solicited* letter of application (responding to an advertisement), or an *unsolicited* letter of application (asking a company if positions are available), researching the targeted company is an essential strategy for success.

You will need to plan your research carefully to get the best results, and you will find many books and job search guides available to help you plan. Visit your college student services centre, your campus library, and your city library for information on careers in both the public and private sectors. You will find, for example, *Canada Prospects*, a publication of Canada Career Information Partnership (CCIP). This newspaper provides career and labour market information to Canadians and contains articles on topics ranging from preparing résumés to managing change. Your college's student services centre and the local Canada Employment Centre will have job postings and probably an automated job bank. Libraries also house trade and industrial directories which contain profiles of companies: products, history, achievements, locations, subsidiaries, current status, and other relevant data.

You will also obtain useful information from companies' annual reports, newspaper business sections, and radio and television programs, both regional and national. Keeping in contact with your instructors, who have direct links with industry and business, and talking with friends and family about your job interests will also bring in helpful "leads." Visiting trade shows and discovery centres will also increase your knowledge of what developments companies in your chosen field are making.

You may be surprised that such job research is essential before you write a job application letter that will get results. However, writing with knowledge of your readers will certainly strengthen your chances: You will be alert to the needs, interests, and specific challenges of the workplace you are applying to enter. Thus, it is important to plan your research, and to record your findings in a file, on index cards, or on disk. You can then draw on this data for your application letters, résumés, and interviews. Remember that a candidate who knows about the job he or she is competing for is more likely to succeed than one who does not. Put yourself in the place of the employer — wouldn't you prefer the person who has taken the time to find out about your company to one who has applied "cold"?

After you have researched a position, you write a cover letter (an application letter that covers or highlights the details in your résumé) for one ultimate reason: to get the job. However, the immediate result of your application letter will not be the job itself; you are never hired solely on the merits of a letter, regardless of how good it is. The immediate purpose of your letter is to present your credentials so effectively that you obtain an interview.

You may want to get your first job as a professional, to change jobs or companies, to relocate, to advance in your field, to change fields, to make more money, or to use your technical, human services, or management skills. To make any career change, you must talk to someone who can make or help make a decision about your future. To get in to talk with someone, you must make a good impression in a letter.

Whether it is solicited or unsolicited, your letter should answer most or all of the following questions:

◆ How you learned of the job opening or vacancy
◆ Exactly what position you are applying for
◆ What you can offer the company
◆ Why you would be a good employee
◆ Where you can be reached
◆ When you are available for an interview

You can allow yourself some leeway with these questions, depending on your background, your experience, and your personality. The discussion which follows is directed primarily at soon-to-be graduates or recent graduates. Persons with a great deal of work experience or community experience will need to vary their letters accordingly. Most personnel officers, however, expect *all* application letters to contain certain information in a standard arrangement.

If you are responding to an advertisement, you should take care to read the position description or requirements extremely carefully. If an advertisement contains the invitation "For more information, contact the Personnel Director," you should do so. Some companies log the names of those candidates who have shown enough interest to collect the information or attend an information interview. Even if such an invitation does not appear, you should telephone the company to express interest in receiving more information, unless, of course, the advertisement ends with "No telephone calls, please."

Reading the advertisement requirements is essential. Personnel directors or members of the hiring committee will have a set of criteria for the successful candidate. They will screen your letter for mention of the required qualifications, experience, and personal characteristics, and will look for evidence of these in the résumé as well. For example, if a firm advertises for someone experienced with Programmable Logic Controllers, you should specifically mention such experience (if you have it) in your cover letter as well as in your résumé.

If you are writing an unsolicited letter, your research and your contacts will help you focus on your reader's interest and needs. You may have learned that a small company has landed a government contract and needs drafters experienced in AutoCAD. Your letter could make early mention of your college courses, your contact training experience, and your knowledge of AutoCAD and other useful software packages.

The Beginning

In the first paragraph, get right to the point. You are an interested applicant for a specific position. Indicate how you know of the vacancy (if, indeed, you do). For example, you might have learned of openings through classified ads, bulletin board notices, fellow employees, college placement services, instructors, employment offices, relatives, or newspaper stories.

In the first paragraph, announce your interest in one or two sentences such as these:

EXAMPLE: Please consider me an applicant for the position of mechanical engineering assistant as advertised in the July 13 *Morning Chronicle*.

EXAMPLE: My two years' training in culinary arts at Watborough Technical College, and my six years' work as sous chef should qualify me for the position of chef which you advertised in the June *International Chef* magazine.

EXAMPLE: A recent *Venture* program aired by the local television station mentioned that Ulysses Aeronautics has landed a government contract to produce aircraft parts for the new Thunderer. If this expansion creates openings for electrical technologists, please consider this application.

Using a person's name as a reference in the opening paragraph is one way of arousing interest. A friend who is employed with the company may have advised you to write for positions which are opening, but you should ask permission to use his or her name. Of course, be careful to name a person who is likely to be known to the personnel manager — and who is known as a reliable, honest person. Your opening might look like this:

EXAMPLE: An accountant in your City Branch, John S. McCready, has told me of a vacancy in the loans department. I would like to be considered an applicant for the position of loans clerk.

When you send letters and résumés without knowing of a specific vacancy, you could arouse interest by using an opening such as this:

EXAMPLE: Do you expect to have any openings in the next few months for a well-trained and highly motivated mechanical technologist with a diploma and two years of experience with a leading tire manufacturer? If so, please consider me for employment.

The purpose of the opening paragraph is to announce in a positive manner "I'm interested in a specific position" and "I have the qualifications and characteristics you are looking for."

The Middle

Whereas the opening paragraph needs to create interest and encourage the receiver to read on, the middle section of the letter must supply evidence to sustain that interest and to highlight the important features of the résumé.

Here, in one or two short paragraphs, you must set yourself apart from all the others applying for the same job. In this section you must say effectively: "Here's why you should interview me. These are my credentials." Then you offer your work experience, your educational experience, and your personality. (Remember that the *tone* of your letter reveals much about your personality; that is why knowing about the employer will be reflected in your confident tone.)

In one or two short paragraphs, tell the reader your general qualifications and mention any specific skills or attributes that match what the company is looking for. Compliment some aspect of the company and show how your skills and abilities can be beneficial. In addition, always refer to your enclosed résumé in this section. Here is an example of a good middle of a job application letter:

EXAMPLE: As a fully qualified instrument and electrical technician (TQ5), I have six years' military jet aircraft experience, and I have a great interest in the aeronautical
industry and aircraft operations in which your company is a leader. I will graduate in June with a diploma
in electrical engineering technology. My program at
Tri-Area College included project management courses
and an introduction to Quality Assurance.

As the enclosed résumé indicates, I have superior
technical presentation skills (oral and written) and a
strong CAD background. My references will confirm my
professional attitude and strong work ethic.

The Ending

The last paragraph of your letter should ask for an interview and give
a telephone number where you can be reached (even though this
number is also on your résumé). Rather than state the obvious "I
shall be glad to come for an interview at your convenience," say
more precisely when you are free. You sound far more responsible
when you write something like this:

EXAMPLE: May I have an interview to discuss my qualifications
further? My class and part-time work schedule
allows me to be available between 12:00 and 3:00 p.m.
every day. You can reach me by phone (123-5435)
at those hours or leave a message at other times at
123-7887.

Letters of application are straightforward announcements of
your interest, your qualifications, and your desire for an interview.
People who read them are looking for employees whose background,
qualifications, and personality meet their needs. Always emphasize
what you can do for the company, rather than what the job might do
for you. Here are some things you should *not* do in your letter:

◆   Do not in any way falsify or misstate your credentials or
qualifications.

◆   Do not say you will take any job open for any salary offered.

◆   Do not say you want to work for the company because of its
location or because of what it can do for you (its wonderful
benefits, good vacations, or unstressful conditions).

◆   Do not indicate any circumstance that could be interpreted as
a potential problem or obstacle (such as babysitting schedules,

long commuting distances, health conditions, or previous
unsatisfactory jobs).

♦ Do not give irrelevant facts or make self-congratulatory remarks.

♦ Do not sound desperate or defeated ("I am anxious to hear
from you").

♦ Do not say you have no experience; emphasize what you do
have to offer.

Activity 7

Below are sentences that have been included in application letters.
Put *Yes* in the blank if you think the sentence serves a useful purpose
in an application letter; put *No* beside any sentence that illustrates
one of the "do not's" (above).

_____ a. I know you receive many applications each year, and I do
not expect you to necessarily answer this letter.

_____ b. I have basic skills in drafting and the fundamentals in jig
and fixture design, progressive die design, mould design,
CNC, and automation operations.

_____ c. Please let me hear from you as soon as possible as I must
arrange for child care before August.

_____ d. All my life I have wanted to live and work in the beautiful
and progressive area near In-Trex Industries.

_____ e. My two years of accounting/management at Forrest
Technical College and my eight years of experience as a
sales associate at Belk should qualify me for the position
of buyer trainee.

_____ f. Although I have had no experience, I am an eager and
willing worker for whatever job you have open.

_____ g. While employed at Royal Metal, I was responsible for
doing a balance sheet each day.

_____ h. I wish to relocate to be nearer my wife's relatives and the
medical facilities of your city.

A complete application letter is shown in Figure 18.9.

Site 14, Box 2134, RR3
Trout Stream, NF A2A 1S9
March 15, 19--

M. H. Deschênes
Engineering Supervisor
Transport Systems International
Montreal, PQ H4B 2W8

Dear M. Deschênes:

Mme. Louise Trottier from the Gascon Employment Agency recently told me that there were openings in your BeauMonde plant for technologists (electrical, mechanical, and electronics). Please consider me an applicant for a position as an electrical technologist.

I am currently enrolled at Tri-Area Community College in the Electrical Technology Program and will complete the required courses in early June.

As a 1995 bursary winner from your organization, I have learned a great deal about automated systems. Currently I am gathering data for my senior technical report, Using PLCs in the Automation of a Subway System. At Tri-Area I have also learned project management with the use of state-of-the-art software, and, as a student volunteer, I am assisting the college to develop its home page on the World Wide Web. With my intense interest in transportation systems, programmable logic control, and computer programming, I know that I can make a valuable addition to your technical team.

Please refer to the enclosed résumé for more detailed information about my experience, education, and abilities. I would like to add that my first language is English, but I am functional in French and am currently upgrading my proficiency in the language.

I would very much like an interview with you to discuss the possibility of employment. My class and work schedule means I can be reached weekdays between 2:00 p.m. and 5:00 p.m. at 555-4567 and at 555-7654 after 5:00 p.m. I am available for an interview any afternoon after 2:00 or all day Saturday.

Sincerely,

Michael C. Gaccioli

Michael C. Gaccioli

Enclosure

Figure 18.9 *Sample application letter.*

RÉSUMÉS

A résumé is a listing of relevant information for prospective employers. Also called a personal record or personal data sheet, the résumé is a pre-evaluation or screening document; employers use it to make initial decisions about whom to interview. Thus it is clearly a selling device. Along with the cover (application) letter, the résumé is the first stage of the employment correspondence process. For any vacancy, hundreds of applicants may think or hope they are qualified, and most may very well be. Nevertheless, after the résumés are reviewed, fewer than 10 persons (usually 4 to 6) may be selected for an interview. They are chosen (assuming no personal or political connections are involved) *solely* on the basis of the written material reviewed by the committee or person doing the preliminary screening of candidates for a position.

Your résumé should represent you at your very best, and it is not a document you can write in a hurry. An effective résumé requires careful thought and planning. To achieve the best results, create a file on yourself either in a file folder or on disk. Think carefully about your education and training, experience, and characteristics that make you employable. Then create appropriate headings under which you will list achievements and dates. You can add to this list, for example, whenever you have achieved a goal, finished a course, attended a seminar, or received an award. Having this information on file ready for selection and inclusion in a targeted résumé will increase your chances of getting the job you want.

Certain components are expected in every résumé, but only you can determine what to include or omit. Whatever you include must be accurate; however, you are not obligated to include any information that may hurt your chances for an interview. Of course, any obvious gaps may raise questions in the interview, but there you can explain omissions. Quite simply, include in your résumé only *accurate* and *positive* data. Omit any negative information and be prepared to answer any questions raised by omissions.

Résumés should contain certain kinds of information in a readable format. Tailor your résumé to display your skills, yet design its format so that it does not distract the reviewer from his or her goal: to determine quickly the best applicants to interview.

Résumés are classified broadly as either chronological or functional. The chronological résumé typically lists work and educational background with dates (years) clearly stated. Functional résumés emphasize skills and abilities that might not be clearly evident in a chronological résumé. Traditionally, recent graduates who have prepared specifically for a certain kind of work and who wish to show specific job experience have used the chronological format. On the other hand, persons whose skills were gained in community or volunteer work or whose educational background is unusual have chosen to summarize their abilities in a functional résumé. However, more recently, job seekers have combined parts of the chronological and the functional into a résumé targeting a specific company and its needs.

Content in Résumés

Since your reader wants to know *who* you are and *what* you have to offer the company, you should always emphasize your educational credentials and your work experience. Stress those skills and abilities you possess that match what the employer needs. The following parts are found in most résumés.

Heading

Put your name, full address, and telephone number(s) at the top of the résumé. The use of the term "Résumé" or "Personal Data Sheet" is optional. A date is not necessary.

Objective

Write a sentence or phrase stating your career objective(s), if you wish, but do not merely restate the job description. Here are sample statements of objective:

EXAMPLE: Objective: Accountant-oriented management position with a national firm with opportunities for professional growth and increasing administrative ability

EXAMPLE: Objective: To use my surgical nursing skills in a progressive and caring hospital

The objective should not imply that in time you may be dissatisfied with the job you are currently seeking. If a statement of objective limits your abilities, sounds presumptuous, or seems unnecessary (depending on the position you are seeking and your goals), omit this section. For entry-level job seekers, a "Position Desired" listing may be more appropriate.

EXAMPLE: Position Desired: Nuclear Medicine Technologist

Education

How much you say about your education depends on how relevant it is to the job you are seeking, how strongly it supports your application, how much education you have, and when you received or completed it. For example, if you graduated from high school two years ago and will complete two years of college soon, list your high school and any college work and diploma. If you have work experience or have attended university courses or earned a degree, omit the high school listing. Remember to list the most recent education first. Here are other practical guidelines to help you determine what to put in the Education section:

◆ If you list your high school, give the year of graduation (and location, if you wish). Indicate any special honours and/or awards such as being valedictorian or receiving a bursary, medal, or scholarship.

◆ If you have dropped out of other colleges, list credits you may have received. Give the course of study if it relates to the position you are seeking.

◆ List any educational experience you gained outside the traditional academic setting, if it seems relevant. For example, you may have studied photography for a year, attended noncredit business or safety courses, or taken courses in the military.

◆ List specific courses or kinds of courses when you wish to emphasize study rather than work experience.

◆ When you list the college you attended, indicate your major area and degree; if you have more education than the degree, use a phrase such as *Further study at Western College* or *Additional courses in electronics at Adult Vocational Training Centre.*

◆ If you are a current student or recent graduate, you may certainly give your grade point average or rank in class, if above average.

◆ Place the Education section first when you are a recent graduate; after you have accumulated relevant experience, place the Education section following the Experience section.

Work Experience

This section contains information about where and when you have worked. It shows what you did (by listing job titles or duties performed or both) and any promotions you gained. If you wish to emphasize your experience, place this section first; otherwise, place it after the Education section. Here are some guidelines for this section:

◆ If you have had only a few jobs, list all of them. As you accumulate experience, drop the less significant jobs or the ones not related to the position you seek.

♦ If you have had a great many jobs of short duration (such as temporary sales clerk during vacations) consolidate them with a statement such as *Various sales clerk positions in local department stores* or *Temporary construction jobs during summer vacations.*

♦ Indicate starting and ending dates by year or by month and year.

♦ List the place of employment, job title, and duties performed if they are not clearly indicated by job title. You may also give your supervisor's name if you wish.

♦ If you worked at the same place in different capacities, list all job titles and responsibilities.

♦ Emphasize any abilities and skills you gained or used that will be helpful in the position.

Summary of Skills (or Skills Profile)

This section is particularly helpful to employers who are scanning your résumé for particular skills. Place this section between the Education section and the Experience section or after both. Here is an example:

Computer	AutoCAD R13 for Windows
	Microsoft Professional Office 4.3, Word 6, Excel 5
	Powerpoint, Access
	Word Perfect 6.1
	Lotus 5
Communications	Technical Report Writing
	Technical Presentation (Oral)
	Leadership
Technical	Machine Design
	Problem Solving

If you have read the job advertisement carefully and researched the position thoroughly, you will be more able to judge which skills to highlight: negotiation, organizational, interpersonal, team building, copy editing, and so forth.

Personal and Miscellaneous Material

Including personal information is optional in a résumé, and many people omit it. If, indeed, you do include date of birth, marital status, height, weight, and health information, some employers will think you have little else to offer, that you are "padding," or that you do not know that such information might infringe on your human rights. You alone can decide whether non-work-related information will benefit your résumé. As you draft your résumé, key in anything you might want to include and then evaluate each item's relevance. The placement of this section is also optional. Typically, you should place it following the Education and Experience sections.

A Personal Data section (should you choose to use one) might include information such as your interests or hobbies, participation in volunteer organizations, membership in professional organizations, special awards or skills, and willingness to relocate or upgrade. (The latter items may be of particular interest to employers.) The Personal Data section can give interviewers a more well-rounded view of you as a person, not just a student or worker. However, some of this information could be included under the heading Other Activities. In any case, this section should not overshadow the more significant parts of your résumé. Here are some examples:

Related courses	CPR, Entrepreneurship
Volunteer work	Fairview Volunteer Fire Department
	Big Sisters Organization
Interests	Mountain climbing, multimedia systems, reading

References

References are those persons who know you and your work and are willing to recommend you. A résumé either states that references are available upon request or actually lists them. Make your decision based on where you are applying, who your references are, and how long your résumé is. For relatively new job seekers who are applying locally, listing references is very helpful. Some people argue, however, that you should first be evaluated in your own right, from the information you provide in your letter and résumé. References are normally checked only when you are short-listed or the winning candidate.

Ask permission of each person you plan to use as a reference. Include at least one person from your educational background, one from the business community, and one from your work experience. Do not list relatives or fellow students. Make sure your references are suitable for your application. If you do not name the references, prepare a list to take with you to the interview and, at the end of your résumé, include the statement "References available upon request."

When you list your references, give their full names, their position or relationship to you, and their current addresses and telephone numbers. Three references are usual, four are fine; five are too many. Be consistent in their arrangement, as shown in Figure 18.11.

A functional résumé, shown in Figure 18.10, stresses the applicant's experience gained in the military, rather than his education. Miranda Nelson chooses to arrange her professional and personal information in a chronological résumé, illustrated in Figure 18.11. The format is easy to follow and stresses her education and work experience. Notice also that the hobbies show an enthusiasm for automotive work.

Figure 18.12 shows how Michael Gaccioli has combined the best of functional and chronological approaches in a résumé targeted to a position in aircraft research and design. He has been busy in his job search: So far he has selected six companies to study and will write a targeted résumé for each.

Design an attractive format for your résumé. The recipient will favour a well-organized and cleanly presented document on good bond paper. You will find templates for résumé formats in various word processors: WordPerfect 6.1 for Windows and Word 6 for Windows provide a number of attractive formats. Remember, though, that many other job hunters will use these too. You might prefer to design your own — but keep it simple.

If you conduct careful job research and write a well-organized, courteous application letter and résumé, you have a good chance of being invited for an interview. Preparation for interviews is discussed in Chapter Nineteen, as they will require you to use the principles of persuasive presentation.

FOLLOW-UP LETTERS

After the interview, you may write a letter to the person who interviewed you. This follow-up letter expresses appreciation for the interviewer's time and reminds him or her of your continued interest. This letter may be a deciding factor in your favour if all candidates interviewed are equally well qualified for the position.

If you do decide to write one, your follow-up letter should include the following points:

♦ Thank the interviewer for meeting with you and indicate the day the interview took place.

♦ Refer to some specific point or item of interest at the company discussed during the interview.

♦ Indicate your continued interest and state that you hope to hear soon about the position.

Gary C. Leinster
102 Turtle Creek Drive
Flin Flon, MB R8A 0N9

telephone
(204) 555-7777

OBJECTIVE:	Supervisory position with leading security and protection firm.
SUMMARY:	Over twenty years of experience in military settings with supervisory duties in security and budget/supplies management. Completed 3 credits in business administration. Retired Sergeant, Canadian Armed Forces.
SECURITY:	Served as a military policeman, with fifteen years as a supervisor both at domestic and foreign (Germany and Cyprus) bases. Last assignment as Flight Supervisor responsible for overall operation of a forty-person military police team.
MANAGEMENT:	Served as budget/supply manager at the squadron level for three years; responsible for accounting, ordering, dispensing, and inventorying. Trained, supervised, and evaluated from five to eight workers.
CURRENT EMPLOYMENT:	December 1993—present: Supervisor, plant maintenance at Camp Hill Veterans Hospital.
EDUCATION:	Business Administration courses at University of Manitoba: three credits with a B+ average. Various service-related courses: personnel management, human communications, budget/supply management. September 1994—present: Athabasca University, enrolled in the Computer Technology Program.
REFERENCES:	References available upon request.

Figure 18.10 *Sample functional résumé.*

Miranda E. Nelson
990 Random Creek Road
Swift Current, SK S1H 2R3
(306) 555-8989

PROFESSIONAL GOAL: Employment in the motive power industry

EDUCATION
1994–95   Cypress Regional Community College
                                      Cypress, Saskatchewan
                                      Certificate from Career Choices Partnership
                                      Program/Pre-Employment

1993–94   Farnsworth College — pre-technology program
                                      Completion Certificate

1989   Mitchell High School — Completion Certificate

WORK EXPERIENCE
1992–93   Hoskins Automotive
                                      Supervisor: Wesley Zachary 555-8987
                                      Position held: Gas Station Attendant and Mechanic's
                                      Assistant (full-time)
                                      Duties: pumped gas, wrote work orders, retrieved
                                      parts from parts department

1990–92   Maplegrove Security
                                      Owner: Russell Martin 555-4726
                                      Position held: Animal Control Officer
                                      Duties: Upheld municipal bylaws pertaining to
                                      domestic and exotic animals

1987–89 (seasonal)   Sweets and Sandwich Shop
                                      Owner: Danelle Martin 555-1143
                                      Position held: Swing Shift Manager (part-time)
                                      Duties: Cashier, hostess, food preparation

Figure 18.11 *Sample résumé in chronological order.*

OTHER ACTIVITIES
1988 (June)   Volunteer Counsellor, Starshine Camp for Children
1985–1989   Girl Guides of Canada
                               Queen's Guide, 1987

HOBBIES: auto repair on own vehicles (1953 Sunbeam Talbot;
                               1986 Ford Mustang), stock car racing, clogging,
                               and reading

REFERENCES
Ms. Eileen Donahoe, Jrny. MVR
Cypress Regional Community College
Cypress, SK S3H 2W4 (306) 555-1212

Steve D. Boehner, Manager
Hoskins Automotive
223 Windwhistle Road
Cypress, SK S5M 3W6 (306) 555-1111

Mrs. Lucy James, Secretary
Starshine Foundation
2305 Third Street East
Saskatoon, SK S7H 3G5 (306) 555-4321

Figure 18.11 *continued*

MICHAEL C. GACCIOLI
Site 14, Box 2134, RR3
Trout Stream, NF A2A 1S9
(709) 555-4567

PROFESSIONAL OBJECTIVE

A permanent position as an electrical engineering technologist
in a challenging career in aeronautical research and design

SUMMARY OF QUALIFICATIONS

Successful completion of two-year electrical engineering technology program
(New Viking)

Instructed junior technicians in efficient laboratory, aircraft maintenance, and
functional procedures and practices

Four years maintaining, calibrating, and troubleshooting (de-snagging)
instrument and electrical systems on military jet aircraft

Top student electrical/electronics class for manual drafting techniques and
AutoCAD R12 drafting system operations

Aided in design, specification, and routing of AC power system for new
AutoCAD drafting room at Tri-Area College

Functional in French language

RELEVANT EXPERIENCE

Electrical   Generation, conversion, and distribution of AC and
                        DC power on jet aircraft
                        Calibrate and troubleshoot vital aircraft flight instruments
                        and flight control systems
                        Overhaul, maintenance, and rewiring of jet aircraft
                        systems
                        Wire routing and installation course for jet aircraft
                        Knowledgeable in lead acid and NiCad batteries for
                        jet aircraft

Figure 18.12 *Sample targeted résumé, combining functional and chronological data.*

Computer	AutoCAD R12 and learning AutoCAD R13 for Windows
	Microsoft Professional Office
	Word Perfect 6.1
	Lotus 5

EMPLOYMENT RECORD

Aug./88–Sept.94	Instrument Electrical Technician on Canadian Forces Jet Trainer Aircraft Department of National Defence
	Honourably Discharged under reduction policy
Nov./87–July/88	Chef's Assistant and Dishwasher
	Silver Dishes Restaurant
	Corunna, Ontario

EDUCATION

Aug./94–June/96	Tri-Area College
	New Viking, Newfoundland
	Electrical Engineering Technology Diploma
Aug./88-Apr./90	Department of National Defence
	Instrument Electrical Technician Program
	Fully qualified military technician

INTEREST AND ACTIVITIES

Learning about "cutting edge" technologies
CPR Heart Start Course
Standard First Aid (Military and Civilian)
Road Racing (running)
Rock Climbing

REFERENCES WILL BE SUPPLIED ON REQUEST

Figure 18.12 *continued*

Above all, remember that the follow-up letter is a reminder — not a new sales pitch. Do not reiterate your qualifications or clutter the letter with irrelevant material. A good example of a follow-up letter is shown in Figure 18.13.

MEMOS

While letters carry messages to the "outside" from an individual or a company, memos communicate information inside an organization. They keep people informed about what is going on in the company and about external events that may have an impact on employees.

You use memos to accomplish the following:

◆ Communicate policies and information
◆ Highlight problems
◆ Congratulate a colleague or department
◆ Raise questions or clarify issues
◆ Request assistance

Memos are ideal for interoffice or interdepartmental communication. They dispense with the formal salutations and closings used in external correspondence. They include headings which set them apart from letters.

Memo Headings

Memo headings are typically arranged in this standard format:

◆ TO: (person or persons receiving the memo)
◆ FROM: (the writer)
◆ SUBJECT: (brief indication of content)
◆ DATE: (month, day, year)

These elements may also be arranged in one of the ways shown in Figure 18.13. Here are some guidelines for writing effective memo headings:

◆ If your company requires a specified form, or if you choose a form, use it consistently.
◆ Include the reader's title after his or her name (for example, "TO: Peter Quiles, Marketing Director")
◆ Include your own title after your name if your reader is not well acquainted with you (for example, "FROM: Lesley Fonteau, Sales Representative — Area 2").

990 Random Creek Road
Swift Current, SK S1H 2R3
May 18, 19--

Mr. B. Dutton
Owner, Dutton Automotive
Mistover Corner
Swift Current, SK S3Y 2S3

Dear Mr. Dutton

Thank you for taking the time yesterday to interview me for the sales position. I know you have a busy schedule and I appreciated the interview, the introduction to your staff, and the personal tour you gave me of your operation.

I was much impressed by the computerized diagnostic equipment you showed me. I'll also look for your team on Stock Car Saturday!

Thanks again for your time and interest. If I can supply you with any further background information or references, please call.

Sincerely,

Miranda E. Nelson

Miranda E. Nelson

Figure 18.13 *Sample follow-up letter.*

◆ Keep the subject line short and clear. (For example, "SUBJECT: Education Fair at Asheville Mall" is better than "SUBJECT: Improving College's Community Image and Disseminating Information at Local Education Fair.")

◆ Initial or sign the memo.

TO: Ruth Leonard, Human Resources Director

FROM: Bruce Neuringer

SUBJECT: Required Credentials for IV Technicians

DATE: April 22, 19--

Figure 18.14 *Types of headings for memos. In this memo heading, the items are lined up flush with the left margin. These headings are generally put in all capital letters.*

April 22, 19--

TO: All Employees

FROM: Harvey S. Gottleib, Vice President

SUBJECT: Change in Dental Insurance Coverage

Figure 18.14 *continued. Types of headings for memos. In this heading, the date is centred and placed above the other headings; this style is often found when a letterhead is used. Lining the headings up by punctuation is often preferred.*

TO: Jason Laredo   SUBJECT: Leave Request

FROM: Kaylene Stevens   DATE: April 22, 19--

Figure 18.14 *continued. Types of headings for memos. Perhaps because this style appears balanced and saves some space, it is gaining in popularity.*

Since memos convey needed or relevant information and since they are received and read at work, they should be completely clear. Readers should not have to guess at the meaning or wonder exactly what they should do.

Here are guidelines for conveying information effectively in the body of the memo:

◆ Keep memos as brief as possible without loss of clarity. Reports in memo form are usually longer, but most memos are best kept to one or two pages.

◆ Make your memos easy to read by using headings for memos of a full page or longer, short paragraphs (when possible) of six or seven lines, and numbered sections or bullets for emphasis.

◆ Use a positive tone and appropriate word choice.

◆ Get to the point immediately.

Figure 18.15 illustrates an effective memo.

Activity 8

After reading the memo in Figure 18.15, answer the following questions:

a. Does the heading section follow the guidelines listed?

August 1, 19--

TO: All A-TEX EMBLEM Employees

FROM: Martha Bayer, Human Resources Director

SUBJECT: INDUSTRIAL FAIR AT ALTAMONT MALL

Can you spare an hour this weekend to answer questions about A-Tex Emblem company, its employee benefits, and its products?

This Friday and Saturday we will participate again in the local industrial fair held at the Altamont Mall. This annual event — sponsored by the Mountain Industries and Technologies (MINT) foundation — gives us the chance to provide information about job opportunities, working conditions, and our product lines.

More than two hundred other businesses and industries in our area are also participating.

The Mall should be crowded this weekend with your friends, neighbours, and visitors to our area.

Will you share your knowledge of A-Tex Emblems with others? At last year's fair, people stood in line to ask questions about our unique flextime and child-care programs, and we distributed thousands of our emblems.

Monroe Cobb is coordinating the Fair for us. Please call his extension (315) and volunteer to share your time.

kl

Figure 18.15 *Sample memo.*

b. Do the readers know what the writer wants of them?

_____

c. List some words that help create a positive, friendly tone:

_____   _____   _____   _____

_____   _____   _____   _____

    Writing letters and memos that get appropriate results is a skill you will often be called upon to demonstrate. Effective external and internal communication results from an understanding of appropriate tone, format, and appearance, as well as from accurate and well-stated content.

QUESTIONS FOR DISCUSSION

1. What must a good adjustment letter do — and how?
2. What should you do before you write an application letter?
3. What are some things you should not do in an application letter?
4. What are the characteristics of an effective résumé?
5. Why are memos so useful?
6. What distinguishes memos from letters?

EXERCISE 1

Rewrite the following letter to improve its clarity, conciseness, and courtesy. Also correct any errors in form and add details, if necessary.

87 Courtney Lane
Abbotsville, BC V3R 2A4
4-2-19--

Mr. Keith Regar
1313 Blakely Ave.
Toronto, Ontario

Dear Sir:

Can you give me some advice on preparing for a career in journalism?

I am interested in being an editor or journalist for a fairly small newspaper, and I would like a list of some schools or colleges and how to approach this career. I would also like to know if it would be beneficial to me if I started to work for a newspaper part-time. How did you get started?

All my life I have been told that I really know how to write and should put my expertise to work in public service. But I don't want to work for no pay, so how much would I make in the newspaper business?

Since I'm desperate to get into a college next month, let me know as soon as possible.

Sincerely yours,

Lance Mitchell

Lance Mitchell

EXERCISE 2

As the branch manager for Quik-Tex Buildings, a firm specializing in prefabricated buildings (with more than 60 different styles and types of buildings available), you receive the following letter:

414 Early Avenue
Winston, Florida 32788
July 5, 19--

Quik-Tex Buildings
6700 Main Street
Omaha, Nebraska 68103

Gentlemen:

Someone told me that your company is the agent for a prefab garage in which I am interested. At one time — maybe five or six years ago — I know that I had all the information on it. Will you please bring me up to date regarding this building?

Sincerely yours,

James Benson

James Benson

Rewrite the letter. Add details and improve the tone and appearance.

WRITING ASSIGNMENTS

1. Find an advertisement in a magazine or newspaper that invites you to send for something (a brochure, product information,

etc.). Write a *solicited inquiry letter* and mail your letter after your instructor approves it.

2. Write an *unsolicited inquiry letter* to a company or organization of your choice asking for information which you are interested in and could logically expect to receive. For example, you might want to know about:
   a. Starting a similar business
   b. Employment procedures at a company similar to yours
   c. Fringe benefits and leave without pay policies
   d. Methods for solving various kinds of problems
   e. Specific information about your major technical project
   f. Job opportunities in your field in a certain region
   Send the letter after your instructor approves it.

3. Write an *order letter* for at least four different items from a catalogue (assume the order slip is missing). Indicate how you will pay and how the items are to be shipped.

4. Think back over the past year or two. At some point you have surely been disappointed (or worse) with a product or a service. Write a *complaint letter* stating the problem and asking for a solution. Invent details or a situation if necessary.

5. Assume that you have been asked by your college president to draw up a set of guidelines (following a study of the situation) for student parents to use in enrolling their children in the college child-care centre. Write a *transmittal letter* to accompany the completed guidelines you send to the president.

6. Write a letter of application for a job that you could apply for at this time or upon graduation. You may find a classified ad or write an unsolicited letter. Your letter should be one you could legitimately send out to a prospective employer.

7. Compose a résumé to accompany the application letter.

8. Find some aspect of your college (or department within it) about which you want to express an opinion or convey information to an administrator. Put your opinion or information in memo form. Here are some possibilities:
   a. Congratulate the winning athletic team and commend its fine sportsmanship at a recent tournament or game.
   b. Ask for an investigation into use of student association fees.
   c. Recommend to your student organization a discounted fee for part-time students who do not participate in college activities.
   d. State your views (assume they've been requested) on improving the quality of library services, preventing vandalism in

student lounges, revising the local bus schedules to campus, creating a stricter attendance policy — or any other subject that interests you.

e. Ask for a clarification of some material in the college catalogue that seems contradictory or vague.

f. Tell your department head (assume you have been asked) which courses are most and least relevant to you — and why.

g. State your opposition to some campus policy such as forbidding children of students in classrooms, requiring complete payment of fines before registration is permitted, or closing labs early on Fridays.

h. Ask the appropriate person about setting up some useful student service such as a book exchange, information booths at campus entrances, or a telephone help line.

9. If you are employed, write a memo to your immediate supervisor or to someone in higher management. Use a topic similar to those listed above, one of the topics below, or any other which is related to your work.

a. Need for more parking and more illumination of parking areas

b. Need for clearly defined policies relating to coffee breaks, personal leave days, attendance at meetings, or harassment of any kind

c. Request additional personnel

d. Request a change in some procedure

Part SEVEN

SPEAKING OF TECHNICAL MATTERS: EFFECTIVE ORAL PRESENTATIONS

Objectives

When you finish Part Seven — Chapter Nineteen — you should be able to do the following:

◆ Recognize workplace situations that give you the opportunity to make oral presentations.

Speaking for yourself (the interview)
Speaking with the team (the meeting)
Speaking for the team (the technical seminar)

◆ Recognize the connections between written and oral presentations.

◆ Discuss the responsibilities of speaker and listener.

◆ Speak for yourself in a job interview.

Preparation
Presentation

◆ Speak with the team in meetings.

Purposes
Roles
Agendas and Minutes

◆ Speak for the team when presenting technical information at a seminar.

Preparing the information
Organizing the information
Delivering the presentation
Responding to questions and comments

Chapter NINETEEN

Interviews, Meetings, and Seminars

"Technologists have the ability to bridge the gap between engineers and production departments. That is one of my main roles here at Zydacron. I make sure that production receives a viable product."

Chris Rogers, Technologist at Zydacron,
Merrimack, NH, and graduate of Nova Scotia
Community College, Institute of Technology

Bridging the gap between departments in any industry requires all the communication skills: writing, reading, listening, and speaking. In your preparation for a technical career, you are investing significant time and effort in writing and reading about technical matters; and you will have already recognized that effective speaking and listening play major roles in any communication process, both technical and general. The Conference Board of Canada's Employability Skills Profile (see Appendix) lists personal management and teamwork as critical skills required of the Canadian workforce. Your ability to speak convincingly and listen actively will enhance your success in getting a job, participating in a team, and representing that team in a highly competitive marketplace. It is important, therefore, to learn how to present yourself at a job interview, how to interact with coworkers at a business meeting, and how to represent your company's interests at a technical presentation.

SPEAKING SITUATIONS IN THE WORKPLACE

Many workplace situations require you to "do some talking." You may be required to give instructions, to make and take telephone inquiries, to receive and assist clients, to explain an event or idea, to report job progress or completion to your supervisor, or to present a proposal. Here are four examples of job situations that call for presenting technical information orally:

Raminder Sharma is being interviewed for her first job, the position of technologist at Savonius Air Conditioning Ltd. She is now preparing to answer the first question: "Why do you want to work for Savonius?"

Electrical technology students Scott McLeod and Cyril Dempsey have completed and submitted their design for an improved security lighting system at St. Brigit's University. Their next task is to present their design proposal to the engineering consultants who are preparing a feasibility report for the university. Although they have talked with the engineers and plant personnel throughout their project, Scott and Cyril will formally present their design at a meeting called by the project manager.

Tuan Ngo is working on a renovation project for a dentist's office in a mall when a problem with the tiling is reported to him. As a construction technologist, Tuan is quite prepared to troubleshoot problems and to expedite solutions on the job. When changes have to be made to specifications, he will telephone his boss, the architect, and the trades involved, so that the change will be negotiated and the change order written and swiftly implemented.

As an apprentice mechanic, Susan Wamboldt has just finished servicing a customer's car. While she is checking off the service order, she notices that the customer, who has been watching through the observation window, is talking angrily to the service manager, Paul Cochrane. In carrying out the work order, Susan had noted the customer's request for a particular kind of motor oil. She has carefully complied, and is now surprised when the service manager asks her to explain why she has used a different viscosity oil. Apparently, the customer saw the wrong oil can on the ground near the car and jumped to conclusions. From a nearby garbage bin, Susan retrieves the can she had used correctly and discarded properly. She then quietly explains to Paul what has happened. Susan has had to act quickly, talk responsibly, and behave professionally.

As these situations demonstrate, people working in technical fields need to prepare for many kinds of oral presentation, ranging from the formal job interview and project proposal to the sometimes less formal routine problem-solving, negotiation, and interpersonal communication.

Formal presentations differ from informal ones in two ways: structure and length of preparation. A formal project proposal, for example, is highly structured, and requires a significant amount of data gathering, analysis, and organization, as well as the preparation of visuals for display on overhead or computer projectors. In contrast, explaining to a customer what has happened in an automobile check is less formal. It is part of the daily routine in a business that depends on accurate work and good customer relations for its success. The information is less rigidly structured and is given quickly and clearly, perhaps with the aid of a hand-drawn sketch.

Activity 1

a. Examine Example 1 above and explain why Raminder's situation is formal:

_____

_____

_____

b. Examine Example 4 above and answer the following questions:

Why does Susan have to act quickly? _____

_____

Why does Susan need to talk responsibly? _____

_____

Why is behaving professionally connected with Susan's response to the situation?

_____

_____

_____

c. Discuss with your class members your responses to (a) and (b).

CONNECTING ORAL AND WRITTEN REPORTS

Oral presentation of technical material is often closely connected with the written presentation. As you saw in Example 2, the two technology students are expected to present their lighting design proposal orally to the engineering and plant representatives. They will have to explain their information and analysis, and justify their recommendations in a meeting that will last an hour or more. For Scott and Cyril, making this formal presentation is a welcome opportunity to contribute to their community and to gain valuable experience.

What you have learned about writing technical reports — planning, determining your objectives, focusing on situation and audience needs, preparing visuals, and so forth — will stand you in good stead for preparing and delivering oral presentations. You should be aware of the advantages of presenting information orally and of the possible drawbacks if the oral presentation stands alone, without the support of a written report or summary notes. Table 19.1 shows the connections and differences between oral and written presentations.

THE RESPONSIBILITIES OF SPEAKER AND LISTENER

In all communications, oral and written, the sender has the responsibility of gaining the receiver's understanding or action. You have studied the ways to do this in writing. In speaking, you have the added responsibility of gauging and responding *immediately* to your listener's response. To do this successfully, you need to study your listeners and to understand their particular motivation for attending your presentation. Researching the audience is key to a successful presentation. You can use the worksheet from p. 591 to identify your objectives and audience in preparing your oral presentation.

Depending on the nature of the situation, both speaker and listener have responsibilities in a technical presentation, which are summarized in Table 19.2.

TABLE 19.1

CONNECTIONS AND DIFFERENCES BETWEEN ORAL AND WRITTEN PRESENTATIONS

Oral Presentations	Written Presentations
Purpose: informative, analytical, persuasive	Purpose: informative, analytical, persuasive
Audience: present listener, observer, and reader	Audience: distant reader
Response: immediate, possibly less thoughtful	Response: delayed, probably more thoughtful; possibly nil
Questions: explanations available immediately	Questions: need to predict and answer in the report itself
More personal	More formal
More control of aggressive or apathetic listener	Less control of aggressive or apathetic reader
More ability to explain or simplify two or three complex ideas	More ability to develop a greater number of complex ideas, but less ability to understand individual reader's difficulties
Need to summarize points more frequently	Need to summarize points, but at the beginning and end of the document
Less chance of misinterpretation	More chance of misinterpretation
Nonverbal communication available for support	Nonverbal communication not available for support

TABLE 19.2

RESPONSIBILITIES OF SPEAKER AND LISTENER IN AN ORAL PRESENTATION

Speaker	Listener
Know the listener's reason for attending	Keep in mind own reason for attending
Gain and keep the listener's attention	Respect the sincere efforts of the speaker; give the speaker a fair hearing
Use language appropriate to the listener's background and level of understanding	Pay attention to the speaker, and note any questions for clarification
Be aware, as far as possible, of language that might trigger negative responses, and avoid it	Be aware of own biases or triggers
Ensure a comfortable atmosphere for the listener, by reducing tension, focusing on topic, and welcoming questions	Contribute to the presentation by disregarding speaker's nerves, focusing on the message, and asking questions
Be totally prepared	Come prepared to learn

In most oral presentations, both speaker and listener have similar responsibilities to ensure the success of the presentation; they each have a part to play. In sales presentations, however, the speaker bears the larger responsibility, for the customer is not obligated to listen or respond. Whatever the situation, the speaker should be aware of words and mannerisms that trigger, or elicit, an undesired response. For instance, using the term "women" is preferable to using the term "girls." While some women are quite comfortable with the latter, others find it inaccurate and offensive. It is therefore inappropriate. Some responses, however, are irrational, in which case the listener needs to identify his or her own triggers. For example, some members of the audience may respond negatively to an unfamiliar accent. It is their responsibility, then, to concentrate on the message and to put aside personal bias. Oral presentations succeed when there is professionalism and mutual respect.

SPEAKING FOR YOURSELF: ATTENDING A JOB INTERVIEW

In most professions, a job interview is a formal occasion on which an employer, personnel officer, or hiring committee follows a set procedure to select the best person for a position. It is also the opportunity you have been seeking since the beginning of your job search. To succeed, you need to prepare your information methodically and present it effectively. Careful preparation will enable you to present yourself in a positive and confident manner.

Preparation

Preparing for the job interview entails at least four steps:

Researching the position and the company
Reviewing your qualifications and experience
Choosing the appropriate apparel
Anticipating questions and planning answers

Research

In sending your application letter and résumé, you will have already done some preliminary research on the company. Once you have been selected for an interview, it is important that you continue learning about the company from newspapers, contacts, and other resources. Knowing any up-to-date news or developments about the company will serve you well in the interview.

Qualifications Review

Study your letter and résumé and be prepared to talk about all or any part of them. Take a copy of your résumé with you, together with the names of references that you promised would be furnished on request. Some candidates take with them a portfolio of work: engineering drawings, technical reports, and even videotapes of technical presentations. Such evidence of achievements can be produced when the interviewer expresses interest.

Appropriate Apparel

The employer is looking for a person who will fit with the company's objectives and culture. Therefore, your appearance — dress, grooming, and deportment — will be noted carefully within the first moments of the interview. You will show and gain respect when you dress in a neat, clean suit, for example. Avoid using scent, as many environments are now fragrance-free. Adopt moderation in hairstyle and jewellery.

Possible Questions

You will be more confident at an interview if you have anticipated some of the questions. To do this, you should read over carefully the job advertisement once again, and you should study the many job search books available. Your local Canada Employment Centre can provide a booklet which contains typical questions asked at interviews. These include the following:

Why do you want to work for this company?

What are your career goals?

Where do you see yourself in five years' time?

What is your major strength?

What situation do you find the most stressful, and how do you handle it?

What kinds of people do you like to work with?

What subject at college do you find the most difficult? the least difficult?

What is your greatest achievement?

Why should this company hire you?

In some situations, the interviewer may give you a problem-solving scenario and ask for your solution. In others, you may be asked to write an accident report or progress report. Be prepared to demonstrate your writing and problem-solving skills.

You will also need to prepare some questions to ask at the interview. It is often a good idea to ask some friends to hold a mock interview with you — you may be surprised at the helpful tips and insights they can provide.

Presentation

Because interviews are an extremely important stage in the hiring process, they will be conducted within a framework that is applied consistently for all applicants. The components vary from company to company but normally include the following:

Introductions
Brief information session
Interviewers' questions
Candidate's questions
Conclusion

Introductions

It is important that you arrive a little early, so that you can sit quietly and calmly in preparation for the interviewer to greet and admit you to the office or conference room. In some cases you will meet only one interviewer, but it is more common, especially for government positions, that you will be interviewed by a board of two to four people. As you are introduced to each person, smile and shake hands firmly. Competent interviewers will soon put you at ease and create a rapport that will help you to present confidently the information they are seeking. Sit comfortably and alertly, take out your résumé, and prepare to communicate.

Information Session

The chair of the interviewing committee, probably the person who greeted you and made the introductions, will then explain briefly the procedure to be followed. The chair will probably explain the criteria by which your interview will be measured, and he or she will mention that the committee members will be jotting down notes. Depending on the situation, the chair will present some brief information on the position itself.

Interviewers' Questions

These questions will determine whether you are the best person for the job. Each questioner in turn will probe a specific area in your qualifications and experience. If you can, answer fully and concisely.

Answer sincerely, and if you do not understand the questions, ask politely for clarification. "Yes" and "No" answers do not do you justice, and your interviewers will find such answers awkward and frustrating. Be prepared to expand on points, but do not ramble on. This is not the time to be falsely modest, nor is it the time to exaggerate. State clearly what you can contribute to the company's projects and activities. You will probably find, as the interview proceeds, that you will be comfortable enough to enjoy the experience and the searching questions posed. Humour will almost certainly enter the exchange and will relieve any remaining tension.

Applicant's Questions

After the main part of the interview is over, you will be asked if you have any questions. These are expected of you, as the interviewers will want to see that you have done some job research. Your first questions should not be about vacations, fringe benefits, and remuneration. These will be covered in an information package or in the conclusion to the interview. You may want to know the specifics of the department you are entering or the kind of immediate preparation you should make if you are offered the position. If the questions you have prepared have been answered during the course of the interview, you should say so.

Conclusion

At the end of the interview, the chair will tell you when you can expect a decision to be made. You may also be asked at that time for the names of your references. You then thank the committee and the chair for the interview and leave the building.

Remember to write a follow-up letter thanking the committee for the opportunity to present yourself as a candidate. This letter will enhance their view of you as a courteous, interested individual, who is willing to take the time to write.

Activity 2

The interviewer asks you the following questions. Check what you consider to be the most appropriate response(s).

"What kind of situation do you find most stressful in the workplace?"

_____ a. Nothing really freaks *me* out!

____ b. I get really annoyed when people come in for a chat when I'm obviously very busy.

_____ c. I get impatient when some people on the team are not pulling their weight. We have to get the job done, and I say so quite diplomatically and firmly.

"What is your major strength?"

_____ a. My attention to detail.

_____ b. Well, I'm pretty good at doing spreadsheets.

_____ c. My ability to build team spirit. I have demonstrated this in my work for xxxxx where we completed the xxxxxx project on time and within budget....

_____ d. I would have to say that I'm a good all-rounder, so it's really difficult to say.

SPEAKING WITH THE TEAM: PARTICIPATING IN MEETINGS

As a member of a team, you will need to take part in formal business or project meetings. These are formal occasions, structured so that the business gets done quickly and efficiently.

Knowing how to participate is a teamwork skill which will help you do the following:

Understand and contribute to the organization's goals.

Understand and work within the culture of the group.

Plan and make decisions with others and support the outcomes.

Respect the thoughts and opinions of others within the group.

Exercise "give and take" to achieve group results.

Seek a team approach as appropriate.

Lead when appropriate, mobilizing the group to high performance.

Developing these skills listed in the Employability Skills Profile will make you a valuable member of your organization.

When you prepare for a meeting, you should do the following:

Study the agenda: it will contain the issues and business to be discussed. Write down your comments and questions.

Read the distributed minutes in preparation for their amendments and approval.

Check the minutes for any actions that were assigned to you, and be prepared to report as required.

When you attend a meeting, be prepared to contribute when asked.

Listen carefully, and do not speak unless you have something to say.

Be courteous, sincere, and businesslike.

Do not make offensive personal remarks to or about another member, even if you have been provoked. The chair will deal with the offender.

Be professional. Do not take professional criticism personally. Learn from others.

Be clear and concise.

Overcome any nervousness by focusing on the task at hand.

In self-directed work groups, you will probably take turns at chairing or taking minutes.

The chair's role is to facilitate the business of the meeting, not necessarily to run the meeting. Keeping the members on track, summarizing points of discussion during the meeting, maintaining focus, controlling members who are out of order — these are all responsibilities of the chair. The chair will also distribute an agenda and any reports for study before the meeting.

The secretary's role is to record the minutes: what decisions are made and who is to act on them. Minutes should be accurate and concise. They form a record of decisions and are often referred to in the course of a project. Figure 19.1 shows an outline of minutes recorded at a regular construction project meeting.

Remember that whatever role you take in a meeting, all attending have a stake in the outcome. On many occasions, and especially when there is a completion deadline, your patience will be severely challenged. Review and take steps to learn more about the teamwork skills listed in the Appendix to this book, and you will be a respected participant at business meetings.

SPEAKING FOR THE TEAM: PRESENTING A TECHNICAL SEMINAR

The workplace will present many opportunities for speaking about technical matters. You may be asked to represent the company at a project meeting, to present a company proposal at a sales meeting, to explain a new procedure or a safety policy to a group of employees, to display your company's product at a trade convention, or to describe your own innovative design at a conference. It is important

BEDROCK FOUNDATIONS LIMITED
MINUTES OF MEETING

Project: Name/Number   Date:
         Location   Time:
Location of Meeting: Jobsite Office   Meeting Number: 3

People Present	**Representing**
Name	Name of Company
Reg Truesdale	Truesdale's Supermarkets
Lou Robitaille (Chair)	Bedrock
Joe MacDonald	MacDonald Architects Inc.
Lynn Allison	Topnotch Construction Ltd.
Willy Morton	Marvel Masonry Ltd. (Site)
Joan Sullivan	Checkvalve Mechanical Inc. (Site)
Janus Starcevic	Skyscraper Steel (Site)

Regrets
Names of absentees who sent regrets

Purpose of Meeting: to discuss any business affecting job progress

Item	Discussion	Action by

Old Business
1.2   (means from meeting no.1, item 2)
Note: Minutes should record the conclusion or decision reached, not everything that was said
2.3

New Business
3.1
3.2
3.3
All parties please advise of errors or omissions in these minutes before the next meeting
Optional: The meeting adjourned (time)

Next Meeting: Location, date, time

Distribution: All present
                 Specific trades reps.
Minutes recorded by:

Figure 19.1 *Outline of minutes for a construction project meeting.*

that you look upon giving an oral presentation as a valuable opportunity, rather than an unwanted chore.

Once you have been assigned the task of giving a presentation or seminar, you will need to do the following:

Define the task.

Identify your objectives.

Target audience needs.

Gather, analyze, and organize information.

Prepare visual aids.

Practise, practise, practise.

If you are working with a colleague, you will be able to share tasks, but you will need to keep in close touch and rehearse the presentation together.

Defining the Task

You need to know the purpose of the presentation: Is it to inform, to present an analysis, or to make a proposal? Review the types of report in Chapter Three, and ask your manager the following questions:

Who is requesting this presentation and why?

What is the time frame?

Where will the presentation take place?

Who will be there?

What is the desired outcome?

Identifying Your Objectives

Once you know the purpose and desired outcome of the presentation, you can define your specific objectives. Let's examine the example of Lorraine MacAdam, who works for an engineering firm that is designing a new waste/resource management system for her city. She has been working specifically on the plan for a sorting plant. The chief engineer asks her to explain her work to the Metro Council and the stakeholders' committee so that they can fully understand the function of the sorting plant, follow its progress, and appreciate its benefits to the metropolitan area.

In her plan, Lorraine takes notes from her meeting with the engineer:

1. Show how the sorting plant fits into the new waste/resource management system.

2. Explain its benefits.
3. Reassure Metro Council members and stakeholders of the value of their investment.

Targeting Audience Needs

Let's follow Lorraine as she prepares for the presentation. She has a good idea of what the Metro Council members need to know, but she has to do some homework on the stakeholders' committee. She finds out that this committee is made up of 40 or so citizens, some of whom belong to a local environmental group. They represent a cross-section of the community, ranging from scientists and environmentalists to residents concerned about using old landfill sites and about finding alternatives to the present garbage disposal systems. She also finds some background information: These concerned citizens have been striving for three years for an environmentally viable alternative to the present landfill site.

Lorraine decides that the audience needs information that will reaffirm the wisdom of this investment and assist their evaluation of the progress being made. She also learns she will be presenting for 45 minutes to approximately 60 people at City Hall. She notes these findings on her objectives and audience worksheet shown in Figure 19.2.

The worksheet format used in Figure 19.2 can be found on pages 93–94 and has been adapted for use in making a technical presentation.

Gathering, Analyzing, and Organizing Information

For Lorraine, this is perhaps the easiest part. She has worked on this project for two months and, being aware of her audience's needs, she can extract enough important points from a substantial stock of material to meet those needs. She will prepare notes on index cards and work from the outline shown in Figure 19.3. Lorraine has followed the steps necessary in developing a plan. If you review Chapters Four, Five, and Six, you will be able to see how readily those steps can be adapted to developing an oral presentation.

Preparing Visuals

Because of the mixed backgrounds of her audience, Lorraine chooses a variety of visuals: a map, flowcharts, and pictograms. Figure 19.4 shows Lorraine's third figure demonstrating how the sorting plant works. Lorraine knows that visual aids must be large enough and

Objectives and Audience

Topic: The New Sorting Plant at Otterbank

Objectives:

My main objectives are to

1. Explain the sorting plant and its place in the new waste/resource management system.
2. Describe its benefits.
3. Demonstrate that waste becomes a resource to be managed.

Audience: _____Mixed_____

My audience's technical level is low, medium, and high
My audience's authority level is medium and high
My audience's purpose in attending my presentation is to

___✓___ Learn   ___✓___ Evaluate   _____ Act

Other ____Monitor progress_____

My audience's attitude toward me is

___✓___ Agreeable   _____ Antagonistic   _____ Apathetic

My audience's major characteristic is _Eagerness to implement project_

Figure 19.2 *Sample of an objectives and audience worksheet for a technical presentation on the new sorting plant at Otterbank.*

**Outline for Presentation to Metro Council and Stakeholders' Committee:
The New Sorting Plant at Otterbank**

Introduction: Review of the history of the initiative

Statement of the problem

Objectives

Discussion

1. What is a sorting plant and where is it to be located?
2. What does the sorting plant achieve?
3. How does the sorting plant work?
4. Current system of waste management:
    Wastes are mixed together.
4. New system: Resources (once considered wastes) are separated.

Conclusion: Waste/resource management system pays tangible dividends to the environment and the economy.

Questions?

Figure 19.3 *An outline for a presentation on a new sorting plant for Metro.*
Adapted with permission from Mirror Nova Scotia, Nova Scotia Business Journal, *January 1996.*
ISSN 0820-2737.

simple enough for her audience. Visuals must be uncluttered and visible. She will also use a Powerpoint slide show for part of the presentation, and a colleague may be helping her with the 3-D graphics and some sound, depending on the time available. However, she does not want to overdo the graphics; she knows that the technology should support her talk, not steal the show. She may opt, therefore, for a simple presentation of coloured overhead transparencies.

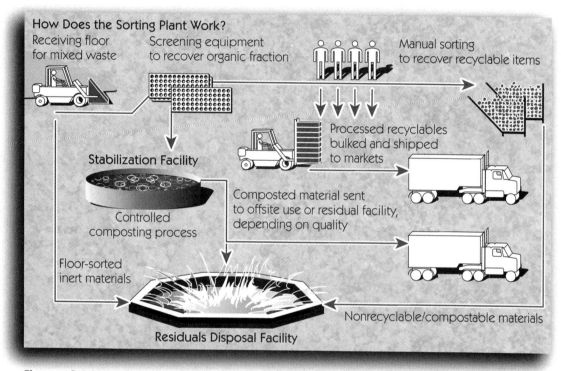

Figure 19.4 *How does the sorting plant work? Figure 3 of Lorraine's presentation.*
Adapted with permission from Mirror Nova Scotia, Nova Scotia Business Journal, January 1996. ISSN 0820-2737.

Practising the Presentation

For Lorraine, practice is one of the most essential steps. She is prepared and she knows her material. However, she has to rehearse the presentation to make sure that it moves smoothly and logically from point to point, and that the visuals are in order.

She also has to deal with her nervousness. She has never spoken in front of a large group before, and she feels slightly apprehensive. Rehearsing the presentation in front of colleague and technologist Van Hofland will help her gain confidence.

Van, who has made several presentations, gives Lorraine the following suggestions:

◆ Rehearse at least three times before the presentation, but do not overrehearse. (That is, do not stay up late the night before. Go for a walk so that you get a good night's sleep.)

◆ Make sure your overhead transparencies are in order.

◆ On your note cards, make cues for your overheads.

◆ Familiarize yourself with the audiovisual equipment.

◆ Make a checklist of things you need for the presentation.

◆ Come to terms with your nervousness by knowing how it affects you (dry mouth, trembling hands, blushing, increased pulse rate, etc.); then realize that none of these manifestations is unusual.

◆ Realize that you can make this nervous energy work for you.

◆ Learn to relax: breathe deeply, tighten muscles and then relax them.

◆ Visualize yourself succeeding.

◆ Focus on your audience and on the need for them to hear your message.

◆ Practise greeting your audience with friendliness and courtesy.

Delivering the Presentation

Delivering an oral presentation is totally different from submitting a written report. Although the preparations for each follow a similar path, the final presentation requires a different skill.

Oral presentations are normally scheduled at major points in a project's timeline. Lorraine has a valuable opportunity to represent her company during the design phase and to review that part of the project for the Metro Council and Stakeholders' Committee. There will be written project reports and a final completion report, but the oral presentation will "bring to life" a part of the project which has been achieved through community commitment.

The success of an oral presentation depends upon the degree of preparedness and the implementation of presentation techniques. Lorraine MacAdam's approach to the presentation demonstrates an understanding of both.

Having prepared and rehearsed the presentation, she is quite confident that she will achieve her objectives. On arrival at City Hall about 40 minutes before the presentation is due to begin, she makes her preparations:

◆ She checks the room and the seating arrangement so that she will feel comfortable.

◆ She checks the audiovisual equipment and the lighting.

◆ She arranges her collection of overheads in the right order.

◆ She arranges for a pitcher of water and glasses (nervousness may make her mouth dry).

◆ She sits quietly and goes through her note cards.

◆ She breathes naturally and calmly.

◆ She methodically relaxes (unobserved) the muscles in her shoulders, arms, and legs by alternately tensing and relaxing them.

◆ She shakes hands with Councillor Seamus Fitzpatrick, who will chair the meeting and introduce her.

After the introduction, Lorraine draws on her knowledge of presentation techniques:

◆ She speaks loudly enough and slowly enough.

◆ She establishes eye contact and smiles at her audience as she begins her introduction.

◆ She speaks clearly and confidently, because she wants the audience to know that she is glad they are there — she has something important to tell them, and she wants them to hear it!

By focusing on the needs of the audience and the importance of the message, Lorraine has created a positive atmosphere and established rapport. She is encouraged by the audience's attention, and is beginning to enjoy the experience.

Lorraine then proceeds with her presentation, being careful not to read information from her notes or from the overheads. She knows that reading her information will lose her audience, for they will see only the top of her head! Her presentation is carefully planned, and she is able to make smooth transitions between points. While she does so, she takes time to observe the audience's response, and can gauge from their body language whether to speed up or slow down. She is careful not to read the lines of her Powerpoint presentations. She is not afraid to pause as the audience silently reads the overheads.

Lorraine's success in her first presentation to a large group can be attributed to her planning, her enthusiasm, and her commitment to the project. At the close of the presentation, she is able to show this commitment by reiterating the main point she wants the audience to remember: that waste has become a resource to be managed, and that the total resource management system depends on the efforts of people like them, the Metro Council members and stake-holders. She then invites questions.

The question period is dreaded by many speakers, even if they are fully prepared. Lorraine wants to be able to answer questions, because that is her job. However, she knows that her boss, the chief engineer, is attending, and that she can call upon him to respond to anything she cannot answer. The audience, she has noted, is not hostile, but eager and excited about the project. The questions are demanding, but not confrontational.

It is highly likely that her careful preparation and her positive attitude have gained the attention and respect of the audience.

Conclusion

Developing oral presentation skills takes time and effort. However, technical presentations, formal and informal, are part of the job. Focusing on objectives and on the needs of the audience will help you achieve success in this demanding arena. Becoming an effective presenter will also contribute to your professional and personal growth.

QUESTIONS FOR DISCUSSION

1. What are the two main differences between formal and informal oral presentations?
2. Name three differences between oral presentations and written presentations.
3. What steps should you take to prepare for a job interview?
4. Name at least four teamwork skills that can be demonstrated at meetings.
5. What are some of the purposes of oral presentations in the workplace?
6. What do you need to consider when you select visuals for your presentation?
7. Why is audience analysis crucial in an oral technical presentation?

EXERCISE

Assume that you have been asked to give an informal introductory three-minute talk to your class on a technical topic of your choosing.

Using a worksheet like the one in Figure 19.2, identify your objective(s) and audience.

SPEAKING ASSIGNMENTS

1. Prepare the three-minute oral presentation you have started to plan in the previous exercise and deliver it to your class.

2. Present the main findings from a lab you have completed in one of your technical courses. Use visuals and be prepared to answer questions.

3. Interview a person whose job includes making technical presentations. Find out

   ◆ the number and kind of presentations.

   ◆ whether the person had received any special training in giving presentations.

   ◆ any advice for dealing with nervousness.

   ◆ any specific problems in presenting information.

   Then, in a short, informal presentation, share your findings with the class.

4. If possible, sit in at a meeting of a local organization or student group. If you are unable to do this, tune in to the local channel that televises your local government council meeting. Observe the procedures and activities of the council, and prepare a short, informal presentation about meeting procedures.

5. With members of your class, prepare a mock job interview that demonstrates what you have learned about successful interview strategies.